BOYD

BOYD

The Fighter Pilot Who Changed the Art of War

ROBERT CORAM

Little, Brown and Company
Boston New York London

First Edition

Library of Congress Cataloging-in-Publication Data

Coram, Robert.
  Boyd : the fighter pilot who changed the art of war / Robert Coram.
    p. cm.
  Includes index.
  ISBN 0-316-88146-5 (hc)
    1. Boyd, John, 1927–1997. 2. Fighter pilots — United States — Biography. 3. United
States. Air Force — Officers — Biography. 4. Fighter plane combat. 5. Aeronautics,
Military — United States — History — 20th century. I. Title.

UG626.2.B69 C67 2002
358.4'3'092 — dc21
[B]

2002022816

10 9 8 7 6 5 4 3

Q-MB

Book design by Bernard Klein

Printed in the United States of America

To John Pennington: my mentor in the newspaper years,
my fellow traveler in the wilderness years,
and my inspiration forever. He died too soon.

Contents

Part 1
FIGHTER PILOT

Part 2
ENGINEER

Part 3
SCHOLAR

Acknowledgments

RARELY has a writer approached a subject where so many people were so anxious to help. This was not because of my winning ways and bubbling personality; it was because John Boyd inspired such passionate feelings among those who knew him and who wanted to be sure his story was told in the proper fashion.

Researching this book brought me into frequent and lengthy contact with the men who were close to Boyd: the Acolytes. The distance I always keep between myself and the people I write about disappeared when I met these men. For my more than two years of researching and writing this book, Franklin "Chuck" Spinney was the "go to" person for everything I needed. Him I owe the most. Chuck Spinney, Tom Christie, Pierre Sprey, Ray Leopold, Jim Burton, and Mike Wyly are as fiery and idealistic today as they were back in the 1960s and 1970s and 1980s. For the endless hours they spent with me going over those white-hot years — and for their friendship — I shall always be grateful.

Mary Boyd, Kathy Boyd, Jeff Boyd, and John Scott Boyd could not have been more forthcoming during many talks about their family. Often it was painful for everyone involved. Mary Ellen Holton, as Boyd's executrix, was particularly helpful in obtaining personal family papers.

It is a measure of the respect Boyd evoked that Vice President Dick Cheney took time to talk about his old friend. The generosity of his comments added much to the book.

Of the dozens of others who helped, a few must be singled out. Jack Shanahan, a brilliant Air Force officer, spent months walking me through Air Force history, Air Force culture, the subtleties of Officer Efficiency Reports (ERs), the intricacies of air combat, and a hundred other details of Air Force life.

Acknowledgments

Grant Hammond was always willing to share the insights that came from spending hundreds of hours with Boyd in the mid-1990s.

Vernon Spradling remains the institutional memory of the Fighter Weapons School as it was in the 1950s and 1960s. He proves that memory does not have to decline with age.

Ron Catton has the wisdom that comes from having a wild youth followed by a distinguished Air Force career and a highly successful business career. His guidance was invaluable.

Chet Richards is a consultant and lecturer on Boyd's ideas as applied to business. He has the keen logic of a mathematician and he saved me from many mistakes.

Dr. Wayne Thompson at the Office of Air Force History provided documents I might never have known about.

At Georgia Tech, Bob Harty, Marie McVay, Debbie Williamson, and Kathy Tomajko brought depth and dimension to the chapter about Boyd's two years at that respected institution. And my friend Grady "Himself" Thrasher spent hours telling me of Tech as it was during his student days in the early 1960s.

Jim Stevenson knows all there is to know about airplanes. He shared his knowledge.

For about thirty years, a group of men has met every Wednesday night in the Officers Club at Fort Myer, across the river from Washington. In few other places in America can you find a room filled with men who have made more of a contribution to national defense than these men have. They are legends all. And they are why I always timed my trips to Washington so I could be there on Wednesday.

A few additional notes.

I happen to have the best literary agent in New York. Mel Berger of the William Morris Agency gets the job done. Quickly.

This book covers a long and tumultuous time in American military history. To insure accuracy, many people mentioned in the book have read part or all of the manuscript. Any errors, however, are mine alone.

I edited the manuscript on St. Catherines Island. No writer ever had a better place to work, and I am forever grateful to my good friend Royce Hayes, the superintendent of that remote island off the Georgia coast.

Finally, my deepest appreciation as always is to my wife, Jeannine Addams. My life has been altogether different because of her.

BOYD

Prologue

Reminiscences

ON March 20, 1997, a somber crowd gathered in the Old Post Chapel at Arlington National Cemetery, across the Potomac from Washington, D.C. They came to attend the memorial service for Colonel John Richard Boyd, United States Air Force, retired.

Winter often lingers in the hills of northern Virginia. And on that Thursday morning a cold rain and overcast skies caused many in the crowd to wrap their winter coats tighter and to hurry for the doors of the chapel.

Full military honors were provided for Boyd — a ceremonial detachment that included an honor guard, band, rifle squad, and flag-draped caisson drawn by six gray horses. Boyd was a fighter pilot. He wore the Air Force uniform for twenty-four years. During that time he made more contributions to fighter tactics, aircraft design, and the theory of air combat than any man in Air Force history. But on that soft and dreary day when Boyd's ashes were laid to rest, the Air Force all but ignored his passing. Only two uniformed Air Force officers were in the congregation. One, a three-star general, represented the Air Force chief of staff. He sat alone in the front row and was plainly uncomfortable. The other was a major who knew Boyd's work and simply wanted to pay his respects.

Neither man had ever met John Boyd.

A chaplain opened the Protestant service. Then, one by one, three of Boyd's oldest friends walked to the front of the chapel.

Tom Christie, a tall, white-haired man, solemnly read the Twenty-third Psalm.

Ron Catton, one of Boyd's former students and a fellow fighter pilot, delivered the first eulogy. He quoted Sophocles: "One must wait until the evening to see how splendid the day has been." As he told what it was like to fly with Boyd back in the old days, his lips trembled and his speech became rushed. Some of those present turned their eyes away, stared at Boyd's linen-draped urn, and remembered.

There was much to remember, for few men have had such a splendid day as John Boyd.

Boyd's friends smiled broadly, a few even chuckled, as they recalled Boyd at his loud, arm-waving, irrepressible best. The chuckles must have puzzled the chaplain. A military funeral with full honors is marked by dignity and solemnity. The slow measured cadences and the history-dictated procedures evoke respectful silence. This is a sacred rite, this final remembrance of a man whose life was spent in the service of his country. Here, levity is out of place.

But Boyd's friends did not come to mourn; they came to celebrate a life that tossed and tumbled those in its wake. And when Pierre Sprey, an aristocratic and reserved man with swept-back white hair, began a second eulogy by saying, "Not many people are defined by the courts-martial and investigations they faced," raucous laughter echoed off the white walls of the chapel. Sprey told how Boyd once snapped the tail off an F-86, spun in an F-100, and how he not only stole more than $1 million worth of computer time from the Air Force to develop a radical new theory but survived every resulting investigation. Chuck Spinney, a boyish Pentagon analyst who was like a son to Boyd, laughed so loud he could be heard all across the chapel. Even those in the congregation who barely knew Boyd wore broad grins when they heard how he was investigated a dozen times for leaking information to the press and how his guerrilla tactics for successful leaking are still being used today.

Boyd's career spanned the last half of the twentieth century. He served in World War II, Korea, and Vietnam. His ideas greatly influenced the prosecution of the Gulf War in 1991. In the aftermath of the attack on the World Trade Center and the Pentagon, there were numerous media stories of "Fourth Generation Warfare," a concept based on Boyd's work. And while Boyd's life was marked by a series of enormous accomplishments and lasting achievements, the thing that meant the most to him over the longest period of time was the simple title he had in the beginning. He was first, last, and always a fighter pilot — a loud-talking, cigar-smoking, bigger-than-life fighter pilot. There is no such thing as an ex–fighter pilot. Once a young man straps on a jet aircraft and climbs into the heavens to do battle, it sears his psyche forever. At some point he will hang up his flight suit — eventually they all do — and in the autumn of his years his eyes may dim and he may be stooped with age. But ask him about his life, and his eyes flash and his back straightens and his hands demonstrate aerial maneuvers and every conversation begins with "There I was at . . ." and he is young again. He remembers the days when he sky-danced through the heavens, when he could press a button and summon the lightning and invoke the thunder, the days when he was a prince of the earth and a lord of the heavens. He remembers his glory days and he is young again.

Some of Boyd's friends at the memorial service remembered the time back in the mid- and late 1950s when John Boyd was the best fighter pilot in America. When he returned from a combat tour in Korea to become an instructor at the Fighter Weapons School — the Air Force's premier dogfighting academy — he became known as "Forty-Second Boyd," the pilot who could defeat any opponent in simulated air-to-air combat in less than forty seconds. Like any gun-slinger with a nickname and a reputation, Boyd was called out. Some of the best pilots in the Air Force challenged him at one time or another. So did the best pilots in the Navy and the Marine Corps. But no man could be found who was better in the air than John Boyd. He was never defeated.

Boyd was more than a great stick-and-rudder man. He was that rarest of creatures — a *thinking* fighter pilot. Anyone familiar with the Air Force can tell you two things with confidence: one, fighter pilots are known for testosterone, not gray matter, and two, military doctrine is dictated by people with stars on their shoulders. But in 1959, when he was just a young captain, John Boyd became the first man to codify the elusive and mysterious ways of air-to-air combat. He developed and wrote the "Aerial Attack Study," a document that became official Air Force doctrine, the bible of air combat — first in America, and then, when it was declassified, for air forces around the world. Put another way, while still a junior officer, John Boyd changed the way every air force in the world flies and fights.

But creating a new standard for air-to-air combat was only the beginning of Boyd's intellectual contributions to the Air Force. Pierre

Sprey told how in 1961 the Air Force sent Boyd back to college for another degree. Boyd chose the Georgia Institute of Technology, one of the tougher state engineering schools in America. Late one night, while studying for an exam in thermodynamics, Boyd went off on a riff about being a fighter pilot in Korea and what it was like to fly an F-86 down MiG Alley. Suddenly what he had learned in thermodynamics meshed with all that he had learned as a fighter pilot and Boyd had the epiphany that became his Energy-Maneuverability (E-M) Theory.

Tom Christie smiled and nodded as he remembered. He was the man who steadied the soapbox for the rambunctious and confrontational Boyd in those tumultuous years of presenting the E-M Theory to the Air Force, the years when Boyd became known as the "Mad Major." After E-M, nothing was ever the same in aviation. E-M was as clear a line of demarcation between the old and the new as was the shift from the Copernican world to the Newtonian world. Knowledge gained from E-M made the F-15 and F-16 the finest aircraft of their type in the world. Boyd is acknowledged as the father of those two aircraft.

Either the "Aerial Attack Study" or the E-M Theory would have given Boyd a lasting place in aviation history. But his greatest and most enduring accomplishments still lay ahead. After he retired from the Air Force in 1975, Boyd became the founder, leader, and spiritual center of the "military-reform movement" — a guerrilla movement that affected the monolithic and seemingly omnipotent Pentagon as few things in history have done. For a few years he was one of the most powerful men in Washington.

Then he went into a self-imposed exile and immersed himself in a daunting study of philosophy, the theory of science, military history, psychology, and a dozen other seemingly unrelated disciplines. He had evolved from being a warrior to a warrior-engineer, and now he was about to move into the rarefied atmosphere of the pure intellectual. He synthesized all that he studied into all that he knew about aerial combat, expanded it to include all forms of conflict, and gave birth to a dazzling briefing titled "Patterns of Conflict."

When Sprey reached this part of his eulogy, he paused and his eyes roamed the chapel and found Christie and Spinney and two other men: Ray Leopold and James Burton. These were Boyd's Acolytes, his most dedicated followers. Their years with Boyd were the pivotal years of their lives. They followed Boyd into dozens of bloody bureaucratic battles and their careers were forever changed, some say ruined, by the experience. These men believe that Boyd's final work made him the most influential military thinker since Sun Tzu wrote *The Art of War* 2,400 years ago. For, like that of an Old Testament prophet purified by wandering in the desert, Boyd's exile ended with a vision so amazing and so profound that it convinced both the U.S. Army and the U.S. Marine Corps to change their basic doctrines on war fighting. As bizarre and unbelievable as it sounds, an old fighter pilot taught ground troops how to fight a war. The results of what he taught were manifested in the crucible of the Gulf War. Everything about the startling speed and decisive victory of that conflict can be attributed not to the media heroes, not to strutting and bombastic generals, but to a lonely old man in south Florida who thought he had been forgotten.

Boyd was one of the most important unknown men of his time. He did what so few men are privileged to do: he changed the world. But much of what he did, or the impact of what he did, was either highly classified or of primary concern to the military. The only things he ever published were a few articles in specialized Air Force magazines and an eleven-page study. His most important work was a six-hour briefing. Thus, there is almost nothing for academics to pore over and expound upon. That is why today both Boyd and his work remain largely unknown outside the military.

The Acolytes work to change that. They work to keep Boyd's memory alive and to move his ideas into the mainstream of American thought. Each Wednesday evening, as they have done for almost thirty years, they meet in the Officers Club at Fort Myer. The basement room where they convene is called, fittingly enough, the Old Guard Room. They talk of Boyd and they replay the old battles and they laugh about the "cape jobs" and "hot platters" and "tube steaks" he engineered. But the conversation often lingers on Boyd's character and integrity. Not that he was an exemplar of all things good and noble. Far from it. Like many fighter pilots, he took a certain pride in his profanity and coarseness and crude sense of humor. He cared little for his personal appearance and could be demanding, abrasive, and unreasonable. And while in his professional life Boyd accomplished things that can never be duplicated, in his personal life he did things few would want to duplicate.

Boyd's Acolytes minimize his faults. They say it is more important that his core beliefs were steel-wrapped and his moral compass was locked on true north, that he never misspent his gifts. His motivation was simple: to get as close as possible to the truth. He would have been the first to admit there is no absolute truth. But he continued chasing something that was always receding from his grasp. And in the pursuit he came far closer to the unattainable than do most men.

Boyd never achieved the one thing he wanted most. He died thinking the people in his hometown never knew of his contributions to national defense. He died thinking he would be remembered, if at all, as a crackpot and a failure, as a man who never made general, and a man whose ideas were not understood and whose accomplishments were not important.

All his life Boyd was pursued by enemies real and imagined. He reacted the only way he knew how: by attacking. The rank or position of his enemy, the size or significance of the institution, none of it mattered. He attacked. And when Boyd attacked, he gave no quarter. Time after time he outmaneuvered his foes and sent them down to ignominious defeat.

The men around Boyd, those who knew him longest and best, say he stood fast against the blandishments of big money. He was a profane puritan who held himself and others to the highest standards. He lived in a world of black and white, of right and wrong, of good and evil. He never broke the faith and would not tolerate those who did. He was an incorruptible man in a place where so many were corrupt. He was a pure man at a time when pure men were needed but so few answered the call.

All this and more the friends of John Boyd remembered that dreary day in the chapel at Arlington National Cemetery. Then it was over and they slowly walked out of the chapel and huddled in small groups against the rain and mist. They were angry at the Air Force. More should have been done to honor the man who had given so much.

If the U.S. Air Force was conspicuous by its absence, the U.S. Marines were conspicuous by their presence. In fact, had anyone passed by who knew military culture but did not know John Boyd, they would have been bewildered to see so many Marines at the memorial service of an Air Force pilot. Particularly noticeable was a group of young lieutenants — rigid, close-cropped, and hard young men from the Basic School at Marine Base Quantico. These were warriors-in-training. From their ranks would come the future leadership of the Marine Corps. Then there was a senior Marine colonel who wore the ribbons and decorations of a man who had seen combat in many places. His presence awed the young lieutenants and they kept their eyes on him.

The colonel's command presence made him stand out — that and the fact he marched alone as the crowd walked down a rain-glistening road between endless rows of tombstones. The damp air muffled the rhythmic clacking of the horses' hooves and the sharp snap of metal taps on the gleaming shoes of the honor guard.

On a green and windswept slope, the cortege halted. The grass was wet and the air was clean and sweet. The crowd gathered at Section Sixty, grave site number 3,660. The Marine colonel took from his pocket a Marine Corps insignia, the eagle globe and anchor. He marched out of the crowd, kneeled, and placed the insignia near the urn containing Boyd's ashes. Someone took a picture. In that frozen moment the light of the flash sparkled on the eagle globe and anchor, causing it to stand out sharply against the bronze urn and green grass. The black insignia drew every eye. As one, and without a command to do so, the young lieutenants snapped to attention. Placing the symbol of the U.S. Marine Corps on a grave is the highest honor a Marine can bestow. It is rarely seen, even at the funeral of decorated combat Marines, and it may have been the first time in history an Air Force pilot received the honor. This simple act is an expression of love — love of the deceased, love of the Truth, love of country, and love of the Corps, all wrapped up together. It signified that a warrior spirit had departed the flight pattern.

A seven-man rifle squad fired three volleys and a lone bugler played the ever-melancholy "Taps." The service was over. Some of those at the funeral turned and walked away. But the young Marine officers remained at attention, a last, lingering sign of respect. Like the Marines, Boyd's friends were reluctant to say good-bye. They tarried in the mist and talked. High overhead they could hear a flight of F-15s prowling around and looking for a way to let down through the clouds and make a flyby over Boyd's grave. But it would not happen; the clouds were too thick. Boyd's friends huddled their shoulders against the rain. Around them, in one of America's most majestic and solemn places, were the graves of thousands who fought and died for their beliefs. It was the proper resting place for the mortal remains of John Boyd. But somehow, some way, his grave should have been set apart from the others. For while America likes to believe that it often produces men like John Boyd, the truth is that men who embody a warrior spirit combined with sweeping and lasting intellectual achievement are rare not only in America, but in any country. They seldom pass among us. And they do so only when there is a great need.

Part One

FIGHTER PILOT

Chapter One

Haunted Beginnings

ERIE, Pennsylvania, is a hard town, a blue-collar town, a grubby and decrepit town that has more in common with its fellow Great Lakes rust-belt towns of Buffalo and Cleveland than it has with Pennsylvania cities. Perched high in the northwestern corner of Pennsylvania, with its face toward the lake and its back toward the rest of the state, Erie is the only lake port town in Pennsylvania. Even people in other parts of the state often are surprised to learn that until the last year or so it was their third largest municipality, after the elegant and history-wrapped city of Philadelphia and the brawny sophistication of Pittsburgh. The town of about one hundred thousand just doesn't seem that big — not so much because it is remote, which it is, but because it is so *narrow,* so *provincial.*

The one natural feature in Erie worthy of note is the glorious Presque Isle Peninsula, which juts seven miles into the lake and forms a bay that in the summer is ideal for boating and in the winter for ice sailing. "The Peninsula," as it is called, offers not only eleven beaches but an untrammeled spot of wilderness, a glorious combination of wetlands and walking trails that draws people by the thousands. It is a unique natural bounty.

But Erie also is suited for being an industrial port, an opening onto the Great Lakes. And almost from its beginning the town has been caught between the polarities of wanting to be a tourist destination and wanting to be an industrial port. The desire to be an industrial city has prevailed to the degree that contamination from local industries may never be removed from the muck at the bottom of the lake.

Erie long has searched for that which made it unique — for events or people in its history worth boasting about to the outside world. Such events and such people have been few and, when viewed from other parts of America, may seem curious. For example, it is a matter of considerable local pride that in the Battle of Lake Erie, an engagement during the War of 1812, Commodore Oliver Hazard Perry sailed aboard a ship built in Erie. Then there was Erie's Colonel Strong Vincent, who stood in the midst of battle at Gettysburg and exhorted his troops with a riding crop — an act that resulted in his being killed by a Confederate sniper. While most historians agree that Colonel Joshua Chamberlain was the Union hero at Gettysburg, people in Erie say Strong Vincent saved the day. And there was the train that carried the body of President Abraham Lincoln from Washington back home to Illinois, a train that passed through Erie.

In the 1920s, Hubert and Elsie Boyd, along with three children — two boys and a girl — lived in a brown, two-story, frame house at 514 Lincoln Avenue on the west side of Erie, only a block from the bay. This was one of the most prestigious parts of Erie, and Lincoln Avenue itself was the sort of street parents longed for: a street of well-maintained homes, a safe street, a street famous for its umbrageous maples and spreading oaks. The homes, most with front porches, breasted against the sidewalk in a neat row. The street ended a long block away at a steep bluff overlooking the bay. Beyond the bay was the Peninsula and beyond the Peninsula was Lake Erie and beyond Lake Erie was the vast horizon and Canada.

Hubert Boyd paid $16,500 for the house. Inside, Elsie had an eye for the fine details. She installed dark hardwood floors in the dining room — not just any hardwood, but narrow tight-fitting boards of dark oak, the best that money could buy. She bought a fine mahogany dining-room table and placed a runner of Irish linen atop it. For the living room, where her growing family would spend long winter evenings, she bought a cast-iron gas heater, and to brighten those winter evenings she covered the walls with pink paper. The living room's other feature was a black Steinway, a gift from Hubert. Elsie liked to play it, having taught piano before she was married.

For Erie in the late 1920s it was a comfortable middle-class home. Hubert Boyd was a traveling salesman for HammerMill Paper Company, and a job at "the HammerMill" was both prestigious and well-paying.

Elsie Boyd was the daughter of Julia and Rudolph Beyer. Her father farmed a small piece of land just south of Erie. Elsie was a German Presbyterian, an ample woman with enormous pride and the self-confidence to freely express her beliefs, many of which were synthesized in pithy expressions such as "The world is not the way you want it to be. The world is the way it is." Or "You have to speak up in this world." Or "Never give up and never give in." Her voice was deep and authoritative, and when she spoke there rarely was any doubt about her meaning.

For his part, Hubert Boyd was the son of Mary Golden and Thomas Boyd. Thomas worked on a boat, probably a fishing boat, that plied the Great Lakes, and his son was a tall, thin, happy-go-lucky fellow with brown eyes and a shock of wavy black hair. Although he was Catholic and had baptized his children as Catholics, he preferred the golf course to church.

It was into this contented and fortunate family that John Richard Boyd was born on January 23, 1927.

When Boyd was born, his mother and father shared the front bedroom. His sister Marion, age eleven, had her own room. The third bedroom was shared by the boys. Bill, who had just turned ten, and Hubert — called Gerry — who was four. John's crib stayed in the bedroom with his parents. On September 23, 1928, Ann was born — the fifth and last child in the Boyd family.

After Ann's birth, the prospect of feeding and clothing five children began to loom large in the mind of Hubert Boyd. He had never gone to college. His quick smile and Irish ebullience had given him a good job at the HammerMill, but he knew that his natural gifts could take him only so far. He wanted his children to have advantages he never had. He preached to Marion the need for a college education. During the fall of 1926 he talked to a neighbor about buying an insurance policy that would pay for his children's education should anything happen to him. But he was young and decided to wait.

In late November of 1929, Hubert spent several weeks "down south" on a sales trip. No one remembers exactly where, only, as Marion says, that it was "somewhere down there where it was warm." He came home to record cold and record snowfall, celebrated Christmas with his family, and in mid-January contracted lobar pneumonia. The family attributed the pneumonia to the drastic difference in temperature between the South and Erie, with the clear implication that the South was to blame. Doctors, however, generally attribute lobar pneumonia either to chronic smoking or to a systemic infection, and Hubert was a heavy smoker.

During Hubert's illness all the children save Ann were farmed out to their father's sisters in south Erie; Mrs. Boyd would take care of her husband and she would do it on her own. The children rarely visited. Marion came home once and found her father had been moved from his cold bedroom into her room. The windows were open to allow the wind off the lake to blow through — the idea, current in the medical community of the time, was to "freeze out" the pneumonia. Marion sat in a chair at the top of the steps, shivered with the cold, and cried.

Icy temperatures and bitter winds were insufficient to cure the pneumonia and Hubert Boyd died January 19, 1930. He was thirty-seven, and was buried on John's third birthday.

When Marion was in her mideighties, she said her father's death was not as painful as it might appear. In most families the father is home every night. But her father was "gone all the time." She said that for months after the funeral she thought, "Oh, Dad's on a trip." But she was a teenager when her father died and her recollection was softened by the passage of seventy years. John was too young to understand the concept of travel and returning home. Even if he could, there had to have been a moment when the painful realization sank in that he would grow up without a father, that he was therefore different from other children.

Hubert Boyd had only $10,000 in life insurance and most of that was used to pay off the mortgage. Elsie faced the insurmountable task of supporting and rearing five children. Ann and John were little more than infants, so whatever work she found would have to enable

16

her to stay at home. But the Great Depression was spreading across America and even a bustling port city such as Erie was beginning to feel the effects.

She had still another burden, a self-imposed burden. As the wife of a salesman for the HammerMill, Elsie had enjoyed a certain lifestyle and a certain community standing. She wanted to maintain both. This meant people in Erie must think she did not really need to work.

She began baking cakes and selling them to neighbors. None of the children remembers the price, but in the early 30s she could have made only a few cents on each cake. She made various sorts but became famous around Erie for her devil's food cake and, at Christmas, her date-and-nut cake. One Christmas she had orders for eighty cakes, and for several weeks the house turned into a bakery. For so many cakes to come from such a small oven in such a short period of time necessitated split-second timing from dawn to dusk. Elsie Boyd did not allow the children to help. They were ordered to stay out of the kitchen.

Mrs. Boyd also began selling Christmas cards and stationery, and found a third job conducting telephone solicitations for advertisements that went inside program booklets for banquets. She did this from the house on Lincoln Avenue and tended to the children between calls.

Marion remembers that when her mother solicited ads from the home telephone, her voice was deep and commanding, "strong, persuasive, and in control." Mrs. Boyd wanted people in Erie to know that even though her husband was dead, nothing had changed. The Boyd family of Lincoln Avenue was doing quite well, thank you.

But events were gathering, momentous events, beyond even the ability of the redoubtable Elsie Boyd to control.

Elsie settled into a curious dichotomy in raising her children. On the one hand she allowed them almost free rein, especially around the house. The postman once reported to Mrs. Boyd that John was running naked through the backyard and playing in the sprinkler. At the dinner table, tempers often exploded and the children shouted at each other. Much about the household was loud and raucous, freewheeling and unrestrained.

If Mrs. Boyd granted her children unusual freedoms within her house, she was more than diligent in imparting rules for outside the house. She inculcated her children with a protective mechanism they remembered all their lives. Over and over again she said if people knew too much about the Boyd family they would use the knowledge in a critical manner. *Never tell people what you don't want repeated,* she preached. *People will seek out your weaknesses and faults, so tell them only of your strong points. No family matters must ever be mentioned beyond the front door.* This resulted in the Boyd children being extraordinarily reticent about all but the most inconsequential of family matters, even when they reached old age.

While Elsie had striven mightily to have people in Erie think she was as comfortable as before her husband died, inside the home she turned poverty into a cardinal virtue. She taught all her children, but especially John since he was at his most malleable age, that they had principles and integrity often lacking in those with money and social position. She hammered into John that as long as he held on to his sense of what was right, and as long as his integrity was inviolate, he was superior to those who had only rank or money. She also taught him that a man of principle frightened other people and that he would be attacked for his beliefs, but he must always keep the faith. "If you're right, you're right," she said.

For several years after her husband died, Elsie maintained a semblance of religion in her household. Because her husband had been a Catholic and because all the children were baptized in the Catholic Church, she encouraged Marion and Gerry to attend church. But she was becoming increasingly annoyed by what she saw as church pressure for greater financial contributions.

Then came the day when Marion, who was studying for her Confirmation, could not remember her catechism. Marion reported to her mother that the priest ridiculed her in front of the class and made her kneel before him "like he was a tin god." Such authoritarian behavior on the part of priests then was the rule rather than the exception, but Elsie Boyd — a Presbyterian and a mother burdened with protecting her children against the world — was furious at the way the priest had humiliated Marion and, by extension, her family. She called the priest and said, "I have enough trouble trying to keep this family together without having a priest pick on my children." When the priest protested, Mrs. Boyd laced into him with even more animus. The priest insisted he was right, at which point Mrs. Boyd ended the conversation by serving notice she was removing her children from the Catholic Church.

John was too young to be troubled by this. But Marion had heard what happened to children who left the church and she thought, "Oh, my. I'm going to hell." Two of Hubert Boyd's sisters, both of whom were devout Catholics, were more than a little disturbed by this theological shift and feared for the souls of the children. Bitter recriminations ensued.

Elsie, as usual, was unbending. These were her children and she would raise them as she saw best. Her dead husband's sisters had no voice in the matter. She summarily tossed them from her house; it would be years before any of the Boyd children were allowed to visit the two aunts.

This was not the last time Elsie was to demonstrate her willingness to sever a relationship with any person or any institution that offended her. She could do it without a second thought, without looking back, without any willingness to discuss the issue. Once she shut the door it was closed forever. John learned by her example, and it was a lesson he would remember.

A few weeks later Elsie withdrew her children from the Catholic Church and decided that John would be raised as a Presbyterian. So one Sunday Marion drove John to the Church of the Covenant in downtown Erie and enrolled him in Sunday School. But it was not long before Elsie decided the Presbyterians were little better than the Catholics. "All they want is money," she complained. She had no money for the church. She severed her relationship with the Presbyterians and withdrew John from Sunday School. For years she inveighed against organized religion. John grew up not attending church and without any religious affiliation. On Air Force records he would later list his religion as Presbyterian, but that was only a word to fill in a blank space.

For several years it seemed that despite all odds Elsie might prevail in her battle to control her world. It seemed she had surmounted the difficulties life had placed in her path. Life settled into a tolerable routine.

Marion graduated from high school and was attending Miami University in Oxford, Ohio, when, on March 20, 1933, she received a letter from her mother. The letter said the depression had forced banks in Erie to close and that John had the measles and had to stay home from school for sixteen days. "It was terrible trying to keep him in a dark room," Elsie wrote. "He is acting like a young colt." She said the front of the house was posted with a large sign saying a case of measles was inside and predicted that Ann would soon have them too.

Ann did contract measles, and a month or so after the disease had run its course, she became sick again, this time with a kidney infection. She stayed for two weeks at a nearby Catholic hospital, and when she came home, she was weak and listless. Eventually Dr. Frank Krimmel, the family doctor, came to the house, examined Ann, and pronounced that she had polio. In 1933 very little was known about polio. It was thought to be a contagious summer disease, perhaps contracted in swimming pools. As was the practice at the time, a large sign was tacked to the front door of the Boyd home saying POLIO MYELITIS. No one could enter except family members. When neighborhood children passed the house, they walked on the other side of Lincoln Avenue and shouted to any Boyd children who might be visible, "We don't want to catch anything!" They treated the house as if it had been visited by the plague.

In later years John would have special reason to remember this.

After Ann was diagnosed with polio, her mother stripped the linen runner from the fine mahogany dining table and the table became a place to perform stretching exercises for Ann's twisted legs. Every day Ann was gently placed on the table and Elsie rubbed and pulled and massaged her tiny legs. Her disease dominated the Boyd household. Elsie wanted to take Ann to the nearby Zem Zem Shriners Hospital where treatment was both good and free, but the hospital rarely admitted Catholic children. She went to a neighbor who was a Mason and asked him to plead Ann's case. He did and Ann was admitted, but the treatment was to little avail. A few months later the doctors said Ann should have surgery on her foot. She was transferred to a clinic in Cleveland, where she stayed a year. Even in the early 1930s such a lengthy stay, combined with complex treatment, was expensive. The surgery and the hospital bill was paid by Hammer-Mill Paper Company. A second operation was performed on a charity basis. Elsie ordered her children never to tell anyone how payment for the operations was handled.

The year Ann was in the hospital was difficult in the extreme for Elsie. Marion transferred to Mercyhurst, an all-girls' college in Erie, and took care of the four children at home. Elsie often drove the one hundred miles to Cleveland, visited with Ann, then returned. She stayed for more than a week after each of Ann's operations.

When Elsie brought Ann home, it was clear that neither the operations nor the treatment was of much benefit. Ann wore heavy braces on each leg and could walk only with the assistance of crutches.

By now Elsie was fighting to maintain control. She forbade use of the word "cripple" in her house. It did not matter to her that doctors said Ann would never be able to walk. She decreed that Ann would walk, that she would be as much like other children as possible.

John stood to the side and watched all this. He heard the arguments between his mother, who was adamantine in her insistence that Ann exercise daily, and Ann, who tried to avoid the uncomfortable exercises. But Elsie prevailed, as she usually did. Ann walked with braces and crutches until she was around eleven years old, and then, as Elsie Boyd had decreed, she put aside the crutches and walked with no assistance. She limped, but it was not obvious that it was from polio.

John was caught in a peculiar place during these years. Marion, Bill, and Gerry were old enough to take care of themselves and of each other. Almost all of Elsie's time and energy and attention were devoted to her three jobs and her baby daughter. John was adrift in between. He had no father, his mother had little time for him, and his older siblings were of an age not to want to spend time with him. He limped for almost a year and doctors could not determine if he had a mild case of polio or if the limp was a sympathetic reaction toward his baby sister. No one wondered if it might have been a way to get his mother's attention.

Many years later Boyd was interviewed by the Office of Air Force History as part of the Air Force Oral History Program. He said, ". . . my mother had to spread herself thin among all of us children. As a result, I did not get a lot of attention." He said this gave him "more freedom" as a child than most. Even then, he remembered his mother's admonition about family matters, and throughout the

21

lengthy interview never explained that the reason his mother had so little time was that she worked three jobs and that Ann had polio.

By 1933 the depression had Erie firmly in its grasp. Half of the workers in the town who had jobs in 1929 were now out of work. The ten banks in Erie closed and four would not reopen.

As Ann's medical expenses continued, anyone could see that the Boyd family was in deep financial trouble. Bill passed his old clothes to Gerry and Gerry passed them to John. And since his mother was busy with Ann in the mornings when he dressed for school, John put together shabby outfits that his mother, had she seen them, never would have let him wear.

In 1933 John entered Harding Elementary School a block and a half from the house on Lincoln Avenue. He failed the first grade because, teachers said, he did not know how to concentrate. But within the next year or so, he was to demonstrate such remarkable powers of concentration that his friends of that time still speak of it, so the teachers' explanation does not ring true. It is more likely that John was the only boy in the class whose father had died, and now, away from home and with other children for the first time, he realized how different he was. His family was poor and bore the stigma of having a child with polio. John's clothes were so tatty that a teacher once asked him in front of the class if he could not wear more presentable clothes. He held back his tears until he could get home and tell his mother what happened. She wrapped her arms around him and said, "Don't let it bother you. Say to yourself over and over, 'It doesn't bother me. It doesn't bother me.' Remember you have something no one else in the class has. You have principle and integrity. That means you will be criticized and attacked. But in the end you will win. Don't let it bother you."

Sometimes when it was too hot to cook, Elsie packed a picnic lunch and drove her children out to the Peninsula. There John learned to swim. Under the protective eye of his mother, his thrashing turned to paddling and then into long smooth strokes. His skills increased with each trip to the beach, until one day he was swimming with power and growing grace.

When John was eight years old, he began asking his mother upon his return from school, "Mom, any mail for me?" She was amused at the idea of her son receiving mail and always said no. When the inquiries continued she said, "What are you looking for?" It turned out that John had seen a magazine advertisement for the Charles Atlas bodybuilding program and returned the ad asking for more information. Then his letter arrived and he came into the kitchen and said, "Mom, can I have fifty dollars?"

"What on earth for?" she asked.

"I want to buy that Charles Atlas bodybuilding program."

Elsie laughed and told John he would have to wait.

During the third grade, John began to show intimations of intellect and concentration as well as a strong interest in aviation. Bob Knox was a fellow student and remembers that John was always one of the first to finish his class work. While the other students continued working on class assignments, John drew pictures of airplanes — not the airplanes of the early 30s, but what Knox remembers as "futuristic" monoplanes with clean, sleek lines, almost as if he had a vision of what fighter aircraft would become in another twenty or thirty years. After he drew an airplane, he would put the drawing on the chair between his legs, rub his hands together, and stare at the picture until everyone else in class had completed their work. During these times he went into such intense periods of concentration that Knox says, "I'd swear he was flying that airplane."

Another friend of those early years was Jack Arbuckle, a neighbor whom John visited after school two or three days a week. When John walked in the door, he began rummaging through magazines, looking for stories or pictures of airplanes. Arbuckle remembers many times when three or four friends would be in his house after school talking about what they wanted to do for the rest of the afternoon, and John would pick up a magazine and sit down and "go off by himself." The boys would decide to perhaps play baseball, but once John was engrossed in a magazine, he was oblivious to their calls. After two or three efforts to get John's attention, Arbuckle would lean over and shout in his ear, "John, we're going to play ball!" and John would jump and look around in confusion.

When John was in the fifth grade, he had a rare experience that doubtless sealed his interest in aviation. Elsie had gone to high school with the half-sister of Jack Eckerd, an Erie man who founded a national chain of drugstores. Eckerd owned a small airplane and once, when he came back to Erie, he offered John a ride. John later told Arbuckle that Eckerd had done steep banks and dives and described a flight bordering on the aerobatic. This may have been true. But it is a rare and unfeeling pilot who does such maneuvers with a passenger who has never flown before. What is more likely is that John's version of events was the first manifestation of what is found deep in the bone marrow of a fighter pilot — exaggeration and the belief that a good story is more important than sticking with the bare facts.

In September 1939, John Boyd and his friend Jack Arbuckle entered junior high at Strong Vincent High School. Arbuckle remembers that he and John were highly competitive and often compared grades. All through Harding Elementary they had been evenly matched, but when they entered Strong Vincent and began taking courses in the sciences, John quickly pulled ahead. He was particularly gifted in math.

During junior high, John tried his hand at running track but soon dropped out. He did not go out for football, basketball, or baseball. He knew he was only average in those sports and he had no time for activities in which he was average. But when he entered the swimming pool, he discovered that the long summer days at Lake Erie had not been wasted. He was an outstanding swimmer. His style and aggressiveness caught the eye of the high school swimming coach, who would later take a personal interest in this talented young athlete.

By the time John began high school, newspapers all across America were consumed by war news. In the *Erie Daily Times,* many of the advertisements, cartoons, and news stories were related to the war. The paper ran a regular column about Erie's men in uniform. Month after month the paper was filled with news of those missing or killed in action. The fare at local theaters leaned heavily toward war movies. John came to maturity knowing that when he graduated he would be going to war.

One of John's favorite stories, one he was to tell all his life, revolved around entering high school on September 2, 1942. He said he took a series of tests, one of which showed he had an IQ of only ninety. When offered the chance to retake the test, he refused. The test gave

John what he later said was a great tactical advantage in dealing with bureaucrats — when he told them he had an IQ of only ninety, they always underestimated him. Boyd now was almost six feet tall with clearly defined features and dark hair — a big rangy kid who moved with the easy grace of a natural athlete. He had a presence rarely found in one so young. His mother had molded and formed him until he was very much her son. He revealed so little about himself that he almost was a two-dimensional figure. It would be several years before his actions began to reveal who he was, and even more years before his accomplishments proved his intellectual prowess. And having grown up without a male role model, he now was, more so than most boys his age, a blank page awaiting a strong hand to write whatever was wanted upon it. In high school he found two such models, two strong hands, two men who would have considerable influence on his life.

The first was Art Weibel, the swimming coach at Strong Vincent. Weibel was a reflection of the brick school where he coached: solid and unshakable. He was firmly grounded in the old-fashioned principles of strong work, individual accountability, and duty. He had a national reputation as a coach, in part because he accepted only the best boys on his team — not just the best swimmers but the best in everything. His swimmers were known for their character, their determination, and their desire to excel at whatever they did. For boys on the cusp of manhood, reaching and searching for the way to become men, Art Weibel was a magnetic figure. He was hard-nosed and rigidly disciplined, and believed that a man should give more than he gets. By today's lights he was old-fashioned with old-fashioned virtues. Not every boy responded well to his rigid discipline, but John needed a man to tell him what to do, to mold him. Art Weibel offered the guidance he craved.

Mindful of his mother's lesson that hard work enables one to excel over those who coast through life, John was in the pool long before other players, and he stayed long after the practice was over and they had gone. He practiced until his stroke became a thing of beauty. He practiced until his muscles memorized the movements of a long-distance swimmer. He practiced until he seemed to skim across the top of the water.

John's skill in the water brought him to the attention of the second man who exerted great influence on him. And this one, although he was only fourteen years older than John, became the father John never had. His name was Frank Pettinato and he was chief assistant lifeguard at the Peninsula.

For young men, being a lifeguard at the Peninsula was Erie's most prestigious summer job. Only about twenty were chosen and it didn't matter how prominent a boy's father might be in the community or what politicians he knew, Pettinato had absolute authority over hiring. He usually hired college students, but most eligible Erie boys were overseas in uniform. Dipping into the ranks of high school students, Pettinato had to be extra careful. The beaches on the Peninsula are subject to storms out of the north, east, and west. Enormous waves can appear within minutes. He wanted boys who saw the job as a sacred calling — as a protector of the young and the innocent and the unwary. He wanted boys who knew right from wrong and who always chose the right. He wanted boys with a strong work ethic. Like Weibel, he expected the boys he chose to be outstanding in every area. And he instilled in his boys the belief that America was a place where the impossible dream could be achieved.

Given that most of the graduating seniors were drafted and few juniors met his standards, Pettinato was forced to search for recruits among the callow boys who had just graduated from the sophomore class, mere sixteen-year-olds. John Boyd was chosen, along with friends Jack Arbuckle and Chet Reichert. Reichert, like Arbuckle, was a neighbor and close friend to John.

When lifeguards reported for work, Pettinato got into a jeep and drove behind them as they went for a one- or two-mile run up the beaches. Then he ordered them into the water to swim back to the starting point. As they swam, he drove along the shore and demanded they swim faster. Sometimes for variety he pointed offshore and said, "Swim out to the fish poles." The fish poles were reminders of the days when blue pike swam in Lake Erie and when fishing boats went more than a mile offshore and tied floats to poles driven into the bottom of the lake. Rainy days, foggy days, windy days when the water was choppy, none of it mattered. Unless a storm was blowing, he ordered them out.

Reichert still shakes his head as he remembers John's power and endurance. John would get a running start, dive into the lake, put his head down, and begin that powerful, tireless, metronomic stroke that propelled him like an arrow through the water.

The lifeguards whom Pettinato particularly liked, the ones he considered the best of the summer crew, were invited to ride with him as he patrolled the beach in his jeep and to hang out with him at the base of the observation platform that was his domain. Almost from the beginning, Boyd rode in the jeep and stood at the base of the tower.

Pettinato's son, Frank Jr., first came to the beach at four or five years of age. One of his earliest memories is of his father talking about John Boyd. And it was for more than John's abilities as a swimmer. Pettinato had never hired a boy so receptive to his ideas and beliefs. John soaked up Pettinato's thoughts, responded to his discipline, and manifested an iron will and a sense of duty that Pettinato had never before seen in one of his lifeguards. No other man in John's childhood had as great an influence on him as Frank Pettinato.

But though he was a star on the beach, John experienced, in his last two years of high school, a mixture of the glory and achievement he had never known and the pain and embarrassment he had always known. Two incidents in high school left an indelible mark. The first was when a teacher said to him, "John Boyd, you'll never be anything but a salesman." Even though John's father had been a salesman, he took the remark as a biting insult; it meant that he was glib and shallow and lacked substance. After he married, he told his wife that he heard those terrible words every day of his life, that throughout his career he was driven to prove he was more than a mere salesman.

The second incident was no less powerful. Even though by 1944 the Army was drafting men in their late thirties, Bill, John's older brother, was twenty-seven and still at home. Bill had tried jobs as an elevator operator, laborer, and security guard. He had quit or been fired from every job. He became depressed that he was not one of the hundreds of other young men from Erie who went away to the war. The family told everyone he could not serve because he had a heart murmur. The truth was something quite different.

The illness that had been festering for years exploded on Saturday, April 1, 1944, when Bill, with no provocation, struck his mother. The next evening he became quite agitated and jumped through a window, cutting his arm and hand so badly that he was taken to the hospital for stitches. Two people were required to hold him in bed and administer sedatives.

His medical records show that on Monday he said he had radar in his teeth. He told hospital workers, "I want to go to see the Pope. I'd turn Catholic if he could help me. I want to go by the way of India." Later that day he complained of a terrible headache and said, "I want to see a doctor. I'm begging for mercy. You have me cornered." Various sedatives were administered and then he was admitted to Warren State Hospital, a mental institution east of Erie. He died there May 3 and was buried in a single plot in the Erie Cemetery. His death certificate says he died after a one-day bout with terminal bronchopneumonia brought on by acute catatonic excitement, and that the excitement was due to dementia praecox of more than four years' duration. In current parlance, Bill was schizophrenic.

Bill's medical records indicate that his maternal grandmother and an uncle both had mental problems and that there was a sister who was "nervous." Although she is not named, this sister was probably Marion.

After Bill died, representatives from Warren State Hospital came to the Boyd home and asked Elsie if anyone else in the family had mental illness, if there were anyone else who should be institutionalized. In the 1940s mental illness was an unbearable stigma. And the shock of people from the mental hospital knocking on her door and asking about mental illness in her family was almost too much for Elsie. Her children were ordered never to mention the visit to a living soul. If anyone asked, Bill died of pneumonia. That was it. No one in Erie knew the truth. Even Jack Arbuckle and Chet Reichert said they never knew what happened to Bill.

At the same time his family was going through such deep personal pain, John was experiencing for the first time in his life the glory of being a superior athlete, of doing something well. During his junior and senior years, he made five letters in swimming and water polo. His swim team won the state championship during his senior season. He placed second in the state in the 220-yard freestyle the same year. He was captain of the water polo team.

No one in his family came to the swim meets. Fathers of other boys sat in the bleachers and cheered. After the meets those fathers slapped their sons on the shoulders and congratulated them. John's victories were solitary and hollow.

John rarely dated in high school. He had little money for dates or social activities. Most of his clothes were still hand-me-downs. His mother told him none of this mattered. Again and again she stressed that if he worked hard and had integrity, one day he would rise above those who snickered at his poverty, ridiculed his clothes, and thought they were superior to him. This would have to be John's consolation. And he took it to heart. During the summers, he and Chet Reichert would paddle their canoe across the bay in all kinds of weather, and John would talk constantly of how he had to prove himself out in the world. He was determined to excel although he did not yet know in what area. He only knew that he had to do something better than anyone had ever done it before. He had to show people in Erie that he was somebody.

John knew from the time he entered high school that he would be drafted during his senior year, and he did not want to go into the Army. He was not one to slog out a battle on the ground. On October 30, 1944, when he was a junior in high school, he enlisted in the Army Air Corps. The terms of his enlistment were for the duration of the war plus six months. He would not report for duty until near the end of his senior year.

By then he had been hammered on the anvil of life far harder than had most young men his age. Whatever the world had to offer could be no worse than what he already had endured. He was ready. He stood six feet tall and weighed 164 pounds. His friends called him "J. B." His high school annual described him as "the strong silent type," "stouthearted," and the "merman."

John missed one of the major rites of passage: he did not attend his high school graduation. America was at war and on April 16, 1945, he answered the call; he reported for duty with the Air Corps.

On his enlistment papers he listed his civilian occupation as "lifeguard."

Chapter Two

The Big Jock and the Presbyterian

BOYD arrived late for his first war.

From Erie he went to basic training at Sheppard Field in Texas, where he applied for the aviation cadet program, a rigid course whereby young enlisted men train to be a pilot and, upon graduation, are awarded both a commission and the wings of a pilot. He was rejected because of "low aptitude."

After basic training he was ordered to Lowry Field in Colorado to be trained as a mechanic for aircraft turrets, but World War II ended that summer and there no longer was a need for such a specialty. Nevertheless, the inexorable momentum of the military was still geared to sending young men overseas; Boyd — after months at a staging area in Arizona — went to Japan as part of the occupation force. He arrived on January 3, 1946, and was assigned to the 8th Squadron of the 49th Fighter Group. His military records show that less than two months later, in order "to meet service requirements," he became a swimming instructor. As a member of the Air Corps Far Eastern Swim Team, Boyd spent his time paddling around indoor heated pools and participating in swim meets around Japan. It was an inauspicious introduction to war for the man who one day would be considered the ultimate warrior.

Little else is known of Boyd's brief service as an enlisted man. About the only thing that has survived is a story he often told, a story where the John Boyd of fact and the John Boyd of legend begin to merge, the first of the countless "Boyd stories" that accumulated over the years. The winter of 1945–1946 was particularly cold and wet in Japan. On the former Japanese air base where Boyd was stationed, officers lived in warm quarters, slept in beds, and ate hot food, while enlisted ranks lived in tents, slept on the ground, and ate K rations. Large wooden hangars suitable for barracks-type housing stood empty and unused. Fed up with this situation, Boyd led a revolt. He and his fellow soldiers tore down two hangars and used the wood to build fires so they could stay warm. Soon after, the Army inventoried base property and discovered the hangars had gone missing. Boyd was identified as the leader of the perpetrators and brought up on charges. A court-martial loomed. Officers believed this would be the quick and uncontested trial of an enlisted man who clearly was guilty. But Private Boyd went on the attack and turned the pending court-martial into a referendum on officer leadership and responsibility. He asked the investigating officer if the Army's general orders were in effect at the time he used wood from the hangars to build fires. When he was told that of course the general orders were in effect, he said one of the general orders stated that the first responsibility of an officer was to take care of his men. Officers were not doing that, not if enlisted personnel were sleeping on the ground while suitable quarters stood empty. Boyd said that if the court-martial proceeded, he would raise the issue of officer responsibility with higher authorities.

The charges were dropped. The U.S. military had lost its first run-in with Boyd. In later years Boyd often told this story, especially to Pentagon subordinates who idolized him. Among the Acolytes, Boyd's most dedicated followers, the story achieved almost ecclesiastical weight. Boyd also told the story to newspaper reporters with the added fillip: "If they had court-martialed me, then they wouldn't have had to put up with me later on."

But when Boyd was interviewed by the Office of Air Force History for the Oral History Program, he did not tell this story. One can only speculate as to why. During the lengthy interview, he told other stories in which he portrayed himself as a frequent violator of Air

Force regulations. But he did not mention destroying the hangars, although, at bottom, both his reason for doing so and the victory he achieved would certainly be worthy of note. Perhaps this was because the idea of enlisted men tearing down two hangars and burning the wood without the knowledge of officers is difficult to believe. It would take weeks, and the fires certainly would be noticed. And why tear them down at all? If the hangars were suitable as barracks, why didn't Boyd and his followers simply move into them? And it can only be called blackmail if Boyd threatened to raise the issue of officers' responsibility to their men with higher authorities. Historically the military has not caved in to blackmail from privates.

The Air Corps did not keep records of threatened courts-martial. But Boyd's Acolytes are unwavering in their belief the story is true. They say Boyd's stories always remained consistent and that had Boyd been fabricating them, little details would have changed over time.

In any case, the story reveals — especially if it is not true — how Boyd saw himself and would continue to see himself: the man of principle battling superiors devoid of principle; the idealist fighting those of higher rank who have shirked their responsibilities; the man who puts it all on the line and, after receiving threat of dire consequences, prevails. His principles win out over his opposition's lack of principles. It is just as his mother said.

Boyd was discharged on January 7, 1947, about two weeks before his twentieth birthday. His military records show he served two years and two months, but this includes the six months from when he first enlisted on October 30, 1944 — when he was still a junior in high school — until he reported for duty the following April. His active duty time was about twenty months.

Boyd grew an inch and gained weight during his time in Japan. His discharge papers show that he now stood 6'1" and weighed 180 pounds. When he arrived home, his mother was amazed at how husky he had become. One of the first people Boyd looked up upon returning to Erie was Frank Pettinato. They probably talked about Pettinato's promotion; he now was chief lifeguard at the Peninsula. And since Boyd was eligible for the GI Bill — a government-financed college education — it is almost certain that Pettinato both encouraged him to go to college and counseled him about which college to attend. They might also have talked about where Boyd could resume his swimming. The bay was frozen but Boyd swam often at the YMCA at 10th and Peach Street in downtown Erie. And only weeks after he returned from Japan, he traveled with the Erie Aquatic Club to Pittsburgh and swam against the famed University of Michigan swimming team. Boyd was the star. He won the 50-yard event in 26.2 seconds and was runner-up in the 100-yard senior freestyle.

When summer came, Boyd returned to his job at the Peninsula, now as assistant chief lifeguard. He spent much of his time patrolling the beaches with Pettinato. Frank Pettinato Jr. was seven years old that summer and remembers that when he came to the beach his father always spoke of Boyd in the most glowing terms. At home his father frequently told Frank Jr. he should grow up to be like Boyd.

When summer ended, Boyd left for the University of Iowa to study economics. He picked Iowa because of David Armbruster, the legendary swimming coach who established swimming as a sport at Iowa in 1917 and who was credited with developing the butterfly stroke and the flip turn. As far back as 1927, Armbruster persuaded the university to build a 50-meter pool. He wrote a textbook called "Competitive Swimming and Diving" and turned more than three dozen swimmers and divers into All-Americans. His swimmers regularly set national intercollegiate records.

One of the more humbling aspects of higher education, both in athletics and in academics, is when a student finds that just because he trailed clouds of glory in high school does not mean he will do the same in college. If Boyd went out for the swim team when the season began in January 1948, he did not make it. The next year at Iowa he found himself competing against the legendary Wally Ris, who began breaking swim records in 1947 and won an Olympic gold medal in 1948. His specialty was the 100-meter and the 220-yard freestyle — Boyd's events.

In 1950, after Ris graduated, Boyd made the varsity team. In later years when Boyd talked about his experiences as a swimmer at Iowa, he always said Coach Armbruster "played favorites." Boyd had been a favorite of Art Weibel and was the favorite of Frank Pettinato. But at Iowa he was not picked out of the crowd. His bitterness toward his college experience was such that for the rest of his life he referred sarcastically to Iowa as "the corn college" and insisted, "I don't know why I went there. I got nothing out of it."

John Boyd met Mary Ethelyn Bruce when both were juniors. She was a prim and petite brunette from Ottumwa, Iowa, and made no secret of the fact she was at college to find a husband. Boyd and Mary met at the Veterans Club. She was there with one of Boyd's fraternity brothers. Mary must have made more of an impression on Boyd than Boyd made on her because when he called a few days later asking for a date, she didn't remember him. After searching through the annual and finding his picture, she decided he was "not bad looking" and agreed to meet him.

In the beginning it seemed they had much in common.

Both had worked as lifeguards. Both came from families of five children — three boys and two girls. Both had mothers who were German Presbyterians, widows who were strong and domineering women. Both came from families that, because of the death of a father, had money problems.

Mary had no trouble finding out all there was to know about Boyd. He told her that she looked like Jeanette MacDonald and then talked mostly of himself. He told her of Japan and how he led a revolt against the officers. He told her of being a champion swimmer back in Erie and he told her of the great Frank Pettinato. He told her how close his family was and how loyal they all were to one another. He said, "In my family we had a tough life. But it didn't bother me. I am not a whiner. I move on." And when he talked he talked loudly and waved his arms and embellished the simplest of stories and made the world new and interesting and exciting.

Iowa was overflowing with older men who had been in the war and there were so many to choose from. But Boyd was different. He made life an adventure. His enthusiasm and joie de vivre mesmerized her. Soon she was dating no one else. Slowly, she told Boyd the story of her life. She was the fifth child of Elizabeth and Albert Bruce. Her mother, Elizabeth Bonar, grew up on an Iowa farm and married Albert Weyer Bruce, a mechanic. Albert was a gentle man whose wants were few. He wanted to work on cars and he wanted to please his wife. But he found he could not do both.

Elizabeth was the antipode of Albert, as hard and dominating as he was soft and accommodating. She had seen enough dirt and grime on the farm and she wanted a different life for herself and for her children. She wanted her family to have a certain social standing in Ottumwa. She wanted Albert to clean the grease from his fingernails and become an executive. Under her ceaseless prodding, he became a consultant and then a superintendent in a company that manufactured equipment for poultry processing plants — equipment that stripped feathers from chickens. And there he was an unhappy man. He did not want to be an executive, even a low-level executive; he yearned to be a mechanic. He died of a heart attack when Mary was eleven and his widow wondered for years if she was the reason. "I wonder if I pushed him too hard," she sometimes said.

These moments of introspection were rare for Mrs. Bruce. She was a woman who had to be in charge. The poultry processing plant sent her monthly checks, but it was not enough to raise five children. She moved the children to the unheated attic and turned the Bruce home into a boardinghouse that she ran with the efficiency of a military operation.

Mrs. Bruce dictated Mary's life to such a degree that Mary had few opinions of her own. She thought whatever her mother wanted her to think. She was a passive person, one of those who stands still and waits to see what life has in store. She almost never argued with anyone; if there was a disagreement, she nodded and agreed but then dug in her heels in small passive-aggressive ways.

When Mary graduated from high school, she attended Parsons College, a small religious school in Fairfield, Iowa. She was there for only a year before transferring to the larger, man-rich University of Iowa, where she majored in home economics. And because she felt she was misunderstood, because she felt there was something wrong in her thinking and how she looked at the world, many of her electives were in psychology.

"Actually, I majored in 'looking for a husband,'" she said. She knew exactly what she wanted. Because her two favorite older brothers were not athletic and not popular, she wanted to marry what she termed a "big jock." She thought an athlete would be easy and accommodating and that after graduation he might become a coach and they could lead a simple life in a small Iowa town. She would be a member of the local Presbyterian church and sing in the choir and life would be uncomplicated.

Boyd fit the bill. He was tall and handsome and dark-haired, just like her brothers. But he was an athlete and very popular as well. She did not question the depth of his faith or whether or not he lived his religion as she did. She was a good Presbyterian and thought he was the same. For her, the world was black and white, good and bad, right and wrong. There were only absolutes, rigid lines that could never be crossed. She looked upon Boyd and put him into a neat and tightly wrapped little box.

The only part that didn't fit her image of him as a "big jock" was that he read so much. He always carried books, not just class books, but books on history and war and philosophy. Mary shrugged this off and considered it a rather quaint affectation. And then there was the military thing. At the beginning of his junior year, Boyd signed up for the Air Force Reserve Officers' Training Corps. He said it was purely financial, as he needed the monthly twenty-eight dollars that ROTC students received. Whatever his reason, he took to ROTC with a passion. He barked orders and took charge of virtually every gathering until the other ROTC students began calling him "Captain Boyd." He was becoming much more assertive, what the military calls a "take-charge guy." He was coming into his own as a man.

When Mary asked Boyd what he wanted to do after graduation, he told her he wanted to go into the Air Force and fly jets. Her brow wrinkled. But she shouldn't worry, he would fly only for a few years and then he would do something else.

After their junior year, ROTC students go to a summer camp that serves as an indoctrination course for young men about to become military officers. Boyd was en route to summer camp in June 1950, when North Korea invaded South Korea. Suddenly America was in another war, this time against Communism. It was the first conflict of the Cold War and it was seen as a contest of good versus evil.

Boyd's last year of college was like his last year in high school, in that he knew when he graduated he was going to war. He decided early on he would go as a fighter pilot. He said in his Air Force Oral History interview that he knew bomber pilots were "a bunch of truck drivers" and "I did not want to be in a crowded bus and have a bunch of people continually telling me what to do." He went to Omaha to take the physical examination and the psychological tests that determined whether or not a person had the capability to become a pilot. He passed them all.

Now that he was accepted for pilot training, he talked to Mary at great length of the airplanes he would fly. After December 1950, there was only one for him — the F-86 Sabre jet.

On December 17, a Sabre had shot down a MiG near the western end of the Yalu River, over a town called Sinuiju, and it made headlines across America. The F-86 suddenly was the most romanticized instrument of war in history, a flashing streak of silver whose guns spoke for America.

By 1950 America had largely forgotten that the Luftwaffe had jet fighters near the end of World War II. And most did not remember that the XP-80, America's forerunner to the venerable F-80, flew in 1944. After World War II, both the Soviets and Americans had access to Germany's research on jet fighters, and both countries went into production on jets based in large part on the German research. The Soviet MiG-15 and the American F-86 Sabre were remarkably similar. Both had swept wings and were about the same size, the MiG being slightly smaller.

Aesthetically the Sabre was the most appealing jet imaginable, with its swept wings and bubble canopy and, in the "D" model, the beak over the air intake that gave it a menacing and aggressive appearance. Here was an aircraft not pulled by a propeller but pushed by fire and thunder. A *jet*. Even the name had a hard new magic about it. In the Sabre, America saw Newton's Third Law in all its glory: light the fire and stoke the burner and the opposite reaction is a burst of amazing speed in a jet that slices through the heavens. Few aircraft had ever gripped America's imagination as did this one.

In what was then considered an amazing display of brute power, the F-86 climbed at a forty-five-degree angle. It flew 680 mph and broke every existing speed record. It was sleek and beautiful and in the skies of Korea it became the very symbol of America's new love affair with jet fighters, of the newly independent U.S. Air Force, of America in the battle against Communism. And it was the last truly great fighter aircraft the Air Force had until almost twenty years later, when Boyd was instrumental in designing a better one.

Boyd told anyone who would listen that this was the only aircraft for him.

Mary listened to all this with one ear. She knew by then that Boyd was the man she would marry. She thought he had been about to propose, but then this war in Korea came along and now all he talked about was jets, jets, jets. After graduating in February 1951, she went home to Ottumwa to await his proposal. She rented an apartment and began looking for a job. She finally became an assistant to a local doctor, giving shots and handling menial chores. And she waited.

Living by herself was lonely and after only a few weeks she moved back home with her mother. She was grown now, but that did not stop her mother from ordering her about. "I did not like Mother telling me what to do," Mary said. "But it was comfortable." She took driving lessons and, at twenty-two, had her first driver's license.

Mary and Boyd often talked by phone. He came down on the bus from Iowa City almost every weekend. He graduated in June 1951 and was commissioned a second lieutenant in the Air Force. Elsie and Ann came to Iowa for his graduation. Mary was also there. She had awaited this event for months, thinking that when Boyd graduated he would propose. She remembers being intimidated by Mrs. Boyd. Mary tried to be nice and solicitous, but Elsie walked about with such a stern expression on her face and with such bold penetrating eyes that it seemed she was angry at everyone except her son. She made it quite clear she thought her son could have done better in his choice of a girlfriend.

Mary had never been around anyone with a physical disability and was terribly uncomfortable watching Ann limp. It was not a good weekend for her. And it was made all the more unpleasant by the fact that Boyd did not propose.

Boyd was ordered to Albuquerque, New Mexico, until the next flight training class opened, and Mary returned to Ottumwa. Maybe Boyd would propose soon. But what if he met someone else? What if he waited until his flight training was over and then he was sent to Korea? The chances of finding a husband in Ottumwa were slim.

Mary would wait.

Chapter Three

Fledgling

SECOND lieutenants, called "butter bars" because of the single gold bar they wear as an insignia of rank, often are given the most menial of jobs, tasks that must be done by officers but that higher-ranking officers would not deign to perform. This is particularly true for second lieutenants about to begin flight training. These young men believe they are Godlike beings, and to nonrated officers they are not only insufferable but will grow more so once they complete flight training and pin silver wings over their left-breast pocket. If there is any group on earth with healthier egos than fighter pilots, they have yet to be discovered. Bureaucrats who run the Air Force personnel system believe that a menial job might teach humility to these fledglings. Over the years they have discovered this belief is founded more on hope than on reality — no fighter pilot ever has been or ever will be humble. But the bureaucrats keep trying.

When Boyd was commissioned, there was a need for an assistant secretary in the officers' dining room at Kirtland Air Force Base (AFB) in Albuquerque. So Boyd went to New Mexico. He was there only a month, but it must have seemed an eternity.

On August 1, he was ordered to report to the 3301 Training Squadron at Columbus AFB, Mississippi, where he would begin flight training. Flying-school classes are numbered according to when the students are scheduled to graduate. Boyd was a member of 52-F. Because experienced Air Force pilots were needed in Korea and were considered too valuable to waste their time teaching basic flying, the instructors at Columbus were civilians. Boyd's instructor was C. Wayne Lemons, an employee of California Eastern, the charter and freight airline that won the Air Force contract to teach young men how to fly. Boyd first went on what was called the "dollar ride," an orientation flight over northeastern Mississippi, where he would be flying for the next several months. He was shown the numerous unpaved auxiliary strips, some of them narrow slices down the middle of a cotton patch. Then he began his classroom work in aeronautics, meteorology, the theory of flight, navigation, cross-country flying, Morse code, radio procedure, and a host of other arcane disciplines.

Boyd was in a class of about forty lieutenants who had received their commissions through ROTC, and about one hundred ten aviation cadets. The forty lieutenants all knew each other after a few weeks, and the camaraderie of learning to fly and the knowledge they soon would be going to war welded them into a tightly knit band of brothers. Many would go on to become high-ranking officers or would achieve great things in combat; some would become legends in the Air Force. But for the remainder of their lives, they would be tied together as members of 52-F.

In the six months he was at Columbus, Boyd became known among the young lieutenants not only for his flying and leadership abilities but for several personal attributes. He could eat an inordinate amount of food, and he could eat it faster than anyone else in 52-F. At the dining room he stacked his plate so high that when he walked to the table, food tumbled to the floor. He sat down, leaned over, and looked neither right nor left as he forked down the food. It was as if he were shoveling coal to stoke a furnace. His hand seemed never to stop in its round trip from plate to mouth to plate. And he apparently did not chew. Usually his squadron mates had barely begun eating when Boyd finished, sighed, rubbed his stomach, pushed his chair back, popped what seemed to be a full pack of Juicy Fruit chewing gum into his mouth, and began talking. He chewed so much gum and chewed so vigorously that he was known to members of 52-F as the "Juicy Fruit Kid." While his squadron mates were still eating,

Boyd expounded on aviation tactics, how frustrated he was about having to follow the Air Force training regimen when he was ready for advanced maneuvers, and how he was going to be the best fighter pilot in the Air Force.

Every morning the students flew the T-6 "Texan," a venerable tandem-seat, single-engine aircraft that in World War II had served as an advanced trainer. The qualities that made it an advanced trainer in an earlier war made it suitable as the basic trainer for men about to transition into jets. The narrow landing gear on the "Terrible Texan" caused many students to lose control after landing and make a sharp horizontal turn known as a "ground loop," a maneuver that could fold or even shear off the landing gear. The common expression was, "There are two kinds of T-6 pilots: those who have ground-looped it and those who are going to ground-loop it." Despite its tendency to bite unwary pilots, the T-6 was sturdy and cruised at a stately 135 mph. The redline, or never-exceed speed, which could be achieved only in a power dive from considerable altitude, was about 260 mph.

From the beginning of his training, Boyd walked around the base as if he were a general. He was not shy when it came to lecturing the other students about aerial tactics. He was independent to the point of being ornery and often argued with his civilian instructor about what he thought was the slow pace of instruction.

During his breaks, Boyd traveled by train to Iowa to see Mary. On one of those weekends, he finally proposed. He and Mary found a ring at a small jewelry store in Ottumwa and she began planning the wedding.

Back in flight training, Boyd quickly went through basic maneuvers and soloed. And then he went out and threw the T-6 around the sky in such a fearless manner that it seemed to others as if he had done it a thousand times. It was difficult for his classmates to accept that he was a student just as they were, that he had never had flying lessons until now. He was, quite simply, a master of the T-6.

To realize the significance of this, one must understand that the first time a young man slides into the cockpit of an aircraft and looks at the strange collection of instruments, a feeling of awe washes over him. No matter how intensely he wants to be a pilot, there is an inherent sense of wonder simply sitting in the cockpit. And when he goes aloft for the first time and realizes he is moving in a three-dimensional world, when he realizes that a moment of inattention can lead to a crash and a fiery explosion, he sometimes finds he has too much respect for the airplane. A pilot can be too cautious. He can be too methodical. He reads and memorizes the specifications, knows the boundaries of the performance envelope, and is careful never to nudge up against the performance limits. But Boyd did not believe the performance specs and had no fear of the aircraft. He jostled the T-6; he pushed it and horsed it around the sky. He flung the airplane up against the outside edges of the performance envelope and then beyond. If the book said the aircraft should never exceed 260 mph, Boyd pushed it to 265 or 270 or 280. He knew intuitively by the sound of the aircraft when it was approaching not the book limits but the true limits, which, for those bold enough to search for them, always are slightly greater. Test pilots do the same thing, but most of them are engineers and highly skilled pilots tuned to a razor edge of proficiency. Few student pilots are so bold.

Pilots who pride themselves on their finesse, who never deviate more than fifty feet from their assigned altitude or more than ten knots from their airspeed, or who fly maneuvers strictly by the book, would say that Boyd was "heavy-handed." And they would be correct. But there is little finesse in air combat. Many civilians and those who have never looked through the gun sight — then called a pipper — at an enemy aircraft have a romantic perception, no doubt influenced by books and movies about World War I, that pilots are knights of the air, chivalrous men who salute their opponents before engaging in a fight that always is fair. They believe that elaborate rules of aerial courtesy prevail and that battle in the clear pure upper regions somehow is different, more glorified and rarefied, than battle in the mud. This is arrant nonsense. Aerial combat, according to those who have participated, is a basic and primitive form of battle that happens to take place in the air. Fighter pilots — that is, the ones who survive air combat — are not gentlemen; they are backstabbing assassins. They come out of the sun and attack an enemy when he is blind. They sneak up behind or underneath or "bounce" the enemy from above or flop into position on his tail — his six-o'clock position — and "tap" him before he knows they are there. That is why fighter pilots jink and weave and dart about like water bugs in a mason jar. They never hold a heading or a position longer than six or eight seconds. Aerial combat is brutally unforgiving. To come in second place is to die, usually in a rather spectacular manner. Most casualties never know they are targets until they are riddled with bullets, covered with flames, and on the way to creating a big hole in the ground. Those who want to engage in the romanticized World War I pirouette of a fair fight will have a short career. Thus, aerial combat favors the bold, those who are not afraid to use the airplane for its true purpose: a gun platform. There is nothing sophisticated about sneaking up on someone and killing him. Aerial combat is a blood sport, a knife in the dark. Winners live and losers die. Boyd instinctively knew this and his flying was, from the beginning, that of the true fighter pilot.

A month before he graduated, he took Christmas leave and, after an engagement of only three months, he and Mary were married in the Presbyterian church in Ottumwa. Boyd wore his Air Force uniform. Elsie and Ann were there. Boyd had little money or time for a honeymoon, so he and Mary drove twenty-five miles to Fairfield, home of Parsons College, and rented a hotel room for several days. Then, together, they set off for Columbus.

During the last months of flight training — when it is clear they will graduate and be awarded the wings of an Air Force pilot — the trainees are divided into those who will go to multiengine aircraft and those who will fly fighters.

Fighter pilots were what the Air Force needed. On the bomber side of the Korean War, the B-29s and B-50s of the Strategic Air Command (SAC) suffered heavy losses flying daytime missions and were reduced to flying almost entirely at night and in smaller numbers. SAC was neither prepared nor equipped to fight a small conventional war; SAC was geared toward delivering nuclear weapons. It was different on the fighter side of the war. Six fighter wings were stationed in Korea, one in Japan, and another in Okinawa — all dedicated to the war in Korea. A wing consists of three squadrons, each theoretically comprising twenty-four to thirty-two aircraft. A fighter wing has about ninety-six aircraft. Thus, these six wings had a theoretical maximum of five hundred to six hundred aircraft, although the actual number was about half that. F-86 pilots rotated to non-combat duty after one hundred missions, and there was always a demand for replacements.

Korea was a fighter war, not a bomber war, and chances are slim that a fighter pilot as skillful as Boyd would have been sent to bombers. But as Boyd tells the story, there was a plot afoot to keep him out of F-86s. Boyd claimed the Air Force told him he was too tall to be a fighter pilot and would have to fly bombers. "Bullshit, I will not go to multiengines. I will not stay in the service if I have to go to multiengines," he recalled telling them. He threatened to resign his commission.

If Boyd did deliver such an ultimatum, a big part of it was bluff. He knew if he tried to resign the Air Force would keep him on active duty, give him a demeaning job, and make his life miserable until he was discharged. Boyd was too committed to flying jets simply to walk away. If indeed he was told he was going to fly bombers, and if he did threaten to resign, the most likely reason is that he wanted to prove the point that he would rather leave the service than fly bombers. This might sit well with superiors who appreciated a passionate approach. Whatever happened, Boyd got his wish and was assigned to fighters, and the story of Boyd's ultimatum, like that of tearing down the hangars in Japan, was valuable primarily for what it revealed about his mind-set. For the remainder of his career, Boyd would see plots and punishment in every new assignment. Again and again there would be a campaign to embarrass or humiliate him with a nonflying job, a bureaucratic battle would ensue, and he, against great odds and with his career on the line, would ultimately prevail.

Williams AFB in Arizona was known as "Willy" or the "Patch" and, as the incubator for fighter pilots, was one of the most famous bases in the Air Force. Here, pilots climbed into jets for the first time. Willy also was the jumping-off point for specialized training. If a pilot was to fly the F-84 fighter-bomber, he would transfer from Willy to Luke AFB, also in Arizona, for combat training. If he was to fly the F-86, he would be sent to Nellis AFB in Nevada.

Instructors at Willy knew that every pilot they trained would be sent to Korea, and they took it as their solemn and sacred duty to make sure the young pilots were well trained and highly professional. Upon arriving at Willy in April 1952, class 52-F gathered in an auditorium for their welcome. A colonel stood in front of them, stared belligerently, then said, "If I had my way, we'd kill half you sons of bitches. The other half would leave here as fighter pilots." He let them chew on that for a moment and then said, "But the goddamn Congress won't let me do that."

Nevertheless, he tried. Class 52-F had more than its share of training accidents and fatalities. The pace was stepped up and the transition to jets and to basic combat training was made as realistic as possible — a prelude to even more realistic training for those who would go to Nellis. But Boyd chafed under the regimen. "A lot of the things they were doing there I had already learned, and I wanted it to go a bit faster to pick up the pace," he recalled. "I felt as if I was being held back — that is, until I got that first jet ride, then I really liked it."

He began his jet training in the F-80 "Shooting Star," a single-engine, straight-winged jet that was slow and underpowered. Early models of the F-80 had no ejection seat, so if the aircraft caught fire or "flamed out" or had a mechanical problem, the pilot was in serious trouble, especially a pilot as tall as Boyd. The least he could hope for was banged-up knees. If he was flying a model of the F-80 with an ejection seat, he would be lucky if his legs were not broken or even amputated.

Tall F-80 pilots were solicitous toward their mechanics.

Boyd found the rules were different when flying a jet. Ease the throttle forward in the T-6 and there is a rising thunder of noise and a surge of power that can pull a pilot through a loop or around the corner in a tight turn. But careless throttle application in a jet caused a new phenomenon known as "flameout." Some of the early jet engines were unreliable and suddenly stopped in flight. And when young pilots pushed the outside of the envelope during tactical engagements, they sometimes overestimated their flying abilities and crashed in the desert.

Boyd never worried about any of this. "I started to do my dirty tricks again — I just could not avoid them," he said. Part of advanced flight training at Willy was what Boyd called "stupid cross-country trips," where the pilot would report in regularly by radio. Rather than flying these trips, Boyd took his F-80 down to where he knew friends from Luke AFB were flying F-84s in simulated air-to-air combat and joined in. Several times when he was supposed to be on a cross-country flight, he went out to where the instructors practiced simulated air-to-air to "bounce" them. They did not like this, especially when he won.

During his Oral History interview, Boyd was asked what he thought about when he found himself on the defensive in those early air-to-air engagements. He manifested both the macho nature of a fighter pilot and the thinking of fighter aviation at the time when he replied, "I had to bend the shit out of that airplane" and "hose" the opponent.

To "bend" an airplane was to pull more Gs than the enemy, to put one's aircraft on the inside of the pursuit curve and gain the advantage from which one could fire.

When a jet fires its guns, tracers allow the pilot to correct his aim. If the jet is pulling Gs, the stream of tracers bends and looks like the stream of water from a hose that is moved quickly. Thus, to "hose" an enemy is to get him in the pipper, follow him with tracers, and — as pilots say — wax his ass.

Halfway through the training, the instructors looked over the best of the young pilots, those who manifested not only stick-and-rudder skills, but who had what has been described as "the spirit of attack borne in a brave heart," and selected them to transition into the F-86 Sabre. Boyd was selected.

On September 13, 1952, Boyd reported for duty at Nellis for combat training in the F-86. If Willy was tough, Nellis was tougher. Nellis was the only base in the Air Force that sent fighter pilots straight into combat. If a pilot were not trained to a sufficient level of skill, the aggressive MiG pilots, many of whom were highly professional Russians, would shoot him down in his first engagement. So at Nellis the idea was to push the aircraft beyond the envelope, to make the training as much like combat as possible. The saying of the time was "The more you bleed in peacetime, the less you bleed in war." This is another way of saying that normal rules of safety and common sense often were ignored. The thinking among pilots was "If you survive Nellis, Korea will be easy."

Nellis was in fact a gladiator school. The pilots were young and cocky and flying the most advanced jet in the U.S. Air Force, and they were about to go into combat. This was not just any war, this was a war to protect the land of the free and the home of the brave from the ravages of Godless Communism. Training *had* to be warlike. And if young men died, so be it. No price was too high. Not when losing meant being overwhelmed by Communism.

Pilots fought in simulated air-to-air combat, always maneuvering to get on the other pilot's six-o'clock position. A siren to rally personnel when there was a crash was located near the flight line, and its wail echoed across Nellis at least once each week, sometimes twice. Soon afterward an official blue staff car would drive slowly down the streets where pilots lived, the driver looking for the correct address. All along the way, the wives — Mary among them — who had heard the siren stood at the window and prayed the car would not pull into their driveway. So many pilots died at Nellis in those days that incoming F-86 students were told, "If you see the flag at full staff, take a picture."

Boyd says that one year, more than seventy pilots were killed. A historian at Nellis says he probably was conservative — that wing commanders sometimes doctored statistics if too many pilots died.

Already Boyd was coming to believe there was more to air-to-air combat than "bending" the jet and muscling it through high-G turns. Embryonic ideas about aerial tactics were beginning to form, not so much in an academic but in a practical sense. He began defeating his instructors, some of whom were combat veterans of Korea.

In December Boyd reached eighty hours of what the Air Force called "applied tactics" and was ready for Korea. His last advice from Nellis instructors was simple: "Stay inside. Hose him down."

Before departing, Boyd was allowed an extended leave because Mary was pregnant and about to deliver her firstborn. Mary and Boyd drove to Ottumwa. She was glad to leave Nellis: the desert and the scrubby bushes and the cactus and the endless wind were not like the familiar green fields of Iowa. Jets took off and landed from dawn to dusk. The smell of aviation fuel, so beloved by pilots, nauseated her.

Stephen Boyd was born February 14, 1953, a child conceived in his father's world at Nellis and delivered into his mother's at Ottumwa. Boyd had a picture taken of him holding his infant son aloft, and he carried it in his wallet until it was creased and darkened with age and falling apart. Often a father is close to his firstborn, especially if the child is a son. But Boyd was unusually close to Stephen, almost as if he were unconsciously aware of what soon would come into Stephen's life and wanted to hold on to the boy so he would have the good days to remember.

Soon it was time for Boyd to depart for combat. He had missed World War II, but he would have a part in Korea. He was doing what the young men of Erie always do when America is at war, but in Boyd's case, this was just the first step of his destiny.

What Boyd learned in Korea would be the foundation for his life's work.

Chapter Four

K-13 and MiG Alley

ONCE again, Boyd arrived late for war.

On March 27, 1953, he and a host of other young men, most of them sporting the silver bars of a first lieutenant on their collars, arrived aboard a C-54 transport at Suwon in South Korea. They looked around with all the confidence of men in their midtwenties who had survived Nellis and who considered themselves to be the best-trained pilots in the world. They looked across the tarmac at the row of shiny F-86s and they were anxious to kill MiGs.

For the first few weeks in Korea, they flew relatively safe and uneventful missions as wingmen or the type of missions older pilots did not want — weather reconnaissance or escort duty. Air Force planes went into combat in flights of four. The flight consisted of the flight leader and his wingman, accompanied by an element leader and his wingman. The flight leader and the element leader were the gunslingers, the shooters, the ones who initiated the attack. The sole and inviolate duty of the wingman was to cover his leader's six-o'clock position, to protect him from enemy aircraft. A new pilot had to fly about thirty missions as a wingman before he could be promoted to element leader and become a shooter.

Suwon was known to pilots as "K-13" and was about thirty miles south of Seoul and two hundred fifty miles south of the Yalu River. K-13 was home of the 25th Fighter-Interceptor Squadron of the 51st Fighter-Interceptor Group. The 25th did no bombing or ground-attack missions; its job was air supremacy. Pilots of the 25th were headhunters. The 25th was the "red squadron" and its F-86s had a red stripe across the top of the tail, while its pilots wore red scarves. Anyone hearing an F-86 pilot identify himself on the radio with a call sign of a bird, as in "Eagle Six," knew he was listening to a pilot from the 25th.

Pilots from the 25th slept in tents bordered on the bottom with cor-rugated siding. The eight-man tents usually had ten occupants. Not even Erie winters compared with the cold of Korea.

Lieutenants newly arrived in Korea were called "smokes." And before a smoke could be unleashed against Communist pilots, he had to go through a few orientation and training flights. Each squadron had its own way of doing this. The 25th sent its smokes to "Clobber College."

Two curricula existed at Clobber College, one formal and one informal. The formal curriculum said the smokes had to crawl into an F-86 and follow one of the combat veterans as he showed them the U.S. side of the combat zone, pointed out emergency fields, and familiarized them with local weather patterns. They performed a few instrument approaches. But most of all they learned the ROE — the rules of engagement — that dictated when, how, and where (mostly where) they could engage MiGs in battle. Under no circum-stances could an American pilot cross the Yalu River and go into Manchuria, where North Korean aircraft were based. American pilots most often encountered enemy aircraft in "MiG Alley," the thirty-mile-wide stretch south of the Yalu where MiGs patrolled. If an F-86 pilot had a MiG in his pipper and the MiG fled across the Yalu, the F-86 pilot had to disengage. Manchuria was a sanctuary that America would not violate.

Or, at least, that was the official policy; young warriors mounted in an F-86 did not always follow the rules. Countless times young pilots chased MiGs back to their sanctuary and shot them down as they were landing. Many MiG kills were disallowed because the gun-camera film showed runways in Manchuria, and for the pilot to claim the kill meant he would be shipped home. (So many MiGs were shot down in Manchuria that pilots said, "No aces are made south of the Yalu.") The proscriptive ROE in Korea foreshadowed the even more rigid rules America would impose on its pilots in the next war.

The informal curriculum at Clobber College called for one of the combat veterans to take up a smoke and see what he was made of — to have the young lieutenant get on his six and see how long he could stay there as the experienced pilot banked and climbed and pulled heavy Gs. Then he would get on the six of the new pilot, tuck in close and tight, and see if the new pilot could shake him. Tactics used by experienced F-86 pilots were essentially the same tactics used by P-51 pilots in World War II but at higher altitudes and greater speeds.

In his oral history, Boyd told what happened when he went up for the informal part of his training. He and an experienced pilot climbed to altitude over K-13 and the combat vet ordered him to get in trail. The lead pilot rolled and snapped and flung his F-86 all over the sky. His intent was to force Boyd to disengage or to throw Boyd out front so he would become the target. The usual procedure for the aircraft in pursuit is to match the fleeing aircraft maneuver for maneuver, to be glued to his six, and to wait for that split second when he can fire his guns. But Boyd didn't play the game. He pulled up and off to the side, and as the pilot came out the bottom of a roll, he pounced on him, still locked on his six, still with the advantage, and with a firing solution.

Then the two reversed positions. Now Boyd was the target. As he tells the story, ". . . I took that son of a bitch and in a crazy roll, I just sent him forward." When a fighter pilot is being closely pursued and slows abruptly in a maneuver that flings his pursuer forward, he is, in fighter-pilot vernacular, "watching the crowd go by." Boyd honked his F-86 into a high-G barrel roll, one that instantly slowed it, and caused the other pilot to shoot past him and become the target.

On a flight designed to show the young pilots a bit of humility and to teach them the dangers of combat, Boyd turned the tables and defeated a combat veteran. He was elated. He considered himself ready for combat, and he believed that once the enemy pilots knew he was there, most of them would park their MiGs and go home.

In early spring, Mary took Stephen on a ten-hour train ride to Erie to show him off to his grandmother. She was nervous about the trip because this was the first time she would be alone with her intimidating mother-in-law. But she thought with Boyd overseas she ought to get to know her mother-in-law and let her mother-in-law get to know Stephen.

Elsie and Mary were puttering about in the kitchen when John's mother asked about her son and what he said in his letters and how he was doing in Korea. Mary dissembled, not telling Elsie she had only written one letter.

"John loves it over there," she said.

Elsie was astonished. She stopped in her tracks and turned her basilisk stare on Mary. "What do you mean he loves it? He's in a war."

"Yes, but he is doing what he was trained to do. He's excited about being there."

Elsie was so angry she flounced from the room.

While in Erie, Mary went sailing several times with Jack Arbuckle. "My son is over there in Korea, at war, and you're out on the lake with another man," Elsie complained. Never one to mince words, she also told Mary she was "irresponsible."

Mary left Erie after five weeks. She thought her mother-in-law would have enjoyed a visit, if not so much from her daughter-in-law, then certainly from her new grandson. But later Elsie said to her, "Five weeks! I thought you would never leave."

Back in Ottumwa, Mary found a letter from Boyd. He wanted to know why Mary didn't write more often. "Some of the guys here get a letter every day," he said.

Mary was casual in her response. "I thought you are where you wanted to be. I thought you were having a good time."

And he was. He might be miffed about not getting as many letters as he thought he should have, but he was having a good time, a great time.

A few weeks after Mary went sailing on Lake Erie, Boyd completed his twenty-ninth mission and logged his forty-fourth combat hour. Any day he expected to be promoted to element leader and thereby become a shooter. He believed he would soon be bagging MiGs in record numbers.

"I was not worried about getting my head pounded in," he later said. "In fact, I thought about that for a couple of nights. Jesus Christ,

I really like this stuff. If I could only get five on a mission. Ping! Ping! Ping! Ping! Ping!"

On June 30, 1953, several weeks before the war ended, Boyd was officially credited with damaging a MiG-15. No details of the engagement could be found, but years later he would tell the Acolytes how he sneaked across the Yalu and shot down a MiG but could not claim credit for the kill. Boyd said a Royal Air Force exchange officer, Jock Maitland, had asked him to cross the Yalu as his wingman on an illegal foray into a MiG-rich environment. They were at 40,000 feet but no MiGs were up, so they descended through dense cloud cover. Shortly after breaking into the clear, at about 19,000 feet, they sighted a gaggle of MiGs, fourteen or sixteen aircraft. Maitland and Boyd dove into the formation. Maitland maneuvered onto the six of a fleeing MiG but did not shoot. He was 200 feet behind the MiG, locked on its tail, and not shooting. Boyd got on the radio and said, "Damn, Jock, why don't you shoot? Goddamn, Jock, those other guys are coming. You have to hose that guy." Maitland did not answer.

The two pilots horsed their aircraft all over the sky, caught in a gaggle of MiGs. What Boyd did not know until later was that Maitland had an electrical failure and his guns would not fire. Then the two pilots came under attack from anti-aircraft fire. They were low on fuel so they disengaged and climbed back to altitude and returned to K-13. Boyd led the descent through the clouds with Maitland on his wing. (Maitland confirms this story.) The two men were fortunate they were not sent home. In the last few months of the war, the 25th sent home six pilots for crossing the Yalu.

By June the hotshot Soviet pilots were no longer flying in North Korea, and American pilots shot down seventy-seven MiGs without the loss of a single F-86. It was a turkey shoot for F-86 pilots, so a question naturally arises: if Boyd was so good, and if he was there at the best time for an F-86 pilot to be there, why did he not shoot down MiGs?

The answer is that he never had the chance. Hostilities ceased before he was promoted to element leader, so he never was a shooter. But even if he had been a shooter, it does not follow that he would have bagged a MiG. Some pilots seemed to find MiGs almost every time they went up. Other pilots flew twenty or thirty missions — one flew fifty-one missions — without seeing a MiG.

The most important part of the Korean War for Boyd was not that he never shot down a MiG, but rather what he did and what he discovered after hostilities ceased. Rarely in the life of a man are successes so clearly stacked one atop the other in a precise, easy-to-see evolution as they are in the life of John Boyd. The accomplishments of Korea are the foundation of that evolution.

First, Boyd's ability as a pilot was outstanding. After hostilities ceased, most of the high-time combat veterans quickly rotated to flesh out fighter squadrons at other bases around the world. F-86s still patrolled MiG Alley, and on the return flights, if there was sufficient fuel, the pilots engaged in simulated air-to-air combat. On days when there were no reconnaissance flights, the pilots slid into their Sabres, climbed to 30,000 feet, and fought until the fuel was exhausted. Boyd clearly was the best F-86 driver in the squadron, so good that on October 20, 1953, he was made the assistant operations officer.

In addition to being known as a "good stick," Boyd became known in his squadron for the appetite that had so impressed his fellow pilots at Columbus AFB. The Officers Club had an all-you-can-eat "steak night" once a week. Jerald Parker remembers that he and Boyd would go to the club together, order a steak, and begin eating. Parker would take only a few bites when Boyd would jump up and go for his second, usually bigger, steak. By now Boyd also was becoming known as a talker, and about the only thing he talked about was air-to-air combat. He had a one-track mind. He talked as fast as he ate, and he could do both at the same time. Sometimes food and spittle flew from his mouth as he talked. Other officers spoke of Boyd's table manners with dismay, even disgust. His behavior was most unbecoming for an officer and a gentleman. Few other pilots wanted to sit near Boyd at the dining table. He leaned close when he talked to them. And if he thought they did not understand, he would reach out with a long finger, poke them in the chest, and demand, "Do you get what I am telling you?"

He talked so much and so often and so loudly about tactics that on November 25 he was made a flight commander and tactics instructor for the squadron. (The Air Force later changed the "tactics instructor" title to "weapons officer.") At this point, what Boyd was teaching was a refinement and an extension of existing tactics. He was simply a great stick with no reluctance to push the outside limits of the performance envelope.

Pilots were intrigued both by Boyd's aircraft handling skills and by his ideas. They asked him to write his tactics down and prepare diagrams of various tactical maneuvers. He eagerly accepted the task and began making notes, putting briefings together, and studying tactics of previous wars. He stayed up during the long cold Korean nights writing lesson plans. Soon he was holding classes.

Even Boyd's fellow F-86 pilots, all of whom were avid and passionate about flying jets, were struck by his enthusiasm and energy. More than one said they had never seen a man before or since who was so single-minded about aviation. He did not see the F-86 as an engine and fuselage and an inanimate collection of esoteric parts; he saw it as a sleek and beautiful and lethal weapon of war, almost a living thing, each aircraft having its own personality, each to be ridden into the heavens in the name of the United States of America.

When Boyd talked of aerial tactics, he grimaced and waved his arms, paced the room, wiggled his shoulders, and snapped his head back and forth. His voice was loud and nonstop. Nervous energy steamed from him. If a person asked him a question, and if Boyd thought the person truly sought knowledge, Boyd would tell him everything he wanted to know about aerial tactics. But he expected those who disagreed to come around to his viewpoint — and quickly. If someone belittled his ideas, they were instantly and forever dismissed from his life. They ceased to exist. He never spoke to them again.

Boyd's ideas about tactics were germinating and sprouting at a time when all the world was agog at America's extraordinary superiority and domination of the skies over MiG Alley. At the end of the war, the MiG was on the losing end of a kill ratio that had been as high as fourteen to one and finally settled at ten to one. The official count for the war was 792 MiGs shot down and 78 F-86s shot down. (Such numbers remain suspect in some quarters. True wins and losses are almost never revealed, even after a war is over. But the ten-to-one kill ratio remains the number published in histories of Korea.) The extraordinarily lopsided kill ratio, while it made Air Force generals puff out their chests and boast, caused great confusion among serious thinkers in the Air Force. The MiG should have done much better against the F-86. In many ways it was a far superior aircraft. It could make harder turns than the F-86, could out-accelerate it, and had better high-altitude performance. The MiG was one hell of an airplane. So what happened?

The confusion was put to rest with a rationale that since has become conventional wisdom. Even today, a half-century later, when people talk of how the F-86s defeated the MiGs, they give as the reason, "Our pilots were better trained than the MiG pilots." And that is true. But it is also true that this logic became an intellectual wastebasket to hide the fact that no one could come up with a better reason.

But Boyd studied the detailed records of each air-to-air engagement and knew there had to be another reason. It took him another decade to figure out what it was. And when he did, it changed aviation forever.

Boyd's brief tour in Korea is put in perspective by what then was called an Officer Efficiency Report — an "OER" or, as it sometimes was shortened, "ER." In the Air Force of the 1950s, an officer's promotions — and thus his career — were dependent almost entirely on his ERs. One bad ER could wreck an officer's career.

An ER was two pages, three if there were additional indorsements. (The Air Force uses "indorsement" rather than "endorsement.") A civilian looking at an ER would say it is straightforward in its language. But this is deceptive, even misleading. Writing an ER is an art form — reading it, for the uninitiated, is like trying to decipher the Dead Sea Scrolls. Language that appears to be the highest praise can in reality be language that ends a career. That is why sometimes even today when an officer is forced out of the military, he waves his ERs to the media, and, not knowing how to read them, the media join the cause and say this extraordinary officer has been treated unjustly.

The most crucial parts of an ER were the first and last paragraphs on the second page. Boyd's squadron commander explained how, after hostilities ended, Boyd "did a commendable job in teaching fighter tactics to the members of his flight." It says he also taught newly assigned pilots techniques of combat flying.

"I consider Lt. Boyd's flying ability superior to the pilots of his rank and experience," the reviewing officer wrote. He added a few lines about Boyd's "nervous energy" and how well he got along with fellow officers. Then came the all-important final paragraph, in which the rating officer evaluated Boyd's ability for higher command and greater responsibilities. The best possible rating would recommend Boyd either for early promotion or for a school that would prepare him for higher command. Such was the case: the final paragraph concluded with a recommendation that Boyd "be considered for enrollment in the Squadron Officers Course."

It was a good evaluation, and it was heightened by an even better indorsement from his group commander, a full colonel who wrote: "Lt. Boyd is an aggressive, capable, dynamic, fearless officer and fighter pilot. The USAF needs more combat pilots of his caliber if we expect to fulfill the responsibility for the defense of our nation for which the Air Force is unquestionably destined. Because of his qualifications and experience, I urge Lt. Boyd's promotion to Captain at the earliest possible date." Boyd clearly had made a good impression on his superiors.

Boyd's combat tour ended and it was time to rotate back to the States. Years later the pilots who roamed MiG Alley would look back and say Korea was a good war, even a great war for fighter pilots — the last war in which pilots were managed by leaders. In the next war they would be led by managers.

The Air Force was only seven years old, but it was fast becoming not only a bureaucracy, but a technocracy that worshiped equipment and gadgets more than any other branch of the military. It was becoming hardware oriented and the goals for its hardware were simple: Bigger-Faster-Higher-Farther. Air Force generals were taking a cold look at fighter pilots. The high speed of jet combat caused generals to believe drastic changes were in order. With the merge speed of fighter aircraft greater than 1,000 mph, guns were a thing of the past, they said. Missiles were the answer.

Boyd received orders posting him to Nellis AFB. He would be there six years. And in that time he would become one of the most famous fighter pilots in the world.

Chapter Five

High Priest

IN the mid-1950s the U.S. Air Force was no place for a fighter pilot.

Men who flew bombers in World War II now were leading the Air Force, and their philosophy of airpower was based on their wartime experience: big, multiengine aircraft plunging deeply into enemy territory and dropping bombs. The very existence of the Air Force as a separate and independent branch of the military was founded on the concept of strategic bombing. Bombers were the favorite — some would say *only* — aircraft of consequence in the 1950s. America's national defense was based on the Eisenhower Doctrine of "massive retaliation," of having enough aircraft and nuclear bombs to act as a deterrent to any foreign power. Only big bombers could carry nuclear weapons to any spot on the globe. Americans built bomb shelters, thousands of them, and every schoolchild practiced what to do if America were attacked by Soviet nuclear weapons. A "limited war" such as Korea was considered an aberration, not a sign of things to come. Now there could be only escalation between superpowers. Escalation meant nuclear and nuclear meant the U.S. Air Force. No other branch of the U.S. military had such a solemn responsibility.

In 1954 the Air Force was seven years old, and like most seven-year-olds it was rambunctious, determined to be heard, and always demanding new toys. The Air Force was procurement-driven. In 1954 the biggest slice of the Pentagon budget — $12 billion — went to the Air Force. (The Army received $9.9 billion and the Navy $8.1 billion. The Air Force continued to receive the largest amount of the Pentagon budget through 1961.) Within the Air Force, most of the money went to the Strategic Air Command. SAC was led by General Curtis LeMay. And if anyone wanted to know what God would look like in a flight suit, let them gaze upon General LeMay. "Flying fighters is fun. Flying bombers is important," he said.

LeMay forged the U.S. Air Force into the most powerful military force in history. He had enormous globe-straddling bombers and he had nuclear bombs and he had the will to use both. If his public comments meant anything, he *wanted* to use both. At any given time, many of his SAC crews were airborne, loaded with nuclear weapons, flying along the edges of Soviet airspace, awaiting a coded command to wheel toward the heart of the Soviet Union. Other SAC crews were on alert, living in bunkers only yards from their loaded aircraft, ready to run across the tarmac, take off, and bomb preselected targets on the other side of the world. A SAC bomber such as the B-47 could fly so high and so fast that no F-86 could reach it. If an F-86 couldn't touch it, the Soviets couldn't touch it because everyone knew that America built the best aircraft in the world.

And because SAC officers had such great responsibilities, they were promoted faster than anyone else in the Air Force. They were responsible for America's safety. And by keeping America safe, they were keeping the free world safe. SAC crews were the chosen few, the anointed ones.

"Peace is Our Profession" was the SAC motto as it prepared for Armageddon.

Thus, during the 1950s the primary mission of fighter aviation became intercepting enemy bombers and delivering tactical nuclear weapons. Fighter aircraft in Europe were cocked and locked — sitting on runways, pilots strapped in the cockpits, with small nuclear bombs bolted to the belly. If war broke out, the job of fighters was to take out targets too small for a B-47 crew to worry about.

Fighter pilots spent most of their time training for the air-to-ground (pilots called it "air-to-mud") mission. Over and over they practiced thirty-degree and forty-five-degree dive-bombing, skip bombing, and strafing. SAC generals believed the best use of fighter aviation was as a mini-SAC. Fighter pilots who talked of dogfights were relics of bygone days. The first air-to-air missiles were in the pipeline and there were whisperings that these missiles could be fired from ten miles away. Missiles could blow up an enemy aircraft before the enemy pilot even saw the American fighter. The next generation of fighters, it was argued, would not have guns. The day of airborne gunslingers was over.

But there remained one place where the flame of fighter aviation was kept alive, one spot in America where the fighter pilot still reigned supreme, one remote and almost forgotten place where the spirit of attack was implanted in brave hearts. It was, literally and figuratively, out in the desert.

Nellis.

Nellis was in one of the least-populated and most remote parts of America, almost as if exiled there by the bomber generals. The air was parched, the wind relentless, and the heat unbearable. Harsh desert and bleak mountains almost surrounded the base, and here and there were the spavined remains of abandoned mining towns. In the Air Force pecking order of the 1950s, Nellis was at the bottom of the list. An officer assigned to Nellis knew his chance for promotion was limited. But to a small group of men, none of this mattered. Nellis was the home of the fighter pilot. And all fighter pilots wanted to do was to strap on a single-engine jet and go romping across the heavens.

The Atomic Energy Commission began using Frenchman's Flat, part of the Nellis bombing range, to detonate nuclear weapons. (The explosions always were announced in advance and one of the most popular pastimes in nearby Las Vegas was watching the mushroom clouds climb high into the clear desert air.) It was not unheard of for a fighter pilot to zoom skyward after dropping his bombs, see a nuclear blast downrange, get on the radio, and say, "Look what I did," before going sky-dancing across the desert. Words such as *Tonopah* and *Sunrise Mountain* and *Indian Springs* and *Texas Lake* and the *Green Spot* began to creep into the fighter-pilot lexicon, dropped like markers to let the listener know the speaker had been to Nellis.

Nellis.

To a fighter pilot the very word was magic.

Much of the land in southern Nevada was owned by the government, and the year-round good weather meant southern Nevada was perfect for dogfighting. In addition to government-owned land, Nellis had rights to the airspace over almost one million acres called the Nellis Range. Airspace was not as controlled then as it is today, and if Nellis pilots wandered off the Range, it did not matter too much. Summer temperatures on the Range regularly reached 110 or 120, sometimes even 130 degrees. To this blast furnace the best young pilots in the Air Force were sent to have their imperfections burned away and to be hammered into the pure gold that was a fighter pilot.

To a fighter pilot, no other place had the mystique of this distant and lonely outpost. There was Nellis and there was the rest of the world. SAC's bomber pilots might be the glamour boys. But to a fighter pilot, flying a B-47 or a B-52 was the aviation equivalent of being a bus driver. Bomber pilots were cautious, methodical team players who climbed high, motored along for half a day, dropped their bombs — often without seeing the target — and came home. The man who drove this aluminum overcast was not even called a pilot; he was the aircraft commander. And he had a copilot, engineer, navigator, and bombardier — a crew to do all the things a fighter pilot did by himself. SAC pilots were "bomber pukes."

Then there were the test pilots over at Edwards AFB in California. The media loved these guys. But fighter pilots snorted in derision at every newspaper article. Sure, test pilots flew hot new experimental airplanes, but they also had little clipboards strapped to their knees and on the clipboards were the altitudes and airspeeds they were to fly and the instructions for every maneuver to be performed and little boxes into which they put check marks when the maneuvers were completed. Test pilots were marionettes whose strings were pulled by controllers on the ground, "golden arms" who could display little initiative and who could never cut loose and bank and yank and turn and burn and fling themselves around the sky the way fighter pilots did. Pilots at Edwards went to their little bar up in the high desert and boasted about pushing the outside of the envelope. But it was big talk about a small envelope. In the mid-50s, most of the test pilots started out as fighter pilots, but they were fighter pilots gone astray. More and more of the test pilots were engineers who were conservative, anal, by-the-book types, not hell-raising warriors.

Test pilots were evaluators. Fighter pilots were applicators.

Test pilots were pessimists who tried to find something wrong with an airplane. Fighter pilots were optimists who looked for something great in an airplane.

Test pilots were detached from the airplane they flew. Fighter pilots fell in love with their airplane.

Test pilots talked of going into space.

Space?

And in a *capsule*?

You don't fly a fucking capsule, you sit in it and watch the instruments. You're a passenger. To *hell* with space. Fighter pilots wanted to get on an enemy's six and hose the sonofabitch.

Fighter pilots held the golden arms in almost as much contempt as they did SAC pilots. Test pilots were "Edwards pukes."

Bomber pukes and Edwards pukes ranked only slightly above people who did not fly, the nonrated bureaucrats known as "staff pukes."

The motto at Nellis was "Every Man a Tiger" and to be called a tiger by a senior fighter pilot was the ultimate accolade. Confident and intelligent men would damn near pop the rivets out of their aircraft during air-to-air combat training just to have one of the Nellis cadre nod approvingly and call them "Tiger." To be called a tiger meant you had stainless-steel testicles that dragged the ground and struck sparks when you walked. To be called a tiger meant you were a pure fighter pilot and that you would not hesitate to tell a bird colonel to get fucked.

Air-to-air training was mostly shooting at a towed target called a DART. But there was always time for a tail chase. Young fighter pilots not only pushed the outside edge of the envelope, they broke through it and operated in the pulsing red danger zone beyond. Pilots scorched across the desert so low they ripped the tops out of Joshua trees and then dropped ever lower and kicked up plumes of sand and came back to base with cactus wedged in the wing roots. They flew about ninety miles north of Nellis and met over a little oasis of grass and cottonwood trees they called the "Green Spot," the only green for a hundred miles in any direction and easily identified from the air. One of the first brothels in Nevada was located at the Green Spot, and oftentimes the employees sunbathed nude.

Over the Green Spot, pilots called "Fight's on" and fought down to the ground and back up again and down again, all the time banking and yanking, turning and burning, as they maneuvered to get on the other pilot's six. They called it "rat-racing" or "playing grabass" or "getting in a furball." One aircraft, one seat, one engine, one pilot — the most lethal combination of man and machinery ever devised.

It only added to the allure of this shimmering fantasyland in the desert that it was one of the most dangerous places on Earth. Rarely did a week go by that a fighter pilot did not crash. And when a fighter crashed at 400 knots, it was for keeps. When a pilot augered in, screwed the pooch, fucked the duck, and bought the farm, then the base siren wailed and the blue car drove slowly and wives stood in the windows and the chaplain consoled and the flag hung at half staff. But it always happened to someone else, never to the best fighter pilot in the world. And if you have to ask who the best is, it sure as hell ain't you. Fighter pilots fly with their fangs out and their hair on fire and they look death in the face every day and you ain't shit if you ain't done it.

Nellis was a place where young men did things at 30,000 feet they would remember all their days. Nellis was Valhalla-in-the-desert.

This was the world Boyd was about to enter — the world he would come to dominate.

In the aftermath of Korea, the Air Force did not know what to do with the sudden excess of fighter pilots. Some were reassigned to squadrons around the world and some were sent to Nellis as instructors. But a surplus still existed, and Boyd almost was assigned to a maintenance squadron where his job would have been supervising mechanics. His Air Force records do not reflect canceled assignments, so the only record of this is in his Oral History interview, where he said, "I just raised hell. Bullshit on maintenance. I don't want anything to do with it." He won the battle and was assigned to Nellis.

By 1954, Nellis was the busiest Air Force base in the world. It was also distinguished by its unusually high rates of courts-martial, sexually transmitted diseases, and those who had gone absent without leave. The nearby town of Las Vegas had begun the decade with a population of about 25,000 and would end it with a population of about 140,000.

First Lieutenant John Boyd, accompanied by Mary and Stephen, reported for duty at Nellis on April 20, 1954. They drove from Iowa, and all during the trip Boyd talked of little but his ideas on aerial tactics and how he was going to change the Air Force. Mary nodded and cuddled with Stephen and made occasional noises of agreement. She understood little and cared less. In all Boyd's years as a pilot, Mary would never see him take off on a single flight. But in this, she was not alone: it is a superstition of military flying, or at least it was in Boyd's day, that the wives of fighter pilots never watch their husbands take off.

Boyd had been assigned to Nellis as a student in the Advanced Flying School, the "hard-polish" school that new jet pilots went through before they were considered combat ready. It seems odd that a pilot fresh from combat and with Boyd's reputation as a stick-and-rudder man would be sent to school. But he was about to become an instructor and he had to go through the school before he could teach. He had to learn the curriculum and he had to learn Air Force teaching methods. So Boyd was a student for nine hours of formation flying, ten point five hours of air-to-ground gunnery, seventeen hours of air-to-air gunnery, and fifteen hours of applied tactics.

Having completed the course, his future, which is to say his chance for promotion, looked good. He was a twenty-seven-year-old combat veteran whose last efficiency report could not have been much better had he written it himself. He was making a name for himself in fighter aviation. And he had ideas — hundreds of ideas — about aerial tactics tumbling around in his head. Nellis was the perfect place to put those ideas to work.

But he and Mary and Stephen had barely settled into the old World War II house they were provided on base, a tiny house with neither telephone nor air-conditioning, when their troubles began.

In June temperatures climbed into the hundreds. Stephen was sixteen months old and slowly learning to walk. One day Stephen developed a high temperature. Mary did not believe it was anything serious — all babies run temperatures at one time or another — but she watched him closely. Stephen did not improve and several days later grew listless and lethargic.

"It must be the flu," Mary thought, and gave him mild medication. Then one morning she went into Stephen's room and he was not sitting up waiting for her, not demanding to be fed. Mary laughed and cooed to him and called him a lazy boy and pulled him upright. His head tilted to the side and he fell back on the bed. Mary pulled him upright again and again his head lolled to the side and again he toppled over.

Mary was a young wife and a new mother and she was far from home and cold terror seized her heart. Something was seriously wrong with her son.

Could it be . . . ?

She could not utter the word.

She rushed Stephen to the doctor.

He had polio.

Boyd had been here before, of course, with his sister Ann. Early stages of the disease caused something known as "foot drop" and, because some muscles in the back were affected and some were not, the victim's legs often twisted outward. Treatment was cruel. Heavy sandbags were lodged against the legs and rigid steel braces held the patient's back and legs firmly in place. Bright stainless-steel hoops pulled the victim's head upright. Almost all patients were confined to wheelchairs. A patient was considered lucky if he could walk well enough to use crutches. Many victims died. But dying was considered by some to be preferable to spending one's life in an iron lung.

Ann had survived to walk again, but Stephen's polio was especially severe. Sandbags went on his legs and braces on his back. Boyd went to a swimming-pool manufacturer and bought a small pump that he installed in the bathtub so Stephen could lie in warm swirling waters. The dining-room table was cleared and turned into an exercise table and every morning Boyd and Mary held Stephen and pulled and tugged and stretched his legs and massaged his atrophying muscles as he screamed with pain. Boyd often used his lunch break to come home and give Stephen additional exercise. Twice Stephen almost died. Mary wept with the pain of what her firstborn son was going through.

When word of Stephen's malady reached Erie, people thought of Ann and of the year John had limped, and a member of Jack Arbuckle's family sent word that polio was hereditary. Boyd must have been going through the agony of the damned. But he never discussed it with Mary. He never talked about feelings or emotions.

When Mary said Stephen's polio might have come from Boyd's side of the family, he squeezed his lips together and nodded and said such speculation was "interesting." He found solace in an unusual place: the music of Wagner. His favorite was "Ride of the Valkyries," which he played over and over at high volume.

Mary remembered seeing the movie clips of President Franklin D. Roosevelt playing in the mineral-rich waters of Warm Springs, Georgia. If Roosevelt went there, it had to be a good place.

Boyd traded in the family car for a station wagon so Stephen could lie down in the back and spread out and be reasonably comfortable. Boyd took emergency leave and he and Mary and Stephen struck out across country. They stayed in cheap motels in Texas and Alabama. For three days Stephen's cloth diapers were washed in motels or at gas stations and hung out the car windows to dry.

After three days of treatment at Warm Springs, the family returned to Nellis. The car had no air-conditioning and it was hot as they motored through the South and the Southwest. Stephen's braces were uncomfortable and confining. The steel brace that held his chin high was painful. Sandbags piled on his neck and legs aggravated his plight. He cried for much of the trip.

This was the first of numerous trips to Warm Springs the Boyd family would make over the years — long, arduous, ten-day round trips that, in the end, had no benefit for Stephen. Boyd was a lieutenant with no money for expensive treatments. Air Force doctors of the time did not have the knowledge, equipment, or ability to treat polio. The March of Dimes and the Easter Seal Foundation paid for Stephen's treatment. Boyd was a proud man and his agony at Stephen's plight must have increased when he realized that his family, like his mother's family, was forced to depend on charity.

There were other concerns, too. Mary was again pregnant. She began a series of gamma globulin shots that doctors said might prevent her from contracting polio. But if polio were hereditary and if their first child had the disease, the same thing could happen to the next child. Mary repeatedly told Boyd of her fear that his family was the source of the polio. He said they would have to wait and see.

To increase Stephen's mobility and to help him have as normal a childhood as possible, Boyd nailed several boards together, attached skate wheels to the bottom, and showed Stephen how to lie on the board and push with his hands. As Stephen grew older, he took to the streets and played with neighborhood children. When Boyd came home from flying jets at 30,000 feet and at more than 400 mph, the first thing he saw when he drove into the neighborhood was his son on a homemade surfboardlike device, gamely pushing himself along the street behind a group of laughing and running children.

The summer of 1954, when Stephen contracted polio, was the last summer America experienced a polio epidemic. Dr. Jonas Salk invented the polio vaccine that year. In 1955 the U.S. government approved polio vaccinations, and for all practical purposes polio disappeared from America. It was good news for America and for the world, but what was even more important news to Boyd was that Dr. Salk said polio was a virus — the disease was not hereditary. Boyd was not responsible. But Stephen would never walk.

That summer, Boyd graduated from Advanced Flying School and was assigned to the 3597th Flying Training Squadron as an instructor. He went through the training aids, the mission plans, the course outlines, and the class structure and announced he was going to "tweak up the tactics section."

Tweak? There was nothing to tweak. SAC generals thought advanced training for fighter pilots, unless it was training in how to put iron on the ground, was useless. The air-to-air portion of the curriculum had dwindled to almost nothing. There was not even a manual of tactics. Everything was a grab bag of tricks passed down from World War I to World War II to Korea.

To understand how this came about, one must go back to the early days of aviation. German pilots in World War I developed the technique of diving with the sun at their backs and firing at blinded American pilots. This maneuver led to the expression, "Beware of the Hun in the sun." American pilots copied the maneuver.

Eric Hartman, the famous German pilot of World War II, simply pounced on slow bombers, unsuspecting fighters, or any crippled aircraft from behind. He was a back-shooter who shot down 352 airplanes and became the leading ace of all time.

Because the P-38 was so unmaneuverable, Richard Bong, the leading American ace of World War II, had to rely on one trick: from a high perch he pushed over and used the blazing speed of his P-38 to dive onto an enemy formation. He pulled in so close he could not miss, blasted the enemy out of the air, then blew through the formation. Bong then used his superior diving speed to zoom back up to altitude and do the same thing again. There was nothing remotely sophisticated about this trick, but he used it to shoot down forty Japanese aircraft.

Combat veterans of Korea were teaching what they learned in MiG Alley, and not surprisingly, it was not that much different from what Hartman or Bong did. That was because new pilots in Korea were told never to get in a turning fight with a MiG and to use their speed to blow through enemy formations. American pilots believed that both they and the enemy had such an infinite number of maneuvers at their disposal that aerial combat could never be codified. Air combat was an art, not a science. After simulated aerial combat, a young pilot would be defeated and never know why. Nor could his instructors tell him. They said something like, "Don't worry, kid. Eventually you'll be as good as we are." Either a fighter pilot survived combat and became a member of the fraternity or he died. In short, aerial tactics — with one or two exceptions — had made no significant advance since World War I. Maneuvers performed in a Sopwith Camel in the First World War or in a P-38 in the Second World War still were performed by F-86s in Korea and taught at Nellis after Korea. The only difference was that the speed and power of jets enabled them to fight in vertical maneuvers that were nearly impossible in aircraft powered by gasoline engines. Even so, F-86 pilots in Korea had only begun to explore vertical maneuvers and most combat was still fought in the horizontal plane.

So when Boyd said he was going to "tweak up the tactics," what he meant was that he was going to develop, and codify for the first time in history, a formal regimen for fighter aircraft. He went about the job with a passion. He worked far into the night devising a series of briefings on fighter versus fighter and began to develop his skills as a lecturer.

No one else in the Air Force was seeking to advance the art of air-to-air combat. Everyone in government, up to and including the president, believed the next war would be a nuclear war. Thus Boyd soon knew more about what he was teaching than did any other person in the Air Force.

Like most people who find a cause, he had little patience for those who did not understand or who disagreed with what he was doing. Boyd never suffered lightly the careerists or bureaucrats or others who did not understand his ideas. Most of the time he showed the proper military courtesy. But he had the aggressive personality of a fighter pilot, and if someone asked a question, they got a straight answer.

Throughout his career Boyd polarized his superiors. There were those who did not like him and thought he was unprofessional and those who had tremendous admiration for him and respect for the contribution he was making to the Air Force. His first ER at Nellis reveals his precarious position. The front page of the ER requires the rating officer to check one of a series of boxes and grade the younger officer in various categories such as "job knowledge" or "leadership" or "growth potential." The idea is to have the front page "fire walled," that is, every check mark in the sixth box on the far right of the page. Boyd's check marks were all in the third or fourth box. It is a mediocre and career-ending rating.

On the more important second page, the rating officer says of Boyd, "He is nervous, talkative, and presents an engaging personality. . . . He becomes very excited and loud during the heat of an argument. . . . [Boyd is] well read and precise on any subject he is familiar with and will discuss it in detail." In the all-important final paragraph, the one that deals with potential for promotion, the officer dismisses Boyd by describing him as ". . . an excellent young pilot commensurate with his grade and experience and would be an asset to any day fighter organization."

Fighter pilots have always been their own worst enemies when it comes to rating each other. One study showed that the toughest evaluators of their peers in the Air Force were fighter pilots, followed closely by nurses. By openly arguing with his superiors, by criticizing them, Boyd only increased this tendency toward harsh judgment. Less than a year after arriving at Nellis, he was in serious trouble.

After a difficult pregnancy and a painful and protracted delivery, Mary Boyd gave birth to her second child on February 8, 1955. She named the girl Kathryn after Kathryn Grayson, a movie star of the 1950s. Mary was filled with apprehension about the possibility of polio and examined Kathy (as the girl became known) daily, feeling her legs and arms and watching for any of the symptoms that preceded Stephen's illness, but Kathy was a healthy baby who would remain free of polio. Her problems would come later and would be of a far more confusing nature.

In the March 1955 issue of the *Fighter Weapons Newsletter,* Major Frederick "Boots" Blesse, a double ace from the Korean War, published an article about fighter techniques used in Korea titled "No Guts, No Glory." The newsletter was the official publication of the Fighter Weapons School at Nellis and usually contained no articles of consequence — but Blesse's article was important for three reasons. First, it was written by a certified MiG-killer, and aces always receive a lot of attention. Second, virtually nothing had been published about aerial tactics — not in World War I, World War II, or Korea. In a foreword, the editor of the newsletter took note of this when he said, "It is a poor testimonial that so little is documented about this vital phase of aerial warfare." He added that ". . . much of this article is an application of known principles." Even though there was nothing original in Blesse's piece, to see an article about fighter tactics written by a fighter ace made Air Force officials nervous, and the issue of the newsletter containing the article was classified "confidential." Finally, the article was important because Blesse's observations would end up overshadowing much of Boyd's original and creative work on aerial tactics.

Boyd pressed on with his research and development of aerial tactics, continuing to test his ideas in the air. The F-86 was temporarily grounded because of structural problems. When it resumed flying, the normal inclination of most pilots was to baby it for a while. But Boyd manhandled the F-86. One of his favorite maneuvers was a snap roll, a violent maneuver that put enormous side loads on the vertical stabilizer. He wanted to teach the maneuver to students, but his superiors considered it too dangerous. If the maneuver was not properly and precisely performed, it could cause a structural failure and a crash. One day Boyd and another instructor were rat-racing when Boyd performed a snap roll. The other instructor looked over and radioed Boyd, "You have some wires flying formation on your tail." Boyd returned to Nellis, made a gentle landing, and parked in a distant corner of the flight line. He was more than a little alarmed to see broken wires protruding from the twisted tail surface. He asked his crew chief to check the damage. Boyd was in the Officers Club when he was called to the front door. The crew chief informed him the main structural mount in the tail of the F-86 had broken and that it was a miracle the tail had not failed. Out of loyalty to Boyd, the crew chief covered up the incident and Boyd was never charged with any offense.

In March 1955, Boyd received another ER from the same major who evaluated him earlier. The report is even more damning than the first. The first page has low ratings. On the second page, the important first sentence reads, "Lt. Boyd is a loud, talkative person who thrives on debates and discussions." The middle paragraphs speak glowingly of Boyd's work: he is a "very successful instructor." His ability as a pilot is "well above average." He is "a diligent worker in motivating his students for combat." And "He is one of the most enthusiastic persons about flying I have ever known." But in the final paragraph, the major says Boyd would be an asset to a fighter squadron as a flight leader or assistant operations officer and that he is ". . . a dependable and typically effective officer." Since Boyd had already served as a flight leader in Korea, the rating officer is saying Boyd would be good at a job he held several years earlier. And to say he is a "typically effective officer" is to say there is nothing special about him; he is not worthy to be considered for promotion — he is one of the herd.

It is a poor evaluation, delivered in a day of inflated ratings, when it was standard practice for most ERs to be fire walled. In fact, most young first lieutenants who received such a rating would seriously reconsider any plans to make a career in the Air Force.

But at the lowest point in his young career, Boyd was accepted as a student at the Fighter Weapons School (FWS) for the class beginning in April. There, he would learn to train instructors in advanced techniques of aerial combat.

The FWS was formed at Nellis in 1949. It had various names and permutations over the years, especially in the mid- and late 50s, but it remained true to its founding belief that air-to-air combat is the noblest and purest use for a fighter aircraft. The idea was to graduate the best fighter pilots in the world and to send those pilots back to their home squadrons to train their fellow pilots in the finer points of aerial combat. But the emphasis on nuclear-bomb delivery and the small number of students attending each three-month class — about a dozen — diluted the potential of the school. (For years Navy and Marine pilots attended the FWS to learn how to become gunslingers. Twenty years after the FWS was formed, the Navy copied the school and called it Top Gun. Because of the movie *Top Gun,* most of the public knows only of the Navy school.)

The FWS has always been the most difficult and demanding school a fighter pilot can attend. Technically, young pilots can apply; in reality they are invited. They come out of basic flying school, are assigned to a squadron, and are watched for four or five years by their superiors and by former FWS graduates. If they are the best fighter pilots in their squadrons, if they are bold and aggressive, if they preach the gospel of fighter aviation, then they might be invited to the FWS.

The FWS is more than a postgraduate school for fighter pilots. And it is more than the top finishing school in the Air Force. The FWS is the temple of fighter aviation. It is for those who believe that fighter aviation is a sacred calling. As is true in most temples of learning, not all who enter complete the course. Those who graduate and march out the front door are awarded respect and honor. Those who "bust out" find that a promising career has ended. The danger of "busting out" adds a certain frisson of trepidation when the highly prized invitation comes to join the FWS.

If the FWS is a temple and if its graduates are priests, then FWS instructors are high priests. They are grand masters of a three-dimensional, high-speed death dance, the most rapidly changing form of combat ever devised.

An FWS instructor has all the outward appearances of a mortal.

But he wears the patch.

In Boyd's day the instructors wore a large badge-shaped patch on the breast of their green flight suits, and in the center of the patch was a crosshair sitting atop a bull's-eye. Across the top of the patch in bold letters was the title: INSTRUCTOR. In most places of higher learning, an instructor is at the bottom of the academic pecking order. But at Nellis there is no more prestigious title. An FWS instructor may go on to become a general; many have. But ask him what gave him the most pride — becoming an FWS instructor or being promoted to general — and he will not hesitate. A general wears stars. But an FWS instructor wears the patch.

FWS instructors also wore black-and-gold checkerboard scarves tucked into the necks of their flight suits. The snouts and the vertical stabilizers of their aircraft were painted in the same checkerboard pattern. Any fighter with the black-and-gold checkerboard pattern instantly was recognized as a Nellis aircraft, and when it landed at another base everyone on the ramp paused and stared as — like a medieval knight flinging aside his cloak — the pilot raised the canopy. Inside flight ops, as the pilot filled out the paperwork, bomber pilots or transport pilots looked over and saw the patch and the black-and-gold checkerboard scarf and their manhood shriveled.

All graduates of the FWS wear the patch, but in the 1950s the graduates' patch was smaller than that worn by instructors and was worn on the shoulder of the flight suit. And whether it is one pilot against another (BFM — basic fighter maneuvering) or two or more flying against one or more (ACM — air combat maneuvering), a patch wearer is expected to win.

In the mid-50s, many of the FWS instructors were combat veterans of Korea, men who had flown F-86s down MiG Alley. "Wombats," the Korean vets were called. To a young student, nothing was better than earning his patch by rat-racing with a wombat.

Well, one thing was better and that was the dream buried in the heart of almost every fighter pilot who ever came to the FWS: the desire to perform so well in the classroom and in the air that six months or a year after he returned to his squadron, he would get the call asking him to return to Nellis as an instructor.

Once in a great while there came along a pilot whose knowledge of air-to-air combat was so great and whose skills were so exemplary that he did not go back to his squadron to await the call. Upon graduation he was asked to stay on as an instructor. These men were seen as the most gifted of the gifted, the ultimate fighter pilots, the pure warriors.

When Boyd graduated from the FWS, he had completed his air work — six point five hours of familiarization and orientation, eleven hours of applied tactics, twenty hours of air-to-ground missions, thirty hours of air-to-air training, and twelve point five hours of training in how to deliver nuclear bombs. On the classroom side, he had twenty-nine hours of instruction on ground attack, twenty hours on aerial attack, twenty-seven hours on how to set up a fighter weapons program, and twenty-four hours on how to instruct young pilots in the fine art of aerial assassination. There is no ER for Boyd's time in the FWS, only a training report showing he completed the course. The best indication of how he performed is that upon graduation he was asked to stay on as an instructor — to become a high priest.

And it was as an instructor at the FWS that John Boyd would become a legend — the man known as "Forty-Second Boyd."

Chapter Six

Pope John Goes
Severely Supersonic

In February 1956, Boyd published an article in the *Fighter Weapons Newsletter* entitled "A Proposed Plan for Ftr. Vs. Ftr. Training." It was the first and one of the few things he ever wrote. The extraordinary thing about the piece is that it is less concerned with teaching tricks or specific maneuvers than it is with teaching pilots a new way of thinking; while it illustrates various maneuvers, it more importantly shows pilots the *results* of the maneuvers.

Original though it is, the article is a shore dimly seen, a tentative effort that only faintly foreshadows Boyd's first great contribution to fighter aviation. He begins by saying the interest in the Blesse article shows that fighter squadrons are not educating their pilots in aerial combat. Delivery techniques for bullets, bombs, and rockets are standardized, but the vital element of how to place a fighter aircraft in the best position against another fighter is missing. Boyd writes that many of the tricks pilots rely on in training could get them killed in combat. He says fighter training must begin with the most fundamental skill of a fighter pilot: "Have student assume in trail position on the instructor and learn how to stay in that position throughout any maneuver." A fighter pilot must know how to hang on to the enemy's six long enough to achieve a firing solution.

Hard turns (a near-maximum performance maneuver while keeping the enemy aircraft in sight) were fundamental in air combat, but Boyd added a wrinkle that indicates his genius as an aerial tactician and hints at far more radical moves to come. Pilots had always been taught to enter a turn by moving the stick, which activated the ailerons, followed by rudder application. But Boyd told students to lead with the rudder because it both slowed the aircraft and tightened the turn. For a pilot on the defensive, beginning the turn with rudder also widened the speed differential between the two aircraft and helped force the opponent to the outside, thus gaining lateral separation. When on the defensive, a pilot's first concern is gaining separation, a tactic that enables him to disengage, then reenter the fight on the offensive. That was not all. He told how to use various tactical combat maneuvers such as the scissors, the high-speed yo-yo, the low-speed yo-yo, the high-G barrel roll, and the vertical rolling scissors to gain the advantage on an opponent.

The effect of the article was instantaneous. The newsletter that had been a somewhat boring and boilerplate publication suddenly was a hot property among fighter pilots. They sent copies to fighter pilots around the world. They pored over Boyd's words, moving their hands, visualizing the maneuvers, nodding as they understood what he was teaching.

What he was teaching was how to think — not just of the maneuver, but of the effect each maneuver had on airspeed, what countermoves were available to an enemy pilot, how to anticipate those counters, and how to keep enough airspeed to counter the countermove. Airspeed preservation enabled a pilot to maintain or to regain the offensive. It was radical, heady stuff, the first effort ever to make air combat a science rather than an art.

Boyd's article appealed most to young fighter pilots; to those who were still green and open to new ideas; to those who wanted to stretch beyond the old way of doing things. His article did not appeal to everyone. Boots Blesse's earlier piece was still being widely circulated, and Blesse loyalists dismissed Boyd's article with, "Yeah? How many MiGs did he shoot down?"

The derision did not deter Boyd, but, at some level, he must have been stung by the criticism. He knew that he was on the trail of something important, and to have it dismissed simply because he was not an ace was galling. Perhaps it was in compensation that he began making outrageous statements in public.

One day Boyd was in a group of officers when someone suggested that a pilot with his knowledge of tactics should join the Thunderbirds, the Air Force flight demonstration team. Inherent in the remark was the jab that Boyd might actually not be good enough to fly with the Thunderbirds, whose pilots were considered among the best in the Air Force.

Boyd stunned the group when he said he had been invited to join but refused.

The officers stared at him in utter amazement as he waved his arms and went off on a cadenza about the Thunderbirds that was nothing short of heretical. "The Thunderbirds are like a goddamned bunch of trained monkeys. They're fucking circus performers. They get out there over the desert and perform the same maneuvers over and over and over. That's not flying. You could take a goddamned bunch of old ladies and train them to do the same thing. Then they go off and do an air show and strut around in their pressed uniforms like they are fucking movie stars. They are good for recruiting; I admit that. They might be the best recruiting tool the Air Force has. But what they do has nothing to do with combat flying. It's all about appearance and not about flying an airplane. I wouldn't have anything to do with that crowd. All they do is work the cocktail and pussy circuit."

He was right when he said being a member of the team is all about appearance. In fact, it may be more about appearance and social graces than it is about flying skills. In truth, it is unlikely Boyd ever was invited to join the Thunderbirds.

Boyd was amused by the astonishment his comments evoked, and over the years he often repeated them. But such views did not sit well with the corporate Air Force. Even bomber pilots looked on the Thunderbirds the way a parent would look upon an exceptionally bright child who is brought out to perform for guests. The Thunderbirds were the greatest public relations tool in the Air Force. One day Boyd would pay for his comments.

But for the moment Boyd was working for superiors who were mature enough to overlook his glaring faults and to appreciate what he was doing for fighter aviation.

One ER begins: "Lt. Boyd is the most outstanding officer with whom I have been privileged to work. He is an expert in the field of fighter aircraft flying and tactics . . . [who] has improved upon the fundamentals of the publication 'No Guts, No Glory' to the extent that he is considered one of the foremost authorities on fighter tactics." The ER is indorsed by a lieutenant colonel who says Boyd's "zealous and enthusiastic nature sometimes causes him to force his viewpoint upon the unwilling." But even more extraordinary is that the ER for Boyd, who still is a first lieutenant, is indorsed by a major general who says, "This young pilot has more get-up-and-go than any other 1st Lieutenant that I know." The general ends by saying, "I recommend that consideration be given him to advance ahead of his contemporaries."

It is one of the best ERs of Boyd's career.

In February 1957, he was promoted to captain and a few months later ordered to Maxwell Field at Montgomery, Alabama, for the four-month Squadron Officers School, a stepping-stone school for young career officers on the way up.

After returning to Nellis, he moved from the antiquated and depressing base housing to a duplex at 11 Cassady Street in North Las Vegas. Boyd's family was now squared away, and his career rested on a solid and expanding foundation. He was ready to hatch a revolution.

Vernon "Sprad" Spradling was an Air Force veteran with 2,000 hours of flying time and a master's degree in public administration — a short fireplug of a man with a no-nonsense demeanor who spent several years observing the nuclear tests at Yucca Flats and working in the highly classified nuclear weapons research facility at Nellis. Then he transferred to the FWS, where his job was to select and train instructors and monitor their performance in the classroom. Before an FWS instructor could stand in front of a class, he had to stand in front of Spradling and demonstrate both his knowledge and his teaching skills. Spradling made sure each lecture hewed to Air Force doctrine and covered all the salient points. And as Spradling's mandate was to improve the quality of instruction, he constantly searched for new ideas and new information and new ways to present both. He liked what he saw in Boyd.

The FWS then consisted of three divisions. To faculty and staff the most prestigious division was Operations and Training, the core of what the FWS was about. The second division was Research and Development, which, like Operations, involved lots of flying. The third and least desirable division was Academics, where the curriculum and teaching methods were developed. If there was a dumping ground in the FWS, Academics was it.

Spradling went to Boyd and said, "John, I want you to head up the academic side; be director of Academics."

Boyd thought for a minute, nodded, and said, "Sprad, I'll do it. But only if you let me tweak up the tactics part of the curriculum."

Spradling had no problem with tweaking up the tactics. In fact it fit in with his plans to upgrade the FWS. But his definition of *tweak* was considerably less ambitious than Boyd's. Boyd wanted to add four more classes to the academic side of the school, and he told Sprad that if the head of the FWS turned him down, he would go back to the training squadron and train pilots who were better than FWS graduates. The head of the FWS knew Boyd could do what he said. Whether he agreed with all of Boyd's ideas about increasing the academic load or whether he did not want other pilots defeating FWS graduates, he allowed Boyd to add the additional classes to the curriculum.

Boyd moved into Spradling's office and took a seat at a facing desk, positions the two men would occupy for about four years. Over those years and many more, Spradling became "Mr. Fighter Weapons School," the institutional memory, the one unchanging element in a school where officers came and went every few years. He was at Nellis twenty-two years and knew the great instructors and the great students, some of whom became heroes in Vietnam or rose to become generals. But for Vernon Spradling the memory of John Boyd burns brighter than that of anyone who passed through the school during those twenty-two years. No one knew Boyd better than he.

By now Boyd realized that his business degree from Iowa had not prepared him for what he wanted to do in the Air Force. But when a fighter pilot with a degree in aeronautical engineering happened to pass through the FWS, Boyd learned for the first time of variational calculus. Math had been easy for him in high school and in college, so he bought textbooks and taught himself calculus. Now he could take his ideas and his research about fighter tactics to a new level. He could reduce the movements of a fighter to mathematical equations of lift and drag and vectors. He could codify in absolute terms what fighter pilots had always believed was an ineffable, unquantifiable art form. Every day Boyd sat across from Spradling, drawing ribbon charts as he developed air-to-air tactics and writing arcane equations, scratching them out, and rewriting them. Spradling and Boyd might be talking and then Spradling would ask a question and get no answer. He would look up from his work to see Boyd staring at the wall, oblivious to the world, for maybe fifteen or twenty minutes. Boyd was, as he described it, "having a séance with myself." Then it was as if a switch had been turned on: suddenly Boyd spun around in his chair and picked up the conversation, waved his arms like a windmill in a hurricane, leaned across his desk toward Spradling, voice rising until he almost was shouting, spittle flying from his mouth.

Some officers who knew Boyd during the Nellis years say he was obsessed. Others say he was "a little crazy." Spradling might have agreed with both.

Boyd had so much nervous energy that he began chewing his fingernails down to the quick, gnawing them until it looked as if he had stuck his fingertips into a blender. Someone told him he should take up smoking, that if he had something in his mouth he would not chew his fingernails. Boyd did not like the smell of cigarettes, so he began smoking cigars. He favored Dutch Masters and began smoking four or five a day. Now he presented a new danger to those he engaged in conversation. When he moved in close and began waving his arms with a lighted cigar in his hand, he trailed fire and ashes in big circles as he talked.

To relieve his tension, Boyd began working out in the base gymnasium. His mother had been unable to afford that Charles Atlas course when he was eight years old, but the government provided everything he wanted for free. He lifted weights almost every day and soon developed large calluses on his palms. His tension unabated, he constantly spread the fingers of his hand, jammed the flap of skin between his thumb and forefinger into his mouth, and chewed off pieces of callus before spitting them out.

It was about this time that Boyd's affection for the telephone began to manifest itself. Three or four nights a week, always after midnight, Spradling's phone rang. He reached over to the bedside table, picked up the phone, and the conversation went something like this.

"Spradling residence."

"Sprad? John."

"Hey, John. What is it?"

"Sprad, I've had a breakthrough."

"What time is it?"

"Sprad, remember that equation I was telling you about this morning?"

"John, tomorrow might be a better —"

"Now I know what was missing. I figured it out."

And off he would go for an hour or two talking about a calculus equation, ignoring all Spradling's efforts to postpone the conversation. Spradling's contribution was an occasional grunt or noncommital "Uh-huh." Initially he thought that if he didn't respond to Boyd's conversation, Boyd would hang up. But after several months of these late-night calls, Spradling realized that Boyd did not want a conversation; Boyd simply wanted to talk. He talked to learn: as he went through his monologues, his thoughts bounced around, various theses were tried and rejected until finally he had gained a better understanding of whatever it was that was on his mind. After an hour or two, Boyd would say, "Thanks for helping me out, Sprad. You've been a big help." And he would hang up.

Spradling's wife did not like these late-night calls. But Spradling tolerated them for two reasons. First, he had monitored so many lectures at the FWS that he had an excellent overall knowledge of the classes and could on occasion offer advice to Boyd. Second, Boyd not only was a close friend, he was the hottest pilot in the FWS and was developing radical new tactics and techniques for aerial combat. In fact, Captain John Boyd was becoming a legend in the fighter-pilot community. Spradling wanted to help. The early-morning calls were a small price to pay.

Boyd's fame as a fighter pilot came on the wings of one of the most quirky and treacherous fighter planes in the history of the Air Force, the F-100 — the first operational aircraft to reach the speed of sound in level flight.

The F-100 was built by North American and was the first of the most fabled series of aircraft ever to see service in the Air Force — the Century Series. Designed and built as a day air-superiority aircraft — a fighter — it was turned into an air-to-mud aircraft by the bomber generals.

The F-100 was called the "Hun," as in "hundred." There would be other glorious aircraft in the Century Series: the F-101, an escort for SAC bombers; the F-102, an interceptor; the F-104 "Starfighter," a fighter with such short wings it was called a "missile with a man in it;" the F-105 "Thud," a tactical nuclear aircraft; and the F-106 all-weather interceptor. But they were all sequels. None had the cachet of the Hun.

The Hun, particularly the A model, was a lieutenant-killer, a widow-maker with a fearsome reputation. One quarter of all the F-100s ever produced were lost in accidents. A forgiving aircraft tolerates mistakes by the pilot; it will not, as pilots say, "rise up and bite you in the ass." The Hun was one of the most unforgiving airplanes ever built. It had to be flown every second; one wrong control move, one moment of inattention, and the F-100 would "depart flight"; that is, it quit flying and assumed the aeronautical attributes of a brick. The departure usually was violent — a sixty-degree pitch-up followed by a hard roll that quickly turned into an out-of-control spin.

The Hun had a number of quirks that pilots found new and troublesome. The least serious problem was the gyroscopic effect of the engine. When the aircraft took off, or when it accelerated out of a slow-speed maneuver, the engine's rotating mass caused a gyroscopic effect that pulled the nose of the aircraft to the side. It could be controlled with authoritative use of the rudders, but it was disconcerting.

There were other annoyances. Hard maneuvering distorted the airflow to the engine. The airflow, rather than going smoothly into the snout of the aircraft, flowed turbulently across the intake and caused the compressor to stall. Fire and smoke belched from both the intake and the exhaust and the aircraft shuddered as an explosive *BOOM! BOOM! BOOM!* shook it with such force that the pilot's feet often were knocked from the rudder pedals. Jets were still new enough that the full dimension of compressor stalls was unknown. For a while there was some apprehension that if the aircraft did not recover quickly enough, it might explode midair. Even after flight tests showed compressor stalls were relatively harmless, they still terrified new F-100 pilots. From the time a pilot taxied out on the runway and advanced the throttle — which caused the engine to begin "chugging" — until he landed, the F-100 was trouble waiting to happen.

Another problem with the Hun was that many mechanical secrets were hidden in its bowels. It came into service when the Air Force was still slicing personnel. Ten tactical fighter wings were deactivated in the years after Korea. This meant some of the most skilled jet mechanics in the Air Force were being forced out of the service at a time when the most complicated fighter the Air Force had ever seen was coming into service. Maintenance problems with the F-100 were chronic.

But the most serious problem with the Hun was adverse yaw. When the F-100 came along in the mid-50s, ailerons were used to increase or decrease the bank angle. But there was a point — and no one knew quite where it was — when an additional touch of aileron caused the F-100 to roll violently in the opposite direction, frequently into a uncontrollable and nonrecoverable spin. The traditional way to counter an unexpected roll was to apply opposite stick. In the F-100, this only aggravated an already-dangerous situation.

Simply put, at low airspeeds and high angle of attack, the down aileron produced more drag than it did lift. As one F-100 pilot said, "If you wanted to go right and the aircraft wanted to go left, the aircraft always won." Suddenly the pilot was out of altitude, airspeed, and ideas — all at the same time. At low altitude, where FWS pilots worked much of the time, there was no room to recover. It was adverse yaw that killed so many pilots and gave the F-100 its fearsome reputation.

Boyd loved the airplane's evil quirks. "It bites back," he said. He thought the F-100 was a great aircraft for students; if they could fly the Hun, they could fly anything. And pilots fell in love with the airplane's ability to reach the speed of sound in level flight. They liked to get out on the Nellis Range, ease the throttle forward until they jostled up through the sound barrier and a thunderous sonic boom trailed them, then stick the nose of the aircraft up over Sunrise Mountain and "boom" Las Vegas.

"There I was, going severely supersonic" became the new phrase among Hun drivers. (No Hun pilot was happy simply announcing he had been going supersonic; it had to be "severely supersonic.") The comment was delivered casually because Hun drivers knew no other pilots in the Air Force could say the same thing and there was no need to remind those lesser mortals of where they fit into the cosmic scheme of things.

In the months after the F-100 came to Nellis, it was not unusual for people in Las Vegas to be sitting quietly at home when suddenly the windows shattered and they were hammered by a sound wave that caused them to think it was the end of the world. One pilot — it was said he was traveling at 815 mph at an altitude of forty feet — boomed a small town out in the desert so vigorously that the main structural wall in the local hospital cracked and the base commander had to go out and apologize and the Air Force had to pay more than $20,000 in damages.

As damage claims rolled in, senior officers cracked down. Supersonic flight was limited to the heart of the Nellis Range, far from civilization, and it became a serious offense to boom a populated area. But since the F-100 was so much faster than its predecessors and took so much room to maneuver, the Air Force also asked for and received air rights over another 750,000 acres of land in southern Nevada.

The edict did not affect Sherrie's — the brothel at the Green Spot — and F-100 drivers liked to point the nose of their aircraft at the whorehouse in the cottonwoods and go booming. For that, it seems, there were few complaints.

The idea that an airplane could outrun its sound startled America. People stood on street corners and talked of how the airplane could fly over and be gone before people on the ground ever heard it. They shook their heads in amazement. And they knew that SAC notwithstanding, as long as America had the F-100, the Communists would think twice before attacking America.

By now the Strategic Air Command was in its full glory. The B-47 Stratojet was the pride of SAC; its wings swept back thirty-six degrees and it could fly almost 600 mph. Curtis LeMay had boasted many times that no fighter could climb high enough or fast enough to reach his bombers. Then one day a B-47 pilot looked out the cockpit and watched a Hun driver do a barrel roll around his aircraft.

The Hun ruled.

And John Boyd was the best Hun driver in America.

Boyd had demonstrated in primary flight training that he had no fear of aircraft. He muscled them around and showed he was in complete control. And the treacherous F-100 was no exception. Most fighter pilots consider the term "heavy-handed" to be a critical commentary about a pilot's skills; it is very close to "ham-fisted," which describes a pilot with no feel for the airplane. But Boyd was heavy-handed in another sense. He was not afraid to muscle the F-100 around. He pushed it to the published limit and then beyond. He had to find out what the airplane would really do, not what the book said it would do.

North American was unable to find a cure for the deadly adverse yaw problem. And there are streets at Edwards named for golden arms who died trying to tame the F-100. The problem was so bad that the standard admonition for F-100 pilots at the end of a preflight briefing was "DBYA" — *don't bust your ass.*

F-100 pilots believed the safest way to fly the Hun was at high speed. But one of the many idiosyncrasies of the F-100 was, as Boyd said, "It will fly slower faster than any other airplane." Not only would it decelerate at an amazing rate, it would keep flying even when the airspeed indicator was at zero. It might be falling at an extremely high rate, but a skillful pilot could pump the rudders and maintain control.

Boyd is the only known Hun driver who liked to work in the dangerous low-speed end of the airplane's envelope. And that was how he solved the adverse yaw problem. He found the solution from a maneuver he developed when teaching tactics to FWS students.

In his article in the *Fighter Weapons Newsletter,* Boyd preached that one of the first teaching tools is to have a student get on the six-o'clock position of the instructor and stay there as the instructor goes through every evasive maneuver known to aviators. And this is how he began his air-to-air training with new students. He was patient with most students, beginning slowly, sensing their level of skill and degree of confidence. If they wanted to learn, he taught them everything he knew. But occasionally there came a student with what Boyd called "an obstruction" — that is, one who thought he was a great pilot and needed no tutelage. Such a student needed to have the obstruction removed so he could fully understand the genius of the man teaching him.

"The only way to get a fighter pilot's attention is to whip his ass," Boyd said.

A student with an obstruction would be put on Boyd's six and then, after one or two maneuvers (during which the student was lulled into a sense of overconfidence), Boyd would demonstrate with one abrupt move why he was considered the best Hun driver in the Air Force. He would seize the stick with both hands, jerk it full aft, and hold it there. This maneuver he called "flat-plating the bird." The maneuver turned the bottom of the aircraft, the wings, and the bottom of the tail surfaces into one enormous speed brake and slowed the Hun from 400 knots to 150 knots in seconds. It was as if a manhole cover were sailing through the air and suddenly flipped ninety degrees to the airstream. Then Boyd, still holding the stick full aft and not moving it a quarter inch in either direction, would stomp hard on the rudder and corkscrew the aircraft violently around in a tight roll. The maneuver spit the student out in front and left Boyd on the student's six. He had set the hook and there was no escape.

It happened so fast that students never knew what happened. One minute they were in a perfect kill position, tight on Boyd's tail, pipper locked on his cockpit, and about to shout, "Guns! Guns! Guns!" into the radio. All they needed was sixteen frames of gun-camera film, the equivalent of a half-second burst, to have a kill. But, as one student remembered, "All at once he did a double outside rat's ass and a two-tone trick fuck and I was a movie star. He had me in his gun camera."

Now it was Boyd behind the student, barking, "Guns! Guns! Guns!" Then there was raucous laughter and, "You just got hosed."

If the student thought this was a fluke and wanted to do it again, Boyd obliged. The outcome was always the same. "Boyd rode his students until they squealed like pigs, then took them home and made fun of them," said one of his former students. When the student realized that continuing the engagement would only add to his humiliation, he signaled he had enough. After they landed Boyd walked up to the student and asked, "Now do you still think you're a great pilot?"

"No, Sir," was the obvious answer.

The elegantly violent slow-speed maneuver does not square with Boyd's admonition to keep up the airspeed for follow-on maneuvers. He used it to prove to students that no matter how good they thought they were, they could always learn. And he taught it as the "desperation maneuver" every fighter pilot should know when he is about to get hosed and there is no other option. He did the maneuver both with wings level and in a turn. He did it over the top and out of the bottom. The maneuver taught Boyd that when the F-100 was at a high angle of attack and slow airspeed, the *only* way to control it was with rudders. Keeping the stick locked in the middle and controlling both rolls and turns with the rudder kept the Hun out of adverse yaw. Nevertheless, most students, even most experienced cadre instructors, were afraid to try it. It was another of the Hun's "JC maneuvers" — one that caused the pilot involuntarily to explode over the radio with a "Jesus Christ." If it was not done exactly right, it could pop rivets and even warp the wing. It also could cause the Hun to depart flight and go into a nonrecoverable spin. Boyd taught that the secret was bracing the elbows on the sides of the cockpit to avoid moving the ailerons and then pumping the rudders.

Boyd sent word to Edwards he had solved the adverse yaw problem. When the golden arms laughed at the temerity of the young captain, he flew an F-100 over to Edwards and made believers out of them. Then he sent word to North American and they, too, laughed in disbelief. What could a fighter pilot, a mere captain, do that the dozens of engineers who designed the aircraft could not do? The senior test pilot at North American came to Nellis and Boyd put him in the front seat of an F-100F and took him up and proved his point. Thereafter it was written into the flight manuals and taught by every instructor pilot in the Air Force: when the Hun is at high angle of attack and low airspeed, don't move the stick laterally. Use the rudders as the primary control for both roll and turn. Afterward, every time a pilot landed the Hun, he centered the stick and worked the rudders. It went against everything a pilot learned in flight training and in flying air-to-air combat, but it worked and became a way of life for Hun drivers. Almost overnight the number of crashes in the F-100 decreased.

It was this quick and violent maneuver that began the legend of "Twenty-Second Boyd." Boyd became so confident of his ability in the F-100 that he had a standing offer for every class that went through the FWS: "Meet me over the Green Spot at thirty grand. Get in trail. Get in close at about five hundred feet. I'll reverse our positions in twenty seconds or pay you twenty bucks."

Wheels were heard grinding in the heads of young fighter pilots when Boyd made his claim: *I'm tight on his six and he rolls right. I hang close. Five seconds. He pulls heavy Gs. I stay with him. Ten seconds. Even if he pulls more Gs and spits me out of a firing position, that's fifteen seconds. He still has to get behind me. I break and go for separation. He can't do it. No way in hell he can reverse our positions in twenty seconds.*

Boyd beat the pilots. But saying he could do it in twenty seconds was, to other pilots, an outrageous statement. Time was the friend of the pilot in the defensive position. The more time he had, the better his chance of throwing the offensive pilot out front. Boyd soon amended his wager to forty seconds and forty dollars. But "Forty-Second Boyd" still beat all challengers in about twenty seconds, a truly extraordinary feat that even today amazes other fighter pilots.

The only counter to the maneuver Boyd used was to do the same thing in the opposite direction. But it had to be done intuitively, instantly, with not a split second of hesitation. And it had to be done as violently as Boyd did it. Even when pilots knew what Boyd was going to do, the reputation of the F-100 prevented them from following through. No one would manhandle the Hun the way Boyd did.

No doubt exists that Boyd beat every young pilot who came to the FWS. This is not as surprising as it might sound, even if the students were the best young pilots in the Air Force. They might be good in their squadrons, but they had little training in air-to-air combat. Even if they had, no one pushed the outside of the envelope like instructors at the FWS. Boyd should have beaten the students. But the legend of John Boyd has it that he also defeated cadre pilots, Navy pilots, Marine pilots, and — beginning in the late 1950s — the foreign-exchange pilots who came through Nellis. He took on all challengers.

Nothing in Boyd's long and tumultuous career causes such a violent reaction among old fighter pilots as hearing about the invincible Forty-Second Boyd. It sets their teeth on edge. They say all this business about being the best is a boy's game and that there is no "world's greatest fighter pilot" — that even the very best pilot can have a bad day. They quote the adage "There never was a horse that couldn't be rode and there never was a cowboy that couldn't be throwed." But if they went through Nellis in the mid- and late 50s, they knew there was someone better. And it still rankles.

Then, too, most fighter pilots operate at the existing skill level. They never improve the state of their art and they never add anything to their profession. Boyd did both. And that rankles even more.

Some fighter pilots from Boyd's day now say Boyd was a one-trick pony, that he had that stupid endgame desperation move, a move that would have gotten him killed in combat. Some say he was easy to beat because he was predictable. But none can come up with the name of a pilot who beat Boyd.

Boyd's standing offer struck fighter pilots at the very core. He was rubbing their noses in his superior ability. The offer was a personal affront to every man who considered himself a fighter pilot. No one could be as good as Boyd was supposed to be. Fighter pilots ached to see him beaten. Word would have swept through the Air Force in days about the pilot who defeated Forty-Second Boyd. Details of the engagement, every turn, every maneuver, the final closure, the triumphant "Guns! Guns! Guns!" would have been played and replayed wherever fighter pilots gathered. The pilot who defeated John Boyd would have been remembered.

The only man who ever came close was Hal Vincent, a Marine Corps pilot who fought Boyd to a dead heat. Vincent was so impressed with Boyd that he applied for and was accepted as a student at the FWS — the first Marine ever to attend. And as is the way of Marines, he was the top graduate in his class.

Boyd fought countless air battles in the mid- and late 50s. He was never defeated. He was the champ, the title holder. *Pope John,* some called him. Others said he was the best fighter pilot in the U.S. Air Force. And they were right.

Chapter Seven

Rat-Racing

DURING the civil rights days of the mid-50s, Nevada was known as the Mississippi of the West. Restaurants and hotels and casinos displayed signs that said NO COLORED TRADE SOLICITED. Nevada congressmen were afraid the federal government might interfere with the burgeoning gambling industry, and they defended states' rights as ardently as did the congressmen of any southern state.

Black people in Las Vegas lived on the west side of town, and it was on the west side that the first major interracial hotel / casino, the Moulin Rouge, opened in 1954. It closed only six months later and ended integrated entertainment in Las Vegas until early in 1960. Sammy Davis Jr. performed at the Moulin Rouge. He and other black entertainers such as Pearl Bailey, Nat King Cole, Louis Armstrong, Harry Belafonte, and Eartha Kitt also performed at the famous hotels on the Las Vegas Strip, but they could not stay in those hotels, nor could they eat in the restaurants. They stayed on the west side at the Apache Hotel or in rooming houses.

In early 1960 the Las Vegas National Association for the Advancement of Colored People (NAACP) told the mayor of Las Vegas that southern-style marches would begin unless the Strip was desegregated within thirty days. Mafia dons who then owned and operated many of the Las Vegas casinos thought black people were after a piece of the action. Dr. James McMillan was a dentist and leader of the Las Vegas civil rights movement. He recalled that a casino owner called the NAACP and passed along the word from Mafia leaders. The word, as it usually was when it came from Mafia leaders, was blunt: back off or you'll be found floating facedown in Lake Mead.

Dr. McMillan replied that he was not trying to cut into the casino business. All he wanted was to make Las Vegas more cosmopolitan. Opening casinos and restaurants to blacks, a new market, would make more money for the casino owners. Desegregation would be good for business.

This the Mafia understood. A few days later the casino owner called Dr. McMillan again. "It's okay. They're going to integrate this town."

The national media picked up the story. Las Vegas would no longer discriminate in public accommodations. Black people could stay at Strip hotels and eat at restaurants there. A formal agreement desegregating all hotel / casinos on the Strip was signed in March 1960, and that is the date usually accepted for the desegregation of hotels and restaurants in Las Vegas.

But three years earlier, John Boyd forced the desegregation of Las Vegas.

It happened this way.

Boyd was becoming more and more interested in math and aerial tactics. He did not want his staff contaminated by the raucous Friday afternoons on base, especially at the Stag Bar behind the Officers Club, so he and Sprad began inviting their staffs to a Friday brunch at the Sahara Hotel. Boyd always was first in line at the enormous buffet for which Las Vegas hotels remain famous. After shoveling the food down, he shoved his chair away from the table, reached into his breast pocket for a Dutch Master, ripped away the cellophane, bit off the end, and struck a match. After a few deep puffs he smiled upon his staff, most of whom barely had begun their meals, and began to expound upon his ideas about the nature of aerial combat and how, if the bomber generals didn't destroy him, he was going to change fighter aviation.

Two hours was the maximum time Boyd allowed for these brunches. His name for the government was "Uncle," as in "Uncle

Sam," and he believed that he owed Uncle a solid day's work. It might be Friday afternoon and fighter pilots might be gathering at the Stag Bar, but the pilots who worked for Boyd would return to the office and stay there until 4:30 P.M.

One day in 1957 a new instructor came to the FWS: First Lieutenant Oscar T. Brooks. He was black.

The next Friday rolled around and by midmorning Boyd's staff was preparing to leave for the drive down Las Vegas Boulevard to the Sahara. Spradling pulled Boyd aside, nodded toward Lieutenant Brooks, who was standing across the room, and said, "John, is this a good idea?"

"Is what a good idea?"

"Taking Oscar to the Sahara. They will throw us out if Oscar goes. He's going to be embarrassed."

Boyd turned to Spradling and his voice was low and urgent and intense. "Sprad, goddammit, he's going. We're going down there as a group and if they kick us out they'll have to kick out the whole base. They'll have to kick out the fucking U.S. Air Force."

"But, John, I was just —"

"Sprad, if they object to Oscar, they have to object to all of us. The Air Force is integrated. We have been for years. We don't have a problem. It's their goddamn problem."

A fighter pilot is a fighter pilot is a fighter pilot. If a man can drive a Hun it doesn't matter what color he is.

Go as a group they did.

Spradling was nervous. He was in civilian clothes but Boyd and the six other pilots wore Class A summer uniforms and were conspicuous in the crowd of about one hundred diners in the large dining room. Spradling wondered if the waiters would refuse to serve them or if the manager would ask them to leave. He wondered how Lieutenant Brooks would react. He wondered most of all how Boyd would react.

The group walked through the buffet line and took their plates to the table. Waiters came with drinks. A manager hovered nearby. But if anyone thought of asking the group to leave, one look at Boyd's glowering face was enough to give them pause. Boyd had on his hard look, the one he had learned from his mother. It was a stern and foreboding visage that brooked no disagreement. He was daring anyone in the hotel to make any sort of scene. He was anxious for battle.

Nothing happened. Everyone was served quickly and courteously and the manager hovered nearby to make sure everything went smoothly.

Boyd and his fighter pilots desegregated Las Vegas that Friday in 1957. It was not a one-time event. They went back almost every Friday until Boyd was transferred in the summer of 1960.

By then the city of Las Vegas had followed their lead.

Boyd became an Air Force legend not only for his flying, but for his abilities as a teacher. A typical day in the classroom went something like this:

At about 8:00 A.M., Captain John Boyd strode briskly into a classroom in the old World War II frame building that served as the Academic Section of the FWS. He stepped up on the platform, walked to the lectern, and picked up two F-100 models mounted on dowels. Then he turned to the ten or twelve young men sitting in straight-backed wooden chairs and said, "Good morning, gentlemen."

"Good morning, Sir," they echoed.

They took the measure of the man they had heard about for so long. He was tall for a fighter pilot and had dark hair, an angular face, and the nose of a raptor. He was rangy and his carriage was loose, more like that of an athlete than a military officer. His uniform was neat and the creases down each side of his shirt lined up with the sharp creases in his trousers. He thrummed with nervous energy as he stood there with the F-100 models in his hand.

Boyd studied the class. The students came from Air Force bases around the world, from Itazuke, Japan, and Clovis, New Mexico; from Kadena on Okinawa and Bitburg in Germany; from Wethersfield, England, and George, California. They were from different backgrounds. Many were on the short side. Most were bachelors in their mid- or late twenties. Each was the best fighter pilot in his home squadron and each believed he was the best fighter pilot in the class. And each ached to meet Forty-Second Boyd over the Green Spot.

Boyd knew each was thinking the same thing: *This guy is getting a bit of age on him. His eyes are not as good as they once were. He can't pull heavy Gs the way I can. When I get him over the Green Spot, I'll pull enough Gs to roll his eyes back in his head and then I'll hose him. Maybe ten seconds. Easy.*

Boyd smiled. They would have their chance. But before they flew against him, they had to listen to him. The platform from which he spoke was a foot high and stretched from wall to wall across the front of the classroom. He roamed this stage like a caged animal and began teaching a subject he knew better than any man in the Air Force: how to fly a fighter plane in combat. In the beginning his voice was soft and compelling, almost as if he were sharing a secret. He stepped forward and prowled the classroom and returned to the platform. He stopped at the edge, leaning toward the students, the tips of his shoes bending as his toes curled downward like a diver on the edge of a swimming pool. Then he backed up, spun around, and began writing equations on the blackboard — long, complicated equations about lift and drag and vectors, math far over the head of most fighter pilots. They didn't care about math. Who the hell could remember this stuff when they were at 25,000 feet in a high-G turn and trying to roll out on a point? All they wanted was to get on Boyd's six and hose him.

Boyd wrote with one hand and erased with the other, occasionally glancing over his shoulder to demand, "Do you get what I'm telling you?"

"Yes, Sir," they said as one.

The old building had no air-conditioning and within minutes he was soaked to the waist. He paused, fired up a Dutch Master, and looked around the classroom. "Are you receiving?" he boomed.

"Yes, Sir."

He puffed on his cigar and remembered what Spradling told him: "Lower the intensity, John. You are just too overpowering to the students. Slow down. Relax."

Boyd took a deep breath and tried to do as Spradling said, but seconds later the admonition was forgotten as he wrote another equation or demonstrated another aerial maneuver. This material was too important; the students had to understand. Boyd taught them aerial maneuvers they had never heard of, maneuvers that even the boldest pilot among them had never considered. He demonstrated with the F-100 models, twisting his body and contorting his arms as he showed maneuver and countermaneuver. There was one maneuver so foreign to fighter pilots, so astonishing in concept, that when Boyd demonstrated it the students frowned in disbelief. He placed the two F-100 models in a tail chase, one tucked in tightly behind the other. In combat, the defensive pilot would be pulling heavy Gs to keep the offensive pilot from getting a firing solution. The usual tactic for the offensive aircraft was to pull tighter and tighter, seeking a better angle in order to loose a burst of gunfire. But Boyd showed how the offensive pilot could roll his wings level, pull up into a climb, and then roll *in the opposite direction*. This happens so quickly and is such an unexpected maneuver that the defensive pilot has no time to react. As the offensive pilot comes out of the roll, he is perfectly positioned on the tail of the enemy.

Boyd bared his teeth. "Then you hose the bastard."

The move was so counterintuitive that it took several moments to sink in. As the students pondered, Boyd placed the F-100 models on his desk, turned back to the class, and said, "The world is divided into hosers and hosees. Your job as fighter pilots is to be a hoser." A feral grin split his face. He leaned toward the class and added, "I, of course, am the ultimate hoser."

By then the pure and elegant beauty of the maneuver sank into their consciousness and they understood and sighed in awe.

One of the students was a first lieutenant named Everett Raspberry. He was known as "Razz" and was considered one of the most promising young pilots in the Air Force. When Razz graduated, he was the "Distinguished Graduate" of his class. He would return as an instructor and become a close friend of Boyd's. Still later he would go to Vietnam and fly F-4s with the 555th Fighter Squadron — the famed "Triple Nickel" — where he would teach the other pilots the maneuver Boyd taught him. One day the Triple Nickel would go up against the North Vietnamese Air Force and have a day of glory that would be remembered for as long as fighter pilots talked of their exploits.

Razz, along with every other student in the class, quickly realized the Boyd legend was based on fact. Boyd clearly was the best aerial tactician in the Air Force. He personified everything the FWS was about. By the end of the first day, all that the students wanted was to learn everything Boyd had to teach.

That afternoon Boyd took his charges aloft. It was time to put into practice what he taught in the classroom. The students put on their green flight suits, zipped up the "chaps" that allowed them to handle more Gs, put on their aviator sunglasses, and strode across the flight line toward the silvery F-100s. Heat waves danced on the runway like dervishes. Off in the distance, west of the Sheep Range, was where they would fight today. As they approached the open canopies of the F-100s, they checked to see that the sleeves of their flight suits were snugged down and tucked into their gloves. Exposed metal inside the cockpit could have a temperature of 140 degrees. Slowly and carefully they settled into the cockpits, fired up the engines, and taxied to the end of the 11,000-foot runway. Then they closed the greenhouse-like canopies and temperatures rose still higher. Air-conditioning in the F-100 did not kick in until the engine was producing almost full power, so they baked and felt sweat running down their helmets, into their eyes, down the small of their backs, and into the cracks of their buttocks and pooling under their thighs while they awaited clearance from the tower. Once cleared for takeoff, they advanced power, and as the throttle passed through 75 or 80 percent, they felt the engine *chugging* for a few seconds. As they accelerated past 100 percent power and ignited the afterburner, the "eyelids" at the rear of the tailpipe opened and a thunderous wave of sound slammed across the base. Fire erupted from the tails as the Huns began their takeoff roll. The students maintained position on Boyd as they climbed out of the pattern in close formation and headed northwest for the Range. The pilots fidgeted with the air-conditioning controls and sought to find the balance between too much and not enough. Not enough and they continued to sweat. Too much and small pieces of ice blasted from the ducts and the canopy fogged over. By the time they reached 30,000 feet and were circling over the Green Spot, everyone was squared away.

Courage, diminished in the classroom under Boyd's intimidating presence, returned. The man who knocked off Forty-Second Boyd would be the most famous fighter pilot in the Air Force, and they were eager to give it a try.

They played grabass. They went rat-racing. They got into furballs. Boyd gave them their chance and one by one he hosed them, and then he nursed them along, teaching, demonstrating how to control the Hun.

At the end of the day, the F-100s returned to Nellis, rolled into place on the ramp, and the pilots dismounted. They were drenched with perspiration, and salt rings stained their flight suits. Their short hair was pressed down tightly by the helmets. They might have lost three or four pounds during the strenuous high-G maneuvers. They were thirsty and longed for a cold beer.

But first they had to catch a ride on the truck that served as the flight-line taxi. They headed back to ops for the debrief, the most important part of the mission. How well a fighter pilot conducted the debrief was one of the most important criteria in evaluating that student as a possible instructor. After the debrief the pilots charged for the Stag Bar.

The Stag Bar sat behind the Officers Club and was surrounded by World War II barracks that had been converted into bachelor officers' quarters. It was a place where pilots could drink without having to change into uniforms. The Stag Bar lacked the formalities of the Officers Club. Lingerie shows were popular and sometimes nude ladies paraded around the club and caused fighter pilots, as one of them said, to be "hornier than a bunch of three-peckered goats." It was rumored that some of these ladies augmented their modeling income with another, much older occupation and that they earned significant amounts of money from fighter pilots.

On Friday nights the bar lacked not only the conventions of the Officers Club, it lacked the conventions of civilized society. Young men carved their names on the tables and on the walls and they bayed at the moon and boasted of being the best goddamn fighter pilots in the whole fucking world. Cigarette smoke was so thick that visibility hovered near zero-zero. Language was wild and rowdy. And just for the hell of it, fighter pilots occasionally attempted to burn down the place.

The pilots often broke out in song — not genteel parlor songs, but the songs of Hun drivers, of men who could go severely supersonic. In the telling, the lyrics are obscene. But they were sung loudly in the spirit of young warriors. The first song often was the elegantly titled "Dead Whore," sung to the tune of "My Bonnie Lies over the Ocean":

I fucked a dead whore by the roadside,
I knew right away she was dead. She was dead.
The skin was all gone from her belly,
And the hair was all gone from her head. Her head.

Boyd sat at the bar, the center of attention, the champion gun-fighter in a room filled with gunfighters, the high priest among high priests, accepting the adulation of his students. He rarely stayed longer than an hour. He might eat fast, but he drank slowly. No one ever saw him drink more than one beer.

Boyd enjoyed these late-afternoon sessions with young pilots. Their adulation was the fuel that kept him going. He sat at the bar and explained various aerial maneuvers and replayed all the air battles he had known and told the students all they wanted to know about the Hun. He told them of MiG Alley. And he listened to the songs loved by every fighter pilot.

Oh, my name is Sammy Small. Fuck 'em all. Fuck 'em all.
Oh, my name is Sammy Small. Fuck 'em all. Fuck 'em all.
Oh, my name is Sammy Small, and I've only got one ball,
But it's better than none at all. So fuck 'em all. Fuck 'em all.

Raucous laughter. Cheers. Another round. By then Boyd had fired up a Dutch Master and was waving it like a baton as he inveighed against the Air Force for wanting to abolish the FWS. There was talk of a new SAC general taking over the Tactical Air Command (TAC) and it was said he wanted to do away with even the vestiges of air-to-air training and have fighter pilots do nothing but deliver nukes.

One pilot turned to another and said, "You made a pussy error on the Range the other day."

There are two kinds of mistakes a student pilot could make when delivering bombs or rockets: "pussy errors" and "tiger errors." Pussy errors are the result of coming in high, shallow, and slow: the pilot is tentative. Tiger errors are the result of coming in low, steep, and fast: the pilot is overly aggressive. Nobody wanted to be known as the pilot who committed pussy errors.

The two men screamed "pussy" and "tiger" at each other for several minutes until Boyd calmed them down. About that time an officer came from the dining room of the Officers Club and registered a complaint. It was unseemly that he and his fellow officers and their spouses must hear such songs and such language. Boyd nodded and said nothing.

As the officer walked toward the door, the fighter pilots made a noise that sounded like a barbershop quartet. *Hmmmmmmmmmmmm. Hmmmmmmmmmmmm.* As the officer approached the door, the sound reached greater volume. *HMMMMMMMMM.* And as the complaining officer walked through the door, the pilots shouted, "FUUUUCK HYMMMMMMMMMMM!"

Glasses were raised on high. More laughter. More drinks.

Oh, there are no fighter pilots down in hell.
Oh, there are no fighter pilots down in hell.
The whole damn place is full of queers, navigators, and bombardiers.
Oh, there are no fighter pilots down in hell.

The Stag Bar was a room filled with mimes. Pilots waved their hands, fingers tight, one behind the other, bending their bodies and twisting their arms, showing how they almost had Forty-Second Boyd. It was *that* close. Next time. Next time.

Boyd smiled and puffed on his cigar. Soon he slipped away. As the door closed, he heard a fighter pilot shout, "Stand to your glasses!" Boyd looked at the stars. In the deep black of the Nevada sky, they sparkled with an almost unnatural brilliance, and he knew there was no place on Earth he would rather be than Nellis. As he reached his car, he stopped and looked over his shoulder and listened. Lilting on the cool night air was the song that comes from the deepest place in a fighter pilot's heart:

We loop in the purple twilight
We spin in the silvery dawn.
With a trail of smoke behind us
To show where our comrades have gone.

* * *

In 1958 Boyd made it official that the Air Force would be his career, changing his status from reserve officer to the regular Air Force. Mary knew her dream of becoming the wife of a small-town coach and living a simple uncomplicated life was over.

On November 2, after another difficult pregnancy, Mary gave birth to her third child, a boy named John Scott, whom she and Boyd decided to call "Scott." He was born prematurely. Mary believed the premature birth came because she had been ill for weeks during the pregnancy with toxemia, a blood disorder caused by ingesting toxins.

After Scott was born, the doctor told her another pregnancy would endanger her health; she might even die. But Mary became pregnant immediately. In fact the shortest time between any of her pregnancies was after the doctors forbade her to have more children.

Jeffrey was born about ten months after Scott on September 4, 1959. Again Mary had a very difficult time with the pregnancy and the delivery, and she prayed Jeffrey would be her last child.

But Boyd had his own agenda.

Chapter Eight

Forty-Second Boyd and the Tactics Manual

BY 1959 Nellis was the largest Air Force base in the world. The airspace over one-tenth of Nevada, more than 3 million acres of gunnery and bombing and air-to-air ranges, was devoted to Air Force use.

Boyd had been at Nellis five and a half years, an unusually long time when a normal tour of duty is two or three years. He believed Nellis was the highlight of his career and often told Spradling that he would always remember the freedom he had and the discoveries he made. But most of all he would remember the flying. When he retired sixteen years later, he had about three thousand hours of flying time, and the greatest portion was from his Nellis tour.

But he was ready to move on. Boyd decided to leave at a time when his career was riding a wave of approval from his superiors. His ERs tell the story. One began with "Capt Boyd is one of the most effective and dedicated young officers I've had the pleasure of associating with." It said he had acquired a "worldwide reputation as an authority on fighter tactics." A brigadier general indorsed the ER by saying Boyd "is definitely in the top ten percent of all Captains known to me and is one of the finest officers I know." The ER said the Air Force had awarded Boyd a commendation ribbon for his ACM research, a prestigious honor for a captain. Another ER said, "Captain Boyd has initiated practically all of the current materials on fighter tactics in use by the United States Air Force and many Navy units." Boyd had made his presence felt throughout the fighter community, something rarely done by young captains.

Boyd's transfer was, as usual for him, attended by conflict and high drama. Boyd wanted to fly F-104s at Tyndall AFB, near Panama City, Florida. "The assignment was set up and then the whole thing fell apart," he said in his Oral History interview. "I do not know what hanky-panky was done, but it was obvious I was not going anywhere." So Boyd decided to return to college, but not to the University of Iowa, which he still despised. His research into fighter tactics was taking him deeper and deeper into mathematics. He knew the research would have more credibility and be far better received if he had an engineering degree to back it up. This time he would go to an engineering school.

In the late 1950s, an Air Force officer wanting to return to college had two choices. He could apply to the Air Force Institute of Technology (AFIT) — the Air Force's scholarship program — or he could go to night school at a university. If he went the AFIT route, the government matched him up with a university and paid his tuition. But AFIT rules were tough. When an officer finished school, his next tour of duty was a "directed assignment" that almost always was on the logistical rather than the operational side of the Air Force. This meant that a fighter pilot would be out of the cockpit during both college and his next assignment. The chances of getting back into the cockpit after such a hiatus were slim. For that reason alone, most fighter pilots returning to college chose night school and paid their own tuition.

Fighter pilots at Nellis were surprised when Boyd chose AFIT. But then they thought about his circumstances; he was supporting a wife and four children — one child with a serious illness — on a captain's pay and had no money for tuition. But there could have been another reason. Considering his chess-master–like ability to plan ahead and considering how the AFIT program and his follow-on assignment turned out, Boyd quite possibly outsmarted everyone, including the Air Force.

The first problem Boyd ran into was the clearly stated intent of AFIT to send officers to college to obtain graduate degrees in the

same area as their undergraduate work. Boyd wanted to go to undergraduate school and he wanted an engineering degree. AFIT
rejected his application. But a month or so later they contacted him;
the AFIT program was not reaching its quota, and, more important,
the 1957 launch of Sputnik had made the Soviet lead in technology a
major issue in the presidential campaign — the Air Force now was
desperate for officers who wanted advanced degrees in engineering
and science. AFIT would relax the rules enough to let Boyd do
undergraduate work in engineering, but, they told him, it had to be
electrical engineering.

"Bullshit on that," he said. "All I would do was worry about gener-
ators and motors. I did not care about that crap." Instead Boyd
wanted to study industrial engineering, a broad course of study across
several disciplines, and he would do it his way or not at all. After a
lengthy exchange of letters and phone calls, the Air Force gave in.
Beginning in the fall of 1960, Boyd could take an undergraduate curriculum in industrial engineering. And he could choose any engineering school in America. He picked the Georgia Institute of
Technology in Atlanta for the same reason he had wanted to go to
Tyndall AFB: it was close to Warm Springs.

When students in the FWS heard Boyd was leaving, they thought
the aerial tactics course would suffer. He realized he would have to
write a tactics manual before he left. But writing the manual would
be a complex and time-consuming job, and Boyd had less than a year
left at Nellis. Boyd told Spradling he would need to be relieved of his
flying and teaching duties until the tactics manual was completed.
Spradling accompanied Boyd to the office of Colonel Ralph Newman, commandant of the FWS. Spradling was there when Boyd sat
down, lit one of his cigars, and told the colonel what he wanted to do
and how long it would take. Newman said Boyd had no mandate to
write a manual and that his job was teaching. "We can't spare you,"
the colonel said. "If you want to write a manual, that's fine. But do it
on your own time."

Boyd's face went rigid with anger. He jumped from his chair and
strode across the room. Standing nose to nose with the colonel, he
began tapping Newman on the chest and loudly reciting his contributions to the FWS during the past five and a half years. He
pounded with such vigor that ashes fell from his cigar and cascaded

down the front of the colonel's uniform. Spradling was horrified. Captains do not raise their voices to colonels. Captains do not poke colonels in the chest. Captains do not dust a colonel's uniform with cigar ashes.

"John," he implored.

Boyd ignored him. Spittle dribbled down his chin as he ticked off all the things his manual would do for the FWS and fighter aviation and the Air Force and why he should be relieved of duty until the manual was completed. He finished, and for a moment he and the colonel stared at each other. Boyd gave the colonel's chest a final tap and said, "Then, goddammit, I'll do it on my own."

Spradling seized Boyd's arm and pulled him from the room.

"Thank you, Colonel," he said.

Once in the hall he said, "John, you don't talk to colonels that way. You just don't do that. You know better."

"Sprad, this goddamn manual is important. It can help fighter pilots. It can change the Air Force."

"I know that, John, but . . ." Spradling shook his head. "You better be glad Colonel Newman is such an understanding and fair man. He could hang you for what you just did."

"Ahhh, he's an asshole."

Boyd could not write the manual and continue flying and teaching; there simply wasn't enough time. Plus, the idea of sitting down at a desk and spending hundreds of hours writing a long document brought him to the edge of panic. He was a talker, not a writer. When he talked his ideas tumbled back and forth and he fed off the class and distilled his thoughts to the essence. But writing meant precision. And once on paper, the ideas could not be changed. This was the first of several times in his life when the need to produce valuable work imposed such pressure and such anxiety that he was stricken with the thought that he, like his brother Bill, would snap. Near the end of his life, he confided to a close friend that when he was faced with the burden of sitting down and writing, he was afraid he would "spin off and lose control."

Spradling came up with the solution. "John, don't make this a big thing. We have some good Dictaphones. Why don't you dictate the damn thing?"

Boyd paused and thought.

"You dictate it and I'll have my secretary transcribe it," Spradling said. "Then I'll edit it for you."

For a month Boyd worked on an outline. Two or three days each week, he moved into the bachelor officers' quarters and worked far into the night. He slept two or three hours, taught in the morning, flew in the afternoon, and worked on his outline until almost dawn. Then one morning about 3:00 A.M., Spradling's phone rang.

"Spradling residence."

"Sprad. John."

"Hey, John. What is it?"

"Sprad, it's time to get that mechanical monster in operation."

"What mechanical monster, John?"

"The goddamn dictating machine."

Several hours later, one morning in September 1959, Boyd began dictating.

The Corvette was the car of choice for fighter pilots in the 1950s. It would not go severely supersonic but it could get close enough, and from the way this one was being driven, it was obvious a fighter pilot was at the wheel. The red Corvette with cream panels held a steady 90 mph as it ripped across the desert of New Mexico and into Arizona, top down, radio blaring. The driver was guzzling Coors beer and was half smashed. Occasionally he reached down and pulled another beer from the six-pack at his feet. He swaggered just sitting there. Only a fighter pilot can swagger while sitting down. When he was down to his final beer, the driver began looking for a place to replenish his supply. He stopped briefly, wedged another six-pack between his feet, and shifted up through the gears and continued westward.

The driver was a slender man with blond hair and a sunburned face. His name was Ronald Catton, First Lieutenant Ronald Catton, and he was a Hun driver out of the 474th Tactical Fighter Wing at Cannon AFB. Not only was he a fighter pilot, he considered himself the best in the Air Force. He was going from Clovis, New Mexico, to Nellis to attend the FWS, and in his heart burned two goals: he was going to clean the clock of this guy named John Boyd, this Forty-Second Boyd he had heard about, and he was going to perform at such a high level both in the classroom and in the air that a few months after graduation, he would receive the call inviting him back to the FWS as an instructor. He was going to wear the patch and then he was going to wear the black-and-gold checkerboard scarf and become one of the high priests in the temple of fighter aviation.

The red Corvette continued its course, now angling a bit to the north as it arrowed on toward Las Vegas. Lieutenant Catton smiled in contentment. He ruled his world.

But after his first morning with Boyd, Catton realized he was in the cage with a man who knew all there was to know about flying a jet fighter. Boyd's overview of tactics and some of the maneuvers he demonstrated with the F-100 models rocked Catton back in his seat. This guy was leagues ahead of every other fighter pilot the lieutenant had ever met. Even other instructors deferred to him. Catton thought Boyd was very intense, cordial to his fellow instructors, and a bit standoffish with students. He heard Boyd call one instructor "Tiger," and from the way the man's eyes lit up, Catton knew this compliment was not one Boyd gave lightly. Just as had been the case with Everett Raspberry, in the space of one class Catton went from wanting to defeat Boyd in the air to wanting to learn all that Boyd had to teach. Great fighter pilots have few heroes, but Ron Catton had a case of hero worship.

Catton's home squadron from Cannon rotated to Nellis for training about the same time Catton arrived at the FWS. He had been on base only two or three days when he met several squadron mates in the Stag Bar and proceeded to knock back a few beers. Then everyone decided to drive into Vegas for a night of barhopping and dancerwatching. Catton lit a cigarette and jumped into his red Corvette and tore through the main gate. The sentry did not salute, probably because the Corvette was only a blur when it passed by. Catton locked the brakes, skidded to a stop, then reversed at high speed, gravel flying. He chewed out the sentry and was off again, the Corvette's rear end skidding as he turned left onto Las Vegas Boulevard and accelerated. As he raced into North Las Vegas, he reached to pull the cigarette from his mouth. But the cigarette stuck to his lip and his fingers slipped toward and closed on the lighted end, burning him and scattering embers all over his beloved Corvette. He whipped across traffic into a service station and leaned down to find the ashes. When he looked up, a policeman was standing beside the car. The cop had the temerity to ask Catton if he had been drinking. Catton was indignant. Nevertheless, the police officer invited Catton to the station. Once there Catton continued to protest but lost all credibility when he puked on the floor.

The police called the duty officer at Nellis and Catton was hauled back to base. The next morning Catton, rumpled and hung over, was standing tall before Colonel Newman and learning the full dimensions of the expression "chewing out." Two things were working against him: the Air Force was cracking down on anyone charged with what then was called DWI — driving while intoxicated — and the city of North Las Vegas was complaining that drunk fighter pilots were endangering local citizens by speeding down Las Vegas Boulevard. The Air Force was being pressured to make examples out of a few pilots. After a lengthy lecture on how Catton had embarrassed himself, his home squadron, the FWS, and the U.S. Air Force, Newman pulled a set of papers from a drawer and threw them atop his desk. His eyes, blue and as cold as arctic ice, stared at Catton. "Know what these are, Lieutenant?"

"No, Sir."

"They're court-martial papers."

Catton's breath stopped. If he stood before a court-martial, it would be the end of his flying and the end of his Air Force career.

The commandant stared at Catton for what seemed like an eternity. Then he said that Catton's squadron commander was a close friend who had saved his life in World War II. "I don't want to embarrass my old friend," he said. He was not going to press the court-martial — not yet. He asked for the keys to Catton's red Corvette. Catton passed them over.

"Lieutenant, henceforth you will walk every place you go," the commandant said. "For the remainder of your tour on this base — and that might not be long — you will not drive, you will not accept a ride from anyone. You will not even put on a pair of roller skates. Except for an F-100, you will ride in nothing with wheels. One more screwup, Lieutenant, just one and . . ." He tapped the court-martial papers.

It was a shaken young man who left the commandant's office.

He stepped outside, looked up at the bright Nevada sky, and wondered how his career could have taken such a perilous turn in such a short time.

By the end of that day, everyone in the FWS knew of his misadventure and was laughing about how he threw up at the police station. He was wounded, and a wounded man has little chance in the FWS. Competition is brutal. He knew what was ahead: students and instructors alike would treat him like a pariah. His fellow students would offer no help and instructors would go out of their way to see that he busted out. There was little chance that he would wear the patch, much less wear the black-and-gold checkerboard scarf. What could he do? Who could help him? There was only one person. Catton stumbled down the street, cursing the hot sun and cursing every beer he had drunk the night before. That took a while. He entered the academic building and knocked on Boyd's door.

"Enter."

Catton stepped inside and saluted. "Sir, Lieutenant Ronald Catton requests permission to speak with the captain."

Boyd nodded.

"Sir, I have a problem," Catton began.

"That's what I hear."

Catton told Boyd his dream and asked what he could do to salvage that dream. For a long moment Boyd did not speak. He turned in his chair and held up his pencil and stared at the tip as if he were looking through a pipper. Then he spun around and looked at Catton. "No one has ever gone through this school with a perfect academic record. I don't know if you have the smarts to do that, Catton. But if you do, you will get their attention. If you don't, you can forget your dream." He paused and repeated, "*Nobody* has gone through this school with a perfect record."

Catton swallowed hard. Nobody had jumped across the Grand Canyon either. And what Boyd was asking him to do was the equivalent. The bust-out rate at the FWS proved it was the toughest course in the Air Force. Pilots were smart guys; they had to be to master the disciplines involved in flying the Hun. But most of them considered themselves lucky to graduate from the FWS. This school had humbled dozens of college graduates, and Catton had received his commission as an aviation cadet; he had only two years of college.

Boyd waggled a finger. "They will be watching you."

Catton left, wondering how he could accomplish the task Boyd had set before him. He would not think about the full academic curriculum; he would not think about the course on air-to-ground, bombs and fuses, gun sight computations, or the course on missiles and rockets. He would not think about any of them, especially the dreaded final course on nuclear weapons. He would think about only one course at a time. And right now he was studying air combat maneuvering, Boyd's course on aerial tactics. It was one of the toughest, designed to weed out every man who was not a tiger. For each hour spent in Boyd's class, a student spent at least two hours studying. Catton settled in. He forgot his squadron mates. He forgot the Stag Bar. He got up at 2:30 A.M. and studied until breakfast. He studied between breakfast and class. He flew in the afternoon, had an early dinner, and studied late, then arose again at 2:30 to start all over again. He was a man possessed.

When he flew with Boyd, he was amazed by the extreme nature of how Boyd handled the Hun, especially the low-speed, high-angle-of-attack flying — the most difficult part of the flight regime for the F-100. But Catton learned. He learned well.

Boyd was right about the lieutenant's being watched. Catton saw the looks every day and he knew the other students and the instructors considered him a screwup. Sure, he was a good pilot, but good pilots were a dime a dozen at Nellis. Every time Catton took to the air, he had to fly better than he had ever flown before. One error in judgment and he was gone. He had already shown his judgment was not the best. But to become an instructor, a man who taught other pilots how to deliver nuclear weapons, he had to be the very personification of good judgment. And he knew the instructors did not believe he had what it took to wear the patch. They were waiting, watching for one miscue. It was a lonesome time for First Lieutenant Ronald Catton.

He took the exam in air combat maneuvering. Boyd smiled as he handed Catton the test results. Catton had a perfect score — the only one in the class.

So far so good. Now Catton saw a grudging difference in the eyes of others. "That screwup Catton got a hundred in Boyd's class. You believe that?"

He finished the course on air-to-ground. Another 100. The flight-line instructors softened a bit. But Catton was still a screwup — just a smarter screwup than anyone had thought.

By the time he took the course on bombs and fuses, word was getting around in the FWS that the guy who got drunk in his Corvette and puked at the police station and was under the threat of a court-martial had made 100 on two courses. He was still laboring over the exam when Colonel Newman called Catton's instructor and asked, "How did Catton do?"

Moments later the instructor called him back and said, "Sir, Catton made one hundred."

Catton and Boyd frequently passed in the hall, and each time Boyd smiled and nodded. The two had a secret; they were the only ones at Nellis who knew what Catton was trying to do. And while Catton did not know it, Boyd was privately defending him with other instructors. "Catton's not a bad guy," he said more than once. "You got him wrong. Wait and see."

After all, Boyd had enormous compassion for the underdog, having been one most of his life. When he saw the instructors and students at the FWS arrayed against Catton, he had to defend the young officer. He saw promise in Catton, just as Frank Pettinato had seen promise in him, and he liked the idea of a man fighting against impossible odds. Plus, he had an old-fashioned belief, instilled in him by Art Weibel and Frank Pettinato, that hard work can overcome all obstacles.

Catton made 100 in the course on the lead-computing gun sight and followed it up with a 100 on missiles and rockets. The word was all over the FWS: Catton's going for 100 in every course. Now rather than ostracizing him the instructors and other students were encouraging him. No one had ever come from so far behind. No one had ever made this many perfect scores in the FWS. Catton had a shot at doing the impossible.

But there was still the last test, the toughest one, the one that consistently lowered a student's academic average. In the dreaded nuclear weapons course, students had to learn not just how to deliver tactical nuclear weapons, but how to arm and disarm them. The course covered the physics and the electronics and the principles upon which nuclear weapons worked. When a pilot finished the nuclear weapons course, he could damn near build an atomic bomb.

Catton studied harder than ever. When he wasn't in class or flying, he was laboring over texts on physics and electronics and explosives. Then came the test. Students finished and waited while the instructor, Captain Mark Cook, graded their papers. Several pilots grimaced as they realized they were not as smart as they thought. After students received their grades, they stood in the back of the classroom and in the hall, watching Catton. Instructors stuck their heads in the door, their raised eyebrows asking the question. "He's not finished," they were told.

The commandant called three times to ask how Catton did. He knew most men would have folded long ago under the pressures the lieutenant faced. They would have busted out and their careers would have ended. But he also knew that a few men, only the best, could grow up and blossom and realize their potential when they were put to the fire. Such men exemplify the highest qualities the FWS seeks to instill in its students. They not only deserve to wear the patch, they honor the patch.

Catton finished and handed the test to Captain Cook. The other students moved forward and instructors crowded into the room. Slowly Catton's instructor checked off the correct answers. The students began to smile and elbow each other. The instructors looked at one another in amazement.

Down the hall Boyd sat in his office, moving papers around, listening to the buzz of conversation. He waited.

Captain Cook reached the last question, checked the answer, and froze. The answer was wrong.

Silence gripped the room.

Cook asked Catton to explain his answer to the final question. Catton had computed the release gyro settings for a nuclear weapons delivery based on the aircraft being an F-100F, a two-seater, while Cook wanted an answer based on the F-100D, a single-seater with a different center of gravity and thus different gyro settings. But the test had not specified the type of aircraft; it simply said F-100.

Cook nodded and reread the way he had phrased the question and rechecked Catton's answer. The answer was correct for the F-100F. Cook ignored everyone in the room as he talked himself through what had happened. No one spoke. No one moved. The classroom waited. Cook decided it was he who had made the mistake. He made a mark on the test and handed Catton the paper. "I'm giving you a hundred."

Students cheered and gathered around Catton, congratulating him and slapping him on the back. The instructors smiled and nodded in approval. They had been present at an event that no one thought they would ever see. Catton pushed through the crowd and walked down the hall toward Boyd's office. He knocked on the door.

"Enter."

The two men stared at each other.

"I heard," Boyd said. He smiled. "You cleaned them out."

Catton bit his lip and nodded. He could not speak.

"Way to go, Tiger."

Catton turned away. A fighter pilot doesn't cry, especially if he has just become the first fighter pilot in history to ace every academic course at the Fighter Weapons School.

Catton graduated and was given a trophy for having the best academic record in his class. He was awarded the patch. Then he drove his red Corvette back across the desert to Cannon AFB in Clovis, New Mexico.

A few months later he received the call.

In early 1960 Boyd stopped dictating. Spradling carefully edited the document. But Boyd was not happy and spent weeks doing further editing, revisions, and more editing. Every sentence had to be right. Every maneuver had to be in the proper sequence. He agonized for hours over single words. He rewrote endlessly. After Spradling sent the document to the printer, Boyd still revised. Dozens of one-page corrections were sent to the printer. When Boyd finally, reluctantly, finished, he had a 150-page single-spaced manual that he called the "Aerial Attack Study" by "Capt. John Boyd."

"Are you going to put that on the cover?" Spradling asked. "Aren't you going to say it is the 'United States Air Force Aerial Attack Study'?"

"To hell with them," Boyd said. "They wouldn't give me time to do it. They made me do it at night, on my own."

Despite his anger, Boyd was, as he put it, "... as proud as a goddamn new father" when he delivered the manual to Newman. The colonel nodded, tossed the manual aside, and said, "We're not going to use this in the school."

"Why not?" Boyd asked.

The colonel showed him a much smaller document — Boyd estimated it was ten or fifteen pages, though it probably was considerably longer — and said it had been prepared by the Training Research and Development (TR&D) section of the FWS and that it was the publication the school would use to teach tactics.

The TR&D people had a mandate to prepare a manual; Boyd did not. His long hours and intensive work of the past four months were in vain. To complicate matters, his manual was classified "secret," which severely limited its circulation. Boyd fought the classification, but since his manual contained both tactics the U.S. Air Force would use in the event of war and specific details on how to avoid missiles, the classification remained in force.

Boyd then took an action that could have ended his career. He went over the colonel's head and sent both the TR&D manual and his manual to a friend at the Tactical Air Command headquarters, a man who could overrule Newman on what was used to teach tactics. His friend preferred Boyd's manual but said to avoid any impression of favoritism, both manuals would be submitted to an independent panel for review.

A request came down from TAC for five copies of each manual — a dead giveaway to Newman. The angry colonel confronted Boyd and demanded to know why Boyd had gone over his head when he already had given his support to the TR&D manual. But then word came down from TAC that Boyd's work would be used as the official training manual at the FWS.

In his Oral History interview, Boyd recounts that he told Newman, "You ought to be glad. This way you are ending up with the better book. It is a better reflection on you as the commander. Why are you protecting a bunch of goddamn losers over there who cannot even do their homework? You know they did not do as good of a job as me. They are losers."

"Get out," the colonel ordered.

But the next day the colonel called Boyd to his office. "I want to apologize to you," Boyd quotes him. "I really never read your manual before last night. Yours really is much better than the one from TR&D." Boyd said the colonel then called TR&D and "ate their ass out" for doing such shabby work.

Several weeks later Ron Catton was passing through flight operations when he saw Boyd and the wing commander, General John Ewbank, standing against the wall. Boyd was smoking his cigar, waving his arms, and talking loudly and in an angry manner to the general. Catton doesn't remember what the conversation was about, only that he was astonished to see a captain publicly haranguing a brigadier general. Then Boyd began poking Ewbank in the chest, jabbing with the hand holding the cigar and dribbling ashes down the front of the general's flight suit.

"General Ewbank put up with a lot from John," Catton said. "If I'd been a brigadier general and he did that to me in public, I'd have court-martialed him."

In 1960 the "Aerial Attack Study" became the official tactics manual for fighter aircraft, and fighter aviation was no longer a bag of tricks to be passed down from one generation of pilots to another. For the first time the high-stakes game of aerial combat was documented, codified, and illustrated. While all other fighter pilots used their hands, Boyd used mathematics.

The "Aerial Attack Study" was seized upon by Boyd's detractors (and by now they were growing in number) as proof that he was a one-dimensional officer, that all he cared about was air-to-air combat at a time when the primary mission of fighter aviation was to be a "baby SAC." Boyd, they claimed, cared nothing for air-to-ground or nuclear weapons delivery or high-altitude intercepts or promoting the new missiles or anything else except air-to-air combat. Decades later, senior Air Force generals would still paint Boyd as someone who simply never understood that the Air Force had moved beyond the air-to-air mission.

But their own closed-mindedness blinded them to Boyd's staggering accomplishment. Before Boyd published the manual, fighter pilots thought the game of air-to-air combat was far too complex to ever fully understand. They believed the high-stakes death dance of aerial combat was too fluid to master. The "Aerial Attack Study" showed this was not the case. When a pilot goes into an aerial battle, he must have a three-dimensional picture of the battle in his head. He must have "situation awareness"; that is, he must know not only where he and each of his squadron mates are located, but also where each enemy aircraft is located. In a swirling furball of jet combat, which can range from 40,000 feet down to the ground and back again, this seems almost impossible. But situation awareness boils down to two things: first, the pilot must know the enemy's position, and second, he must know the enemy's velocity. (Boyd would later change "velocity" to "energy state.") The amount of airspeed or velocity or energy available to the enemy dictates what that enemy is able to do, which maneuvers he can perform. Boyd was the first to understand the cognitive aspect of aerial combat, that it was possible to isolate not only every maneuver a fighter pilot could perform but also the counters to those maneuvers. And the counter to the counter. This meant that when a fighter pilot bounced an enemy pilot, he could know, depending on the altitude and airspeed and direction of the attack, every option available to the enemy pilot. And he knew the counter to each option. And if an enemy pilot bounced him, whether it was a high-side or low-side or head-on attack, he knew every available counter and every available counter to his counter.

Everything a fighter pilot needed to know was in the "Aerial Attack Study." The most prescient part was called "Basic Limitation of AIM-9 Against Maneuvering Targets." Even though the Air Force had an unshakable belief in the omnipotence of missiles, Boyd showed — and he was the first to do so — that missiles could be outmaneuvered by a maneuvering target (i.e., another fighter). His specific reasons for why they could be outmaneuvered were why the "Aerial Attack Study" was classified. The fact that missiles could be defeated was of crucial importance; it meant the dogfight was not dead, as SAC generals believed.

As soon as pilots saw the manual, they knew this was what they had always wanted. The first 600 copies disappeared almost overnight. Although classified "secret," manuals were taken home by pilots who hid them and studied them and prepared for the inevitable day when war would come and they would be in an aerial gunfight.

For the "Aerial Attack Study" Boyd received the Legion of Merit, an award usually given to senior officers. The commendation said the

"Aerial Attack Study" was the "first instance in the history of fighter aviation in which tactics have been reduced to an objective state." The commendation further stated that Boyd had demonstrated the maneuvers in a way that showed he was "undisputed master in the area of aerial combat." Finally, the commendation said Boyd had assembled the manual "with a zeal seldom equaled" while performing his regular duties "in a superior manner."

Demand for the manuals was so great that several years later the Air Force removed the material on missiles, changed the language in a few sections, and printed a nonclassified version. Air Force squadrons rotating through Nellis took copies back to their home bases, where copy after copy was made and passed around until they became tattered.

Hal Vincent of the Marine Corps, the pilot who fought Boyd to a dead heat in simulated aerial combat, used the manual to train Navy and Marine pilots. Foreign pilots training at Nellis as part of the Mutual Defense Assistance Pact took copies back to their countries, where it was studied as if it were Holy Writ. They agreed that the U.S. Air Force was truly an amazing organization if a mere captain could write such a document. Within ten years the "Aerial Attack Study" became the tactics manual for air forces around the world. It changed the way they flew and the way they fought. Forty years after it was written, even with the passage of the Vietnam War and the Gulf War, nothing substantial has been added to it.

And it was written by a thirty-three-year-old captain who was not happy with it.

Boyd believed the "Aerial Attack Study" could be formulated another way, that there had to be a better method of articulating the contents, maybe even something beyond the maneuver-countermaneuver strategy, something that went even beyond the mathematical formulae to the core, the very essence, of combat flying.

"One day I'll have a breakthrough on this," he told Spradling.

While most thought Boyd was a great pilot, others — including at least one of the pilots who checked his flying proficiency — thought he was so heavy-handed that he was dangerous to himself and to others.

Harold Burke was a chief warrant officer and the man in charge of aircraft maintenance for the FWS in 1960. He was a passenger in the backseat of a Hun one day during a firepower demonstration for VIPs visiting Nellis. Boyd was flying off the right wing in a second F-100. Both aircraft were loaded with bombs and rockets.

As the two aircraft flew out to the bombing range, the element leader decided he wanted Boyd on his left wing. Rather than easing off on the power, sliding backward, then moving into position on the other wing, Boyd simply rolled inverted across the top of the lead F-100 and settled into position on the left wing. Burke looked up through the canopy at Boyd's head, about twenty feet away. The element leader was angry at the proximity of two fast-moving aircraft loaded with enough bombs and rockets to blow a big hole in southern Nevada. This was the most stupid and dangerous thing he had ever seen a pilot do.

"Dammit, Boyd. Don't be horsing around," he radioed angrily.

"One G is one G," Boyd said. "It doesn't matter what position I'm in."

The point was that he flew the Hun as smoothly in the roll as he could have flown in level flight. It was a casual demonstration of extraordinary flying ability — a maneuver only a highly skilled and supremely confident fighter pilot would perform. Others believe it is one of the dumbest things they ever heard of a fighter pilot doing.

On June 1, 1960, Boyd was flying an F-100D, serial number 56-2931A, at 25,000 feet in a remote part of the Nellis Range. The aircraft entered an unusual series of maneuvers. Boyd jerked the stick full aft and performed a maneuver called "wiping out the cockpit." He moved the stick full right forward, full left forward, full left rear, full right rear. The Hun lost airspeed and wallowed and lurched about the sky. Boyd selected afterburner. The Hun shook as it was racked with one compressor stall after another. It stood on its exhaust flame and indicated zero airspeed but was still flying. Then Boyd jammed the stick full forward and dumped the nose. The extreme maneuver blew out the pressure seals on the primary and then the backup flight-control systems. The Hun was no longer an aerodynamic object, simply a fourteen-ton collection of metal and electronics falling rapidly toward the desert. Boyd had no options. He ejected.

He led off his accident report by saying he had discovered a design deficiency in the F-100, and that deficiency was the reason he lost the airplane. General Ewbank was almost apoplectic. He planned to court-martial Boyd for gross negligence, for performing an illegal and dangerous maneuver that resulted in the loss of an airplane.

Boyd said he could duplicate the hydraulic failure and prove there was a design flaw. What he had learned would make the F-100 a safer aircraft. Boyd thought he should get a medal rather than a court-martial.

Spradling was hearing talk that Boyd didn't hear. The long knives were out.

"Sprad, don't worry," Boyd said. "They can't touch me. I do my homework."

A board of inquiry was convened. If the board said the loss of the aircraft was Boyd's fault, it would be the end of his career.

The general ordered a static test that would replicate the conditions Boyd experienced. He went to the flight line and personally chose the F-100D that was to be tested. He thought if Boyd selected the aircraft, he would pick one with weakened seals.

Harold Burke set up the test. The F-100 was lifted on jacks and a hydraulic line attached. "We had an inert aircraft but active hydraulics," he said. Boyd crawled into the cockpit. Many of the FWS cadre and a group of students were on the ramp watching the test. It was Forty-Second Boyd against the Air Force and this time the betting favored the Air Force. When Burke said the F-100 had hydraulic pressure, Boyd wiped out the cockpit, held the stick full aft, then shoved it forward. Hydraulic fluid gushed from the belly of the F-100 and pooled on the ramp.

Boyd had won the first round, but now the general said the maneuvers that caused the hydraulic failure were reckless and negligent.

Boyd pulled out the aircraft manual compiled by engineers at North American and showed there was nothing in the manual that proscribed the maneuvers he had performed. Then he pulled out the Air Force Technical Orders (T/O) on the F-100. Every aircraft in the Air Force has a T/O. This is where pilots learn what the aircraft will do and not do. There was nothing in the T/O prohibiting the maneuvers. Nor were there squadron or wing prohibitions. Boyd won. The Air Force decided that he had, after all, discovered a design deficiency in the F-100.

Boyd's last ER at Nellis, dated July 22, 1960, began with "Capt.

Boyd has done an outstanding job as the Academic Supervisor for the USAF Fighter Weapons School. . . ." Of the "Aerial Attack Study" his rating officer wrote, "This is the first manual of its type in existence. TAC has accepted the manual in its entirety and will issue the manual as an accepted doctrine for all TAC F-100 equipped units." He ended by saying, "I recommend that he be promoted to the temporary grade of Major ahead of his contemporaries."

The astonishing thing about this last ER is that it was indorsed by General Ewbank. The general said Boyd "enjoys an outstanding reputation with respect to his speciality within tactical aviation circles. I consider Captain Boyd to have an exceptionally high potential in the Air Force, and one who should go far in his career. I know him to be fully qualified for promotion and recommend that every consideration be given to his early advancement to the next highest rank."

It was extraordinary, especially for someone with Boyd's reputation for impatience and outspoken nature.

Now it was time for the next step in his career, the beginning of his evolution from a warrior to a warrior-engineer. Early in August he packed the station wagon, and he and Mary and their four children prepared for the long drive to Atlanta and Georgia Tech. Mary was pregnant again, and early next year there would be a fifth child. Lashed to the top of the station wagon were clothes and personal items the family would need until the household goods arrived in Atlanta. It was a hot day and the wind off the desert was blowing hard. Spradling helped Boyd tie down the last items atop the overloaded station wagon and made sure all was secure.

"Sprad, I'll call you when I have that breakthrough," Boyd said.

"Anytime, John."

A flight of Huns took off and Boyd watched as they slipped the reins of Earth, tucked in close, and climbed for what the poet called the "long delirious burning blue" of 30,000 feet and a game of grabass over the Green Spot. The maneuvers they used would be maneuvers Boyd taught them. They had read his manual. There were only a few FWS-trained fighter pilots, but if war came, they would be ready.

Boyd shook hands with Spradling and looked around the dusty expanse of the spartan base and shook his head. "It will never be this good again."

As stated earlier, this is an especially good maneuver by which to slide into an opponent's GAR-8 angular velocity cone, since it provides the attacker a better opportunity to launch GAR-8 against a maneuvering target.

Procedures for the Barrel-Roll Attack

1. Stalk your target and attempt to reduce angle-off as much as possible. If this is impossible, employ the procedures outlined below.

2. Dive below and inside your opponent's turn radius, maintaining nose-tail separation throughout the maneuvers. The dive below should be initiated far enough out so the forthcoming zoom may be played inside or outside the defender's turn.

3. Pull up and zoom inside your opponent's turn radius if you feel he is not strongly oriented toward the scissor maneuver (sometimes this is difficult to determine).

4. Barrel-roll, nose-high, in a direction away from your opponent's turn. If he turns right, barrel-roll left, and vice versa. The roll will reduce vector velocity and the height of the yo-yo apex, yet maintain a higher aircraft velocity.

5. Continue the roll and employ bottom rudder as the aircraft comes through the nose-high inverted position. This will provide a 270° change of direction and place you with longitudinal separation, at a reduced angle off above your opponent, diving toward a six-o'clock-low position. The longitudinal separation will be less than that acquired from an ordinary yo-yo.

6. Do not employ bottom rudder if your opponent rolls away from the turn and pulls up into the attack. Instead, employ top rudder and continue the roll from the inverted position. This will place you in a nose-high attitude at six-o'clock-low - a perfect set-up for a GAR-8 launch.

7. Pull up and zoom to the outside of your opponent's turn radius if you feel you can sucker him into a turn-reversal. If he reverses, continue with the following procedures.

8. Roll in a direction opposite your opponent's turn-reversal. This will reduce your vector velocity and help maintain longitudinal separation.

9. Play top or bottom rudder, according to whether your opponent pulls up or dives away after the reversal. If he pulls up, employ top rudder. This will allow you to roll nose-high toward a six-o'clock-low position. If he dives away, employ bottom rudder. This will allow you to roll nose-low and prevent your opponent from obtaining extreme longitudinal separation.

80

A page from the "Aerial Attack Study." Dark spots at top and bottom cover the former "secret" classification.

Part Two

ENGINEER

Chapter Nine

Thermo, Entropy, and the Breakthrough

On September 14, 1960, Boyd began classes at the Georgia Institute of Technology. He was almost thirty-four years old, had four children and a pregnant wife, had served in two wars, and had spent the past five years or so teaching men the business of aerial assassination. All in all, not the background of the typical undergraduate.

But Boyd shared a surprising number of similarities with many students at Georgia Tech. To appreciate those similarities, one must first know what the school was like in 1960. Some 6,488 students were enrolled. Tech was considered a men's school, a place where men studied hard during the week and partied hard on weekends. Most students wore tee shirts and shorts and flip-flops to class, while some fraternity boys, particularly the SAEs, ATOs, and Kappa Sigs, dressed as they thought students at Ivy League colleges dressed: Weejun loafers and Gant shirts during the week and three-button suits when attending Saturday football games at Grant Field.

About half the students at Tech were from Georgia, with the remainder from all over the world. (One of the largest contingents of foreign students, until the Bay of Pigs debacle, was from Cuba.) The first female students — both of them — were admitted to Tech in 1952. Two more enrolled in 1953. By 1960 Tech had twenty. A male student could go through four years at Tech and never have a class with a woman. The Rambling Wrecks of Georgia Tech called female students "co-odds" or "co-techs."

Tech was ranked one of the top state engineering schools in America and was said to accept only one of eight applicants. The academic program was the intellectual version of advanced jet training and with an even greater bust-out rate. At freshmen orientation, students were told to shake hands with the person on either side and say "good-bye," because half of those present would flunk out their first year. "You are too dumb to graduate from Georgia Tech" was a frequent comment of professors. Students who survived their four years did not talk of graduating, but rather of "getting out."

The 1960s were years of protests and demonstrations on college campuses across America. But not at Georgia Tech. In 1961 the president of Tech called a mandatory all-student meeting and announced that the first black students had been accepted, that all students would welcome them in friendship and cordiality, and any student who behaved otherwise would be dismissed and there would be no appeal. Thus, Tech became the first major state university in the South to desegregate peacefully and without being forced to do so by court order. Tech and its students were too serious about academics to become sidetracked by such issues. During the 1960s the most avant-garde activity at Tech was the English professor who sometimes held classes at Harry's Steak House on Spring Street. This professor's "liberalism" was the talk of the campus.

All in all, Georgia Tech was a place of high standards, a place for serious students to obtain a first-rate engineering education, a place where the 1960s did not arrive until about 1975. It was a place where competition was tough and where only the dedicated and committed survived. Like Boyd, the school was intolerant of the slothful or the second-rate.

Boyd wore civilian clothes to class and no one knew he was an Air Force officer; he was simply an older guy, someone else to compete with in class. The biggest difference between Boyd and other students was one of attitude. Many Tech students were impressed with the fact that they had been admitted to Tech. The school's demanding academic standards and its willingness to kick out those who did not perform made them walk around campus as if on hallowed ground.

Not Boyd. He walked as if he owned the campus. His voice could be heard a block away and his language could peel the paint off the old buildings. One man who was in a thermodynamics class with Boyd said, "I'd love to have introduced him to my brother or my daddy, but not to my mama. That was the cussingest man I ever met."

The new year brought in a series of events that later would have a profound impact on Boyd's career and personal life.

President John F. Kennedy took office on January 20, 1961. His secretary of defense, Robert McNamara, was hardly in office when he ordered the Navy and Air Force to coordinate plans to build a new tactical aircraft. General Curtis LeMay became the Air Force chief of staff in 1961, a promotion that led to SAC virtually taking over the Air Force and causing even greater damage to the Tactical Air Command. And in a curious twist of history, it also laid the foundation for one of Boyd's greatest achievements.

On the personal side, the Boyd family welcomed another child, a daughter named Mary Ellen, born February 12, 1961, at Piedmont Hospital on Peachtree Road. She was the fifth and last Boyd child. Those who were close to Boyd later in his life see only coincidence in the fact that Boyd came from a family of five children — three boys and two girls; that Mary was one of five children — three boys and two girls; and that Boyd stopped when he had five children — three boys and two girls. They say he never talked of such things, that he was too pragmatic and too fixated on his work and too devoid of the emotion surrounding family to plan for five children.

Nevertheless, he impregnated his wife twice after the doctor said having more children would endanger her health. And after Mary Ellen was born, he did two things that indicate he knew his family was complete: he had a vasectomy, and he began looking for a house.

Two months later, in April 1961, he bought a house in Doraville, a lower-middle-class industrial suburb in northeast Atlanta about a half-hour drive from Georgia Tech. The three-bedroom ranch house at 2860 McClave Drive cost $16,400, the loan being repayable in monthly installments of $105.67. The house cost $100 less than his father paid for the property on Lincoln Avenue more than thirty-five years earlier.

Mary liked the idea of having a house of her own. But she did not understand why Boyd bought a house when he would have a new assignment in little more than a year. Boyd replied that the house was a good investment.

Living on McClave Drive was similar to living in the home where Boyd grew up. The ranch house was on a quiet, tree-shaded street and was so small and so filled with children that it always seemed crowded. Mary and Boyd had one bedroom, the two girls had another, and the three boys shared a third. The dining-room table was used as an exercise table for Stephen.

Stephen entered the first grade that year. The curvature of his spine made it too painful for him to sit up all day, so the school supplied a chaise longue for him. He had a difficult time in class and it appeared he might have a learning disability. Then the teacher realized Stephen could not see what she was writing on the blackboard. In addition to having polio, Stephen was almost blind. Glasses brought an immediate improvement in his vision but not in his classroom work. He missed much of the first year of school because he was in the hospital at Warm Springs. Stephen swam in the warm waters and had his braces adjusted and his young body pulled and stretched and examined by the doctors. But he did not improve. And Mary, who was never quite sure about any decision she made, began to wonder if she should have picked some other place for treatment.

Boyd was in Atlanta to go to college and did little except study, while Mary handled all the traveling back and forth to Warm Springs. When Mary Ellen was born Boyd was at the hospital, but he was in the hall, bent over his books. He did not swim and he stopped working out. The Georgia Tech annual contains no class picture of Boyd during the two years he was there, nor was there any graduation photo. The single mention of Boyd in the *Blueprint* is when his name appears in agate type among the list of 1962 graduates.

In addition to his studies, Boyd always kept in mind his desire to expand the "Aerial Attack Study." There had to be a way to reduce the 150-page narrative to the purity of a mathematical formula. Boyd often called Spradling or Catton and talked of the ideas swarming through his mind, about the breakthrough he hoped to find. Spradling and Catton listened for hours. It seemed as if each session took Boyd one step closer to a dim and distant goal. Spradling and Catton were proud that Boyd called them, even if it was in the middle of the night.

Spradling knew Boyd was walking a high-wire. While Boyd was obsessed with pushing the "Aerial Attack Study" to a higher level, his first priority had to be keeping his grades up. The Air Force would take a dim view of an officer who was sent to college at taxpayers' expense and did not do well.

Spradling was right to be concerned. Boyd's transcript from Georgia Tech shows his grades were erratic, ranging from A to D, with several dropped courses. But he doubled up enough in later quarters to receive his degree one quarter sooner than expected. His Air Force Training Report — the equivalent of an ER — said his academic performance was "above average" and that "he complied with Air Force Institute of Technology directives promptly."

What his transcript cannot reveal is the profound and lasting contribution Boyd made to aviation during the winter of 1962. In one sense, all that happened in Boyd's life up to this point was laying the groundwork; the real story of his life was about to begin. He was about to take the first faltering step in a process that would change aviation forever. What he discovered late one night in the second-floor classroom of an old building is today as fundamental and as significant to aviation as Newton was to physics.

One of several disciplines associated with mechanical engineering is the study of thermodynamics. *Thermo,* as the course at Georgia Tech is commonly called, was in 1962 and remains today near the top of the list of the toughest classes on campus. Thermo is a physical science that some define as the study of energy. Thermodynamics encompasses but then goes beyond Newtonian mechanics. A big part of thermo is the mathematical relationship between the amount of energy that goes into a substance and the resulting change in the properties of that substance.

Thermo can be peeled layer by layer, with new revelations at every level. The first law of thermodynamics is usually studied in physics and concerns the conservation of energy. The best layman's explanation is a checkbook analogy: money goes into a bank account, money goes out of the account, but a balance must be maintained. Energy, like money, does not disappear; it must be accounted for.

The second law is unique to thermo and puts limits on what is physically possible in the conservation of energy. It is called the "law of entropy" and applies to all systems but is most easily introduced by its effects on a closed system — that is, one not acted on by outside forces. The second law postulates that the expenditure of energy does not ebb and flow like the bank account. It says that in a closed system, the transfer of heat goes only in one direction, from a high temperature to a low temperature. A good example is an ice cube and a small amount of water, both within a sealed enclosure. As heat is transferred from the surrounding water, the ice melts until all the water in the container is the same temperature. The transfer of energy ends. The system is closed, stable, homogenous, uniform. But it is considered to be in a greater state of disorder than before the ice melted.

The first law seems simple and obvious, when in fact it is extremely complex and one of the more difficult parts of thermodynamics to understand. The second law was the first nonreversible law in physics — something almost beyond the pale of science. It says the universe goes from order to disorder. Separate cold and warm bodies represent a higher state of order. When the warm body has heated the cold body to an equilibrium temperature, disorder has increased — a concept difficult for many to grasp.

The second law is one of the weirdest creatures in all of science. Interpreting and defining the second law, playing with its implications, can become one of those endless academic exercises for which there is no answer. For instance, what if the second law, this one-way system, this order-to-disorder, is the arrow of time that is reality? That means the world we think of as real is instead an aberration.

Some even use the second law to try to prove the existence of God. This argument has it that God established order (low entropy), and since then the universe has progressed and continues to progress to disorder (high entropy). Since this has been a one-way evolution, there had to be a God to establish the order in the first place, otherwise there would be nothing to decay into disorder.

In the winter of 1962, Boyd wrestled with thermo.

Charles E. Cooper was nineteen — a junior majoring in aeronautical engineering and fascinated, indeed, mesmerized, by anything and everything to do with aviation. He was from southwest Atlanta and had the southerner's respect for all things military. Thermo was easy for him, just another course between the really great classes in aeronautical engineering, where he could work with lift and drag coefficients, structures, propulsion, and flight control systems, and spend long hours over a drafting table designing military aircraft. One day he might work for defense contractors and with aviators. All America was talking about the "Space Race" and there was even talk of going to the moon. As a graduate of Georgia Tech with a degree in aeronautical engineering, he could be involved in whatever course America took.

The student sitting next to him in the classroom on the second floor of the mechanical engineering building was an older guy who walked around the campus as if it was his personal property and who talked as if he learned the English language in a New Orleans whorehouse. The older man introduced himself as John Boyd. He was having trouble understanding thermo in general and the second law in particular — especially the mysterious, bewildering idea of entropy, of unavailable energy. How in the hell can you have energy that is not available? Cooper and Boyd talked, and Cooper explained what the second law meant and how it was relevant.

For weeks the two talked after class, and Cooper's tutoring kept Boyd abreast of classroom work. One afternoon, the two men walked across Hemphill Street to the Yellow Jacket, a small restaurant named for the Tech mascot and a convenient place for Tech students to buy hamburgers and hot dogs. They nursed a couple of sodas and talked. Finally Cooper raised the subject that had been on his mind since he first met Boyd. "You're older than most students. Why did you wait so long to go to college?"

Boyd said he already had a degree from Iowa and that he was an Air Force officer seeking an engineering degree.

"What do you do in the Air Force?"

Boyd beamed down at Cooper and said, "I'm a goddamn fighter pilot."

From his tone of voice it was clear there was nothing better in the world to be, nothing higher to which one might aspire. It so happened that Cooper agreed. Forty years later he still remembered the gist of the conversation.

"What do you fly?"

"Fly 'em all. Been flying an F-100 for the past few years. Flew a fucking F-86 in Korea. I was in goddamn MiG Alley. We'd fly up to the Yalu and the Communist sons of bitches would be up forty-five or fifty thousand feet where we couldn't climb, but when they came down we kicked their asses."

Cooper was a nineteen-year-old college student talking to a thirty-four-year-old Air Force fighter pilot who had romped triumphantly down MiG Alley. He had no idea that Georgia Tech would expose him to such things. He put down his soda and stared. This was more exciting than designing space vehicles. He was talking to a *war hero*.

Boyd must have sensed Cooper's awe because suddenly he was off and running. He loved to talk and now he had an appreciative, even worshipful, audience. And it was okay, too, that everyone else in the restaurant could hear.

"I landed in Korea at a place called K-13. Came in there in a goddamn C-54 with a load of lieutenants, all F-86 pilots about to go into combat. We land and we hear sirens and we see the air police racing alongside the airplane and we wonder what the hell is going on. Then the door opens and this full colonel comes up the ramp. He's got APs [air policemen] in front of him and APs behind. They're guarding him, making sure he gets on the damn airplane. They're sending him home. Turns out he crossed the Yalu and shot up half of Manchuria. He told his flight, 'Turn off your goddamn radios.' And they went across the river and shot them up. It happened a few days later to another colonel. Then another one. In three days I had three full colonels gone. They went across the Yalu and hosed them down good."

Cooper shook his head in amazement. And other students in the restaurant listened and nodded, apparently delighted to know the truth of what had taken place in Korea, and glad to know our boys had done what had to be done in fighting the Communist menace.

It is true that pilots sneaked across the Yalu and shot up Communist airfields in their Manchurian sanctuary. And it is true they were transferred if they were detected. But colonels did not do this, certainly not three colonels in three days at one base. This was a war story, an instance of Boyd laying it on thick when talking to civilians — but this does not mean it was a *lie*, as most people define the word. Cooper as a southerner understood this. Southerners and fighter pilots know the story is more important than the facts. If a story is not true it can become true in the telling. So even if Cooper had known Boyd was telling a war story, it wouldn't have mattered. Cooper went on to work in the defense industry and would repeat the three-colonels story hundreds of times in later years when Boyd became famous.

Boyd and Cooper ordered hamburgers. Boyd wolfed his down in several bites and kept talking, telling stories of his Nellis days, his loud raucous laughter ringing out triumphantly across the restaurant. He told Cooper of this thing he was working on, this idea he first had back at Nellis when he wrote the "Aerial Attack Study." It concerned the performance of fighter jets and it was something like driving along the expressway and deciding whether or not to pass the car ahead. At some speeds the driver knew he had the power to pull out and pass the car in front. At other speeds passing the car was far more difficult. The same idea could be applied to an aircraft in combat. The pilot with the most airspeed or the most power could put himself on the six of an enemy and be in position to win the dogfight. If he did not have the airspeed or power, he better not try to outmaneuver the enemy.

Finally it was time to get back to studying, and the two men returned to the John Saylor Coon Building. They found an empty classroom on the second floor and there, on one of the long desks that ran almost the width of the room, they opened the thermo textbook *Engineering Thermodynamics* by Jones and Hawkins. It was a relatively small book, but its equations had bested some very bright young men. Cooper began talking about the second law, explaining how more usable energy always goes into a system than comes out, because there is unavailable energy called *entropy*. Boyd nodded. After a while he stood up and began pacing. Cooper went on for several hours, but Boyd could not concentrate. Something was swirling through his mind, pushing at the edges of his consciousness — but what? Boyd continued pacing. He grimaced as if he were in pain.

All entropy means, Cooper said, is that no system is one hundred percent effective; if it were, you would have a perpetual-motion machine. The professors make it too complicated with all the talk of unavailable energy and states of energy and systems.

It was almost midnight when Boyd threw wide his hands in exasperation and said, "Goddammit, I understand about airplanes. Why can't I get this?"

"Then think of it in terms of an airplane," Cooper said. "It's the same thing. *Entropy* is unavailable energy. Energy can increase and decrease. If you put ten units of energy into a system and only eight units are available to do work, the result is an increase in entropy."

Cooper continued. He loved to talk about thermo. But Boyd wasn't listening. He was hearing something else. In his Oral History interview he said that suddenly he found what he had searched for so long, that his hair stood on end and his skin tingled. All that he had been wrestling with for years suddenly made sense. The clean and simple and elegant majesty of the idea almost overwhelmed him. Thermo laws about the conservation and dissipation of energy are like the tactical give-and-take of air-to-air combat. In a dogfight it is not power or airspeed that enables a pilot to outmaneuver an enemy. It is *energy*.

Energy!

If he was at 200 knots at 30,000 feet, he was carrying little kinetic energy but a tremendous amount of potential energy. If he saw an enemy fighter at 20,000 feet and dived to engage, his airspeed rose, because he was trading potential energy for kinetic energy. He built up speed, like Richard Bong in a P-38, to slash through an enemy formation and be out of gun range before the enemy knew what was happening. Then he could use the kinetic energy (or speed) of the dive to climb back to altitude. But as he climbed he lost airspeed and converted kinetic energy back to potential. The only way to regain airspeed was performing a maneuver that might make him vulnerable, such as straight and level flight or diving again.

He had energy but it could be temporarily unavailable.

Boyd searched frantically through his books and found a yellow legal pad and began scribbling notes and ideas and equations and theories and questions. If he could look at air-to-air combat in terms of energy, he could devise equations for the performance of an aircraft.

The test was forgotten. Boyd wrote and mumbled and nodded and went into long periods of silence. Cooper tried a few times to talk to Boyd, but it was clear the older guy was in a different place. Cooper went home. Boyd went to the library — it was open until 1:00 A.M. — and continued working on equations. He made a list of what had to be done next, which equations had to be written and solved, what theories must be followed up and developed. He filled sheet after sheet of his yellow legal pad.

When the library closed he drove up Buford Highway, turned onto McClave Drive, entered his home, and continued working. Then he called Spradling. It was about 4:00 A.M. in Atlanta, three hours earlier in Las Vegas.

When the phone rang, Spradling knew it was either Boyd or a family emergency.

"Spradling residence."

"Sprad. John."

"Hey, John. What time is it?"

"Sprad, I had the breakthrough."

"What breakthrough?"

"The one I've been after ever since I got here. It happened tonight, Sprad."

Boyd talked for more than an hour. He slept several hours, then drove back to Tech and took the thermo test. (He must have done well, as he made a B in the course.) After class he rushed home and pulled out his legal pad "to see if all I had done was a bunch of shit or whether it made sense."

It still made sense.

He added more notes, more thoughts, more equations. And then he put it away and went into what he called his "draw-down period," thinking, "Oh, hell. Somebody has already done this." If what he had discovered was work done by someone else, he did not want to waste more time. What he had come up with was so simple, so obvious, that someone had to have discovered it before. He was casual when he mentioned his ideas about energy to Cooper and other students at Tech. He wondered if they had heard of similar work. They had not. His thermo professor knew of no work in this area. Boyd could find nothing in the library along the lines of what he was working on. Then it registered: if someone had reached the same conclusions he had reached and applied it to tactics, he would have known about it when he was at Nellis. Anything to do with fighter tactics wound up at Nellis. And since he had been the head of the Academic Section at the Fighter Weapons School, he would have seen the material. But he had never seen any papers, any research, any reports.

It had not been done before.

He became excited all over again. The enormity of what he was in the process of discovering would change aviation forever. He knew it.

But he had one more quarter at Tech before he graduated. And he had to do well. His attention had to be on his studies. Nevertheless, he always carried his legal pad for jotting down new ideas. He already had orders for his next assignment. He was going to Eglin AFB down in the Florida panhandle. At Eglin he could devote full time to these ideas about excess energy. But how could it be applied? What could he do with it? Would the Air Force be interested?

Boyd graduated from Georgia Tech after the summer quarter of 1962. Soon afterward he was promoted to major. All his promotions had been in or below the zone; that is, he had been promoted on schedule or faster. He was ahead of many of his contemporaries.

It was an exciting time to be in the Air Force. The country was enamored of its new president, who had declared that America was going to put a man on the moon. The Space Race was going strong and the Air Force had big plans for its engineers. A new general was in charge of the Tactical Air Command, a General Walter Campbell Sweeney who had been on Curtis LeMay's staff — a real bomber general who probably would dismantle the FWS.

Boyd put the house on McClave Drive up for sale, but it was February 1963 before a buyer came along. The buyer made no down payment; he simply assumed the mortgage. This means that Boyd made payments on the house for twenty-two months and then unloaded with no return on his investment.

Mary looked at her husband, a man who had a degree in economics from the University of Iowa and a degree in industrial engineering from the Georgia Institute of Technology, and demanded an explanation. "You said the house would be a good investment," she charged.

Boyd shrugged and said, "We lived in that house rent free."

It was the only house Boyd would ever own.

Chapter Ten

$$P_s = \left[\frac{T\text{-}D}{W}\right]V$$

IF Nellis was the most remote and isolated Air Force base in America, Eglin ran a close second. But Eglin did not have the throbbing and pulsating city of Las Vegas; Eglin had the lethargic hamlet of Valparaiso, called Val-P, and nearby wide spots in the road such as Fort Walton Beach, Shalimar, and, yes, Niceville. Eglin was so bucolic that white-tail deer grazed along the base's main road. Eglin's primary connection to the outside world was Southern Airways and the two DC-3s it flew each day into the Okaloosa County Airport. The civilian airport and Eglin shared the same runways.

Eglin has hundreds of thousands of sandy acres covered in pine trees to the north and west of the base. To the south is the Gulf of Mexico. The remoteness of the base made it the perfect place to test guns, bombs, and rockets. Some of the most secret missions of the American military have been practiced at Eglin and the little ancillary bases squirreled away in the pine forests. In World War II, Jimmy Doolittle came here and trained his B-25 crews for the raid against Tokyo. Tactics used to destroy German rocket installations were developed here. A few years later, a mission to rescue POWs in Vietnam was practiced here.

The very attributes that make Eglin such an ideal place to test munitions, develop tactics for delivering those munitions, and practice top-secret missions make it a terrible base for the spouses and children of military personnel. The nearest town of any size to the east is Tallahassee. To the north is Montgomery, Alabama. New Orleans is about two hundred miles west. All in all, in the summer of 1962, the western end of the Florida panhandle was a sleepy backwater of America that was virtually untouched by the outside world and influenced by little except the relentless heat of the southern sun.

Tactical aviation was in serious trouble when Boyd arrived at Eglin. Bomber generals, hanging on to the coattails of General LeMay, were at the peak of their power. They boasted of having the biggest and fastest and most high-flying long-range bombers. They were increasingly dogmatic about strategy: one airplane, one weapon, one enemy. The Air Force leadership in 1962 had essentially the same guiding philosophy as did the Air Force leadership in 1947; in existence only fifteen years, the Air Force was ossified.

But things were about to change. President John F. Kennedy had been profoundly influenced by Maxwell Taylor's book *The Uncertain Trumpet,* in which Taylor asserted that the Massive Retaliation approach to war, the Eisenhower Doctrine, actually increased the possibility of conventional war. Taylor said because the United States lacked a capability for conventional warfare, it would be extremely cautious about risking nuclear war on trivial matters. The book so influenced Kennedy that he decided America must have a more balanced approach to warfare; America needed options, and conventional warfare must be a big part of future plans. Replacing the doctrine of Massive Retaliation with one of Flexible Response put the bomber generals and the Kennedy Administration on a collision course. Already Secretary of Defense McNamara and his Whiz Kids had cancelled the F-105 program; no more of the low-level, high-speed nuclear bombers would be built. McNamara had ordered the Air Force to buy F-4 Phantoms. But Phantoms originally were built for the Navy; they were interceptors designed to take off from a carrier and shoot down whatever might be threatening Navy vessels. Air Force pilots ridiculed it as a "Band-Aid aircraft" and said every bend in its wing and every angle in its tail covered a design flaw (which was true). It had two engines and two crew members — one too many of

$$P_s = \left[\frac{T-D}{W}\right] V$$

everything. And its shape — my God, that bulky, fat fuselage with the bent wings and angled tail! Air Force pilots said the F-4 proved that with enough power, anything could be made to fly, that if it were pushed sideways through the air, the drag coefficient was no different than in normal flight.

Having a Navy aircraft, a "saltwater airplane," forced on it was the most humiliating thing that ever happened to the Air Force. So it was decided that the Air Force must have a new fighter, one designed by Air Force people to fit the Air Force mission. In the back rooms the generals began planning a new fighter, something called the F-X.

If the Air Force was in trouble, so was Boyd. In his Oral History interview, Boyd recalled that when he finished Tech he wanted to return to Nellis but found himself in a "skunk fight" with a general who insisted he come to Eglin. He recalls that the general called and said, "You are going to get court-martialed unless you stop that shit. . . . Drop all that goddamn other hanky-panky you are playing." The general finally grew tired of Boyd's wrangling and asked Boyd if he were able to choose the base he wanted, "Will you stop all that crap you are pulling?" Boyd says he then picked Eglin.

This story is another example of how Boyd embroidered reality. First, Boyd knew that inherent in the AFIT program was the follow-on directed assignment to a base in the Air Force Systems Command. Second, generals do not negotiate assignments with captains. Third, Mary says that months before Boyd finished at Tech, they had discussed his next assignment and that Eglin was their first choice. The reason was as simple as it was personal: Warm Springs was only a six-hour drive.

When Boyd arrived at Eglin, he was bounced from job to job, from standardization and training to the operations staff to a job briefing distinguished visitors. For a while he was the base locator — the man in charge of housing assignments. But his overriding interest was in developing this theory he had begun back at Tech. Every officer who came to him for a housing assignment heard of his work. When Boyd briefed distinguished visitors, he delivered a tumbling cascade of ideas about how to maneuver jet fighters. He waved his arms so vigorously that he pulled his uniform shirt from out of his trousers. Little wonder he was pushed from job to job — each boss thought Boyd was trouble and wanted to move him along to someone else. Eventually he was assigned to maintenance, a job that fighter pilots consider one step up from sweeping floors, and he responded with, "Bullshit. I did not come down here to spend four years in maintenance." He told the colonel he worked for, directed assignment or not, bad ERs or not, he was going to work himself out of the maintenance assignment and in six months would have another job.

About this time the first copy machine came to Eglin. Until then, in order to make multiple copies of a document, secretaries cut a stencil and ran it through a mimeograph machine. Now a document could be placed in the new machine, a button pressed, and out came numerous copies. When Boyd first saw the new machine, he stared, thought for a moment, then said, "What do you call this machine?" This is a copy machine, he was told. He shook his head and said, "No, that's an antisecurity machine." Boyd instantly sensed that people who would not go to the trouble to cut a stencil to make copies of a document could now easily make copies, or, as Boyd called them, "little brothers and sisters." And he was right. Ultimately the copy machine had more to do with opening up government than did the Freedom of Information Act.

After a day at whatever his present job might be, he went home and worked on his yellow legal pads far into the night, developing equations, asking questions, refining what he called his theory of "excess power." Lunch hours and weekends were devoted to endless hours on the legal pads trying to reduce the theory to a simpler form. He used legal pads by the dozens. Around Eglin he was getting the reputation of a man who might not have both oars in the water.

Spradling and Catton received updates several times a week — always in the wee hours of the morning. Fighter pilots from Nellis and throughout TAC often came to Eglin to test weapons. Boyd grabbed them and talked for hours of how airplanes could maneuver against each other, about how he was trying to quantify their performance. In the middle of a conversation he suddenly would stop, pull out a scrap of paper, and scratch out an equation or a few notes. The more he talked, the more he understood about what he was trying to do. Each soliloquy was another step toward wherever it was he was going.

Boyd was metamorphosing from Forty-Second Boyd into the "Mad Major." He knew there were enormous holes in his work, glaring inadequacies that he could not resolve. He spent weeks testing an

$$P_s = \left[\frac{T-D}{W}\right] V$$

equation only to find in the end it was wrong. At this pace it would take years to refine and crystallize the research. He could see the far shore but could not reach it. What he needed was a computer to crunch the numbers, to quickly test a theory. Then, if it did not work, he could come up with new numbers and crunch them again. But the Air Force was just beginning to use computers and access was limited. Boyd went to the civilian who controlled the computers and asked for access. He wanted several hundred hours of time, maybe more. The civilian held a rank equal to that of a one-star general. He stared at Boyd in disbelief. "Major Boyd, what is your job here at Eglin?" he asked.

Boyd grinned that wide-open grin of his, waved his cigar, and said in effect, "Well, I've had several jobs since I got here. Right now I'm a maintenance officer. And I have some other duties. But I don't intend to have any of these jobs much longer. Once the Air Force understands what I'm doing, they're going to tell me to spend all my time developing these theories of mine. I'm going to change everything people think they know about aviation."

The civilian threw Boyd out of his office.

The mind-numbing and trivial jobs humiliated Boyd. He had an engineering degree from Georgia Tech and the Air Force needed more engineers to compete in the Space Race, but he was being used as a goddamn maintenance officer. All the night hours with the yellow legal pads were for nought. His theory might die before it was fully born.

Then Boyd met the "Finagler."

During Boyd's life he became close friends with six men. They were his Acolytes. In many ways these six men are quite different. What they share is that all are extraordinarily bright, all have an almost messianic desire to make a contribution to the world in which they live, all are men of probity and rectitude, and all — while independent in the extreme — are devoted followers of Boyd. They are important because they were so close to Boyd that oftentimes their work cannot be distinguished from his. The story of Boyd's life is by necessity the story of their lives.

The first and in some ways the most important of these men is Thomas Philip Christie. Born May 28, 1935, Christie was the first of five children. He grew up in hard times. His father was a gambler, a drunkard, and an inveterate womanizer, and when drunk, he beat his wife. When Christie came to his mother's defense, he, too, was beaten. The family was embarrassingly poor, raising chickens to get by. Christie missed out on the dating and parties that were part of growing up. As the child of an abusive alcoholic father, Christie learned survival techniques early in life, and he learned to keep from being noticed by those who could harm him. In spite of his difficult childhood, he managed to excel in the classroom and on the baseball field, and eventually escaped from Pensacola on a scholarship to Spring Hill College — a small Jesuit school in Mobile, Alabama, where he studied mathematics. In 1955 he graduated with honors, and soon after he applied for a civilian job at Eglin AFB, where he was hired immediately as a GS-5, earning $4,000 annually.

Almost from the time Christie went to work at Eglin, he began taking graduate courses in math and statistics. The Air Force had the AFIT programs to encourage officers to seek higher degrees, but it offered little to civilian employees. In 1961 Christie became one of the few civilians picked by the Air Force to go to graduate school. The Air Force told him to choose any school and they would pay his way. Christie picked New York University and earned a master's degree in applied mathematics. When he returned to Eglin in 1962, he was assigned to the Ballistics Division of the Air Force Armament Center, where his first job would enable the Air Force to make its final break from the Army.

The Air Force was still trying to find itself, to establish itself. Connections with the Army had been broken one by one, but the Air Force still used Army Air Corps bombing tables, the mathematically computed trajectory of bombs dropped from various altitudes with the variables of wind and speed and temperature figured into the equation. These complicated formulae were reduced to tables used by bombardiers. Christie's job was to develop bombing tables for the Air Force so the old Army tables could be tossed in the waste can and the Air Force could, at long last, be free of its most embarrassing tie to the Army.

In the beginning Christie had a junior officer and one civilian assigned to him. But that would change. An organization would grow around him. He was young and relatively inexperienced in the ways of

$$P_s = \left[\frac{T-D}{W}\right] V$$

the bureaucracy, but already he had mastered the system. It was almost intuitive. He was the adult child of an alcoholic and he knew how to operate below the radar of those who could shoot down his projects. While older and senior Air Force officers fumed at their failures, Christie quietly achieved his goals. His voice was so soft and his manner so self-effacing that few saw him as a potential rival. He was such a brilliant navigator of bureaucratic swamps that one of his nicknames was the "Finagler." He could get anything done. And he could do it in such a gentle unobtrusive way that few ever became angry or jealous.

Christie was engaged to a Catholic girl from Pensacola and soon would be married. His life was good. But he was restless. He knew all there was to know about putting iron in the mud; after all, he had written the tables. But the tables were merely an update of what the Army Air Corps had done long ago. He wanted to work where no one had worked before. He wanted to move away from pure math and develop something new. He wanted a job that would tax his abilities, one that would enable him to make a contribution to science, to the Air Force, and to his country.

The opportunity came, as it almost always does, from an unexpected source and in an unexpected manner. One Friday night Christie and his staff were enjoying their weekly visit to the Officers Club when his attention was drawn to a group of men at the bar. They were in civvies but clearly were fighter pilots; no one else uses his hands the way fighter pilots do. And they acted as if they owned the bar. The center of attention was an older guy, tall and gangly, maybe in his midthirties, waving a cigar and spewing profanities in a voice heard all over the club. Fighter pilots generally show deference to no man, but the look on the faces of the young pilots around this man could only be described as idolatrous.

Christie walked over to an officer he knew and quietly asked, "Who is that officer at the bar?"

The officer did not have to ask who Christie meant. "John Boyd," he said, as if that explained everything.

Christie's eyebrows moved upward an eighth of an inch, for him quite an emotional display. "I've heard of him. He did some good work out at Nellis."

"You should have him brief you on what he is doing now," the officer said, and offered to bring Boyd over.

A moment later Boyd sat down at Christie's table, leaned forward until he was nose to nose with him, and began talking as if Christie were across the flight line. His Dutch Master described circles in the air as he told Christie about his ideas regarding the trade-off in kinetic and potential energy and how he believed new tactics could be developed from this "excess power" theory.

Christie nodded in agreement. "That makes sense," he said.

Boyd talked of the equations he was developing, equations that would quantify his theory, equations that would define a jet aircraft's performance at various altitudes and various G-loads, equations that would reduce the entire performance envelope to a set of graphs.

"I think you are right," Christie said.

Boyd said everyone told him that there was nothing new about his work, that it had been done before or it was not important. But goddammit he knew it was fresh and innovative. "I can't get anybody else to go along with it," he said. "I've been all over this base and they think I am nuts."

Christie sipped his beer and chewed on a handful of munchies. In his soft voice he said, "I haven't heard anything like it before."

Boyd was surprised. He had found someone who not only understood what he was trying to do, but agreed with him about its importance. He leaned closer to Christie and asked, "Just what is it that you do here at Eglin?"

Christie explained how he worked with tactical aircraft-performance data to prepare bombing charts and how he developed maneuvers for pilots to deliver nuclear bombs and then escape the blast. He worked in ballistics, studying bullets and bombs. He told Boyd of his collection of aircraft-thrust data, angle of attack data, computations about fuel and altitude and airspeed, and all the other variables of aircraft performance. It was the greatest collection of such information anywhere in the Air Force.

Boyd nodded. "Falling bombs and active bullets. Ballistically they're not that much different from an airplane in flight, are they?"

Christie agreed. Bombs, bullets, and airplanes have only two kinds of energy: kinetic energy, the *ooomph* due to speed and motion, and potential energy, the *ooomph* due to altitude. "They're pretty much the same," Christie said.

Boyd's eyes widened. "Goddamn," he said.

$$P_s = \left[\frac{T-D}{W}\right] V$$

Then Christie told how he was using computers to develop even more sophisticated aircraft-performance data. For him, an aircraft held no secrets. The computers revealed all.

"Goddamn," Boyd repeated.

As Boyd remembered later, "I cleaned the shit off the tablecloth and began writing all over it. This was happening just like in the movies. I started laying out these equations and shit." He wrote formulas and diagrams and charts on cocktail napkins and gave them to Christie. He insisted Christie hold on to them.

Christie listened attentively. He knew nothing of air-to-air maneuvers. This could be the challenge he sought. The odds were insuperable, but that made it all the more interesting. And this Major John Boyd might be on to something. He appeared a wild man. His reputation was like the shock wave in front of an aircraft; it rode ahead of him and disturbed everyone it washed over. It left people rolling in its wake, confused and often angry. Boyd's methods were the very antithesis of how Christie operated. And yet . . . there was something about him. Boyd was a man possessed. He had an idea bigger than himself — a cause. And that was what Christie wanted. A cause.

"Why don't I come by your office Monday morning?" Boyd said. "We'll see what we can do."

"Come on by."

Boyd stood up and pointed at Christie. He nodded and a smile beamed across his face. "Tiger, we're gonna do some goddamn good work."

Rarely in the Air Force has an introduction resulted in such a productive, long-term, synergistic explosion of creative thought as when the Mad Major met the Finagler. The Air Force would never be the same. It was more than ambition and the desire to do good and significant work that bound these two men together. Neither man talked about personal or family matters, yet each must have sensed at some level the parallels in their childhoods: the embarrassing poverty, the dysfunctional families, the athletic prowess, the overpowering desire to get up and get out and to be somebody. Christie, though eight years younger than Boyd, would be more of an indulgent uncle.

Boyd was a fighter pilot and operating with a fighter pilot's passion and aggression and desire to do battle. His primary form of social intercourse was confrontation. He had not yet acquired subtlety and bureaucratic skills. He needed a protector, someone to — in Air Force parlance — fly top cover. Christie was that man. The friendship that began that night in the Officers Club lasted until the day Boyd died.

It is impossible to separate the contributions of the two men to the work they were about to do — work that would, in the end, do just what Boyd predicted: change people's fundamental understanding of aviation. The idea was Boyd's. But Christie's background in advanced math and his skill with computers, along with his skills in handling the bureaucracy, made possible Boyd's great and lasting contribution to aviation. Boyd simply could not have done what he did had it not been for Christie — not at that time and not at that place.

In the beginning they talked of pursuit curves. How many Gs would a pilot have to pull to get the correct angle to shoot an enemy aircraft and how much would aircraft performance be degraded by pulling those Gs? Christie listened to Boyd, asked questions, and began developing new equations. Boyd was a reasonably good mathematician, but he was not in the same league with Christie. Yet he insisted on understanding every equation. "I don't understand," he said. "Tell me one more time. I'm a dumb shit." Christie patiently walked through the equation again. "Do it again," Boyd said. It almost drove Christie mad. He believed time could be better spent simply by plowing the equations into the small Wang computer in his office, seeing where the equations led, developing new equations, and always moving ahead. But Boyd wanted to go over the math, dissect each equation, and explore the full range of every theorem until he was as familiar with it as was Christie. Hour after hour Christie stood at a blackboard with Boyd and walked him through the equations.

Boyd's ideas changed every day. "Let's look at this," he would say. Or "Let's try it this way." He was never satisfied. For months there was not even a name for what the two men were working on. Then one day Boyd walked in and said to Christie, "I'm calling it the 'Energy-Maneuverability Theory.'"

Christie nodded. He didn't care what Boyd called it, as long as he would move ahead. Christie wanted a pamphlet, a briefing, a book,

$$P_s = \left[\frac{T-D}{W} \right] V$$

something codified that he could hold in his hand, something that could be presented to the Air Force. But Boyd was such a perfectionist that he would not write anything. What was the use of writing it if it was going to be changed five minutes later?

Over and over, day and night, Saturdays and Sundays, they pushed data through Christie's computer until the Wang was overwhelmed and it became obvious a bigger computer was needed. If the Wang was overwhelmed, so was Christie. Because the E-M Theory had nothing to do with Boyd's assigned job, all the work had to be done in the evenings and on the weekends. Christie lived forty miles away in Pensacola and came to work in a carpool. If he was driving, he had to go to Pensacola, then return to Eglin and work late into the evening. And chances are when he walked into his house at 2:00 A.M., the phone would be ringing. It was always Boyd.

Christie was in effect working two jobs — his regular job and the Boyd job. Saturdays and Sundays he spent in his office with Boyd. His fiancée did not look with favor on this after-hours work.

The biggest computer on base was an IBM 704. To use it, one had to come to the computer shop as a supplicant. The proper way to obtain computer time, the Air Force way, the only way, was first to have a project that met all the criteria for computer usage. Then whoever was in charge of the project delegated someone to take the data to the computer office. There a program was written and the information placed on punch cards, which then were fed to the computer. The printouts were returned to the supplicant. Boyd wrote letter after letter asking permission to test his E-M data. The civilian in charge refused each request. Boyd again went to see the civilian. "This thing I'm working on will benefit the Air Force," he said. "It will enable fighter pilots to devise new tactics. It will enable America to dominate air combat."

The civilian reminded Boyd that he was only a major, a man being bounced from job to job, someone whose job description had nothing to do with computers. Computer time was too valuable to waste on some harebrained idea. Besides, Eglin was a weapons-testing base. Theories about energy-maneuverability, or whatever the hell Boyd's idea was called, came from Wright-Patterson AFB.

Again, Boyd was at an impasse.

"I have an idea," Christie said. "Let me see if I can work it out."

Almost half of the computer work done by the IBM 740 was done for Christie. He went to his boss and said he had some ideas he wanted to run through the base computer. He was somewhat vague about these ideas, but his boss did not press the issue. Whatever Christie wanted was okay. His work was important and it had the attention of Air Force generals. If he wanted to run some ideas through a computer, fine.

Christie and Boyd worked out long lists of equations and then Christie took the equations to the computer shop. "These are my inputs," he said. "This is what I want my outputs to look like." He was asked for an authorization code. His office had dozens of such codes, one for each project. He picked a number. The computer technician checked a long list of approved project codes and, yes, there it was. He ran the equations and by the next day Christie had a stack of printouts a foot tall, row after row of data, pages and pages of nothing but numbers. (An E-M chart is a state condition, a snapshot of an aircraft state at a given moment.)

When Boyd saw them, he reacted as if he had been handed the Ten Commandments. He sat down and reverently turned the pages. Christie realized that Boyd had the ability to look at pages of numbers and visualize their meaning. He could look at what to most people would be a confusing jumble of arcane math and see an airplane with the variables of altitude, airspeed, temperature, angle of bank, and G-load. As Boyd sat at the table, his head moved and his shoulders rolled and his fist pulled back on the stick and he mumbled as he flew the numbers. He said to Christie, "The charts sing to me. I hear music when I read them."

Boyd had begun working out at the gym again and had returned to his habit of chewing calluses on his hands. People in Christie's office were horrified. They were working on what sort of blasts are generated by bombs of a given size, what sort of damage bomb fragments might do to given targets, how many bombs of a given weight must be dropped to destroy, say, a bridge, and over in the corner was Major Boyd, working on an unauthorized project that could get the entire office in trouble, mumbling and chewing on his hand and spitting skin across the office.

Boyd scanned page after page of numbers and missed nothing. When a computer operator hit the wrong key and a printout had one

$$P_s = \left[\frac{T-D}{W}\right] V$$

wrong number, Boyd erupted. The slightest anomaly, the slightest perturbation on one of maybe five hundred pages, he instantly picked out. "Goddammit, Christie, they fucked up over there in the computer shop," he yelled. "I'm going over there and kick that civilian's ass."

"Now, John," Christie said in his soft conciliatory voice. "Let me handle it." Above all else Christie had to keep Boyd out of the computer shop. Each new collection of data led to more iterations that were integrated with earlier work and then sent back to the computer shop. Now Boyd was making progress.

Reduced to its basics, Boyd's work hinged on thrust and drag ratios. An airplane at a given altitude, given G, and given speed has a defined drag. The engine has a maximum potential thrust at that altitude and that temperature. If the engine puts out enough energy to match the drag, the aircraft's total energy is unchanging — the energy rate is zero. All is balanced. But Boyd wanted to know how fast a pilot could gain energy when he fire walled the throttle. At a given altitude, given speed, and pulling a given amount of Gs, how much *ooomph* did he have in reserve? And the answer he sought had to be normalized so every aircraft could be seen in an equal light, independent of its weight. That is why Boyd chose to look at how fast a fighter gained or lost *specific* energy, not total energy.

A B-52 and a Piper Cub, both flying at the same speed and same altitude, have the same specific energy — that is, total energy divided by weight. How fast either aircraft gains or loses specific energy depends on the difference between the engine's available thrust and the airplane's drag. For example, an aircraft in level flight is pulling one G. Say the aircraft has 2,000 pounds of drag. If the pilot racks the aircraft up in a tight bank and pulls hard on the stick, he might pull six Gs. Now the aircraft is generating 12,000 pounds of drag. As the G-load increases, drag becomes enormous — much greater than thrust — and airspeed bleeds off rapidly. Tactically, the ability to quickly slow down is as important as the ability to quickly speed up.

The E-M Theory, at its simplest, is a method to determine the specific energy rate of an aircraft. This is what every fighter pilot wants to know. *If I am at 30,000 feet and 450 knots and pull six Gs, how fast am I gaining or losing energy? Can my adversary gain or lose energy faster than I can?* In an equation, specific energy rate is denoted by "P_s" (pronounced "p sub s"). The state of any aircraft in any flight regime can be defined with Boyd's simple equation: $P_s = \left[\dfrac{T-D}{W}\right] V$, or thrust minus drag over weight, multiplied by velocity. This is the core of E-M.

Elegance is one of the most important attributes of an equation. The briefer and simpler an equation is, the more elegant it is. $E = mc^2$ is, of course, the ultimate example. Boyd's theory is not only elegant, but it is simple, beautiful, and revolutionary. And it is so obvious. When people looked at it, they invariably had one of two reactions: they either slammed a hand to their forehead and said, "Why didn't I think of that?" or said it had been done before — nothing so simple could have remained undiscovered for so long.

Boyd now could do more than imagine and believe; he could actually *see* the potential impact of his work. In the beginning the entire thrust of his theory had been to understand the full performance envelope of American aircraft, with the goal of developing new tactics for aerial battles. Then he realized that if E-M could quantify the performance of American aircraft, it could — for the first time — do the same for "threat aircraft," for the MiGs and Sukhois flown by the Soviets. Finally, if E-M could quantify aircraft performance, why couldn't he back up the theory and use it to *design* fighter aircraft?

Upon first learning of Boyd's early work with E-M, people naturally ask if he had a "target P_s" or an "ideal P_s." This is not only wrong, it is meaningless. More is usually better in a fighter, but "target" or "ideal" smacks of optimization and Boyd despised optimization. He wanted E-M to explore possibilities across the entire flight envelope. He then tweaked designs, made small variations, and saw how they compared, always keeping the improvements and discarding the degradations. He evolved his way to a design by trial and error. He did not know what he was looking for before the fact. He selected improvements as a basis for further variations and tests — very Darwinian, which by its nature put him on an unpredictable path. The end result emerged when variations no longer yielded improvements. The result was an artistic balance and compromise, not an optimization.

Boyd's E-M research had an unexpected result on his personal appearance. He no longer was the spit-and-polish officer he had been at Nellis. The creased shirts and trousers and the crisp military look were gone. Wearing civilian clothes for two years at Georgia Tech

$$P_s = \left[\frac{T-D}{W}\right] V$$

may have contributed to this; pouring all his energy into his research couldn't have helped. Although Boyd was rumpled and disheveled and badly put together, he still saw himself as he was at Nellis. When he and Christie walked from one office to another, he oftentimes chewed out enlisted personnel for looking sloppy. He stood there, his own shirttail hanging over his belt and his trousers wrinkled, and lectured enlisted men about the importance of respecting the uniform and making a good appearance for the Air Force. Christie shook his head in disbelief.

Boyd was developing a curious reputation at Eglin. In addition to the E-M and his slovenly appearance, his dining-room habits were following him. There was talk of submitting his name to the *Guinness Book of World Records* after he was clocked downing two eggs, a slice of ham, two pieces of toast, and a cup of coffee in twenty-two seconds. And for such a profane man he had a paradoxical streak of the puritan. He once attended a bachelor party, and the sexually suggestive language, the gag gifts, and the gyrations of a nude female dancer so embarrassed him that he left.

Boyd was so focused on his research that very few things in the daily course of events registered with him. But after he saw the movie *El Cid,* he talked for weeks of the final scenes. El Cid is gravely ill, but if Spain is to be saved he must lead his troops in battle against the Moors. El Cid dies one evening and the next morning his body is dressed in armor and tied to his horse and sent out ahead of his troops, causing the Moors to flee in panic.

The movie had two themes that must have resonated with Boyd: El Cid is a man of unbending principle and patriotism, and he sees duty as more important than family. Boyd lived by these same lights. But what Boyd could not know was that after he died, his friends remembered his great affection for the movie and talked of how he, like El Cid, was causing confusion among his enemies even after death.

Boyd still had no mandate from the Air Force to work on the E-M Theory. Nevertheless, he was determined to have his work acknowledged. But he had two big problems. First, he had to have the weight, thrust, lift coefficients, and drag polars for every fighter aircraft. He had to have what engineers call "the numbers." Second, he had to find a way to translate pages and pages of complex mathematics into something that was informative, persuasive, and interesting — something that, as he kept saying, "even a goddamn general can understand."

Getting the numbers was an almost insurmountable obstacle. The weight of an airplane is a good example. Obtaining the weight seems simple. But what weight? The ramp weight (what an aircraft weighs sitting on the ramp) is one of the most common measurements. But the ramp weight, depending upon the amount of fuel or the external racks and weapons, can vary by thousands of pounds. What is the fuel state of the aircraft when it fights a MiG? What missiles are aboard? The variables for the weight of an aircraft are endless. The manufacturer and the Air Force always offer stripped-down and misleading figures because the less an aircraft weighs, the better its performance — and they want the performance to look better than it really is. But the foundation of E-M is based on having correct numbers. To use spurious data would endanger pilots. Boyd had to have the correct numbers, and those numbers were at the Flight Dynamics Laboratory at Wright-Patterson AFB in Dayton, Ohio.

At the time the Air Force was divided into three broad categories: the operational Air Force, the supply Air Force, and the acquisitions Air Force. Wright-Patterson was the heart of the acquisitions Air Force. Wright-Patterson actually is two bases: Wright Field and Patterson AFB. But usually this distinction is not made, and the facility is referred to simply as Wright-Pat. The base is the crown jewel of Air Force bases — what those in the Air Force call a "heartthrob base." Named for the Wright brothers, it is one of the oldest bases in the Air Force. The Air Force Museum is at Wright-Pat. And the base has the cachet of being the intellectual center of the Air Force, the home of the Propulsion Laboratory and the Flight Dynamics Laboratory, where the Air Force does basic research into aircraft and engines. Wright-Pat has a higher percentage of advanced degrees and a higher ratio of officers to enlisted men than any other base in the Air Force. Wright-Pat and Eglin both were in the Air Force Systems Command (AFSC). But the difference between the two bases was the difference between an Ivy League university and a trade school. People at Wright-Pat looked at Eglin as that place down in the Florida panhandle where pilots played with their airplanes and dropped bombs and tested guns; it was a hobby shop. The heavy lift-

$$P_s = \left[\frac{T-D}{W}\right] V$$

ing, the work of consequence, was done in the cloistered confines of Wright-Pat.

While the denizens of Wright-Pat have always had a very high opinion of themselves, that opinion is not universally shared. A story is told of how a group of former high-ranking German officers was touring military facilities in America and was taken to Wright-Pat. The officers saw the labs and talked with professorial officers and experienced the lofty mustiness of the base, and then one of the German officers turned to his host and quietly said, "Now I know why we lost the war."

His host from Wright-Pat smiled and waited.

"We had *two* bases like this."

It was this atmosphere that Boyd entered. He flew to Wright-Pat and was driven to the Flight Dynamics Lab, where he explained what he wanted. The officer with whom he talked must have been bemused by the intense major from Eglin who believed he was working on some revolutionary idea about aircraft performance. It was as if a first grader had gone to his father and asked for engineering data on the family auto. But the officer had been told to provide the data. Besides, no harm could be done by giving this major from Eglin the data. It would be amusing to see just how much he understood. After all, he was only a fighter pilot.

Then Boyd went to the Foreign Intelligence Division, commonly called Foreign Tech, and asked to see the highly classified performance data of Soviet aircraft — not how high a MiG-15 can fly or how fast a Sukhoi can go, but the same thing he had asked for in American aircraft: weight, thrust, lift, drag coefficients, and drag polars. This data was too sensitive for Boyd simply to throw it in the backseat of his T-33 and carry it to Eglin; it would be sent by special courier.

Boyd was elated when he took off from Dayton the next morning. Rather than flying south to Florida, he flew northeast for about 350 miles — less than an hour in the air — and landed at Erie.

After talking with his mother for a while, Boyd called his sister Marion and asked her to meet him at their father's grave. He liked to visit the cemetery on West Lake Avenue when he was in town. The two met and stood near the grave in silence for a while. Marion sometimes wondered why her younger brother never asked about her memories of their father. But he was not the sort of person to whom Marion could say, "John, don't you want to know about our father?" So they talked of other things, mostly Boyd's work at Eglin.

Then Boyd grabbed one of his old bathing suits and drove out to the Peninsula. He and Frank Pettinato walked the beach and he told Pettinato about the Energy-Maneuverability Theory he was working on and how the Air Force didn't understand what he was trying to do and all the high-ranking people who were trying to stop his work. Frank Pettinato Jr. was there too, working as a lifeguard for his father, and remembers how Boyd then dived into Lake Erie, swam a few hundred yards offshore, turned and swam effortlessly down the beach for several miles, his long arms slicing deep into the water, legs kicking tirelessly. Boyd was in his midthirties — to Frank Jr., an old guy — but he never slowed his pace.

Boyd talked more with Frank Pettinato and then was gone. A half-hour later a small silver jet appeared low over the bay and only a few yards offshore. It roared along in front of Pettinato's lifeguard tower, then pulled into a steep climb and a wingover and the pilot came back, this time lower, skimming the surface of Lake Erie. Observers swore the jet was so low that the turbulence stirred the water. The aircraft climbed out toward the south.

The little straight-wing plain-Jane T-33 was an old and underpowered training jet. There were so many of them they were used by many officers just to maintain their flying status. But to people in Erie it was a jet fighter. And it was flown by an Erie man who used to be a lifeguard out at the Peninsula and who had been a combat pilot in Korea. Frank Jr. remembers that his father was very excited and came over to him and grabbed his arm, pointed at the jet, and said, "See that fighter plane? That's John. That's John Boyd."

After buzzing the beach, Boyd climbed up to altitude, adjusted the throttle and the trim, and settled back for the flight down to Eglin. He must have been quite happy. The data from Wright-Pat would be along soon. Frank Pettinato was proud of him. He knew that Erie was talking about his buzzing the beach at the Peninsula. The poor boy in ragged clothes, the boy with no father, had grown up to be somebody. He was more than a salesman.

Back at Eglin in the modest house on the corner lot at 11 Bens Lane, Mary waited. When they arrived at Eglin, he had said to her, "I

$$P_s = \left[\frac{T-D}{W}\right] V$$

want you to try and be more social here than you were at Nellis." And she had promised. "I'll change," she said. "I'll go to parties at the club with you and I'll meet your friends."

And she did try. She went to a few parties at the club. She followed Boyd around, almost hiding behind him, trailing in his wake. She was very shy and her Presbyterianism weighed heavily on her. Boyd insisted on introducing her by saying, "This is my wife, Mary. I found her in an Iowa cornfield." Everyone laughed but Mary. Once she turned away in tears, but an angry Boyd said, "Mary, you can't be a big baby. You have to be tough. You have to face up to things. If you don't want to do that, why don't you just stay at home and feel sorry for yourself?"

Mary frequently stared at Boyd with her big Ottumwa eyes and asked him questions about his childhood and not having a father and being poor. She reminded him that she had taken several psychology courses at Iowa and she knew about these things.

"You're always trying to find out about my weaknesses," he said.

"I'm not looking for weaknesses. But children who grew up as you did almost always have scars. And you don't. You just seem unreal to me."

"Mary, you are my wife and I want you to be on my side. Not against me."

But in their time at Eglin, Boyd and Mary did begin to drift apart. Boyd's work became more important to him than his family. It is almost as if Boyd believed his family obligations were over once he had finished his job of fathering five children. Mary's job was to raise the children while he went about his life's work.

Mary began spending two or three days each week at the fabled talcum-powder beach of the Florida panhandle. Stephen liked the beach. He climbed down from his wheelchair and rolled in the gentle surf and was free. He often became sunburned, but he had so much fun that Mary paid little attention.

Chapter Eleven

The Sugarplum Fairy
Spreads the Gospel

IN late 1962, Harry Hillaker was one of the most important men in the defense industry. He worked for General Dynamics and was project engineer for the F-111, the aircraft that Secretary of Defense McNamara decided to make the universal aircraft for the Navy and Air Force. In theory, the multipurpose aircraft exemplified the cost-effectiveness so beloved by McNamara. It was hyped as the aircraft that could perform close air support, air-to-air combat, air-to-ground, and nuclear-attack missions. It could do everything but dust crops.

A combat aircraft is a peculiar combination of design, avionics, and power plant. Prudent designers usually make significant technological advances in only one of the three categories when they plan a new aircraft. But the F-111 was a high-tech wonder with two bold innovations, both of which were later to cause enormous problems. The F-111 was the first combat airplane to have an afterburning turbofan engine. Until then, combat aircraft used turbojet engines. The primary difference is that all of the air entering a turbojet engine goes through the engine core, while the airflow of a turbofan engine is split between the engine core and a duct that bypasses the engine and goes straight to the afterburner. The split airflow means back pressure from the afterburner affects the compressors at the front of the engine. The turbofan is very sensitive to airflow distortion.

The second innovation was the wing. The F-111 was the first combat aircraft to have a variable-geometry wing, commonly called the "swing wing." The small narrow wings extended straight out for takeoff and slow-speed flight, then folded back for high-speed runs.

The F-111 — Harry Hillaker's baby — was the pride of the Air Force. More than five thousand people at General Dynamics worked on the airplane, and the Air Force had more than two hundred people monitoring development and construction. So Hillaker can be forgiven if he was a bit full of himself that night when he visited the Officers Club at Eglin. He and an Air Force officer were at a table having a quiet drink, talking of the wonders of the F-111, how the British had ordered a large number, how the Navy was going to cover its carrier decks with the airplane, and how the F-111 was on the way to becoming the greatest airplane in the history of the Air Force, the envy of the world. Hillaker found he was constantly being distracted by noise from the bar. A group of young fighter pilots clustered around an older guy who was holding court, talking in a voice heard all over the bar and waving a cigar as he described various fighter maneuvers. Occasionally the young pilots broke out in uproarious laughter.

Hillaker tilted his head toward the bar and said, "Now there's a man who thinks he's the greatest fighter pilot in the world."

His host looked toward the bar, then turned back to Hillaker and smiled. "He might well be. That's John Boyd."

Hillaker shrugged. "Never heard of him."

"I'll introduce you."

"No thanks. I don't like loudmouths."

But the officer had already moved toward the bar and was talking to Boyd, telling him about the VIP, and asking Boyd to meet him. The two men were walking back to the table. Hillaker took a deep breath and hoped that after the introduction Boyd would return to his cronies. Before Hillaker could say a word, Boyd made a head-on attack. The first words out of his mouth were, "My name is John Boyd and I'm a fighter pilot and I understand you work on the F-111 and what I want to know is why you guys built a goddamn eighty-five-thousand-pound airplane and called it a fighter."

"It's a fighter-bomber," Hillaker said, somewhat taken aback.

Boyd poked Hillaker in the chest three or four times, took a puff off his cigar, and said, "Yeah, well last time I looked, an *F* in front of an airplane meant it was a fighter. That thing is a piece of shit. It's too big to be a fighter and that goddamn little wing it's got, it must take two states to turn the thing around. I'll tell you something else. The pilot can't see behind and he can't see out the right window. He has to depend on his copilot to tell him what's out there."

Hillaker gritted his teeth. The project manager for the F-111 did not have to listen to this from a loudmouthed fighter pilot. Before he could reply, Boyd was off again.

"It's too goddamn big, too goddamn expensive, too goddamn underpowered. It's just not worth a good goddamn." He moved closer to Hillaker. His voice rose. "How much extra weight does that swing wing add to the airplane? Twenty percent?"

Boyd didn't wait for an answer. He poked Hillaker in the chest again. "The entire weight of the wing goes through that pivot pin and you hide it all in that big glove. You'll be getting fatigue and stress cracks in that fucker before it's got five hundred hours on it. And the amount of drag you've created is aerodynamic bullshit. That pivot adds weight and degrades performance, plus you can't sweep the wing back fast enough in combat to make a difference. The low-speed performance is lousy, the high-speed performance is worse, and the goddamn thing won't maneuver."

Hillaker stared at Boyd. Fighter pilots usually talk in generalities when they criticize an airplane; they say it is a "pig" or that it needs five miles of runway to get off the ground, but they don't know enough to hone in on design specifics. An engineer trying to get hard information out of a fighter pilot is like a man trying to nail Jell-O to a tree. Thus, Hillaker was more than a little shocked to hear the loud-mouth pilot ask about the things that were only beginning to be whispered about in the back rooms of General Dynamics.

Hillaker did not know he was looking at the only man in the world who knew more about the capabilities of the F-111 than he did. Boyd had done some preliminary E-M calculations on the F-111 and knew what a terrible mistake the Air Force was making. Boyd knew that, left to its own devices, the bureaucracy always came up with an aircraft such as the F-111. The Air Force looked at technology rather than the mission. And if they did consider the mission, it was always the fashionable mission of the day.

Hillaker pulled out a chair. "Sit down, John."

Hillaker was supervising construction of what would turn out to be one of the most scandal-ridden aircraft in U.S. history. Boyd was the first to publicly say what in a few years everyone would know. The Air Force was seduced by swing-wing technology, a technology that ultimately would ruin two generations of airplanes. (The under-powered Navy F-14 Tomcat is a swing wing and the performance is so poor that pilots call it the "Tom Turkey." The B-1 Bomber, one of the most trouble-plagued aircraft in the Air Force inventory, is a swing wing. And the U.S. version of the SST, which Boyd and his friends managed to have cancelled, would have been a swing wing.)

After only a few minutes of a highly technical engineering discussion, Boyd and Hillaker had cleaned off the table and began writing on cocktail napkins and passing them back and forth, covering them with engineering data, formulae, drag polars, and lift coefficients. They exchanged ideas about fighter aircraft, about what each considered the *ultimate* fighter aircraft, a nimble little fighter such as the world had never seen, about the fighter that, if they had no restraints, they would build.

Hillaker was a company man who hewed to the company line. But that did not mean he did not have a dream of his own. A few years later he and Boyd would have their chance to build the ideal fighter aircraft. They would join together in the most audacious plot ever conceived against the U.S. Air Force.

The engineering data from Wright-Pat dribbled into Eglin. Boyd was not confident of the numbers, but at least he had something to work with. Now his second problem in developing E-M — how to present it to Air Force brass — was becoming paramount.

About 4:30 P.M. each day he went to Christie's office, sat down, and leaned back. He gripped a pencil between his thumb and forefinger, then held the pencil at arm's length, staring at the eraser. As he stared at the eraser, it became a pipper. He twirled in his chair as if maneuvering to get a tracking solution on an enemy fighter. Then one day he stopped twirling and tossed the pencil on the desk. He had the answer; he knew how to translate the reams of charts and formulas and engineering data from Wright-Pat into a simple form. He would show graphs of the *differences* between each American fighter's energy rate and the energy rate of its Soviet counterpart. Blue areas represented where the differences favored the American fighter, red where the Soviet fighter had the advantage.

Blue is good.

Red is bad.

Even a goddamn general can understand that.

It is a matter of delicious irony that one of Boyd's duties at Eglin was supervising the graphics shop. The purpose of the graphics shop was to provide services for every harried officer who wanted briefing charts or lettering placed on photographic slides or a fancy graph. Managing the graphics shop was one of those menial and embarrassing jobs no pilot wanted, but for Boyd it would pay off.

Boyd put two people to work doing nothing but E-M briefing charts. To say he was a perfectionist is an understatement of epic dimensions. Far into the night he pored over every detail on every slide. Each letter had to be exactly right. Every line in the cross-hatched performance chart had to be shaded correctly. Each slide had to be cropped precisely so. And if at 1:00 A.M. or 2:00 A.M. he found the slightest imperfection, something that no one else would have noticed, he called one of the technicians to come down and correct the slide. Not later during normal working hours. Now.

After one such all-night session, he told the female technician he would approve the overtime on her time sheet. But the colonel who was the base comptroller not only denied the overtime, he chewed out the young woman in front of her coworkers and told her that whatever it was Major Boyd was working on was unauthorized and the Air Force had no money to pay overtime for unauthorized projects.

When the young woman reported her humiliation to Boyd, he steamed over to the base commander's office. The base commander was not only the comptroller's boss, but unbeknownst to everyone he was a friend of Boyd's from the Nellis years. Boyd told the base commander what happened and said, "I want this taken care of."

The base commander called in the comptroller. "If there is no money in the account, find it, even if you have to pay it out of your own pocket," he ordered. He ordered the comptroller to apologize to the technician in front of the same people who had been present when he criticized her.

"I hosed that son of a bitch," Boyd gloated to Christie.

But the price of his victory would be high. Boyd made an enemy not only of the comptroller but of the comptroller's friends. And there would be a day of reckoning.

When the Air Force believes enough in an officer's potential to admit him to the AFIT program, it is an acknowledgment both that the officer intends to make a career of the military and that the officer is a bit special. The officer's first ER after AFIT should reflect this. But Boyd's first ER at Eglin was mediocre. He had bounced around too many jobs. There was a vague reference to Boyd's E-M work, though it was not called that. The rating officer said Boyd had "developed a qualitative-quantitative analysis in which energy considerations can be effectively applied to fighter tactics . . ." that ". . . for the first time will provide a valid basis for designing tactics against hostile fighters."

Generals rarely become involved in ERs of majors. But, luckily for Boyd, Brigadier General A.T. Culbertson added an indorsement that contradicted the rating. Boyd, Culbertson said, "represents the sort of productive, creative thinker that is so critically needed in this Command and the Air Force. I rate him as truly outstanding and worthy of rapid promotion." As had happened again and again in Boyd's career, his immediate supervisor gave him a poor or mediocre rating, one that signaled it was time to get out of the Air Force, and again and again a general officer rescued him.

By the summer of 1963, when Boyd received his first ER at Eglin, the E-M charts were beginning to come together. At the same time the Air Force was pressing for a report that went beyond briefings, a comprehensive document that told all there was to tell about E-M. Christie wanted Boyd to prepare the report, but Boyd wanted to begin briefing.

Boyd's briefing charts were things of beauty, pieces of art, clean and elegant and simple; they had enough data to inform but not enough to overwhelm, and were creative in appearance but not so creative as to detract from the information being presented. As Boyd honed and refined the charts, he realized something was wrong. The people at Wright-Pat had not given him the correct data.

He went back to the general who had helped him with the overtime problem and told him he was going up to Wright-Pat and straighten them out. "You might get a phone call," he said.

The general looked at Boyd and shook his head. "Try to be diplomatic, John."

But Boyd rarely was diplomatic. And when he arrived at Wright-Pat, his arm waving and profanity and accusations of incompetence quickly broke up the meeting. The colonel who chaired the meeting stalked off in a huff to call Boyd's superiors at Eglin.

The colonel did not get a sympathetic ear. The general told him to give Boyd the correct data or he — the Eglin general — would call the general who commanded the Flight Dynamics Lab and ask why he was not getting any cooperation. After all, they were all in the same Air Force.

The colonel knew not to give reason to one general to call another and complain. The fraternity of generals is tight and closed. A colonel who wants to be promoted does not fare well by confronting a general.

Boyd got the data, and this time it was correct. He also created another enemy in the colonel at Wright-Pat.

Boyd flew his T-33 back to Eglin. As he approached, he heard a B-52 pilot talking to the control tower. Fighter pilots called the B-52 the "BUFF" — big ugly fat fucker. Boyd knew the BUFF pilot was returning from a lengthy mission and that the crew was doubtless exhausted. He decided to show the B-52 pilot what to expect in a real shooting war. He swung wide, eased forward on the stick, and lined up on the nose of the huge bomber — it was the size of a barn door — then pushed the throttle forward.

The B-52 pilot was cleared for the final approach. He knew his aircraft could be seen for miles and probably was thinking of landing, plodding through the debrief, and having a good meal and ten or twelve hours of blessed sleep. What he got was a window filled with a T-33 and a fiendish voice on the radio shouting, "Guns, guns, guns!" and the blur of the T-33 rolling inverted and passing under him so closely he could count rivets on the belly. Then a raucous cackle on the radio and a triumphant voice saying, "I hosed you."

A man driving a B-52 loaded with enough nuclear bombs to destroy several large cities has to be a cool customer. But a B-52 pilot also knows how dangerous a head-on pass is. There is no room for error. The slightest miscalculation in judgment and there is a collision that scatters the remains of two aircraft and their crews over a wide section of countryside. The BUFF crew erupted into near panic as the pilot got on the radio and complained to the tower. Then the B-52 pilot began shouting at Boyd and telling him he would be reported for this safety violation.

Boyd circled around and pulled into the B-52's ten-o'clock position about a half-mile away, while the B-52 driver continued to bluster and complain and threaten. Boyd decided the SAC pilot had an obstruction. He needed to realize he had just lost a battle with the best fighter pilot in the Air Force and that it was no accident. Boyd kicked in right rudder and pulled hard on the stick, racking the T-33 into a slashing high-G turn toward the B-52. "Guns, guns, guns!" he brayed over the radio as he zoomed across the cockpit. The B-52 crew involuntarily ducked and then they heard that cackling, nerve-jangling laughter.

When the B-52 pilot landed, he was so spiked with anger that he forgot his fatigue. He registered a complaint against the T-33 pilot and was backed up by the crew in the control tower. The guys in the control tower rather liked the little air show, but they had to report what they had seen.

Boyd was grounded.

But he knew that the BUFF driver had a new and altogether different understanding of the hell, death, and destruction that could be wreaked by a fighter pilot. And for that, it was worth it.

A military briefing is a slow, antiquated, and terribly inefficient way to present information. Nevertheless, it is an art form upon which an officer's career can rise or fall. Many men have risen to high rank on their ability to, as the military says, "give a good brief." A certain charm school manner surrounds a good briefer. He almost always is junior in rank to those being briefed, but not too junior. Generals, for instance, usually are briefed by a lower-ranking general or by a full colonel. A brief is wrapped in unwritten rules. The briefer has a pointer, which he should not use too often. He stands on a stage but should not move about too much. He has a lectern upon which he should not lean. He has slides or charts but is expected to know the material far beyond what is displayed. He tells the higher-ranking officers what he is going to tell them, then he tells them, then he tells them what he has told them, and finally, if he hasn't been ripped to shreds by adversarial questions, he closes. One of the most rigid of the unwritten rules is that the briefer be prepared to answer every question quickly and confidently. A man who cannot answer a question asked by a superior officer has a mental picture of his career going down in flames. It is obvious that most people can read and assimilate information faster than they can learn something by listening to a dog and pony show. But the U.S. military culture is an oral culture and the bedrock of that culture is the briefing. Many very smart officers learn most of what they know through briefings. But no matter the type of briefing, the briefer rarely presents information that contradicts the beliefs or the position of the person being briefed.

With his new information from Wright-Pat and with his elegant briefing charts, Boyd put together two E-M briefs — one for Air Force officers and one for defense contractors. *Dazzling* is the only way to describe the briefs. Boyd's years as an instructor at the FWS gave him unusual confidence as a speaker. With the exception of Tom Christie, he knew the material better than any other person. When he delivered an E-M brief, he was spreading the gospel. His voice began very low and controlled as his eyes roamed over every person being briefed. He had an actor's ability to know when he had seized their interest, and once that happened he let loose the full repertoire of his oratorical gifts. His voice ranged from conversational to bombastic. When he made a point, he jutted his chin, paused, and stared. For a man who could be crude and coarse among his friends, he could, when giving a brief, be as smooth and professional as any officer in the Air Force. He spoke with fire and enthusiasm; he even spoke over the heads of those he was briefing. But he had such far-ranging knowledge of the new and fascinating subject that he could do this without antagonizing those in the audience. Serious questions he entertained in a serious manner. The truth is that no one knew enough about E-M to go head-to-head with Boyd, but it is the nature of the military that some tried. Boyd loved hostile questions. He treated hostile questioners as if they were pilots who had just bounced him over the Green Spot. He reverted to Forty-Second Boyd and began running up the score. Later he would sidle up to Christie and say, "Did you see that, Tiger? I carved him a new asshole."

Christie had great admiration for Boyd's briefing technique, except for one thing: Boyd roamed the stage and bounced on his toes and waved his arms about with such passion that he reminded Christie of a ballet dancer. "Stand still, John," he said again and again. But Boyd could not. Christie began calling him the "Sugarplum Fairy," a nickname soon shortened to the "Plum," which is how Boyd was thereafter known to his friends at Eglin.

Pilots from throughout the Air Force passed through Eglin on temporary duty. Boyd hunted them down and briefed every one he could pack into a room. He went to Nellis and briefed. He even briefed Chuck Yeager.

As more people listened, more began to sense that Boyd's E-M Theory was a new way of thinking about aviation. In the past, when pilots thought of maneuvering, they thought strictly in terms of airspeed. Good pilots intuitively understood energy, though they could not articulate it. In World War II, for instance, they knew never to get into a turning fight with a Japanese Zero; in Korea, never turn with a MiG. Now, thanks to E-M, they could look at a chart and know at what altitude they could best fight. They knew how many Gs they could pull at a given altitude and still maintain not airspeed but excess energy. And they sensed that if Boyd was right, he had developed a theory that would change aviation.

As word continued to spread about this new E-M Theory, the rank of those wanting to hear the brief increased. Now majors and lieutenant colonels and colonels asked for a session. If a superior officer congratulated Boyd on his brief, Boyd's response was always the same: "Sir, I do my homework."

Boyd had regained his flying status and often flew a T-33 to Nellis, where his former student Everett Raspberry had developed a new maneuver to emerge victorious in a canopy-to-canopy vertical rolling scissors. It was called the "Raspberry Roll" and used what Boyd had taught about slow-speed control of the aircraft. Raspberry began flying E-M profiles for Boyd, proving in the air what the E-M charts said was the performance of various aircraft, and he often assisted Boyd in the E-M briefings, handling the projector and flipping charts while the Plum roamed the stage.

Boyd and Christie began making trips all around the country to brief defense contractors. Heretofore, a fighter aircraft had been the result of a point design: that is, a group of generals got together and decided they wanted an aircraft that would do, say, 400 knots at 30,000 feet and have a combat radius of 500 miles. E-M changed that. Boyd told the defense contractors, "One day soon, the Air Force will come to you and say that in this airplane when we pull four Gs at twenty thousand feet, we want this excess energy rate. Or the Air Force will tell you we want to have a sustained five-G capability up to thirty-five thousand feet. Or if we are doing point nine Mach at ten thousand feet, we want enough excess power to climb at five hundred feet per second."

It was a revolutionary, not evolutionary, way to design aircraft. But defense contractors, especially those interested in the F-X — the new fighter aircraft the Air Force was talking about building — saw the simplicity of E-M and knew that what Boyd said was true. To help them reach that conclusion, Boyd and Christie told the defense executives about the computer program they had developed to fold E-M into the design process and even gave them copies of the program. The executives could also come to Eglin and use the computer there. And when modifications were added, they could have those modifications. Defense contractors adapted E-M with such alacrity that Boyd and Christie had a never-ending stream of them pouring into Eglin.

Air Force generals who worshiped at the shrine of high technology believed if an American pilot saw a blip on his radar, he pressed a button, launched a missile, and the blip disappeared. *Poof!* It was that simple. Push-button warfare was the thing of the future, and the probability of kill (P_k) was near 100 percent. Boyd and Christie used E-M data to run computer simulations and discovered that the reality was far different. Performance of U.S. missiles was nowhere near what it was advertised to be, and Boyd and Christie became the first two men in the defense industry to talk about the limitations of missiles. When Boyd briefed fighter pilots, he taught techniques to defeat enemy missiles and to raise the P_k of U.S. missiles. And he told the pilots the best way to defeat surface-to-air missiles as well.

As Boyd probed deeper into the comparisons between American and Soviet aircraft, he began to notice a disturbing trend in the chart overlays. Blue was good and red was bad and there was entirely too much red in many of the charts. This meant that in a big part of the performance envelope, Soviet aircraft were superior to U.S. aircraft. This could not be true. U.S. fighter aircraft were the best in the world. If Boyd briefed this — if he showed, for instance, that the F-4 Phantom was too heavy and did not have enough wing to win a turning fight with a MiG-21 at high altitude — and he was wrong, it would be the end of E-M. If he said, as the E-M charts showed, that the only place for an F-4 to successfully fight the MiG-21 was at low altitude and high speed, he had better be right. And the F-111 chart was one that would cause serious heartburn to any general who saw it — the chart was solid red: Soviet aircraft could defeat the F-111 at any altitude, at any airspeed, in any part of the flight envelope.

Boyd and Christie went over the calculations again and again and the numbers came out the same. Perhaps the data from Foreign Tech was wrong. U.S. aircraft could not be inferior to Soviet aircraft in so many areas. Boyd returned to Wright-Pat and went over the data with intelligence specialists. A few corrections were made, but Soviet aircraft were still superior.

"If I brief this and someone calls you to check it out, will you stand by this data?" Boyd asked.

"Of course," the officer said.

Boyd and Christie rewrote the computer program at Eglin and recomputed the data. Still the Soviet aircraft were superior. They brought in an outsider, a mathematician who had no connection to E-M, and said, "Find where we made mistakes." The outsider crunched the numbers, checked them, recrunched them, and announced he could find no mistakes.

Now the E-M Theory had ecclesiastical weight.

Boyd was too busy tuning the brief to work on the official energy-maneuverability report the Air Force wanted, so Christie did almost all the writing. Boyd asked that Christie make sure to give credit to three articles he used in his research. The first was published in 1954 by E. S. Rutowski and was titled "Energy Approach to the General Aircraft Performance Problem." The article expounded an optimization theory about the quickest way for an aircraft to climb to a given altitude. It had nothing to do with the maneuverability of an aircraft, with combat flying, or with the design of an aircraft. The second article was written by H. J. Kelley and published in the October 1960 issue of the *Journal of American Rocket Society* and titled "Gradient Theory of Optimal Flight Paths." It was, in essence, a mathematical way to find the most effective flight paths. The third article was a Raytheon study by A. E. Bryson and W. F. Denham titled "Steepest Ascent Method," which explained a method to optimize aircraft performance. In the "secret" E-M report published in May 1964, all three of these reports are cited.

Boyd's second ER at Eglin is dated September 7, 1964, and is nothing short of phenomenal. This is one of the few times in Air Force history, perhaps the only time, when an officer has created a radical new theory and then been told his job was to develop that theory. Under "Recommended Improvement Areas," the rating officer calls for "improvement of his manners and skills in human relations. He often shows open disdain for persons who have not gained his respect professionally." But the rating officer ends by saying of Boyd: "He is the most dedicated officer that I have known."

Boyd no longer was a maintenance officer. He did as he had said; he had worked himself out of every job except developing E-M.

In early 1965, shortly before the Air Force began the longest bombing campaign in its history, Boyd went to Vietnam and briefed F-105 pilots, telling them if a MiG got on their tail and they could not outrun it, they should dump energy immediately by flat-plating the bird. F-105 pilots were highly skeptical. The Thud — the pilots' name for the F-105 — was not a bird that took kindly to such maneuvers.

Boyd returned through Europe, where he briefed E-M to a group of wing commanders. Boyd said the outstanding safety records of the European wings showed they were not training hard enough; they were not preparing pilots for combat.

But safety was becoming paramount in the Air Force. A commander was more concerned with maintaining a good safety record than with improving the air-to-air skills of fighter pilots. Few commanders wanted to risk their careers over a little rat-racing. Dogfighting was becoming an arcane and almost lost art in the Air Force.

The effectiveness tests conducted by Boyd proved to be the last step before he began briefing top generals on E-M. The tests were flown by a group of young pilots, several of whom would go on to extraordinary achievements. Tom McInerney was the primary pilot. He eventually became a three-star general. Douglas "Pete" Peterson, later to be shot down in Vietnam and still later to return to Vietnam as America's ambassador, also flew E-M profiles. Perhaps the most colorful member of the group was Bobby Kan, a Korean who signed documents as "WGOFP" — World's Greatest Oriental Fighter Pilot. Kan was shot down in Vietnam, and when the rescue helicopter came to pick him up, the crew saw his Asian features and thought a North Vietnamese was trying to get aboard. The helicopter quickly departed. Kan released such a stream of creative profanity over the radio that the helicopter crew knew the man on the ground had to be an American and returned to pick him up.

McInerney had heard a great deal about Boyd when he arrived at Eglin. Boyd took McInerney to his office, showed him stacks and stacks of mathematical computations, laughed and said he had stolen hundreds of hours of computer time to prepare the charts. He then told McInerney in great detail how the tests would be flown. The purpose of each flight was to verify Boyd's theoretical computations, to see if an airplane would do in flight what the E-M charts said it would do.

Each day at 6:00 A.M. one of the pilots took off from Eglin in an F-100, F-105, or F-4 and flew over the Gulf of Mexico to the "start box." A computer was bolted to the rear seat. Each mission had a precise profile. If the pilot was flying an F-4, he would climb to about thirty thousand feet (the exact altitude depended on the temperature), light the afterburner, point the nose down at a certain pitch angle (usually about five degrees), and descend until he was indicating six hundred knots. This usually happened at about twenty-six thousand feet. Then he pulled the nose up to about fifteen degrees and held it until he was indicating Mach 2.

Boyd called the slight dive followed by a climb the "dipsy doodle." It was derived by Boyd and Christie's computer-optimized flight paths and was the quickest way for an F-4 to reach Mach 2. After the pilot reached Mach 2, he came out of burner, noted his fuel weights, and did another dipsy doodle. Another mission was to verify the optimum airspeed and G-load necessary to sustain a 360-degree turn. Every maneuver, every variation, was laid out in careful mission profiles. Boyd had worked on this for several years and knew exactly what needed to be done.

When the pilots landed, Boyd was waiting. A van that served as the flight-line taxi stood nearby, engine idling. Boyd took the data from the computers, jumped into the line taxi, and raced across the base to have the information compared to E-M charts. With the exception of inaccurate performance data from Wright-Pat and small errors induced by variations in aircraft performance, every mission proved almost exactly what the E-M charts predicted. (Years later, when he was ambassador to Vietnam, Douglas Peterson said the pilots who flew E-M profiles for Boyd knew from the beginning this was not another busy-work project of the Air Force. He said everyone involved "sensed that this was breakthrough work that would ultimately impact on aircraft design and, as we saw immediately, on air-combat tactics.")

People in the Flight Dynamics Lab at Wright-Pat heard of Boyd's work and were working day and night to disprove the E-M Theory. It was embarrassing in the extreme to have a fighter pilot from Eglin develop a theory that should have been developed there at Wright-Pat. The comptroller at Eglin was lying in wait; he knew that sooner or later Boyd would make a mistake that could not be shielded by a general. But now that the E-M report was circulating and its information had been backed up by flight tests, Boyd could not be held back. The Mad Major was ready to take on the U.S. Air Force.

Chapter Twelve

Pull the Wings Off and Paint It Yellow

THE last half of 1964 and the first half of 1965 was a glorious time for Boyd.

It began when Boyd briefed a group of pilots from TAC headquarters. Because they were fighter pilots and because they were from TAC headquarters, he included for the first time data showing the superiority of Soviet aircraft. The pilots were stunned. Naturally they asked Boyd if he was sure of his facts. He told them about going back to Foreign Tech and reconfirming all the inputs, of reprogramming the computer, and of having an outsider check everything. "If it's wrong, I can't find where the mistakes are," he said.

The headquarters people shook their heads in dismay. "Wait until Sweeney hears this," one said. "He is going to come unglued." Sweeney was General Walter Campbell Sweeney Jr., head of the Tactical Air Command.

One Thursday in the fall of 1964, Boyd received a phone call from a colonel serving on General Sweeney's staff. "The general has heard of your briefing," the colonel said. "I believe you call it energy-maneuverability. He would like you to deliver the brief Monday at o-eight-hundred in his office at Langley."

"Yes, Sir," Boyd said.

The colonel hung up before Boyd could ask any of the questions swirling through his mind, the most important being: "How much time do I have?" The E-M brief, depending on the number of questions asked, could last three or four hours. Would Sweeney block out that much time? Who else would be in the room? Did Sweeney simply want information or was this to be a decision briefing?

Whatever the answers, Boyd was elated. Sweeney "owned" every fighter aircraft in the Tactical Air Command. If Boyd could show how Sweeney's fighters compared with Soviet aircraft, and if Sweeney accepted the briefing, not only would E-M become part of Air Force doctrine, but the Air Force would have a powerful argument in convincing Congress to fund its proposed new fighter.

Four-star generals rarely receive briefings from someone as far down the food chain as a major. It was presumptuous enough for a major to come up with a radical new theory that caused so much talk, but now he was stepping into the office of one of the most powerful generals in the Air Force. This would be the most important briefing of Boyd's life. Sweeney would be accompanied by his retinue — bright people all, most of whom would consider it their bounden duty to disprove this new E-M Theory.

Boyd had one unsettling thought: at Eglin he was under the ultimate command of General Bernard Schriever, head of the Air Force Systems Command, who had not yet been briefed on E-M. To brief the four-star who headed another command before briefing the four-star who headed his own command was a serious breach of military protocol. Not only that, but Sweeney would call Schriever and want to know why the hell he was giving TAC inferior airplanes.

Unfortunately, Schriever was out of the country, but at Boyd's request his deputy called Sweeney and postponed Boyd's briefing. Then Boyd delivered his brief to Schriever's top people, all of whom demanded the information be checked and confirmed. Even after Boyd told them of the laborious process he had gone through, one of the officers left the briefing, called Foreign Tech, and was told Boyd's data were correct. The briefing quickly became acrimonious, and Boyd was the target.

"You are trying to say we do not know what we are doing," said an angry colonel. "You are telling us we are buying the wrong airplanes when we have the best minds in the Air Force on this." Across the room a general was going through a book that listed Eglin research projects. "I am missing something here," the general says. "Where in the hell is this energy-maneuverability project? Did you list it under another name?"

"It's not in there," Boyd says.

"I just heard you talk about the resources to make this thing go. There is no way you can get those resources in the computer without having a project."

"I can steal computer time on any computer in this command and you would never know it," Boyd said.

"Are you telling me you stole the computer time?"

"I am being honest with you."

The general locked eyes with Boyd and barked, "Everybody out but Boyd."

"If you are wrong," the general told Boyd, "we are going to court-martial you." In the end no one could find any mistakes in Boyd's briefing, and he was cleared to brief General Sweeney.

Now the resources of TAC were his to command. He flew to Nellis to gather more information and pick out additional slides for the briefing. Nothing but the best for General Sweeney.

"You're going with me," he told Raspberry. "You flip the charts and advance the slides while I do the brief." The two men sorted through and rearranged a stack of slides Raspberry estimated to be more than a foot tall. Boyd worried over every selection, worried that the slides and graphs could be of better quality. Finally the two men gathered all the briefing equipment, climbed into an F-100F, and flew across country to Langley AFB in Virginia. They arrived late in the afternoon.

A young major, the aide to General Sweeney, met them on the ramp. "I hope you are prepared for a full brief before General Sweeney and his staff," the aide said.

Technically speaking a briefing is a briefing. There is no distinction between a brief and a full brief. Nevertheless, the phrase "full brief" gives pause. It implies a more serious briefing, greater formality, all the unwritten briefing rules peculiar to each commander, and — most of all — an uninhibited salvo of questions. A full brief can be bloody. If it goes wrong it can wreck a career.

"How much time do we have?" Boyd asked.

"Twenty minutes."

Boyd grimaced. "Twenty minutes? That's not enough time to —"

"Twenty minutes." The aide handed a set of car keys to Boyd and pointed to a blue Cadillac Coupe deVille gleaming in the afternoon sun. "My car. Use it tonight. Go out and get a good meal. I'll see you at o-eight-hundred tomorrow."

"Good meal" sounded too much like "last meal" to Boyd and Raspberry. They checked into the visiting officers' quarters, ate quickly, then came back and practiced the brief far into the night. Razz threw questions at Boyd, the questions Sweeney's staff was most likely to ask.

If told to shorten a four-hour briefing to twenty minutes, most officers would simply condense the briefing. Not Boyd. He would start at the beginning and proceed as if he had all the time he needed. By a few minutes after seven the next morning, Boyd and Razz were in the briefing room down the hall from the big corner office that is the lair of the TAC commander. Boyd tested the projector, adjusted the screen, chewed on his hand, made sure the slides and charts were in the proper order, moved the lectern a quarter inch, slid the pointer a half-inch down its rack, and chewed on his hand some more. He paced, practicing the brief in his head.

By 7:45 A.M. most of General Sweeney's staff was seated. A colonel noticed Boyd was not wearing the lapel microphone placed atop the lectern.

"Major, the microphone is for your use," he said.

"I don't need a microphone," Boyd said.

"Our rules are that briefers wear the microphone."

"Yes, Sir." Boyd clamped on the microphone.

At precisely 8:00 A.M. the general and his aide entered.

"You may begin, Major Boyd," the general said.

And the Plum was off and running — smooth, easy, confident, and professional. He had to turn down the volume on the microphone several times. Sweeney was attentive. But the briefing clearly pained him. He was agitated, shifting in his chair and grimacing.

At 8:20 Razz gave Boyd a signal. Boyd stopped, said, "Thank you, General. Unless you have questions, that will be all."

"Where do you think you're going?" asked Sweeney.

"Sir, your aide said we had twenty minutes. We've used up our time."

"Continue the brief."

"Yes, Sir."

Sweeney turned to his aide. "Cancel my appointments for today." He glared at Boyd. "What you're saying can't be right."

"I believe it to be correct, Sir."

"Who else have you briefed on this? What was their reaction?"

Boyd told Sweeney whom he had briefed and said their reaction was "the same as yours, General."

Sweeney turned to one of his staff members and said, "Get my intelligence guy on this. And call those people in Foreign Tech and make sure these numbers are right."

A few minutes later Sweeney's intelligence specialist returned and said, "They have a copy of Major Boyd's brief, Sir. They say his data is correct."

"How many airplanes did you run this on?" Sweeney asked.

"All of them, Sir. I've just shown you the interesting ones so far. But I'll be glad to run them all for you."

"Continue."

And continue he did. All that day Boyd briefed Sweeney. He whispered, he cajoled, he confided. He could not smoke while briefing a four-star but he could roam the stage and wave his arms and raise his voice. As the day wore on, he grew cocky. This was the brief that would change the Air Force. When Boyd was at his best — and he was at the top of his form that day — he was one of the best briefers in the Air Force. The Plum was in full bay.

During breaks, aides rushed in and out and the general delivered orders. And the briefing resumed. The questions grew tougher and more frequent, but Boyd answered them all courteously, completely, and confidently. General Sweeney followed each exchange and occasionally nodded.

The office of a four-star general is not unlike the court of a pasha, replete with all the trappings of high rank as well as intrigue and constant jockeying for favor. The general controls the careers and lives of those on his staff. For an outsider to seize a day of the general's time and to have the general's undivided attention is seen by some on his staff as a threat. Several members of Sweeney's staff began to ask questions designed to embarrass Boyd, to throw off his timing, to reveal how shallow this new theory was.

That was fine with Boyd. He looked on the questions as if they were bullets fired during an air-to-air engagement. Before more than a few words were out of a man's mouth, Boyd knew where a question was going, and he knew how to respond. Like any fighter pilot he turned into the fight, confronting every question head-on. And because he knew his material better than any other person in the room, no one touched him.

Sweeney sat impassively through it all. In such a situation, generals imagine underlings as gladiators in a pit. The gladiators are encouraged to do battle. The last man standing, the man to crawl over the edge of the pit and emerge victorious, is the general's favorite. Sweeney must have hoped someone on his staff could leave Boyd in the pit. He did not want to know his warplanes were inferior to those of the Soviet Union. The animosity toward Boyd reached its climax late in the afternoon when the most hostile interrogator, a colonel who wore no silver wings over his left breast pocket, a colonel aching to exchange the eagle on his shoulder for a star, suddenly interrupted Boyd and said, "All of this work, this so-called theory of yours, has been done before." He paused. Everyone in the room turned to look at him. "And it has all been proven wrong."

Sweeney nodded. His best gladiator was in the pit.

Boyd expected something like this from a nonrated staff puke and he was ready. He smiled. "Colonel, show me the source document that says this has been done before."

Boyd saw the colonel not as a gladiator but as an angry bull. His demand that the colonel reveal the source document was what Boyd called a "cape job," beckoning the colonel to charge ahead with his proof. Boyd had dealt with this criticism for months and knew there was only one possible name the colonel might raise.

"It was done at Edwards and disproved." The colonel spoke with great authority.

Again Boyd waved the cape. "Colonel, do you have the source document?"

For a moment the room was quiet. Sweeney looked at a two-star sitting near him, a general who had recently transferred to his staff after a lengthy assignment at Edwards. The general smoothed the crease in his pants and said, "Sir, if it had been done at Edwards I would have known about it." He looked at Sweeney. "This work is new to me."

The colonel was wounded and the others sensed it. One extended what was apparently a helping hand. "Do you have the name of the person at Edwards who did the work?"

Boyd flicked the cape. "Perhaps there is someone, Sir. If you'll give me his name and show me that he did this work, I'll walk away from this project today."

Boyd was doing more than saying he would walk away from E-M; he was laying his career on the line. If the colonel came up with a name, Sweeney could, with one phone call, drive Boyd out of the Air Force.

"Rutowski," the colonel said.

"Hmmmm," Boyd said, bending his head as if in deep thought. "In the index of my briefing I refer to a 1954 article by E. S. Rutowski entitled 'Energy Approach to the General Aircraft Performance Problem.' Is that the same Rutowski?"

The colonel charged ahead. "It is."

"He developed what we know as the 'Rutowski Curve,' which, if I understand it, is an optimization theory about the quickest way to reach an assigned altitude. The airlines find that information useful but I don't believe it has anything to do with fighter aircraft, with pulling Gs, with maneuvering against an opponent." Boyd paused. "If I've overlooked something, Colonel, I'd be glad to hear about it."

The colonel had charged over the cliff and was in free fall. Many superior officers were to experience the same thing in coming years.

After that the questions were less adversarial. Boyd had proved he was not intimidated by rank and he knew his subject. No one else wanted to meet the same fate as the colonel. The questions shifted and were now asked in the spirit of understanding or for clarification. Late in the afternoon, Sweeney stood, signaling the briefing had ended. He looked at Boyd. "Major, I want you back here at o-eight-hundred tomorrow."

"Yes, Sir."

The colonel who said Boyd's work had been done earlier was not in the briefing room the next morning. The other officers were almost cordial. Boyd knew from the look on the face of the general that he had prevailed. He had won over the head of TAC.

The briefing was winding down, but Sweeney had one more question. "Major, yesterday you said you had run the numbers on all U.S. aircraft. But nowhere did you mention the F-111. Did your research cover that aircraft? If so, what conclusions did you draw?"

Boyd clicked the slide projector. His final slide was an E-M diagram of the F-111. Boyd did not speak. The general and his staff had seen enough E-M diagrams in the past two days to grasp the implications of the F-111 display. Even so, they studied the solid-red slide and then looked at Boyd in disbelief.

Boyd gave them the numbers that showed how at any altitude, any speed, any G-load, any part of the flight-performance envelope, the F-111 was inferior to the Soviet threat. If the F-111 faced a MiG, it would be shot down. Period. End of story. The F-111 was, in the traditional phrase of fighter pilots, a dog.

The general thought for a moment. Maybe there was something the charts did not reveal, something he could salvage. "Major, based on your extensive research, do you have any recommendations regarding this aircraft?"

Boyd did not miss a beat. "General, I'd pull the wings off, install benches in the bomb bay, paint the goddamn thing yellow, and turn it into a high-speed line taxi."

Sweeney's acceptance of Boyd's briefing meant E-M had the imprimatur of the Air Force high command. In the coming months Boyd briefed a series of four-stars, the USAF Scientific Advisory Board, and the secretary of the Air Force. When he briefed the Air Force Science and Engineering Symposium, a convocation that lasted almost a week and included dozens of the best briefers in the Air Force, he was given the award for having the best presentation. Boyd even briefed the president's Scientific Advisory Board, the most respected and one of the most influential groups of scientists in America. It was an extraordinary streak of high-level briefings for anyone; for a major it was unprecedented.

Boyd was a model of decorum during these briefings. The Air Force chief of staff sent down an order that he not include the F-111 slide in any of the briefings and that he particularly leave out the comment about turning it into a line taxi. Boyd complied, and with Christie's calming influence, his briefings became slightly more decorous.

The briefing to the president's Scientific Advisory Board is noteworthy in several respects, the most obvious being that there is no higher body to which a technical brief can be presented. Nevertheless, Boyd embroidered the event in a way that perhaps reveals his deep insecurities. He wanted people to think he hosed one of America's preeminent scientists.

It began when one of the scientists took a long look at the basic E-M diagram and saw what appeared to be an anomaly. On a standard day the temperature at sea level is fifty-nine degrees Fahrenheit and the speed of sound is 1,117 feet per second. For each 1,000-foot increase in altitude, temperature decreases at three point five degrees and speed of sound decreases at about four feet per second, until the tropopause at about 36,000 feet. At this altitude the temperature is minus sixty-eight degrees and the speed of sound is 971 feet per second. Upward from the tropopause, these values remain constant until about one hundred twenty-three thousand feet. At the point where the values stop changing and become constant, there is a bump in the E-M diagrams. The bump is called the "tropospheric discontinuity" and is well known among scientists.

But when Boyd displayed the diagram, one member of the board affected a "gotcha" air and queried Boyd about the bump. The scientist's attitude was condescending and gave the impression that if such a fundamental flaw was obvious up front, how could anything from this upstart fighter pilot be believed?

Christie was present and says Boyd was taken aback that one of America's top scientists was ignorant enough of atmospheric physics to ask such a question. Nevertheless, he was respectful and courteous. He knew this was a tremendous opportunity to advance the cause of E-M. But when Boyd later told the story, he said he answered, "Sir, *everyone* knows the troposphere is here and that it accounts for this discontinuity." And he said that when he and Christie emerged from the briefing, he turned to Christie and said, "Guess I hosed that dumb son of a bitch."

On April 4, 1965, forty-eight F-105s attacked the Thanh Hoa Bridge in North Vietnam. They attacked in flights of four. One flight was holding over the initial point ten miles south of the bridge when it was bounced by four MiGs. The F-105s fled. One pilot could not shake a pursuing MiG and in desperation flat-plated his bird and caused his pursuer to overshoot. Later the pilot told debriefers he had never done the maneuver before.

Two other F-105s were shot down by cannon fire.

When four MiGs attack four F-105s and the score is 2–0 in favor of the MiGs, people at the highest levels in the Pentagon want to know what the hell is going on. How can the U.S. Air Force so decisively lose an air-to-air engagement with MiGs? Was the problem with the pilots, the aircraft, or the tactics?

Several months later four F-105s were lost in a single strike against a surface-to-air missile (SAM) site.

Boyd and Christie were summoned to the Pentagon.

One Saturday morning they marched down the long halls to the E-Ring office of Dr. John Foster, the third-ranking official in the Department of Defense and the man responsible for all research and technology as well as for developing and testing new weapons.

Boyd showed Foster how and why the primary Air Force aircraft in Vietnam — the F-105 and the F-4 Phantom — were the wrong aircraft for the jobs they were doing. The F-105 was being used as an air-to-ground aircraft. The F-4C was a big, heavy, twin-engine aircraft whose smoke trail could be seen for miles. It had no guns but was being used for air-to-air combat. Its missiles were virtually useless in a tight turning fight. It was simply no match for a MiG. And at most altitudes and airspeeds, neither was the F-105.

Boyd and Christie expanded the regular E-M brief to show how woefully inadequate were America's air-to-air missiles, the Sparrow and the Sidewinder. The Sidewinder missed its target and plowed into the ground so often that pilots called it the "Sandwinder." And the Sparrow could be defeated by the simplest of avoidance maneuvers.

Foster was shaken by the briefing. It was clear America needed a new fighter aircraft.

These were heady days for Boyd. His name was becoming known throughout the Air Force, and not just as a fighter pilot, but as a thinker, as a theoretician, as the man who developed a radical new theory. Even the Navy was using his E-M Theory. They took his name off it, and they did not call it E-M, but it was Boyd's work.

Given the success of E-M, Boyd had been invited to be part of the group whose job it was to develop a design for the new fighter the Air

Force wanted to build. That group, however, was dominated by people at Wright-Pat who were so embarrassed by Boyd's E-M work that they made sure he had no influence. That did not matter to Boyd. If the Air Force was indeed serious about building the new fighter, he knew what would happen. He would wait.

In addition to being recognized for his accomplishments, Boyd was becoming widely known in the Air Force as a man who could be difficult to get along with. Sometimes it seemed he went out of his way to be obstreperous. The man just would not bend, even on things that did not matter to most people. One example was when the Air Force launched a Zero Defects Campaign, and the base commander at Eglin wanted every person on base to sign a pledge saying he would make no mistakes during the coming year. Most organizations at Eglin already flew a flag saying the office was 100% FOR ZERO DEFECTS. But Boyd knew, as did almost everyone who signed the pledge, that he and everyone else would make mistakes. He thought Zero Defects was a stupid idea and refused to sign. A group of lieutenants working for Christie not only followed his lead but raised a flag that proudly proclaimed they were 100% AGAINST ZERO DEFECTS. Hints that people would be fired and threats of courts-martial drifted down from above. But then Boyd sent word that if there were any retaliations he would, in his words, "create an epic shit storm." The base commander decided it was okay to have a few mavericks at Eglin.

Then there was the day Boyd and Christie were in the coffee shop at Eglin, talking and laughing with the easy confidence of two men sure of their future, when in walked the civilian in charge of the computer shop. Boyd's laughter ended and his face became hard and angry. He stuck his cigar in his mouth, stood up, and stalked toward the civilian. Christie sensed the danger, but it was too late to stop Boyd.

Boyd took the cigar out of his mouth and said, "Guess you heard I briefed Sweeney."

"Yes, I did," said the civilian.

"And Schriever, and the secretary of the Air Force, and the president's Scientific Advisory Board, and Dr. Johnny Foster?" Boyd's voice rose with each addition to the list. The civilian nodded. Now people in the coffee shop were looking up and listening.

Boyd tapped the civilian in the chest. Hard. "You didn't think my work was important enough for your goddamn computer and now I got four-stars calling me for briefings." Tap. "Everybody in the Air Force has heard of energy-maneuverability." Tap. Tap. "You." Tap. "Don't." Tap. "Know." Tap. "Shit." Tap.

The civilian smiled tightly and tried to step around Boyd.

Boyd pushed his cigar against the civilian's tie. A round hole appeared and smoke blossomed. The crowd in the cafeteria stared in shocked silence. The civilian slapped at his smoldering tie, gave Boyd a venomous look, and flounced out of the coffee shop. Boyd was on his six and firing steadily. "You're a loser. A fucking loser. Go on, get out of here. Run." His raucous laughter followed the man. As the civilian strode through the front door, Boyd stopped and shouted in a voice heard throughout the building, "You're a fucking loser!"

Boyd watched the civilian walking across the parking lot. Twice the civilian looked over his shoulder as if afraid Boyd was still in pursuit. Boyd smiled and puffed on his cigar.

He had hosed another one.

Boyd did not see the dangers inherent in deliberately seeking conflict with others. In his mind he had been wronged by the civilian. The fact that he had briefed top people in the Air Force and in government proved he had been right and the civilian wrong. But to be right was not enough. He had to have a redress of grievances and he had to publicly embarrass the person who wronged him. He had to be the last man standing. "People did things to me when we were young," he once told Mary. "They did it because we were poor. But they're not going to do it now."

But when Boyd hosed the civilian, he created another enemy. A powerful enemy. And payback time was rapidly approaching. The Air Force is a collection of coalitions, and by late 1965 there were strong anti-Boyd coalitions at Eglin, at Wright-Pat, and in scattered pockets around the Air Force.

One day word came down that the inspector general (IG) for the Air Force Systems Command was coming to Eglin to investigate Boyd's illegal use of computers. No one knew the origin of the investigation, but chances are it was initiated by the comptroller or the civilian who controlled the base computers or else someone at Wright-Pat — all of whom realized Boyd could not have developed the E-M Theory without countless hours of computer time. Plus, Boyd, with a wink and an elbow to the ribs, had told dozens of people about stealing computer time. Whatever the source, the IG was well armed. He said he was investigating allegations that Boyd had bilked the government of around $1 million in illegal computer usage. The IG investigation did not mention Christie, who was a civilian in another chain of command. Boyd was the sole target.

If the investigation showed Boyd used government computers for an unauthorized project and without proper authority, the military equivalent of felony charges would be filed and a court-martial would follow. If convicted, Boyd could face a prison sentence, be asked to repay the $1 million, and be tossed out of the Air Force with loss of all benefits and allowances.

Boyd was not worried. "I did my homework," he said to the few people who asked about the investigation. After he was questioned by the IG team, he and Christie left Eglin for an extensive tour of the West Coast, where they briefed defense contractors on E-M. When Boyd returned, the investigation was over and the IG team wanted an exit briefing. Considering the high rank and influence of those behind the investigation, the ending was almost anticlimactic. The colonel in charge of the investigation sat down with Boyd and said, in effect, "Major, we know thousands of computer hours went into developing your E-M Theory. But we can't find any evidence of computer misuse. Everything is accounted for."

Boyd smiled.

"My report will recommend that no charges be filed."

Boyd nodded. It was as if the colonel were a not-too-bright child who had slowly worked his way to the only possible conclusion.

"But, Major, we would like to know how you did it."

"And no charges will be filed?"

"No."

"Okay, but first I want to show you something." Boyd pulled from his desk several dozen letters he had written not only to the civilian in charge of computers at Eglin, but to people at Wright-Pat, telling all the benefits his theory would bring to the Air Force and asking for computer time. He showed the letters denying him use of computers. And he told how the civilian had twice tossed him out of his office.

"Colonel, my goal here was not personal. My work was for the best interest of our country. I tried to do it the Air Force way and was refused at every turn."

The colonel nodded.

"Then I did it my way."

Boyd told the colonel of his subterfuge in gaining access to the computers. Then he told the colonel about the people he had briefed on E-M and all the changes taking place in the Air Force because of it. When Boyd finished, the colonel was silent. He looked again at the stack of letters Boyd had written. "Thank you, Major."

Several weeks later the IG issued a report. A copy was sent to Eglin. The report exonerated Boyd of culpability. It said his original and creative work was of overwhelming significance to national defense and that the benefits of E-M had spread throughout the Air Force and would have great influence for years to come. But an IG report must have a villain, even if no charges are filed. The report excoriated the civilian who denied Boyd use of the computers.

Boyd was euphoric. What he did not know was that a few months later would come a day of reckoning. And this time he would not escape.

By 1965 Boyd had been in the Air Force fourteen years. He was not yet up for promotion to lieutenant colonel. But each year the Air Force selects a few promising officers from each rank and promotes them "below the zone" — that is, before they have the time in grade. It is the best way the Air Force has to acknowledge talented young officers and to show that they have a promising future. Boyd looked back at his accomplishments at Nellis, researching and writing the "Aerial Attack Study," gaining an engineering degree, and the impact his E-M Theory was having throughout the Air Force, and he knew that if ever a man deserved early promotion, he was that man. The Air Force owed him a debt of recognition and the best way to recognize an officer is to promote him. He was confident that he soon would be wearing the silver oak leaves of a lieutenant colonel. But Boyd's name was not on the early-promotion list. That, by itself, disappointed and angered Boyd. But what sent him over the edge was the list of men who were promoted. He read down the list in disbelief. Many of those promoted were "horse holders," aides to generals.

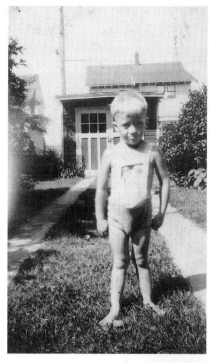

Three-year-old John Boyd in the driveway of his home in Erie.
Photo courtesy of Marion Boyd

Boyd and sister Ann on the running board of the family car, summer 1932.
Photo courtesy of Marion Boyd

Lifeguard John Boyd with Frank Pettinato on the beach at Lake Erie.

Photo courtesy of Marion Boyd

Boyd during his high school years.

Boyd family photo

Enlisted man John Boyd in Japan after World War II. This photo was taken about the time he says he burned down two aircraft hangars.

Photo courtesy of Marion Boyd

Mary Bruce as a student at the University of Iowa.
Boyd family photo

Second Lieutenant John Boyd after receiving his wings in 1952.
Photo courtesy of Marion Boyd

Stephen, dog "Tiger," and Kathy at Nellis AFB, 1958.
Stephen's polio necessitated the steel collar around his neck.
Boyd family photo

A Hun taking off from Nellis AFB, circa 1958. Note the
checkerboard pattern on the nose and tail.
USAF photo

The high priests of fighter aviation in 1959; cadre of the U.S. Air
Force Fighter Weapons School at Nellis. Boyd is kneeling,
fourth from the right.
USAF photo

Boyd's house on McClave Drive in Doraville, Georgia. This is the only home he ever owned.
Photo by Chester W. Richards

Major John Boyd and Tom Christie receive the U.S. Air Force Scientific Achievement Award for 1964.
USAF photo

Armed Forces Day at Eglin AFB, 1965. Captain Tom McInerney stands with Boyd. Left to right: Steve, 12; Jeff, 6; Mary Ellen, 4; John Scott, 7; Kathy, 10.
Boyd family photo

Boyd and Franklin "Chuck" Spinney.
Boyd family photo

Boyd after retirement from the Air Force.
Photo courtesy of Marion Boyd

These three photos of Boyd were shot in 1995 at the West Virginia cabin of Congressional Aide Winslow Wheeler. When Boyd journeyed from Florida to Erie each summer, he stopped over here for long weekends with his friends. Wheeler still hosts a biannual gathering of Boyd's closest comrades.
Photos by James P. Stevenson

Mary Boyd at the dedication of Boyd Hall at Nellis AFB, September 17, 1999.
USAF photo

JOHN R BOYD
COL
US AIR FORCE
KOREA
VIETNAM
JAN 23 1927
MAR 9 1997

Boyd's grave in Arlington National Cemetery. Section sixty, grave site 3,660.
Photo by Chester W. Richards

The Acolytes, Boyd's closest friends and greatest legacy.

Thomas P. Christie
Department of Defense photo

Pierre M. Sprey
Photo by Katherine Frey, *Prince Georges Journal*

Dr. Raymond J. Leopold

Franklin "Chuck" Spinney
Photo by Alison Spinney

James Burton
Photo by Howard Allen

Colonel Mike Wyly
U.S. Marine Corps photo

Others were nonentities whose contributions, if any, were unknown to Boyd. There was not one person on the list who had made the contributions to the Air Force and to national defense that he had made.

Boyd was deeply affected. This was a pivotal event in his career, as well as a personal epiphany. Often, when a man is young and idealistic, he believes that if he works hard and does the right thing, success will follow. This was what Boyd's mother and childhood mentors had told him. But hard work and success do not always go together in the military, where success is defined by rank, and reaching higher rank requires conforming to the military's value system. Those who do not conform will one day realize that the path of doing the right thing has diverged from the path of success, and then they must decide which path they will follow through life. Almost certainly, he realized that if he was not promoted early to lieutenant colonel after all that he had done, he would never achieve high rank. And in light of a speech he was to give in coming years to young officers, his famous "To Be or to Do" speech, he likely realized that while he might *do* big things, he would never *be* at the top of the Air Force hierarchy.

It was clear to Boyd's friends what had happened. Those whom Boyd had belittled and denigrated had sent out the word, and the word had percolated among various coalitions until it reached the promotion board: sure, Boyd has done some good things for the Air Force, but he is unprofessional, lacks basic military courtesies, and is unfit for rapid promotion. These people had lost battles with Boyd, but they won the war. They affected his career and his life in the most hurtful way possible.

Boyd's public reaction to what he saw as a personal and grievous slight was entirely out of character. He went to the Officers Club and got rip-roaring, knee-walking, commode-hugging drunk. He sat alone at the bar, not holding court, not talking about fighter tactics or E-M, but just staring at the wall, smoking his cigar, and drinking. And drinking. And drinking. It is the only time he is known to have gotten drunk.

A few months later Boyd was awarded the Air Force Systems Command Scientific Achievement Award, the highest scientific award in the AFSC. Then he was awarded the Air Force Research and Development Award for Aeronautical Engineering, the highest scientific award the Air Force gives to an officer. And in Boyd's ER — dated September 7, 1965 — which covered his work of the previous year, he received the highest possible ratings in almost every category. "This brilliant young officer is an original thinker," said the ER. "His production comes from about 10% inspiration and 90% a grueling pace that his cohorts find difficult if not impossible to keep up with. He is extremely intolerant of inefficiency and those who attempt to impede his program." It ends with "Maj. Boyd should be promoted to Lt. Col. below the zone of primary eligibility at the first opportunity."

In the spring of 1966, Boyd was granted his heart's desire: he was ordered to Thailand as an F-4 pilot. At long last he was going into combat and this time he would be in the thick of it. It was about time. He missed World War II and he arrived late for Korea, but now, by God, he would be a Phantom driver in Vietnam. The air war in Vietnam was white-hot. F-105s were going up North to the area around Hanoi — "Route Pack VI" it was called — where they were being shot down by the dozens. The previous year, 171 American aircraft were lost in North Vietnam. That year the number would rise to 318.

The Air Force had said F-105s were fast enough and deadly enough to fly missions alone; they needed no fighter support. But that policy changed and now F-4C Phantoms flew MiG cover for the Thuds. The F-4C was too big and heavy to get into a turning fight with the nimble little MiGs, so a Phantom driver had to take the fight down low and keep his airspeed up if he was going to hose a MiG. The Phantom also had no guns and its missiles were virtually useless in many air-to-air scenarios; the launch envelope was so narrow that a pilot had to be a very hot stick to get a kill. Boyd was not worried. He told everyone he met that the first five enemy aircraft he sighted would be history. Forty-Second Boyd was going to wax some Communist ass.

Boyd was packing, getting his shots, making arrangements for Mary and the children to go to Iowa, and handling the myriad details a pilot must endure before a combat assignment when he received word his orders for Thailand had been cancelled.

The new fighter, the F-X, was in trouble.

The Bigger-Higher-Faster-Farther syndrome that had plagued the Air Force since its earliest days had resulted in an F-X design that reminded many of the F-111. The proposed new fighter was a swing-wing behemoth of some seventy thousand pounds. While the Air Force publicly praised the F-111, they were finding it more and more difficult to hide the fact that the airplane was as bad as Boyd had said, maybe worse. The Pentagon took a hard look at the design for the F-X and realized it could only lead to embarrassment. The Air Force probably would lose the fighter and be forced by Congress to fly another saltwater airplane.

Boyd was ordered to the Pentagon.

In the summer of 1966, before he transferred to Washington, Boyd spent part of his accrued leave in Erie. These summer trips to Erie had become a practice he would follow for the rest of his life. But this was the first time he had taken Mary and all five children home at the same time. Naturally he expected everyone to stay at the house on Lincoln Avenue. But when he drove up to his mother's house and children began falling out and running across the yard, the redoubtable Elsie Boyd told her son they couldn't stay. I don't want five children underfoot, she said. They make too much noise and the noise will bother me.

For one of the few times in his life, Boyd had nothing to say. He stared at his mother. This was his home. And he was turned away.

"You can come by with the children every day, but I don't want you staying too long," his mother said.

"Mother, where do you want us to stay?" Boyd was almost plaintive.

"In a motel."

Boyd was crushed. Almost every day he was in Erie, he told Mary of his disbelief. His dear mother, whom he often said was the most important person in his life, had turned him away from her door.

It was a fresh reminder of how tough his mother could be, how unbending. It was a lesson Boyd learned well and one he would need during the next few years.

Boyd's last ER at Eglin, dated September 7, 1966, was both good and bad, and it signaled again that Boyd, despite his contributions, was not a company man. The ER praised Boyd's original work on E-M but added, "He is an intense and impatient man who does not respond well to close supervision. . . . He possesses a lot of nervous energy. . . ."

Worse for Boyd, the colonel who indorsed the report downgraded the promotion-potential block, showing he did not concur with the reviewing officer. This is unusual. What is even more unusual is that a second colonel signed an additional indorsement saying he agreed with the downgrade.

Boyd had established a pattern: no matter what his contributions to the Air Force or to national defense might be — and there were significant contributions yet to come — his outspoken nature, his lack of reluctance to criticize his superiors, and his love of conflict with others would hinder his promotion throughout his career.

Boyd and Christie went to Washington on temporary duty shortly before Boyd moved there from Eglin. They met with a series of defense contractors to talk about E-M. Christie also talked to Boyd about the Pentagon and cautioned him about what to expect. The people at Wright-Pat still were angry and would do everything in their power to undercut him. The coalition at Eglin also was angry at how he snookered them on computer usage and then humiliated the civilian in charge. The defense contractors who favored swing-wing construction would put unimaginable pressure on him. And although they had not yet revealed their hand, top Navy officers — far more skillful at both bureaucratic infighting and public relations — would engage him in a form of battle even more deadly than rat-racing over the Green Spot. Hundreds of millions of dollars and thousands of careers would be at stake once the F-X contract was let.

Christie was a master at bureaucratic maneuvering and had sheltered Boyd at Eglin. But now Boyd would be on his own, and Christie wondered if he would survive.

One night Boyd and Christie and a defense contractor went to dinner and afterward went to a movie. Boyd liked aviation movies and action movies, so he picked the newly released *Blue Max,* a story of German fighter pilots in World War I. The movie has many air-to-air combat scenes, and during one of them Boyd began mumbling, "Hose him. Hose him."

Christie and the defense contractor smiled. Boyd was being Boyd. But then Boyd's voice grew louder. "Hose him!" People seated nearby turned to look. Christie elbowed Boyd. "John," he admonished, "it's just a movie."

Boyd was quiet for a few moments. But during the next aerial engagement, as the German fighters played a deadly game of grabass with British fighters, Boyd disapproved of the tactics.

"Break left! Break left!" he shouted.

Now people for several rows around were turning to look. "John," Christie said. He was so embarrassed he almost moved to another seat.

Boyd was so intense in evaluating the air-to-air combat that he forgot he was in a movie. Finally he could take no more. He stood up, waved both arms, jabbed one hand toward the screen, and shouted at the top of his lungs, "You missed the goddamn shot! Hose him, you stupid bastard!"

Christie shook his head in dismay. Not for Boyd, but for those in the Pentagon. They were bureaucrats. Boyd was a warrior.

Chapter Thirteen

"I've Never Designed a Fighter Plane Before"

A STORY is told in the Pentagon of a colonel waiting in the outer office of a four-star general. The colonel's face is twisted in anguish. He looks at his watch and he looks down the hall and he looks over his shoulder at the general's door. Everything about the colonel shows a man twisted and torn by powerful emotions.

Moments earlier a subordinate had rushed to inform the colonel that his wife called to say their house was on fire. Her call was suddenly cut off, presumably by the fire. The colonel did not know if his wife was safe, if his children were safe, or if his house was burning to the ground. Every ounce of his being as a husband, every iota of his soul as a father, dictated that he drop everything to rush to his family. Yet he stayed. The chance to have a one-on-one meeting with a four-star general, the chance to advance his career, is more important.

Such is the way of life for many in the Pentagon.

From Eglin AFB to the Pentagon is a long way, not so much in distance as in style and pace and atmosphere. The distance was especially great for Boyd. He was a thirty-nine-year-old major who had demonstrated at Eglin that he did not care about military politics, human nature, and the ways of the world. He wore the ribbons and decorations of two wars on his chest and he wore commendation ribbons rarely found on young majors. He also had a reputation as a pilot and a thinker unmatched by any man in the Air Force. Physically, he was in his prime. Regular workouts had widened his shoulders and deepened his chest. When he spoke, which was often, there seemed to be no filter between what he thought and what he said. He was not intimidated by the Pentagon. He still was angry about not being sent to Vietnam. Soon the anger would be ameliorated by the joy he found in shooting down generals.

The Pentagon is tricky and treacherous, and can be immensely rewarding. No assignment in the military is more desired, more detested, and more necessary to an officer's advancement. It is said that Air Force careerists — "Blue Suiters" — would put on track shoes and climb up the backs of their mothers for such an assignment. If an officer is to be promoted rapidly, he must have a protector, a guardian, a rabbi — what the Navy calls a "sea daddy" — to prepare the way. No better protector can be found than a man with stars on his shoulders. A general who bestows his blessings on a young officer can see that the officer receives assignments that prepare him for ever-higher commands. A general's support automatically puts an officer's career on the fast track. For a Blue Suiter who craves face time with generals, the Pentagon is the ultimate assignment.

All the things that make the Pentagon so prized by careerists make it loathed and detested by warriors. The self-promotion and sycophancy and backstabbing treachery are all anathema to a warrior. A warrior wants his country to be prepared for war, to win against all enemies, to prevail at all costs. *Duty* and *patriotism* and *honor* are not buzz words to a warrior; they are his creed. A warrior speaks the truth to generals and congressmen. Being promoted is not the top priority of a warrior. Thus, warriors do not fare well in the Pentagon.

But then, there are few true warriors in the Air Force.

There are officers of great patriotism, however, who are appalled by what they see in the Pentagon. They say to themselves, "I'll go along for now. But when I get to be colonel, I'm going to change things." What they don't realize is that they will be promoted to colonel only if their superiors think they *won't* make changes. Study after study shows that the higher in rank a military officer ascends, the less likely he is to make change. It is sad indeed to look upon a patriot whose ideals have been destroyed by the Pentagon. But even sadder are those who simply stand aside and do or say nothing, allowing those who sold their souls to have their way.

Those who work in the Pentagon call it the "Building" — a 6.5-million-square-foot structure covering twenty-nine acres and containing more than twenty thousand workers, the bureaucratic nerve center for a worldwide network of airmen, soldiers, sailors, and marines who operate weapons of scarifying lethality. The Pentagon has clothing stores, bookstores, bakeries, and a shopping mall; it even has its own battery-powered ambulances called "white wagons." The need for ambulances is not surprising when one considers the plague of interservice rivalries in the Building. The depth of these rivalries is difficult for civilians to understand. Even an Air Force officer who has never served in the Pentagon is amazed when he arrives and finds his primary job is to see that his branch of the service gets more money than any other branch of the service. He finds the real threat facing America is not a despotic foreign power or rogue terrorist groups; the real threat is that an officer from the Navy or Army or Marines might cut a deal with Congress that gives his branch of the service more money.

Officers of all ranks are found in the Building, but the preponderance are lieutenant colonels and above. If the Building could be squeezed, generals would pop from every orifice. So many generals are here that full colonels are often little more than errand boys or coffee pourers. Senior generals have access to helicopters or well-appointed jets and are treated as royalty when they visit military bases. They have retinues of horse holders whose jobs are to see that the general's path is paved with convenience and covered with roses. A general is a sovereign whose look of disapproval can banish an officer from his presence and wreck that officer's career. Generals rarely are reluctant to use their powers. Blue Suiters and warriors alike find that the Building is more dangerous than an unmapped minefield. The slightest misstep can wreck a career.

Boyd was near the bottom of the food chain when he walked into the Building. Yet he was about to demonstrate how one man could seize control of the Building's bureaucracy and have a profound influence — far out of proportion to his age and rank — that is still being felt today.

Boyd also was about to demonstrate how he rarely met a general he couldn't offend.

Boyd came to the Building at a pivotal time in Air Force history. The swashbuckling World War II generals who led the Air Force were retiring in large numbers and being replaced by a new breed of officer, graduates of the Air Force Academy, men who could hold their own with Research and Development intellectuals, men who were far more sophisticated in dealing with defense contractors but just as anxious to get the maximum number of dollars for the Air Force. Paradoxically, while the type of Air Force leader was changing, the dogma of Bigger-Higher-Faster-Farther was as entrenched as ever. The best example was the deeply troubled F-X project.

The Navy was a big part of the Air Force problem. Navy admirals earlier snookered Secretary McNamara by saying they would accept the Air Force's F-111 for Navy duty if they could continue development of their favorite jet engine, the TF30, and their favorite anti-bomber missile, the Phoenix. McNamara agreed. The Navy plan, brilliant in its bureaucratic manipulation, was to dillydally for another year or so over whether or not the F-111 was carrier compatible, turn down the aircraft, then go to Congress and say, "We have a good engine. We have a good missile. Give us the dollars we would have gotten for the F-111 and we will use them to build a truly great Navy airplane." That airplane was the F-14. Now there was a very real danger that the Navy would impose the F-14, or the F-14 follow-on, on the Air Force.

The Air Force knew Congress would never fund a new aircraft that looked like the F-111, and the F-X was a virtual carbon copy. In addition to obvious F-X design problems and a looming fight with the Navy, the air war in Vietnam was becoming intense. Air Force leaders were stunned to discover that big, expensive, complex F-4s and F-105s were the wrong aircraft for that war. Not only that, but in a development predicted by Boyd and ignored by Air Force tacticians, the vaunted missiles that were to have ended the era of the gunfighter had proven highly unreliable. A pilot was lucky to get one hit out of every ten missiles launched. The Air Force had long advocated that maneuverability be built into the missile rather than the airplane, and now it suffered the consequences. If a gun-firing enemy is on his six, a fighter pilot can disengage and go for separation. He can dive and outrun the enemy. But a jet can't outrun a missile. Vietnam proved that a pilot has to be able to turn and burn in order to defeat a missile chasing him across the heavens. In fact, missiles meant that fighter aircraft should be *more* maneuverable than in the past.

The host of troubles facing the Air Force allowed Boyd to take over the F-X project. His takeover was de facto rather than de jure, as he was far junior in rank to people who made design and acquisition decisions and to those who, on organization charts, led the F-X program. Later, some senior officers would question the significance of Boyd's role in developing the F-X. To prove their point they would say, "He was only a major." But Boyd's contributions depend upon the power of the microscope used to examine his work. If someone looked at the F-X project through a Pentagon microscope, the four-star generals who led the Tactical Air Command and the Systems Command were the decision makers. A two-star general was directly in charge of the F-X. Under him was a one-star, numerous full colonels, and, somewhere down near the bottom, Boyd. Each of these officers has a different perspective when he talks of the F-X. But if one uses a more powerful microscope, if one knows which decisions about the F-X were crucial and who made those decisions, one sees that Boyd was driving the train that would deliver the F-X. He knew more about fighter tactics and what made a great fighter aircraft than any man in the Air Force. Government, industry, and academia were now developing E-M techniques for optimal aircraft maneuvers and beginning to apply them to fighter design. The calculus of variations, optimal control theory, dynamic programming, differential game theory, and steepest-descent techniques were being discussed at a floating crap game that moved between the Air Force Flight Dynamics Laboratory at Wright-Pat and the Air Force Academy. Boyd attended most of the meetings, and even though he had more than his share of enemies at Wright-Pat, his E-M work made him the center of every meeting.

In addition, Boyd had support from the top, invaluable in a bureaucracy. Few in the Building knew that Air Force Chief of Staff John McConnell was a Boyd fan. It was General McConnell who cancelled Boyd's Vietnam tour and brought him to the Pentagon. He knew of Boyd, the legend: fighter pilot and creator of the E-M Theory. But he needed Boyd, the maverick: the obstreperous and independent officer who cared more for his work than for his career. Only such a man could save the F-X from being cancelled and prevent the

Air Force from being outmaneuvered by the Navy. Only such a man could save the Air Force from itself.

From the moment he walked into the Pentagon, Boyd was embroiled in conflict.

According to a monograph from the Office of Air Force History, the colonel for whom Boyd worked gave him a copy of the F-X design and asked for comments. The monograph says Boyd "summarily rejected it."

What actually happened is far more graphic. Boyd's boss was about to become known as the man who caused the Air Force to eat another saltwater airplane. The nervous colonel looked with curiosity at the famous young major who had been brought to the Pentagon to bail out the F-X. He pointed to a voluminous stack of design studies.

"Your first assignment here is to review these requirements and the design package for the F-X," the colonel said in effect. "We're having trouble getting it approved by Congress. Take two weeks and report back to me with recommendations."

The colonel expected Boyd to do what subordinates in the Pentagon do when given a big project: they compile a lengthy briefing to demonstrate how smart and how diligent they have been, or they do a bit of cosmetic work on an old report and pretend that it is new.

Boyd said, "Yes, Sir," gathered the papers, and carried them to his office. He pored over them day and night, growing ever more disgusted with the intransigent and hidebound nature of the Air Force R&D bureaucracy. The weight had been trimmed down to about 62,500 pounds, but the fighter was still overweight and underwinged, too complex and far too expensive. And because it was a multirole aircraft, Boyd knew it could do none of its jobs very well. A fighter is designed one way, a low-level nuclear bomber another, and an all-weather interdiction bomber still another. Put all these requirements inside the skin of one airplane and all you get is trouble. Imagine designing a high-performance sports car that must also haul gravel and take a family across country and you get the idea.

Boyd's first objective was to cut back on the weight of the F-X. This would both lower the cost and improve maneuverability. "You pay for airplanes just like you do for potatoes," he said. "The heavier they are, the more expensive they are." The more Boyd studied the

F-X plans, the more he realized that everything the Air Force had done would have to be tossed out. Everything prepared by generals and bureaucrats at Wright-Pat, everything from the generals of the Tactical Air Command and the Systems Command and their staffs — it all had to go. The Air Force simply was going about this the wrong way. As Boyd later explained, "You gotta challenge all assumptions. If you don't, what is doctrine on day one becomes dogma forever after."

Boyd wanted a far smaller aircraft, maybe with only one engine, a high-performance hot rod of an airplane with a thrust-to-weight ratio that would make it the purest air-to-air machine the world had ever seen, an airplane that could dump and regain energy faster than any aircraft ever known, a fighter so maneuverable it could, in Boyd's less-than-elegant but highly descriptive phrase, "fly up its own asshole." Boyd did not care about Bigger-Higher-Faster-Farther. He wanted only one thing: a fighter that would dominate the skies for decades.

He was thrumming with excitement when he returned to the colonel's office. He stacked the reports and design studies neatly on a table. He brought in no new papers, no easel to hold the flip charts, no slides, no projector, no stacks of documents. He simply returned what he had been given and said he was reporting as ordered.

"Where is your report?" the colonel asked.

Boyd smiled and tapped a long forefinger against his temple.

The colonel's eyebrows rose. The most crucial acquisition project in the Air Force was at stake. He wanted to see something new and startling about how to save the F-X. And this boy wizard from Eglin was standing there, grinning and tapping his temple.

"You don't have a briefing?"

"Sir, you asked me to review the design package and report to you. I'm ready to do so."

"If you have no briefing or no report, you are not prepared."

"That is incorrect, Sir. I have a report — a well thought-out report."

The colonel stared long and hard at Boyd. He leaned back in his chair. "Proceed, Major."

Boyd rocked on his heels. He looked the colonel squarely in the eye. In his most earnest and sincere tone he said, "Sir, I've never designed a fighter plane before." Then he paused and nodded toward the design studies stacked on the table. "But I could fuck up and do better than that."

An outspoken and confrontational officer such as Boyd rarely lasts long in the Building. In later years one of Boyd's favorite stories — which may or may not have been true — was how he was fired soon after coming to the Pentagon. Being fired in the military can mean the officer was simply transferred from one job to another. But it also means the officer's career has ended.

All his life Boyd told the story of how a colonel not only fired him, but humiliated him by conducting the firing in front of a half-dozen people. Boyd was banished to another office to perform unknown duties. He languished in exile while the F-X and the Air Force were threatened by the Navy. Then the chief of staff heard about the firing, said Boyd was irreplaceable on the F-X project, and ordered the colonel to bring Boyd back. Boyd said the colonel offered him his old job but that he refused unless the colonel publicly rehired him in front of the same group present when he was fired. Boyd always ended the story by laughing and saying, "I got my pound of flesh."

Boyd's ERs do not reflect his being shifted from one job to another. Nor does Christie remember the name of the colonel who supposedly fired Boyd. And given that Boyd was the fair-haired boy sent to the Pentagon to save the F-X, it seems improbable he was fired, especially by a colonel whose own job depended in part on how well Boyd performed.

None of this matters. Because this story, like the story of tearing down the barracks in Japan, is more revealing if it is not true.

Boyd was in the Building several months when he was called on to silence a white-haired "Whiz Kid" named Pierre Sprey, who had become a thorn in the Air Force's side. This brilliant young civilian from Systems Analysis, an office that reported to the Office of the Secretary of Defense (OSD), had spent a year preparing a report for the secretary of defense and the president on the Air Force's structure and budget for waging war in Europe. The Air Force force structure was based on the World War II doctrine — "interdiction bombing," it is now called — of bombing bridges, railroads, highways, industry, and infrastructure to prevent Soviet forces from overrunning Europe. The civilian's heretical report said the interdiction mission was flawed, that even if the Air Force had three times as many aircraft, it could not keep Soviet forces from pouring into Europe. The report said the role of tactical air forces in Europe should be twofold: supporting ground troops — close air support, or CAS, as it is called — and maintaining air superiority so that the CAS airplanes could do their jobs without interference. Interdiction should be a minor mission, if pursued at all.

Even among McNamara's Whiz Kids — the highly educated and extraordinarily bright young men brought into the Building with a mandate to impose rational thought on both the military and the military budget — Pierre Sprey stood out. Some Whiz Kids traveled on their reputations. Not Sprey. He entered Yale at fifteen and graduated four years later with a curious double major: French literature and mechanical engineering. Then he went to Cornell and studied mathematical statistics and operational research. At twenty-two he was running a statistical consulting shop at Grumman Aviation. He wanted to design aircraft but knew it would be years before Grumman gave him that freedom, so he went to work for Alain Enthoven, the leader and best known of the Whiz Kids.

Sprey is not a physically imposing man. He is about 5'8" and slight of build. His white hair sweeps back theatrically from a high forehead. His speech is slow and considered. He speaks French and German fluently. Women find him gallant and rakish. Men often find him intimidating. He has an intellect as clear and cold as polar ice. If one of Sprey's friends is asked to describe him, the respondent's first words are about how smart Sprey is. Some very smart people are said to have a computer for a brain. Sprey is an atomic clock, relentlessly dependable at penetrating to the essence of a subject or a person and laying both bare. He is an absolutist in all things. Sprey's wit is both biting and erudite. He has an immediate recall of almost everything he has ever read. He knows more about tactical aviation and the history of warfare than do 99 percent of the people in the Air Force. More than one bombastic and patronizing general has been stopped short after a single exchange with Sprey. He is a rarity, a civilian who can take on the Air Force on its own turf and prevail. Unlike many civilians who worked in the Pentagon, Sprey was not intimidated by rank; in fact he thought there was an inverse relationship between the number of stars on a man's shoulders and his intelligence.

Sprey brought his searing intellect and unbending rectitude to the Building at the height of the McNamara era. His hours were those of a vampire. Whatever issues he raised had to be taken seriously by the military because, like other issues raised by Systems Analysis, they were codified in Draft Presidential Memos sent to McNamara and then to President Johnson. The military services hated and were afraid of Systems Analysis, and they were especially afraid of Pierre Sprey. He was one of the most formidable men in the Building.

Air Force generals read Sprey's report and became almost apoplectic. Interdiction bombing was sacred doctrine. It was the rationale for separating the Air Force from the Army back in 1947. Close air support, ever since those days, was anathema, for it reminded the Air Force that its primary purpose had once been to assist ground forces. There was nothing of the wild blue yonder about close air support, no white scarves, no glory.

Sprey's report imperiled two-thirds of the Air Force budget, including $8 billion allocated for the F-X. Thus, the report was not only a dangerous violation of sacred doctrine but, even worse, it threatened the Air Force's budget and top fighter project. Debunking his report was a top priority of Air Force leadership.

But there were two big problems. First, Sprey had used targeting information from the Joint Chiefs of Staff. To attack the targeting part of the study would be to attack the Joint Chiefs, and that simply was not done. Second, the data on the number of bombs needed to destroy a given target had come from the Joint Munitions Effectiveness Manuals (JMEMs) computed by Tom Christie down at Eglin. Christie — thanks partially to his work on E-M — was a rising civilian star in the Air Force, and his research was so meticulous that all four services had signed off on the JMEMs at the four-star level.

Nevertheless, a colonel was ordered by superior officers to declare war on both the report and the civilian who wrote it. Pull out all the stops. We don't want to know the details; just do whatever it takes to get the job done. But neutralize that civilian son of a bitch.

The colonel went to Sprey and said, in effect, "This report is not bad work. But it involves lots of tedious hand calculations. Let's agree on a computer model and then let the computer verify your work."

But Sprey knew the ways of the Building. He knew the colonel had a large staff and that he could program computers to spit out whatever results he wanted. "Not unless I can do the same calculations by hand," he said. It proved to be a wise move. He began having nighttime visits from conscience-stricken young captains and majors who worked for the colonel and who said they had been ordered to program the computers to give false results in order to discredit the report. Sprey demanded a meeting with the colonel. He could not keep the disgust from his voice as he cited chapter and verse on how the colonel doctored the numbers. "Your numbers are a lie," he told the colonel in front of a packed conference room.

The colonel was furious at being embarrassed by a young whippersnapper, particularly a civilian analyst. He responded in the way of most military men: he attacked. He went up the chain of command all the way to Secretary McNamara and said Sprey had insulted his dignity. He demanded an apology. Word came down for the colonel and the civilian to work out their differences. Sprey not only refused to apologize but stepped up his attacks, saying the colonel was a "slimy creature" who "oozed mendacity."

Sprey was nonrated; that is, he was not a pilot. And he had never been a member of the armed services. The outraged colonel therefore assumed he knew nothing of fighter tactics and Air Force doctrine and shifted his attack accordingly. Remembering that this new guy in the Building, this Major John Boyd, was the Air Force's resident expert on fighter tactics, the colonel decided Boyd's rare combination of operational experience and intellectual accomplishment could demolish this pesky civilian.

The colonel who arranged the meeting between Boyd and Sprey must have been like a man locking up two heavyweight champions in a room, then backing up and listening for sounds of battle. He must have wanted to be the fly on the wall and feel the tension, hear the first volleys, and see the blood on the floor.

If so, he would have been terribly disappointed. He had only a one-dimensional understanding of both Boyd and Sprey. Boyd was not influenced by other people's judgments. The very idea of being told to attack a man's intellectual accomplishment simply because it threatened the Air Force budget was humorous. Boyd was anything but hostile that day.

And the colonel was so locked into his judgment of Sprey as an uncontrollable attack dog that he did not know two of Sprey's more important attributes. First, Sprey had great respect for the officers he met whom he considered men of integrity. Second, Sprey was a curious man. He was aware of Boyd's reputation and wondered if Boyd really knew the inner working of air combat or if he simply was there to parrot the Air Force line.

The meeting was anticlimactic.

As background for his interdiction study, Sprey had read widely about the combat histories of World War II and Korea. He could talk for hours about air-to-ground and air-to-air combat. So the two men quickly found common interests. When Sprey talked of the combat records of various fighter aces, Boyd's eyes lit up and he leaned forward, amazed at Sprey's interest and understanding of an area so dear to him. When Sprey mentioned Richard Bong as America's leading ace in World War II, Boyd nodded in agreement but then lifted an admonishing finger as he told Sprey that Bong was a one-trick pony. When Sprey said the Air Force needed air-superiority fighters to protect aircraft flying close air support, Boyd agreed. But then he added, "We can't fly those air-superiority missions in a predictable way; we can't be like a taxi going up there on schedule. We have to be unpredictable."

The conversation went on for hours. Sprey lobbed an idea and Boyd fleshed it out, added perspective, and bounced it back. Boyd told Sprey about the F-X and how he proposed to change it. Ideas ping-ponged between the two men, each adding a twist or new bounce until both sat back with smiles on their faces and respect in their eyes. Boyd was fascinated by Sprey's knowledge of math and statistics. Sprey could help him hone the E-M Theory into a tool for designing the finest fighter aircraft the world had ever known. And Sprey was excited by Boyd's profound ideas about fighter combat and by his intellect and rectitude. He had finally met an Air Force officer of fire and conviction. Sprey was not the sort of man who followed other men, but he could follow Boyd.

Boyd had met the second of the Acolytes.

Many people think they understand Boyd's E-M Theory. But few men truly grasp the theory in all of its elegant simplicity. Sprey would come to understand E-M and how to use it as well as Boyd and Christie.

The meeting between Boyd and Sprey in the Pentagon paralleled, in some respects, the meeting between Boyd and Christie at Eglin. But while Christie became an indulgent uncle, Sprey became a brother.

Both Christie and Sprey sensed an innocence and purity about Boyd. They believed not only that he would make enormous contributions but that he was a man who often needed protection. A few generals also knew this. But Boyd relied almost daily on Sprey and Christie, while the generals usually appeared at times of crisis.

When the colonel who had unleashed Boyd asked how the meeting with Sprey had gone, Boyd smiled, gave him an evasive answer, and said he was going to get back with the civilian and finish the job. The colonel went away pleased.

The F-X now became as much a part of Sprey's life as it was Boyd's. After most people departed the Building, Boyd and Sprey were still at their desks. And then around 7:00 or 8:00 P.M., Boyd wandered down to Sprey's office. In the beginning they met maybe once a week, then twice, then three and four nights. The men pored over E-M charts for the F-X, new designs, and arcane engineering data until long after midnight.

Then Boyd began showing his briefings to Sprey and asking for an opinion. Sprey often ripped the briefs to shreds. And he did it in such a calm and irrefutable manner, reason stacked atop reason, logic atop logic, that it was impossible to disagree. Boyd referred to a Sprey critique as the "Pierre Sprey buzz saw." But he knew Sprey was making his work stronger and more focused and virtually impervious to attack. "We've got to do our homework, Tiger," Boyd often said to Sprey. "One mistake and they will leverage the hell out of it."

Boyd's acceptance of Sprey was signaled when he began calling at 4:00 A.M., tossing out new E-M iterations and new ideas about how to use those ideas in the design process. Sprey realized, as had Christie before him, that being Boyd's friend meant dedicating one's life to Boyd's causes. Very few men were ever invited by Boyd to join forces with him. None ever refused. Each sensed intuitively that he was being offered a rare gift. Each was to pay a terrible price for his friendship with Boyd. Each would have paid more.

It was seven years before the remaining Acolytes met Boyd. Each would know in his turn the opprobrium that Sprey was about to experience. The calumny Sprey had received because of his interdiction study was nothing compared to what was about to come his way because of Boyd. The Blue Suiters came to view the Boyd / Sprey relationship as a friendship forged in hell. And they would unleash the seemingly omnipotent bureaucratic powers of the Building against the two men. The careers of many would change; even the Pentagon would change.

Boyd and Sprey formed the nucleus of what in a few years would be the most famous, most detested, and most reluctantly respected ad hoc group in the Building, a group that history would know as the "Fighter Mafia."

Chapter Fourteen

Bigger-Higher-Faster-Farther

BOYD was caught between the proverbial rock and a hard place.

On one hand was Boyd's belief that E-M could produce the most remarkable fighter in history. On the other hand was the implacable and relentless nature of the Bigger-Faster-Higher-Farther fraternity to make the F-X bigger and heavier — and more expensive — by loading it with every high-tech gizmo known to man.

Boyd was a man possessed. He bulldozed ahead, knocking over people and ideas and long-cherished beliefs. He was so intemperate in his speech and actions that it seemed to many he was out of control. He was still angry and hurt about being passed over for lieutenant colonel below the zone. "I'm a mere major," he said again and again. The F-X was a glorious opportunity for him not only to show the Air Force the practical value of his work but to serve as the vehicle that could ensure he made lieutenant colonel within the zone.

To accomplish his goals, Boyd had to conquer a host of institutional obstacles. First, he had to overcome the technical incompetence at Wright-Pat, where engineers had proven they were unable to produce a simple conceptual design for the F-X. At the same time, he could not ignore Wright-Pat, as they were the only official Air Force source for basic engineering data on the aircraft. He suspected much of the data was incorrect, but he had to use it. Second, he had to make people understand that E-M was not just the best way, but the *only* way to measure air-to-air performance in an airplane. Even though both the Air Force and industry were enamored of E-M, not everyone yet grasped the full dimensions of what it could accomplish. It was new and different. And anything new and different is feared by a bureaucracy. Finally, Boyd had to upgrade E-M from the area of tactics and move it more firmly into the area of aircraft design.

Preaching the gospel of E-M was an ongoing and ever-changing process, much of it dictated by day-to-day discoveries and iterations and permutations as Boyd pressed ever deeper into an area of aeronautical engineering where no one had gone before. This could not have happened without having Tom Christie at Eglin. On Christie's staff was an Air Force lieutenant who did nothing but E-M computer work. From the Pentagon, Boyd called the lieutenant three and four times daily about revisions and upgrades for the E-M computer program and E-M charts. One night Christie's phone rang and he knew it was Boyd. He looked at his watch. The hour was late, and Boyd was so intense that Christie knew if he picked up the phone that he would be held captive for hours. So he did not answer. He and his wife, Kathy, sat and talked and read and shook their heads in wonderment as the phone rang for thirty-two minutes before Boyd gave up.

Christie's work brought him to the Pentagon almost on a weekly basis. Every time, his briefcase was filled with new E-M data. One Monday, Boyd told Sprey about the "Wild Hog" (as Christie was known because of his large appetite), and Sprey suggested they go to Don Quixote, a restaurant in Shirlington that on Monday night served all the filet mignon a customer could eat for a fixed price. Sprey, a refined man, ate two small steaks. Boyd's competitive side was in full flower that night, and he matched Christie steak for steak until the count was at five each. Christie sighed and sat back. Boyd grinned in satisfaction and rubbed his stomach. He had eaten as much as the Wild Hog and to him that was a victory. But Christie was only taking a break, allowing his food to settle to make room for more. After resting a moment, he again tucked into the steaks. Boyd watched in amazement as Christie ate four more. Boyd was unusually silent as the three men walked to the door. Christie knew he would pout all evening. It was only a dinner, but Boyd saw it — as he saw most everything — as a contest. The three men stood in the door and looked across the parking lot for their car. Christie smiled and turned to Boyd and said, "What say we go out for some pizza before we go back to work?"

Christie's office kept preparing new E-M charts, and with each one came a new insight, a new approach, a new way to display information. The deeper Boyd moved into the design applications, the more he had to experiment or explore new aircraft performance fields such as agility or persistence. Incredible as it may seem, the F-X was the first fighter in U.S. history designed with *any* maneuvering specifications, much less E-M specifications. That is, the F-X was the first U.S. aircraft ever designed with dogfighting in mind. (Aviation aficionados often say the P-51 of World War II and the F-86 of Korea were pure fighters. But the P-51 was designed for range and speed, not maneuvering. It became the premier fighter of World War II only because the British — over the vehement objections of the Wright-Pat bureaucracy — replaced its puny power plant with a big Rolls-Royce engine. The F-86 was designed as a high-altitude interceptor. To reach high altitude, it had to have big wings, and because it had big wings, it became, serendipitously, a great maneuvering fighter.)

Boyd was guided in his work by one simple principle: he wanted to give pilots a fighter that would outmaneuver any enemy. He did not become fixated on technology or "one-point" numerical solutions. For instance, he did not say the F-X had to have a certain top speed or a certain turning capability. He knew that it must have a high thrust-to-weight ratio if it were to have neck-snapping acceleration. And he knew it had to have lots of wing in order to maneuver quickly into the firing envelope. It had to have the energy to disengage, go for separation, then come back into the fight with an advantage. It had to have the fuel to penetrate deep into enemy territory and sustain a prolonged turning fight. But all these criteria were vague. The closest Boyd came to defining a specific technical solution was when he said the aircraft should pull enough Gs at 30,000 feet to "roll down your goddamn socks."

Boyd faced opposition at every step. He constantly took things off the airplane to lower the weight. He had no specific figure, but he wanted the F-X to weigh somewhere around thirty-five thousand pounds, maybe less. But while Boyd worked daily to remove things from the F-X, seemingly everyone else in the Air Force — the fire-control people, missile people, electronic-warfare people — wanted to add something. Maintenance people even insisted the aircraft carry a built-in maintenance ladder. They said the aircraft might operate in a forward area where there would be no ladders for mechanics.

"Tell them to get some goddamn orange crates and climb on those," Boyd growled, trying with little success to explain the term *growth factor*. A twenty-pound maintenance ladder does not simply add twenty pounds to the aircraft — not if the aircraft is to maintain the same performance. Dozens of subtle additions are caused by the ladder until finally the ladder adds not twenty pounds but perhaps two hundred.

Boyd wanted the F-X to carry a small radar. But electronics people wanted a radar that could acquire and track a MiG at forty nautical miles, a criterion that meant the aircraft must carry an enormous radar dish. The size of the dish was driving the size of the fuselage, which was driving the size of the F-X. Wright-Pat's structural engineers also wanted a stronger wing, which meant more weight. The Tactical Air Command was calling for more fuel and a top speed of Mach 3. Because the Air Force had been flying the Navy F-4, which had a tail hook, someone decided the F-X, even though it had extraordinary short field landing performance, needed a tail hook. Boyd insisted the F-X have an internal gun, while Wright-Pat's electronics gurus wanted only missiles. Boyd's early design work indicated that while a swing-wing aircraft had certain aerodynamic benefits, the extra weight and drag inherent in the swing-wing design destroyed more performance than was gained. Still the Air Force insisted on the heavy swing-wing design.

Boyd was being pecked to death by a thousand ducks. He drank about ten cups a day of what he called "smart juice" — black coffee. He smoked a dozen or so Dutch Masters. Several times each day he loped down to the concourse and bought dozens of chocolate candy bars. He arrived for work at 11:00 A.M. or noon, usually unkempt and unmilitary in appearance. Several times his boss said, "John, get a haircut or get lost." Once he added, "While you're at it, get your shoes shined and your uniform pressed." He thought about telling Boyd to adopt regular working hours, but he knew Boyd was staying at his desk until 3:00 or 4:00 A.M. He knew because several nights a week Boyd called to exult over a new equation he had derived or to shout about a design problem he had solved.

One man who knew Boyd at the time said he was like a radio in which a button is locked down so it cannot receive; it can only transmit. "Boyd is on *transmit* today" became a warning phrase for visitors.

For several years, the defense industry had been involved in preliminary design work on the Air Force's new aircraft. Now, as the design process gathered speed and the defense industry realized the Air Force was approaching the big-money decisions, representatives of America's biggest defense contractors began making their way to Boyd's office.

Harry Hillaker, the project director for the F-111 and the man who met Boyd at Eglin, was one of the first. Hillaker and Boyd had stayed in touch and found they had much in common in their beliefs about fighter aircraft. Each wanted to work with the other. Hillaker had an extra incentive, as General Dynamics was reeling over the bad press about the F-111 and was seeking a way to redeem itself. But the company was not agile enough, could not move quickly enough, and didn't invest enough design effort and soon was thrown out of the running. Eventually, they would have another chance.

Defense contractors had a cozy relationship with the Pentagon. Their friends were congressmen and senators, cabinet officers and administration officials, and top generals. But it was a peculiarity of the military that to get something done, the contractors had to go through young project officers, usually lieutenant colonels or full colonels. They were used to swaying these men by taking them to expensive Washington restaurants and ordering lobster and steak and wine and picking up the tab. Defense contractors are powerful men. And they thought this young major, this John Boyd, could be easily influenced.

When the contractors came into Boyd's briefing room, he was loaded with smart juice and smoking a Dutch Master. He stood atop a small platform, looked over his congregation of contractors, and preached a new gospel, the gospel of E-M. When the contractors understood, when they had a vision of the promised land, Boyd's high, bugling laugh could be heard far down the halls. But when they did not understand or, even worse, when they ignored his vision and presumed to tell him what his ideal fighter should be — usually a modification of one of their existing airplanes — he held a clenched fist in the air and moved it up and down and shook his head and scornfully said, "Stroking the bishop. You're just stroking the bishop."

When contractors said some of Boyd's engineering specifications could not be met or that a fighter could not do what Boyd wanted it to do, he listened, chewed on his hand, and stared unblinkingly at the contractor. When he had enough he stopped chewing, spit out pieces of skin, jabbed the contractor in the chest, and exploded. "You are the dumbest son of a bitch God ever made" or "You don't know what the fuck you're talking about" or "You stupid fuck. That will never work."

Defense contractors are not used to being talked to in such a fashion. Often they sat there a moment in shock. Boyd moved even closer and shouted louder, "Do you get my meaning?" or "Do you hear what I'm saying to you?"

Almost every time a defense contractor left his office, Boyd turned around and said to all in hearing, sometimes before the contractor was through the door, "The one thing you can always expect from a contractor is that he will hand you a load of shit." If he suspected a contractor was trying to deceive him, he looked for evidence. He prepared for a confrontation. When he found the evidence, he did not say he had found the proverbial smoking gun. Instead he walked into his office, threw his arms wide, and trumpeted, "I have found the dripping cock."

Secretaries wept at Boyd's language. Several threatened to quit. When generals complained about Boyd's language, he said he did not mean to sound disrespectful. "I'm just a dumb fighter pilot. I don't know any better. I had an IQ test in high school and they gave me a ninety." For several months Boyd was not allowed to brief generals and members of Congress. But the Air Force had to have the F-X and no one else preached the gospel as convincingly as Boyd. Soon he was back, briefing VIPs. And his language was the same.

Boyd was impatient and wanted to get a fixed design and see it move into production and into the air. All these needless requirements and senseless questions he saw as part of the conspiracy at Wright-Pat to foul up his airplane. It was the same conspiracy that had kept him from being promoted below the zone to lieutenant colonel.

Wright-Pat was a constant barrier to Boyd. An early and continuing roadblock in the F-X design was the presentation of drag polars. Drag polars — or polars, as they are commonly known — show estimates of the total drag of the airplane as a function of the airplane's angle of attack (i.e., how high the nose is relative to the airstream). Accurate polars are a critical part of the design process and vital to E-M calculations. It is almost a given in aircraft design that an aircraft never has the thrust the contractor says it will have and always has more drag than the contractor predicts. Wright-Pat sent Boyd a collection of polars for the new design that simply looked too good to be true. He began calling the engineers at Wright-Pat to question their estimates, and with each call they grew more patronizing. They had been estimating polars for years on all sorts of aircraft and no one else had complained. To them Boyd was a Pentagon desk jockey who simply did not understand polars.

Finally Boyd demanded a meeting. He checked out a T-33 and flew to Dayton. A group of lieutenant colonels and full colonels, along with several high-ranking civilians, were sitting around a conference table in the Flight Dynamics Lab when Boyd walked in. He got straight to the point. He said the data he had been given were wrong and that this time he wanted good data. He cited chapter and verse. From his briefcase he pulled the drag polars Wright-Pat had derived. Their polars showed that the smaller the wing, the greater the lift. This is dumb, Boyd said. People in the Flight Dynamics Lab need to get on the ball.

The senior colonel stared at Boyd, then made it clear that data from the Flight Dynamics Lab were Air Force gospel. The lab was not at fault if the major could not understand. The level of acrimony escalated. The lieutenant colonels joined the fray and then the civilians.

Finally an exasperated Boyd jerked his wallet from his hip pocket and threw it onto the middle of the conference table. It skidded to a stop in front of the colonel. The conversation stopped and everyone stared at Boyd. He looked around the table, staring each man in the eye. Then he pointed at the wallet. "Everything in there says you fuckers are lying."

When Boyd returned to the Pentagon, a full colonel was waiting. He chewed Boyd out for insulting a senior officer. He said the general in charge of Research and Development for the Air Force was so angry that he was about to transfer Boyd to Alaska. The two men marched down the hall to the general's office. Boyd was still carrying the briefcase he had taken to Wright-Pat.

"Major Boyd, I have just one question," the general said. "Did you tell that colonel at Wright-Pat he was a lying fucker?"

"Yes, Sir, I did."

"You are out of here. You are being transferred." The general launched his own chewing-out session about respecting senior officers and insubordination and how lucky Boyd was that he was only being transferred. When he paused, Boyd said, "Sir, do you want to know why I said that?"

"No."

"I think you do. Give me one minute." He opened his briefcase.

Reluctantly, the general looked at the drag polars. "Know how to read these, General?"

"Yes."

The general moved his finger over the polars. "They're saying . . ."

"Yes, Sir, they are saying the smaller the wing, the greater the lift."

"That means . . ."

"Yes, Sir, that means the greatest lift would come if there were no wing at all."

The general picked up his telephone and called Wright-Pat. And Boyd swears that as the general picked up the phone, he muttered, "They *are* lying fuckers."

Once again Boyd was protected by a benevolent general. And his list of enemies grew longer.

Even Sprey suggested that perhaps Boyd was a bit confrontational. "Tiger, I've got to have accurate information," Boyd responded. "There is no such thing as being too careful about information. I need the right information to separate the wheat from the chaff. Those who can't separate the wheat from the chaff don't matter."

Trade-offs are the heart and soul of aircraft design. If an engineer wanted greater range, he knew acceleration would be diminished. If he wanted greater speed, the wings would have to be smaller, and that, in turn, would decrease turning ability. If he wanted a small airplane, the engine, wings, or range would shrink. All things have to be wrapped inside the skin of a fighter. Design discipline is the key. The engineer must remember the mission.

By using E-M and ever more sophisticated computers, Boyd was able to consider a virtually limitless number of variables. His trade-offs were orders of magnitude more complicated than had ever been done before. He was going through thousands of designs. The slightest variation in one performance area had an impact all across the design spectrum.

Boyd's trade-offs using E-M and computers were a turning point in aviation design and aviation history. He was working with the entire maneuvering envelope of a proposed fighter, something that had never been done before. Sprey was there every step of the way. Soon he would have the chance to put into practice all he was learning from Boyd.

Boyd's first ER in the Pentagon covered the period from September 8, 1966, through June 9, 1967. Rarely has there been an ER with such disagreements between the reviewing officer and the indorsing officer. On the front side the colonel who wrote the ER gave Boyd less than top marks in four categories. The colonel dwelled on Boyd's scientific and research contributions to the F-X program and said, "If Major Boyd were evaluated solely on technical competence, he would be rated absolutely superior." This sounds complimentary. But the ER of a major being considered for promotion should not talk about technical competence; rather it should talk about his ability to lead, to obtain the maximum work from his subordinates, to show a potential for higher rank and greater responsibilities. Talking about a major's technical competence is a signal to the promotion board that this officer is not qualified for further advancement. The colonel who wrote the indorsement ended by saying, "Maj. Boyd is very opinionated and at times tends to be argumentative." It is a damning, career-stopping ER.

But once again a superior comes to Boyd's aid. The officer writing the additional indorsement says that Boyd is not opinionated and argumentative but is advocating a new advanced fighter, that there are many designs and systems, and that Boyd usually is right in what he wants. "He has made himself an authority on the subject and is more knowledgeable and informed in this field than his rating officials." Adding heft to the colonel's additional indorsement is still another indorsement from a major general. The general says Boyd is a "promising officer, strongly motivated and one who gives his best effort toward any assignment." He says Boyd "... should be promoted to Lt. Colonel immediately."

Not being promoted below the zone to lieutenant colonel still weighed on Boyd. He brought up the subject in conversation, sometimes in an unusual fashion. In the summer of 1967 he went to Europe and the Pacific to brief top commanders on the F-X. During one briefing in Europe to a four-star general, the general mused on how this new aircraft would require intensive pilot training. The general then boasted about the safety record of fighter pilots under his command and told how he had had no training accidents for several years.

"General, if you're not having accidents, your training program is not what it should be," Boyd said. He told the general about Nellis and how realistic the training was — and how it resulted in a ten-to-one exchange ratio in Korea. "Goddammit, General, you need more accidents," he said. "You need to kill some pilots."

The general stared at Boyd, horrified at what a training accident would do to his career. The general made it clear that Boyd was not only flirting with insubordination but advocating dangerous and irresponsible ideas. He hinted of disciplinary action.

"I don't know what you can do, General," Boyd said. "I was only responding to what you said."

"Promotion boards can be influenced," the general said.

"I've been passed over," Boyd said.

But he became a lieutenant colonel soon after.

If there was a turning point, a time when even the most jingoistic Air Force general at last understood that Communist forces could build fighter aircraft superior to anything that America put in the air, it was Vietnam in 1967, the worst year of the war for the Air Force. It finally sank in that, as Boyd had said for years, the Air Force had no true air-to-air fighter. It is said that combat is the ultimate and unkindest judge of fighter aircraft. That was certainly true in Vietnam. The long-boasted-about ten-to-one exchange ratio from Korea sank close to parity in North Vietnam; at one time it even favored the North Vietnamese. When the war finally ended, one Air Force pilot would be an ace. North Vietnam would have sixteen.

While 1967 was a dismal year for the Air Force, it was also the year that two of Boyd's former students from the Fighter Weapons School at Nellis proved that while America might not have superior aircraft, it had superior pilots.

When old fighter pilots gather to retell the stories of their glory days, they sometimes forget who declared mechanical problems and aborted the mission, and they sometimes forget who led the great missions, and they sometimes make themselves gunfighters when they were actually wingmen. But in every war there are bigger-than-life men whose exploits are so far beyond what most mortals can accomplish that they are in a separate category. Merely to fly with such men is enough glory for most pilots. Every maneuver and every detail of certain missions flown by these men are told and retold, are taught to young pilots, and are held out as the pinnacle of what a fighter pilot can accomplish.

Two of Boyd's former FWS students, Everett "Razz" Raspberry and Ron Catton, wrote their names large in the history of aerial combat in 1967. For different reasons, both became legends in the fighter-pilot community. And for as long as old fighter pilots gather to tell and retell the stories of the long-ago days when they strapped on jet aircraft to do battle in the heavens, they will talk of what Razz and Catton did that year.

It is the way of fighter pilots that Razz and Catton rarely talk of the events of 1967. But when they do, they always talk of Boyd's influence on what happened. Razz was first. He found glory on what would be the most celebrated date of the Vietnam War for the Air Force: January 2, 1967 — the day of Mission Bolo.

At the time, the North Vietnamese Air Force was shredding the ranks of F-105 drivers. So many F-105s were shot down along a mountain range near Hanoi that the pilots called it "Thud Ridge." The North Vietnamese knew the refueling corridors flown by Thuds, the electronic signatures, radio frequencies, and the peculiar idiom of Thud drivers. Most of all they knew how vulnerable the heavily laden Thuds were as they approached the target. But again and again the Thuds went up North loaded with bombs, sluggish, barely maneuverable, and found MiGs waiting.

The legendary Robin Olds, commander of the "Wolfpack" — the 8th Tactical Fighter Wing at Ubon, Thailand — grew weary with the F-105 mortality rate and came up with the plan for Mission Bolo. Like most great battle plans, it was simple in the extreme: his F-4s would pretend to be F-105s. Their target (via the heart of the infamous Route Pack VI, the deadliest collection of AAA, missiles, and enemy fighters the world has ever known) was the North Vietnamese air base at Phuc Yen. They would fly the same refueling tracks flown by Thuds, use the radio frequencies, automobile call signs, and even the specialized lingo of Thud drivers. They would attach electronic countermeasure pods to the F-4s so they could send out an electronic signature like that of the Thud. And if the gods of war smiled upon them, MiG pilots would be waiting. But instead of finding F-105s wallowing around trying to escape, the MiG pilots would confront Phantom drivers anxious for payback.

It was a bold plan. It was also dangerous. Except for the element of surprise, much of the advantage seemed to be with the MiGs, which were so nimble that in a turning fight they could eat an F-4 for lunch. MiG drivers were highly experienced pilots who fought year after year and were not rotated home after one hundred missions as were Air Force pilots. In addition, most of the Air Force pilots being assigned to Vietnam had been trained under SAC doctrine of intercepting enemy bombers and delivering nuclear weapons. Their rat-racing skills left much to be desired. To make this situation worse, transport pilots and SAC pilots were being assigned to Vietnam to get their tickets punched — to fly the one hundred missions and go home as combat veterans. They often had little time in fighters.

Razz was in the 555th Fighter Squadron, the Triple Nickel. Because he was an FWS graduate, it was his job to teach tactics and train the pilots throughout the wing. The F-4C had no guns and the missiles were virtually useless. In fact, of all the tactical weapons employed in Vietnam, air-to-air missiles ranked among the most disappointing. Sparrow missiles performed so poorly they were considered little more than extra weight; more than one pilot punched them off his aircraft as soon as he was away from his home base. And the

213

AIM-9 had such a narrow launch envelope — no more than two positive Gs or one negative G — that it was useless in a turning fight.

Razz had his work cut out. The success of Mission Bolo depended in large part on him. Then he remembered the maneuver John Boyd taught at the FWS, the one that had so astonished him with its elegant simplicity: the roll to the outside in order to gain the tactical advantage. It was a maneuver contrary to everything a fighter pilot thought he knew about aerial combat, but a maneuver that put a pilot tight in on his adversary's six, well within the narrow missile-launching limitations. Razz briefed more than sixty pilots in the wing. And after every mission up North, he had pilots practice the maneuver on the way back to Ubon. Again and again they practiced.

Then came January 2.

Razz was to lead Ford Flight. But Chappie James, vice commander of the wing, came to him the night before and said, "Razz, I got good news and I got bad news. The bad news is I'm taking over the lead of Ford Flight. The good news is you'll be flying my wing."

"Oh, shit," Razz thought.

Razz had been up North many times. But it seemed that every time Chappie James headed toward Route Pack VI, the vice commander developed mechanical problems and had to return to base.

Razz took off and checked his eight missiles. Seven indicated malfunctions. Only one came on-line and he selected it to fire first. Ford Flight entered Route Pack VI at 17,000 feet, the altitude used by F-105s and an altitude that, coincidentally, gave the F-4s an abundance of energy. The flight crossed the Black River and flight lead radioed, "Green 'em up" — the command given by a Thud leader that told his pilots to set their switches for bomb delivery.

North Vietnamese radar operators observed and heard. MiGs were vectored to the six of every flight approaching Phuc Yen. Chappie James was Ford 1 and Razz was Ford 2. Ford 3 and 4 were far out of position, several miles off to the right. Razz and Chappie James were alone when Razz saw a MiG maneuvering to attack James.

"Ford lead, break right," Razz radioed.

Chappie James motored on.

The MiG was almost in position.

Maybe Chappie James had forgotten his call sign.

"Chappie, break right!"

214

Chappie James motored on, wings level.

Razz did what wingmen are trained to do: he protected his leader. He moved between James and the MiG and rocked up on a wingtip to clear before engaging. The MiG pilot did the same. Razz and the MiG pilot were canopy to canopy, pulling heavy Gs, spiraling down and then up, maneuvering to get on the other's six. The MiG pilot was good, but he was rat-racing with the man who invented the Raspberry Roll and he never had a chance. Razz gained the advantage. The MiG pilot went for separation and pulled heavy Gs. Razz rolled to the outside and came down on the MiG's six. The MiG pilot reversed his turn, a fatal mistake. Razz unloaded his Gs, got a strong aural tone, and squeezed the trigger. As the missile left the rails, the sun glinted off the MiG cockpit and the missile went straight toward the light. It exploded in the cockpit and Razz had his first MiG.

Wolfpack pilots shot down seven MiGs that day, plus two probables (MiGs that disappeared into an overcast with missiles tracking strong and true). January 2, 1967, was the greatest day the Air Force had during the Vietnam War. Bolo went into the history books. But what Razz remembers is that six of the seven kills that day were done by pilots who used John Boyd's outside roll at some point in the engagement. Razz says Boyd was the father of that great victory as surely as if he had led the mission.

Back in the Pentagon, where Boyd's office kept close track of aerial engagements in Vietnam, there was rejoicing. Fighter pilots throughout the Building quickly learned the details of the engagement and were amazed at the roll-to-the-outside maneuver. Boyd prowled the halls telling one and all that "Razz is a great fighter pilot. He was one of my best students at the Fighter Weapons School. We used to do the E-M briefing together."

A few months later Razz got into a screaming low-level chase up near Thud Ridge, hanging tight on the six of a MiG. The MiG was at 300 feet and Razz was below the MiG when he fired his AIM-7 into the tailpipe. That kill put Razz into the record books: during the long air war in North Vietnam, no other Air Force pilot had a missile kill from a lower altitude.

Boyd, perhaps because he had given up his dream of being an ace, got a vicarious kick from the exploits of former students. "Yeah, Razz was up there not too far from the Chinese border," he told people in his office. "I bet our guys are sneaking across the border the way we did in Korea." Boyd beamed with pride. "If that MiG was only at three hundred feet, Razz must have been down in the weeds when he launched." He paused. "Goddamn F-4 is a Navy airplane; it's not a fighter. They give us shit for airplanes and we win anyway."

Ron Catton came to Ubon a few weeks after Bolo. He was a flight leader in the 433rd Tactical Fighter Squadron, "Satan's Angels." He soon had fifty-five missions in Route Pack VI, at that time more than any other Air Force pilot in a single combat tour. Usually, once a pilot flew ninety missions, his last ten missions before rotating to another assignment were in the relatively safe skies of the southern Route Packages. But Catton had come to fly and fight.

Once, Catton was leading a flight of four F-4s on what was supposed to be a routine bombing mission in Laos. A forward air controller radioed that he had discovered what he believed to be an enormous training area for enemy troops. Catton's flight was diverted to bomb the area. Catton's arrival over the target area elicited a virtual blanket of 57-millimeter flak, a phenomenon rarely seen in Laos and an indication that the forward air controller was correct in his assessment of what he had found.

Air Force policy was clear about how pilots dealt with heavily defended areas in North Vietnam and Laos. They were to descend no lower than 7,500 feet, make one bomb run, and then depart. "Shoot and scoot," the Air Force termed it. Pilots referred to it as "One pass, haul ass." That day Catton changed the policy. He ordered multiple low-altitude attacks. His flight was so low that all the pilots were taking ground fire as well as flak. It was the proverbial hornet's nest. Catton set his pilots up in a wagon wheel over the target. Each aircraft made several passes through an air-defense system almost as intense as that in Route Pack VI. One of the F-4s was always rolling in hot, switches set to pickle off a pair of 750-pound bombs. The target was smoking when Catton's flight departed.

The next day a team of Special Forces soldiers went in to assess the battle damage. They estimated that more than nine hundred enemy soldiers had been killed. The pilot who a few years earlier had been famous for puking on the floor of the police station in North Las Vegas and for almost being tossed out of the FWS proved once again what he was made of. Major Ron Catton was awarded a Silver Star for that day's work.

Catton was one of the Air Force's golden boys. His record at the FWS and during a tour with the Thunderbirds had been extraordinary. Now he had topped it off with a significant combat decoration. Catton was on his way to becoming a general. Near the end of his tour, he was nominated for another Silver Star because of his record number of missions into Route Pack VI. After six more missions, he would be reassigned as an instructor pilot to the FWS, where his combat experience would be invaluable to students. Then came his ninety-fourth mission, the day he commanded a force of fighters in Route Pack VI. His job was to protect the Thuds. The MiGs rose up from several locations and threatened the strike package. Catton recognized the feints and refused to be lured away from the Thuds. He recognized the main thrusts of the attack and deployed his F-4s against them. It was a masterful orchestration of pilots and aircraft performed by a master of battle. Every Thud put its bombs on the target that day. Every Thud returned home. It was a grand and glorious day for Catton and his men. Coming home Catton decided to celebrate with formation victory rolls. Two F-4s collided and the crews bailed out.

Usually a combat leader would face a court-martial for losing two aircraft in this fashion. Catton had been away for several days before the mission, and while he was gone the commander issued new operating procedures forbidding victory rolls. But the sergeant major had not posted the new rules on Catton's squadron bulletin board, so Catton was not brought before a court-martial. But the Air Force withdrew the second Silver Star, and the prized Nellis assignment was cancelled. A man who lost two F-4s is a poor example to students. Catton was ordered to the Pentagon, where sober and responsible senior officers could keep an eye on him.

He reported for duty in December 1967. When he walked into the personnel office, an elderly woman, a civilian who had worked there for dozens of years, smiled at him and said, "You are Major Ron Catton? I've been dying to meet you." Catton looked at her in bewilderment.

"In all the time I've been here I've never had an officer report in who was on the control roster."

The "control roster" was a way the military had to keep track of problem children. It meant Catton could not be considered for promotion during the next year and that he would have more frequent ERs. Someone would always be looking over his shoulder. He called Boyd and the two men met in a cafeteria. Boyd was feeling particularly proud because a few weeks earlier he finally had been promoted to lieutenant colonel. Shiny silver oak leaves adorned his collar.

Catton congratulated Boyd on his promotion and said, "Sir, I've got a problem."

Boyd clapped Catton on the shoulder and smiled. "So I hear. Don't worry, Tiger. You've been there before. You'll come out from under it."

Once again Boyd was right in his assessment of Catton.

During the summer of 1967, the Soviets introduced two new fighters: the swing-wing MiG-23 and the MiG-25. American fighter pilots laughed at the MiG-23 and said the only good thing about the F-111 was that the Soviets had copied it and thereby lost at least one generation of aircraft to bad technology. But the Air Force inflated the MiG-25 into a serious threat. Word leaked out that the aircraft could reach Mach 2.8 and altitudes far above the ceiling of the F-X. What the Air Force did not reveal was that if the MiG-25 reached Mach 2.8 it immediately had to land because the fuel was exhausted and the engine had to be replaced. Nevertheless, the "threat" of the MiG-25 meant the F-X suddenly had a much greater priority.

But a fundamental decision about the F-X had not been resolved. Boyd insisted that the aircraft be armed with guns as well as missiles, but the Air Force said this was the age of missiles, that guns were a backward step, and that the F-X should have only missiles.

The guns versus missiles argument is one of the most emotional arguments in the Air Force. It is utterly incomprehensible to non-pilots, most of whom probably think missiles are the best possible armament for a fighter. The rules of engagement in Vietnam, combined with poor-performing missiles, had shown what happened when fighter aircraft had no guns. The rules dictated that a U.S. pilot visually identify an enemy aircraft before firing a missile. But the minimum missile-launch range was far greater than the range at which an aircraft could be identified as friend or foe. That meant the pilot had to get in close, identify the enemy, then back off far enough to launch his missiles. Missiles could be evaded by the simplest of countermeasures. There was no countermeasure for a gun. Signs began showing up on the walls in the Pentagon: IT TAKES A FIGHTER WITH A GUN TO KILL A MIG-21.

Nevertheless, while it defies all logic, high-ranking Air Force officers ignored the lessons of history. After World War II, the Air Force said dogfights were a thing of the past. In the 1950s, Air Force generals said Korea was the last hurrah for the gunfighter. Then came Vietnam, which was supposed to be a push-button war that made dogfights obsolete. But Vietnam proved Boyd had been right about serious inadequacies in the new missiles. America needed a fighter with guns.

Then in the fall of 1967 there came to the Building one Mordecai Hod, head of the Israeli Air Force (IAF). He came to buy F-4 Phantoms. And he came wearing the aura of a man who was an icon in the fighter-pilot community. Under his leadership the IAF had done three things that got the attention of the U.S. Air Force. First, in the Six Day War of June, the Israeli Air Force shot down sixty Arab jets while losing only ten fighters — an exchange ratio of six to one. Second, *every Israeli kill was a gun kill.* And third, the Israelis — as the name of the war indicates — had moved quickly, decisively, and thoroughly at a time when the Americans had been at war in Vietnam for several years, and the war was escalating with no end in sight.

There was still another unspoken issue, a very big issue. Behind the issue were two assumptions: first, that Arab pilots and North Vietnamese pilots operated at roughly the same skill level. Second, that U.S. and Israeli pilots operated at roughly the same skill level. So how did the IAF achieve a six-to-one kill ratio against the Arabs while the Air Force was operating at near parity against the North Vietnamese?

The foundation for this line of reasoning was flawed in that years of combat made the North Vietnamese much better pilots than the Arabs. Nevertheless, either the Air Force was not nearly as good as it liked to believe or the Israelis were far better than the Air Force wanted to believe. A convocation of senior Air Force officers gathered to hear Hod deliver a classified briefing about the Six Day War.

When he had finished, a fighter pilot stood up and asked how the IAF got sixty gun kills.

Hod paused, shrugged, and said, "Why waste a missile on an Arab?"

Hod used humor and a diplomatic response to avoid saying Israeli pilots used guns because missiles didn't work. He depended on the United States for fighter aircraft and knew the Air Force was infatuated with missiles. His facetious response drew laughter. But behind the laughter was an unavoidable fact: the day of the gunfighter had not passed.

Chapter Fifteen

Saving the F-15

MARY Boyd says her husband changed after he went to the Pentagon, that he became more intense, less gregarious, and always on the defensive. Boyd was constantly angry about what he saw as careerism and corruption, and he brought the anger home.

When Boyd moved to Washington, he was so anxious to jump into the F-X fray that he would not take time to look for a place to live. Mary, taking care of the five children, did not have time to look either. For more than a month the Boyd family lived in a single room at the Breezeway Motel in Fairfax, Virginia. Then one day Boyd showed up and said to Mary, "I found us a place to live. It's over in Alexandria."

"Oh," Mary said. She couldn't generate enthusiasm for anything in Washington. She had not wanted to move from Eglin, where the broad and virtually empty beach was nearby and where Stephen rolled in the surf and found one of the few pleasures of his life. She had not wanted to drive up in the station wagon with five children while Boyd went on ahead in his Corvair. She had not wanted to live in an apartment.

Boyd drove her and the children to 4930 Beauregard Street, a new apartment project then called Brighton Square. It was only minutes from the Pentagon. He pointed to the door of a ground-level apartment, number T-3, and said, "I think you'll like this place." The apartment project was filled with young couples and children. Nearby were forests and open lots where children played without supervision. The apartment had three bedrooms: one for Boyd and Mary, one for Kathy and Mary Ellen, and one for Scott and Jeff. The den was converted into a bedroom for Stephen, who was now twelve. Big sliding glass doors covered one wall of the den-cum-bedroom and Stephen could enter and leave via his own door. For a boy wanting independence but who was forever bound to his wheelchair, this small measure of freedom was important.

The apartment project had no sidewalks and in the summer Stephen rolled his wheelchair through grass that rarely was mowed. In the winter he sometimes had to push his way through snow. "Why doesn't Dad get us a better place?" he asked his mother several times.

Mary smiled down at her son and said, "I'll talk to him about it."

Boyd would brook no argument. "What if we buy a house and are stuck with it?" he said. "What if we can't sell it when we leave? That happened in Atlanta. Houses always have expenses. But just paying the rent is no hassle. Besides, we are only going to be here a few years." When Mary continued to ask about owning a house, Boyd settled into a stock response: he nodded and said, "Yeah, we'll have to do that" and changed the subject.

The apartment on Beauregard Street became a symbol of how Boyd's family suffered because of his devotion to his work. In the years following the move, Boyd's family life devolved into a state of disarray from which it never recovered. Stephen began repairing television sets and stereos and various electronics. His sadness about his handicap had left him withdrawn and fiercely independent. Kathy's quiet and gentle nature slowly changed into a clinical depression. Jeff, shy and gentle, was hammered in discussions with his father. He found refuge with his collection of spiders and poisonous snakes. John Scott and Boyd had tumultuous arguments that turned into scuffles and, in at least one instance, into a fight. Mary Ellen was more like her father than any of the others; she was his "Snookums," and she broke his heart when she became ensnared in the drug culture. For years they did not speak. And all the children say today that their anger toward their father is rooted in his insistence on living in the tiny apartment.

The first time Mary met Sprey was at 10:30 one evening when he and Boyd left the Pentagon early. Boyd got up from the table and began making phone calls while Sprey and Mary were still eating. Mary confided to Sprey that people asked if she had ever thought of getting a job so there would be more money for the family. "They told me if I worked I would have more input into what went on around here," she said. She shrugged. She knew that was not true. "I can't take care of five kids and work. I'm not that efficient." She said a few people at the Pentagon asked Boyd why he lived in an apartment. After all, the mid-60s were a propitious time to invest in the Washington real estate market. A lieutenant colonel could buy a home that would only appreciate in value. But Boyd brushed off every such question with "I don't like to cut the grass."

Mary seemed bewildered by all that was going on around her. She told Christie and Sprey that when she and Boyd met at Iowa, she thought she was marrying an athlete who would become a coach and they would live in a small town in Iowa and join the country club and buy a little house and lead a quiet uneventful life. It was as if she had stepped onto what she thought was a sedate merry-go-round and found it was instead a cyclonic roller coaster.

She nodded toward her husband and with a rueful laugh said, "Look what I got."

Boyd and his family would live on Beauregard Street for the next twenty-two years.

Most fighter pilots fly until they are too old to pass the physical or until they are promoted into a nonflying job. Some even refuse promotions that would take them out of the cockpit. Once they lose their flying status, the rest of their life is anticlimactic. They often live near airports and turn their eyes upward and stare longingly at every passing jet.

It was not that way with Boyd. Few pilots have been as deeply involved with all aspects of fighter aviation as he. Yet in 1968 he lost interest in flying. As a Pentagon staff officer he was not allowed to fly fighters, only the venerable T-33 that fighter pilots looked on with considerable disdain. He did not always fly enough to maintain his flight-currency requirements and twice his boss took him up in a T-33 to regain currency, to enable him to keep his flying pay. But eventually his currency lapsed and Boyd did not regain it. Fellow pilots who knew his background were puzzled. "Why?" they asked. He shrugged and said, "I've done that."

It was as if he realized that not only had he moved beyond being a fighter pilot, but that he was about to move farther and deeper into other, more complex, and more important areas of his life and that he had to clear his mind of all extraneous matters.

Almost daily he brought new E-M graphs or new slides or the outline of a new briefing to Sprey. "Hey, Tiger, this is what I put together. What do you think?"

Sprey took the graphs and slides and briefings and studied them. After a while in his soft calm voice, he might say, "John, this slide is no good. Do you have a better way of showing this?"

Then the fight would begin. Sprey would explain why the slide was no good and Boyd would shout that it was perfect. Sprey would answer in his irrefutable and thus maddening manner. After Boyd had all he could take, he would slouch off to his office. About 4:00 A.M. Sprey's phone would ring and when he picked it up he barely had time to say "Hello" before Boyd barked, "What did you mean when you said that slide was no good?"

Sprey would calmly list the reasons. Boyd would argue and shout and finally end the conversation with a grunt and slam down the phone. He never said to Sprey, "You are right." But he would change the slide and later boast to Sprey of how strong his briefing was.

Time after time he came back from a briefing in exultation. One time he burst into Sprey's office and relived every exchange of his latest cape job. "Goddamn, Tiger, you should have been there. I hosed those sons of bitches. I stacked those goddamn generals up like cord wood."

Sprey was amused. "I think you like the body count."

Boyd stared at Sprey, thinking, and a wide grin sliced across his face.

Boyd won battles not only in the open and more or less public arenas, such as briefings, but also in the corridors and offices of the Pentagon, where politics is both byzantine and deadly. Here, one of his greatest weapons was his secret back-channel communication to the Air Force chief of staff. The chief often followed the Franklin Roosevelt theory of management, bypassing sycophantic generals and seeking out from among relatively junior officers a few men who would tell him the truth. The chief knew the culture of the Building and knew that, in many ways, he was the most ignorant man in the Air Force. Dozens of high-ranking officers put their fingers in the wind before they talked to him. Then they told him what they thought he wanted to hear. Boyd, and presumably a very few others, told him what he needed to know. Occasionally a colonel from the chief's office dropped into Boyd's office and said, "Can I buy you a cup of coffee?" And the two men sat in a corner of the cafeteria and the colonel said, "The chief wants to know . . ." And because Boyd gave him straight answers, the chief came to him again and again.

Boyd used these clandestine meetings to put forth his agenda for the F-X. The chief had enough confidence in Boyd's integrity that he agreed with Boyd about keeping down the weight of the aircraft. He sent down the order that Boyd asked for: the F-X will have a maximum weight of 40,000 pounds.

Since the F-X had sprung forth at 62,500 pounds and since many generals believed bigger was better, those generals now thought of the F-X as a lightweight fighter, almost a toy. Yet Boyd *still* was not happy. He wanted the F-X to weigh under 35,000 pounds.

Sprey never understood the way a real fighter pilot feels about a small aircraft until the day he and Boyd went out to Dulles Airport to fly a pylon racer, a small but very fast aircraft. Many pylon-racer pilots are the size of jockeys. It took Boyd several minutes to shoehorn himself into the cockpit. His shoulders were scrunched together and his knees were up around his neck. He had to bend forward so the canopy could be closed. Sprey thought Boyd must be miserable. But when Boyd looked up there was an expression of absolute glee on his face. "I love it! I love it!" he shouted through the canopy. And Sprey realized that for a true fighter pilot, a fighter aircraft cannot be too small.

By 1968, people in the Building did not know if Boyd was a genius or a wild man. The most favorable light that can be put on much of his behavior is that it was not that of the typical lieutenant colonel seeking advancement. Boyd's manner went beyond the coarseness, the close-in spittle-flying conversations, the arm waving and loud voice, the long hair and disheveled appearance, and the nocturnal work habits. If a superior gave Boyd an order and Boyd believed that order had implications deleterious to the F-X, he smiled and said, "Sir, I'll be happy to follow that order. But I want you to put it in writing." Generals like to issue verbal orders. That way if the results are not what the general expected, he can always deny he issued the order. While Boyd was within his rights to ask for written orders, his doing so infuriated generals. It clearly indicated he thought the general was wrong.

Once, he accosted a general in the corridor and began an intense conversation about lowering the weight of the F-X. Boyd was smoking a cigar and waving his arms and jabbing his finger. The general grew bored and turned and began edging away just as Boyd reached out to emphasize a point. The cigar burned a hole in the general's tie. For a moment those passing by froze as they stared at the tableau of an astonished general looking down at the hole in his tie. The hole smoldered on the edges and grew larger and larger and smoke rose around the general's face. He slapped out the burning tie, then spun and walked away. Boyd did not know the reason for the general's abrupt departure until someone said, "Damn, John, you just set the general's tie on fire."

Boyd looked down the hall after the general. "Yeah?" He chortled. "Bet that's the first time that ever happened to him."

Then there was the trance thing. Boyd would be in the middle of an intense conversation when suddenly his eyes would glaze over and he would stop talking and stare at the ceiling or the wall or out the window. It was as if he had been dealt a stunning blow to the head. He did not respond to questions. It might be two or three minutes before he awakened and picked up the conversation.

"What the hell happened?" someone occasionally asked. "What are you doing?"

"I just thought of a new E-M iteration" or "Something just occurred to me" or "I just got the answer to something I've been working on for several weeks."

Finally there was the pipper. For a while no one knew what he was doing. Then one day a secretary could no longer take the suspense and asked, "Colonel, are you all right?"

Boyd gave her a beatific smile and said, "I got the son of a bitch in my pipper."

A day or so later there was a rash of hot platters and cape jobs and Boyd won another battle and his triumphant laughter was heard in the halls.

Afterward, when Boyd put his feet atop his desk and began moving his pencil around and staring at the eraser, someone would say, "Oh, God. He's got somebody in his pipper." They knew hell was about to break loose all over again.

TAC always has seen speed as a vital part of air-to-air combat and wanted the F-X to have a Mach 3 top speed. Never mind that combat always starts at subsonic cruise speed and almost never reaches supersonic speed. Never mind that the trade-offs necessary for an airplane to reach such speeds would seriously degrade dogfighting performance. As for range, there is no faster way to degrade performance on a fighter than to ask for too much.

The Air Force feeling about weight was demonstrated during a meeting when the TAC colonel in charge of fighter requirements stood up and said, "I don't give a damn what the airplane weighs. The specs we gave you are the absolute validated TAC requirements. We have to have these things and I don't care about the weight. Besides, everyone knows a good big airplane is better than a good little airplane."

This was the very antithesis of what E-M revealed to Boyd.

In late spring of 1968, the Air Force was still so influenced by the F-111, so mesmerized by the heavy and expensive variable-geometry wing, that it had not made the fundamental decision as to whether the F-X would be a swing-wing or a fixed-wing design.

By now Boyd was losing major design battles. The Air Force insisted on a speed greater than Mach 2. The Air Force insisted on a radar with a thirty-six-inch dome — a requirement that dictated a much larger fuselage than Boyd wanted. Despite orders from the chief of staff, the F-X was now at an estimated 42,500 pounds (actually, it was much larger), and the performance, while unprecedented, was far degraded from what it could have been.

Sprey called the heavy and expensive additions "gold-plating." He had no patience with those who wanted to add so many heavy items that had nothing to do with shooting down another airplane — everything from nose wheel steering to boarding ladders to tail hook. "If you take off all the nonkill horseshit — everything not necessary to kill another aircraft — you can't believe how the performance goes up."

Boyd and Sprey were desperate. They decided to make one final effort to save the F-X. They would go back to the ideal aircraft. Night after night they labored at the Pentagon, drawing plans for an airplane they called the "Red Bird," a 33,000-pound stripped-down version of the F-X. Boyd briefed the Air Staff at the Pentagon. On July 18, 1968, Sprey wrote a letter to General James Ferguson, head of the Systems Command. The letter became famous and was passed around the Pentagon, where a few young officers saw it as a masterful dissection of how the Air Force had gone wrong. They admired the brilliance of the man who wrote it and privately wondered if they would have the courage to do such a thing. Others saw the letter as the bitter fulminations of the infamous Boyd / Sprey collaboration. The letter, classified "secret," said the Air Force had exercised no design discipline on the F-X, no willingness to forgo items that did not directly contribute to shooting down MiGs, but only added weight. Sprey detailed items such as the tail hook, nose wheel steering, and maintenance ladder and said the Air Force was so anxious to add gold-plating to the F-X that it was ignoring the ever-rising cost of the airplane. Accompanying the letter was a twenty-three-page, single-spaced list of technical recommendations to clean up the F-X.

Then Boyd and Sprey briefed General Ferguson, the man who would make the final decision on the F-X. The general agreed with everything Boyd and Sprey said. He liked their plans for the Red Bird and said it clearly was superior to the F-X.

Then the general dropped the other shoe. He said all the three-stars who worked for him wanted the bigger and heavier version of the F-X and that he could not go against their recommendations. He tried to console Boyd and Sprey by saying the F-X would be the best maneuvering fighter in history; why should they get wrapped around the axle trying to make it the perfect airplane?

Once again, the school of Bigger-Higher-Faster-Farther had won.

The Air Force was so busy fighting Boyd that it neglected to stay abreast of what the Navy was doing. A few weeks after the Ferguson meeting, the Navy announced that its version of the F-111 — the

F-111B — had turned out not to be carrier compatible and would not be accepted. The Navy told General Dynamics to cancel its F-111. Then Great Britain cancelled its order for the aircraft. This meant the Air Force was left holding the bag containing the expensive remains of the F-111 program. (The Air Force liked the airplane and continued buying it until the mid-1970s.) But that was not the half of it. Admirals testified to Congress that just because the Navy could not accept the F-111B, it did not mean the Navy could not continue to perform its vital role in national defense. In fact, they announced, the Navy had been secretly working on a plane called the F-14 Tomcat and if Congress would give the Navy the money already allocated for the F-111B, the Navy could go ahead and build the F-14.

The Navy theory about interservice politics is that once the enemy is down, they should slash his throat, burn his remains, bury the ashes, then sow salt over the land where the ashes are buried. So not surprisingly, the Navy told Congress the F-X had a fundamental flaw, a flaw so serious that development should be stopped: the F-X could not reach the high speeds or high altitudes of the MiG-25 and thus could not shoot down the most serious threat presented by Soviet aircraft. But America should not worry. If the Air Force was unable to design an aircraft capable of meeting the Soviet threat, the Navy was glad to help out. This phantasmagorical aircraft we are developing, this F-14, will do everything and more than the F-X is supposed to do. We will be glad to sell the F-14 to the Air Force.

The Air Force countered the first Navy attack by saying the Mach 2.5 "burst speed" of the F-X and the addition of Sparrow missiles meant the F-X could handle the MiG-25. But the Navy had powerful friends. Some of those friends in Congress had serious questions about the F-X. The Navy's offer to sell the F-14 to the Air Force quickly gained acceptance.

An Air Force general was summoned to testify about the F-X to an ad hoc Tactical Aviation Subcommittee that was part of the House Armed Services Committee. Boyd was the expert on the F-X, so he accompanied the general. Representative Mendel Rivers of South Carolina, a state about to sink into the Atlantic from the weight of the Navy bases located there, chaired the House Armed Services Committee. His presence dominated the Tactical Aviation Subcommittee. Boyd and the general were testifying before a group that openly believed the F-14 was superior to the F-X. And Rivers was always willing to help out the Navy.

As the general answered question after question, Boyd realized where the queries were leading. The survival of the F-X would be based on a single issue: whether or not it was a swing-wing design. The subcommittee and the committee and Representative Rivers were not going to approve a swing-wing design for the F-X when the Navy was building a swing-wing aircraft that was farther along in production.

A member of the subcommittee scratched his head and in a non-committal tone, almost as an aside, asked the general if the Air Force had made a decision about the wing design.

The general paused. Boyd knew that the future of the nonnuclear Air Force hung in the balance; all the work he had done on the F-X was crystallized in that one frozen moment. He leaped into the breach. "Yes, Sir, we have. The Air Force does not believe a variable-geometry wing is the answer. In fact, we believe the fixed-wing air-craft is a superior design. The F-X will be a fixed-wing aircraft."

It is difficult to know who was the most surprised — the general or the members of the subcommittee. The general stared at Boyd in disbelief. No decision had been made on the wing design. And now a lieutenant colonel on his own initiative had made a decision that was the prerogative of a four-star general.

"General, is that correct?" asked a member of the committee.

Boyd whispered to the general what was happening. The general thought for a moment, looked at the congressman, swallowed, and said, "That is correct. The Air Force has decided our aircraft will be a fixed-wing design."

Upon his return to the Pentagon, Boyd immediately called the colonel who worked for the chief of staff and told him why he had made the decision. "I don't have the final numbers," he said. "Wright-Pat is sitting on data I need. But I believe the weight penalties of the variable-geometry wing more than offset the aerodynamic benefits. I believe the fixed wing is better. If we had said anything else, the committee would have forced the F-14 on us." The chief agreed.

Which is how the F-X came to be a fixed-wing aircraft.

Which is how John Boyd saved the Air Force from having to eat another saltwater airplane.

No transcripts from either the Senate Armed Services Committee or the House Armed Services Committee indicate when the F-X became a fixed-wing aircraft. It is clear from the transcripts of both committees that the Air Force wanted the variable-geometry wing until late 1968. (The ad hoc committee kept no transcripts.) But both Tom Christie and Pierre Sprey talked with Boyd immediately after the hearing and are convinced events took place as Boyd described them. Also, from the day of the hearing onward, there were no more Air Force references to the F-X being a swing-wing aircraft.

History has proven Boyd correct in picking the fixed-wing design. The variable-sweep wing was one of the major aviation engineering blunders of the century. Hollywood and the movie *Top Gun* notwithstanding, the F-14 Tomcat is a lumbering, poor-performing, aerial truck. It weighs about fifty-four thousand pounds. Add on external fuel tanks and missiles and the weight is about seventy thousand pounds. It is what fighter pilots call a "grape": squeeze it in a couple of hard turns and all the energy oozes out. That energy cannot be quickly regained, and the aircraft becomes an easy target.

Navy admirals strongly discourage simulated battles between the F-14 and the latest Air Force fighters. But those engagements occasionally take place. And when they do, given pilots of equal ability, the F-14 always loses.

After the Air Force was locked into the fixed-wing design for the F-X, the "X" designation was dropped in favor of a numerical designation, and since the Navy had the F-14, the F-X became the F-15.

Boyd was disgusted. He could tell that his dream for the pure fighter aircraft had vanished. Yes, he had cut some weight, and yes, he had killed the variable-sweep wing. But it had taken just about everything out of him to fight and fight and fight for so much that was so obvious. He knew that in its inexorable way the Air Force would add more gold-plating, more missions, to the F-15 until one day it would be barely recognizable. On October 24, 1968, he submitted papers saying he would retire the next year.

Chapter Sixteen

Ride of the Valkyries

THE year 1969 was a curious and bewildering one for America. It was the year Neil Armstrong walked on the moon, the year of Woodstock, and the year *Sesame Street* made its debut on public television. It was the year of war rallies and the year the My Lai story broke — the year a humiliated Lyndon Johnson left Washington to be replaced by an exultant Richard Nixon, who announced the beginning of troop withdrawal from Vietnam.

The year 1969 was also the year that Pierre Sprey demonstrated just what sort of men were these Acolytes, these men beginning to gather around Boyd and devote their lives to his goals and ideals. Sprey was even more bitter than Boyd over what happened to the F-15. He had come to the Pentagon from the defense industry solely because he wanted to have an impact on the bloated defense budget and be part of acquiring better weapons for soldiers and airmen. His first effort, born in high idealism and great hope, had been gold-plated by Blue Suiters and transmogrified into something far less than it could have been. The F-15 was a learning experience that prepared him for an even more difficult task. He was about to loose his considerable talents on developing another airplane, *an airplane the Air Force did not want.*

To fully appreciate what Sprey did, one must remember that close air support — bombing missions that support ground troops — has never been a priority mission for the Air Force. Nevertheless, the Air Force officially owned the CAS mission, and no branch of the service wants to lose a mission, because losing a mission means losing money. The Air Force paid lip service to the CAS mission, making just enough effort to prevent the Army from taking it over. The best way to show how the Air Force looked upon CAS is that it *never* — not in World War II, not in Korea, and not in 1969 — had an airplane dedicated to CAS. Air Force practice was to take one of the worst aircraft in its inventory and designate it a close air support airplane. The F-84 in Korea is an example. In Vietnam, the Air Force used a cast-off Navy airplane: the propeller-driven A-1, which was forced on the Air Force by Secretary of Defense McNamara. The Air Force was embarrassed by the A-1, never mind that it turned out to be one of the best CAS aircraft used in combat up to that time. But in 1969 the Air Force learned that the Army wanted to develop a new helicopter called the "Cheyenne." The most startling thing about the Cheyenne was that it was so technologically complex that it cost more than an F-4. This frightened the Air Force. This meant the Army was going to make a run at taking over the CAS mission *and* the CAS money.

In order not to be stigmatized as the chief of staff who lost the CAS mission, the Air Force chief had to develop a CAS airplane and it had to be cheaper than the Cheyenne. The idea of a dedicated CAS aircraft was anathema to all senior Air Force officers below the chief of staff. Blue Suiters would fight the chief tooth and claw, but the fight would not be out in the open. The chief knew that his subordinates would pledge their support but then, in the bureaucratic warrens that are the refuge of the careerist, would wage a sub-rosa war to sabotage the project.

Thus, whoever directed the CAS program must be strong enough to stand against the generals. He would have to be smart and supremely focused, with the self-confidence of a buccaneer and the armor of a dinosaur. The chief thought he knew such a man. He sent an emissary to Pierre Sprey with the question, "Were you serious about what you wrote in your interdiction study about the need for close air support?"

The question rankled Sprey. He would not have worked seven days a week for a year on something he was not serious about. "Of course."

"Then you have another job if you want it."

The big problem was that Sprey's involvement could not be made public. He was still Public Enemy Number One to the Air Force. People who cared about their careers were not seen entering his office. Few people spoke to him in the halls. If his role in the CAS project became public, the long knives would come out. No, Pierre Sprey would have to stay in the background.

So Sprey's new job was a night job. He worked in Systems Analysis for the secretary of defense during the day and then about 5:00 P.M. began his unofficial job for the Air Force on an airplane now designated the A-X. He led the technical design team working for Colonel Avery Kay, an Air Force hero who had been lead bombardier on the Schweinfurt raid in World War II. Sprey wrote the specifications for the A-X; it was his responsibility, his airplane.

The A-X was one of the more bizarre acquisition projects in the history of the Air Force in that it was developed solely for bureaucratic reasons. The Air Force usually takes a deep proprietary interest in its new airplanes. They are touted as the best of the species and another example of how the U.S. Air Force is the best air force in the world. But the A-X was the most unpopular airplane the Air Force ever built. Because it was unpopular, TAC and Wright-Pat and the Systems Command and all the people who gold-plated the F-15 did not want their fingerprints on it. The A-X was a leprous project led by a pariah.

Usually there are no cost constraints on an aircraft-design program. Politically there are often many reasons to maximize costs. In all the history of the Air Force, the A-X was the single exception. It *had* to be cheap. It *had* to cost less than the Cheyenne.

Few men are as methodical as Sprey. He began by wanting to know what functions were needed in a CAS airplane. To find out he sought out A-1 pilots who flew CAS missions in Vietnam. These young officers were energized by the chance to have their recent combat experience considered in designing the first designated CAS airplane the Air Force ever had. None of this "one pass, haul ass" stuff for these guys — to protect troops on the ground they needed loiter time over a target. They needed an airplane, they said, with long legs. Much of the time hard-to-see targets and the smoke and haze of the battlefield mean a CAS pilot must work low and tight and slow, so they wanted maneuverability at slow speeds. When friendly forces are in dire straits, they need an airplane that can wreak hell, death, and destruction, an airplane the very sight of which will turn an enemy soldier's bowels to water, so they wanted lethal weapons, preferably cannon. Working low and tight as a good CAS pilot must do means the "gomers" will shoot at them with everything from rifles to AAA to missiles, so they wanted an airplane that could take hits and still bring its pilot home. They wanted survivability.

Survivability was an issue that particularly resonated with Sprey. In doing research for his interdiction study, he read how more than 85 percent of all aircraft losses in World War II and Korea were from fire or loss of control. Several bullets in the right place and crucial aircraft systems were burned or destroyed. It was almost impossible to get out of the airplanes once they were damaged or on fire. Thousands of good men had died because of bad design, and Sprey was determined not to let that happen on the A-X.

Sprey was fascinated by Hans Rudel, the legendary tank-killing German pilot of World War II who still is considered the greatest CAS pilot of all time. Sprey insisted that everyone on the A-X project read *Stuka Pilot,* Rudel's wartime biography that told how he flew 2,530 missions and destroyed 511 tanks.

Because maneuverability is so important in CAS, Sprey used Boyd's E-M Theory and ideas about trade-offs. Time after time, Sprey was now the one who took the charts and diagrams to Boyd and said, "Hey, John, check out what I'm doing." Boyd had the vision to understand the importance of CAS, although, like most fighter pilots, he had little personal interest in the mission. He glanced at the paperwork, slapped Sprey on the back, and said, "Good work, Tiger. Keep it up."

The colonel who was Boyd's boss detested everything about the A-X and openly criticized the project. As the man in charge of fighter requirements, his was a respected voice. Then one day the colonel from the chief of staff's office dropped by Boyd's office and invited him for a cup of coffee. The two men sat in a corner of the cafeteria and the colonel said in effect, "Your boss's comments about the A-X and his obstruction of the project have reached the chief. Tell your boss this criticism has to end. The A-X project is about saving a mission for the Air Force."

Boyd went to his boss, shut the door, and said, "There are high-ranking officers in the Building who want you to lay off the A-X. The senior leadership is behind it." He emphasized the "high ranking" and the "senior leadership." The colonel ignored the message and continued his bitter denunciation of the airplane. A few weeks later he was summarily fired and given twenty-four hours to clean out his desk.

Sprey exercised on the A-X perhaps the tightest design discipline that has ever existed on an Air Force project. He worked in a strange confluence of serendipitous forces. Sprey had an iron will and passionate belief about what would make a great CAS airplane, and all those Air Force decision makers who could have gold-plated the airplane had a fervent desire to keep their distance. Tactical Air Command and Wright-Pat didn't even attend A-X meetings. Sprey pushed through an austere design in which he got everything he wanted — almost.

He lost two significant battles. He wanted a single-engine airplane, while the Air Force insisted on two engines. And he wanted a small maneuverable aircraft, while the Air Force wanted a much bigger airplane. In the end the airplane was bigger than necessary and its maneuvering performance was degraded by the insistence on carrying too many bombs.

Once the A-X concept formulation package was finished, the secretary of the Air Force and the secretary of defense approved the design. Congress appropriated the initial R&D money, and a request for proposal (RFP) was sent out. In the RFP, Sprey told the contractors they could not respond with the usual two-foot-tall stack of documents. The response had to be limited to thirty pages and confined to pure design — no smoke and mirrors. Even more unprecedented, airplanes from two contractors would be picked and the Air Force would supervise a combat-type fly-off between two flying prototypes. Specifications demanded that the fuel and the engine be in separate parts of the aircraft. Fuel tanks had to be explosion-proof. To make sure this was done, sections of the wing and fuselage would be fired at with Soviet weapons. And, oh yes, this must be done under simulated flight conditions with wind blowing over the prototypes being fired upon. Wright-Pat said no facility existed for such tests and that the resulting explosions would be too dangerous. Sprey told them to take the propeller and engine off a World War II B-50, attach them firmly to a solid stand, run up the engine, and let the prop wash go over the fuselage and wings. They did and several years later proudly took credit for what they termed the world's first ballistic wind tunnel.

Rather than having flammable and vulnerable hydraulic controls, the A-X would have mechanical cables and push rods — redundant dual cables — to control the flight surfaces. Sprey insisted that the A-X must be able to maintain flight even with half the control surfaces shot away. As for armament, the A-X was built around a radical new cannon that fired banana-sized depleted uranium bullets. To protect the pilot, the cockpit was surrounded by a titanium bathtub.

The Air Force loathed everything about the A-X, which soon would be known as the A-10. Jokes were made that it was so slow that it suffered bird strikes — from the rear — and that instead of carrying a clock, the cockpit had a calendar. The aircraft was so ugly it was called the "Warthog." Many in the Air Force said no airplane could perform or survive in combat as this airplane was supposed to perform. It would be almost twenty years before the A-10 had the chance to demonstrate just how wrong its detractors were.

It was in 1969 that Boyd laid the cornerstone for one of his greatest bureaucratic victories.

Two players crucial to the victory, Defense Secretary Melvin Laird and Deputy Defense Secretary David Packard, moved onstage early in the year. But the drama was not yet ready to be played out. One character was missing.

He was a full colonel, a volatile, hand-waving test pilot and fighter pilot named Everest Riccioni. Riccioni took over the Development Planning Office, part of the department where Boyd worked in early 1969. Boyd and Sprey briefed Riccioni on their early work with the F-X and found a receptive audience. Riccioni had long favored the idea of a lightweight, high thrust-to-weight fighter similar in some respects to what Boyd and Sprey wanted.

Riccioni is a curious fellow. He is a professional Italian in whom both tears and laughter are always near the surface. He is so sensitive that his feelings can be hurt with a harsh look, and he has an unending need for recognition. Riccioni flew P-38s and P-51s in World War II and then got an undergraduate degree in aeronautical engineering and a master's degree in applied mathematics before going to MIT to work on a doctorate in astronautical engineering (he did the course work but dropped out without writing a thesis). He was an instructor at the Air Force Academy, where he taught Astronautics 551 — a course dealing with the mathematical physics of space motion, perhaps the most advanced course at the Academy. Both Riccioni's brilliance and naïveté were manifested at the Academy when he wrote a book called *Tigers Airborne,* a book on aerial tactics. In the book Riccioni said Air Force tactics not only were stupid, but could get pilots killed in combat. He said it in such a harsh and unequivocal fashion that the Air Force had to respond: he was not allowed to publish the manuscript, and, unbeknownst to him, his superiors sent the manuscript to Boyd for comments. Boyd then was stationed at Eglin and did not know Riccioni, but he sensed that the Air Force was looking for a reason to end the man's career. And he knew that if he — as author of the "Aerial Attack Study" and the man whom the Air Force acknowledged as its supreme aerial tactician — criticized the manuscript, Riccioni's career would be over. He read the manuscript and said he disagreed with Riccioni's conclusions but that only by being exposed to a wide variety of thought on aerial tactics could American fighter pilots remain the best-trained pilots in the world. His refusal to pan the manuscript and his strong recommendation not to fire the author saved Riccioni's career.

It was one of those curious twists of fate that Riccioni now became the spark plug that helped Boyd resurrect the glory that could have been the F-15. Riccioni was in a Pentagon R&D job where he could contract for research studies. Boyd and Sprey told Riccioni how their idealized lightweight fighter had been gold-plated and was becoming heavier by the day. Boyd said he was certain the F-15 would not perform as predicted and that many of the onboard high-tech gizmos would not perform as advertised. And when that happened the Air Force would not be able to justify the ever-escalating costs, and the airplane would again be in jeopardy. The Navy could once more go to Congress and try to scuttle the F-15 and force the F-14 on the Air Force.

Boyd said the Air Force needed an alternative, a backup airplane in case the F-15 project failed. Riccioni had the vision to see that a great fighter could be built by wrapping a small airplane around the F-15 engine. Sprey was pessimistic about using the F-15 engine; he thought it wasn't good enough to make a great fighter. For his part, Boyd wasn't optimistic, but thought no harm could come from Riccioni's proceeding.

The new lightweight fighter would be the airplane of the future, a small, highly maneuverable, deadly little wasp of an airplane. Since the Air Force did not know it needed a backup airplane, Boyd's plan had to remain a secret. The Air Force would view any backup airplane as a threat to the F-15. And Congress would never fund another fighter, not when the F-15 was in production.

Then Boyd's uncanny ability to look ahead and plan move and countermove gave him another thought. If high-tech equipment was not going to work on the F-15 and if performance criteria were not going to be met, wasn't it possible that the Navy's F-14 was facing the same problems? And if so, might not the Navy be thinking of an alternative to the F-14?

Riccioni drafted a memo to a general in charge of Research and Development and dangled the threat of a small, high-performance Navy aircraft. Nothing galvanized an Air Force general more than being told the Navy was on his six. The general told Riccioni to press on.

Boyd laughed. "We don't care what the Russians are doing. We only care about what the Navy is doing."

Boyd had expected the general's reaction. Riccioni wanted to apply for a study proposal, the ostensible purpose of which would be to determine if E-M data and trade-off studies could be a tool for advanced-fighter design. The study proposal would leave the clear impression that this was nothing more than a research project. Actually, the real purpose was to design a superhot and supersmall fighter. Boyd showed Riccioni how this could be done with the E-M trade-off approach. Boyd and Riccioni and Sprey drafted plans for a study with the cumbersome and soporific title "Study to Validate the Integration of Advanced Energy-Maneuverability Theory with Trade-Off Analysis." Something so arcane and academic and ponderous had to be innocuous. The Air Force gave Riccioni $149,000 to fund his research.

When Boyd and Sprey thanked Riccioni for resurrecting the light-weight fighter, Riccioni suggested the three men consider themselves partners. "We should call ourselves the Fighter Mafia," he said. Since all this was his idea and since he was Italian, he would be the godfather. Boyd was fine with that; all he cared about was that the $149,000 would allow him and Sprey to resume their work on the lightweight fighter. Besides, even if Riccioni was a full colonel and called himself the godfather, it was Boyd who led the group. While Riccioni liked to talk about his role in the Fighter Mafia, Boyd was wise in the ways of the Building and knew theirs must be an underground guerrilla movement. Once the true purpose of the Fighter Mafia was discovered, the Air Force would consider it an enemy of the F-15 and therefore an enemy of America.

It was about this time that the Office of the Secretary of Defense, on Sprey's recommendation, recognized that Tom Christie was too valuable to remain squirreled away in the piney woods at Eglin. His work on the effects of bombs had been adopted by every branch of the military. In addition, he was a wizard in managing people: every time the Air Force shoved a problem child over to Christie, he turned that person into a creative and productive worker. In 1969 Christie was offered the job of running TacAir, the old Whiz Kid shop that reported to the secretary of defense. But he was a cautious man and not sure he wanted to move to Washington. In a compromise move, for four months he spent three weeks of every month at TacAir. Then the man whom Christie would have replaced was fired. Christie returned to Eglin. It would be four more years before he came to the Building to run TacAir.

Not long after Christie returned to Eglin, Boyd came down on temporary duty. He visited Christie, who, along with his wife, Kathy, was hanging curtains in his house. Boyd was so intense about the chance to build a new airplane that he would not stop talking. Christie knew Boyd liked Wagner so he played "Ride of the Valkyries." Boyd's eyes widened, he stopped talking, and suddenly was transported. He waved his arms as if conducting an orchestra and began dancing about the room. For several hours Boyd stayed in the room alone, listening to the music. Thereafter when Boyd visited, Christie kept a Wagner record nearby.

Riccioni was close to Boyd for a while, but he never was one of the Acolytes. Soon the relationship would be seriously strained. Riccioni would be sitting at his desk when Boyd's big hand would slap him on the shoulder and a loud voice would say, "Tiger, let's go strafe the concourse." The two men went to the shops on the concourse, loaded up with bags of chocolate candy, then returned to the office, where they passed out candy to the secretaries. The secretaries stashed the chocolate in their desks. And in the evening after the secretaries had gone home, Boyd went from desk to desk, retrieving the candy.

One day as Boyd paced up and down the hall worrying about getting more drag polars from Wright-Pat, Riccioni passed by. He spoke to Boyd and continued on his way. But Boyd's internal radar had suddenly locked on a target. He wheeled and followed Riccioni, talking intently about polars. He tugged at Riccioni's elbow, stopping him, then tapping Riccioni in the chest and shouting that he had to have the drag polars and the sons of bitches at Wright-Pat were blocking him. "John, I have to go to the bathroom," Riccioni said. "Can we talk about this later?" Boyd kept talking. He followed Riccioni into the bathroom. Riccioni stood at the urinal, Boyd at his shoulder still going on about drag polars and the sons of bitches at Wright-Pat. Riccioni turned and walked into a stall. Before he could lock the door, Boyd was squeezing in with him, still talking. "Dammit, John, I want to do this by myself," Riccioni said. He pushed Boyd from the stall. As he slammed the door, Riccioni had a quick glance at Boyd's face and knew that Boyd had not realized what was happening. He was unaware of anything but Wright-Pat and drag polars and numbers and data and charts.

Several days later the two men were driving to Andrews AFB outside Washington when Boyd went into one of his trances. He stopped talking and stared out the window. A few minutes later he snapped out of it, turned to Riccioni, and said, "Tiger, I'm plotting some E-M data and I need to know how to take a derivative of —"

"You're plotting E-M data?" Riccioni interrupted. "In your head?"

In the mathematics doctoral program at MIT, Riccioni had studied disciplines and schools and theorems that Boyd had never heard of. But Riccioni could not plot E-M data in his head. He could not visualize the charts. He could not hear the music.

Riccioni told Boyd how to find the derivative of whatever it was he was after and Boyd returned to his reverie. With the Fighter Mafia's secret project, he had been given another chance to develop the purest jet fighter the world had ever known.

There was so much to do.

Chapter Seventeen

The Fighter Mafia
Does the Lord's Work

BOYD'S retirement date was drawing closer when, in May 1969, he received an extraordinary ER. His boss, Colonel Robert Titus, fire walled the review on the front side. On the second page he said Boyd's E-M work "has been the single most important link making the acquisition of the F-15 Advanced Tactical Fighter possible." He talked of Boyd's "unbounded enthusiasm," said Boyd was a "tactical and technical innovator who has no peer," and said Boyd's "active and searching mind seemingly never rests as it seeks out ever broader and farsighted fields of inquiry." He ended by saying Boyd was a "gifted, resourceful and adroit" officer who should be promoted to full colonel below the zone.

The indorsing officer said Boyd had "contributed immeasurably to the Air Force F-15 program." A major general provided still another indorsement saying Boyd was "recognized by the military and industry as an outstanding authority in the field" and that he recently had received the Citation of Honor for his pioneering development of fighter tactics. The general concluded by urging that Boyd be promoted to colonel below the zone and said he was ". . . one of the two best candidates of all the Lt Colonels that I know."

Boyd's retirement date was pushed back from October until December. Then, in July, Boyd asked that his retirement again be pushed back, this time until February 1, 1970. Usually when an officer submits his retirement papers, it means he wants out quickly. Not so with Boyd. He submitted papers for retirement a year early, then added more time. There had to have been a reason. A cynic would be justified in thinking Boyd was using the threat of retirement as leverage for his promotion to full colonel, an idea the Acolytes strenuously oppose. They say Boyd simply did not care about rank. But their view is from the benefit of hindsight and of Boyd's later expressions about rank. None of them knew at the time he was submitting and extending his retirement dates.

In August, Boyd was transferred from the Pentagon to an office in Systems Command headquarters at Andrews AFB, where his job was to monitor the work of the F-15 program manager at Wright-Pat. He was humiliated by the assignment. At the Pentagon he had back-channel communications with the chief of staff and often dealt with members of Congress. At Andrews he was in a nonjob. In addition, the Air Force had changed the fundamental nature of the F-15. Boyd was beginning to look at the aircraft — even though the first one had not rolled off the assembly line — as a transition aircraft, a cumbersome misapplication of technology. On the other hand, the lightweight fighter he secretly was working on was a rapier that embodied all the concepts of his updated E-M Theory. It was simple and small, with less drag, less weight, less visibility, and with much greater performance than the F-15, a day fighter that would not even carry a radar. It was a pure fighter with no bomb racks. It would be a 20,000-pound airplane, half the weight of the F-15; in fact, it was the aircraft the F-15 could have been. The design requirements Boyd set up meant he knew what would come from the contractors even before they set pen to paper. He knew the turning capability, the specific energy rate at every altitude, the rate of climb, and the range. And best of all, the aircraft would be so inexpensive that the Air Force could build several thousand, enough to flood a future battlefield. This was what he called his "Grand Strategy." Reduced to its basics, the Grand Strategy was to take on the U.S. Air Force, develop the new lightweight fighter in secret, build a prototype, then force the Air Force to adopt the aircraft.

It was one of the most audacious plots ever hatched against a military service and it was done under the noses of men who, if they had the slightest idea what it was about, not only would have stopped it instantly, but would have orders cut reassigning Boyd to the other side of the globe. Boyd knew this. He told Sprey and Riccioni they should never make a reference, on the phone or even in private conversation, to the fighter they were designing. Anything and everything to do with the lightweight fighter should be referred to as the "Lord's work."

Developing a new fighter aircraft is a long and tedious proposition. The F-15 project existed six years before a hardware contract was issued. In retrospect, the idea that three men could secretly design a new lightweight fighter is laughable. To think they could push it toward production against the wishes of the Air Force is sheer lunacy. At no other time in history could such a plot have the remotest chance of success. But Boyd was about to prove that fortune indeed favors the bold.

The $149,000 study grant obtained by Riccioni was split between Northrop and General Dynamics. This probably was illegal, since no other contractors were offered a chance to participate and since Northrop and General Dynamics soon were spending their own money in anticipation of a future contract. These two contractors knew if the Air Force discovered the true nature of the contract, it would be killed. So they kept quiet, knowing one of them eventually would receive a multimillion-dollar contract.

Northrop said it needed $100,000 to justify putting its engineers to work designing a new fighter to be called the YF-17. General Dynamics received $49,000 to design what it called the YF-16. General Dynamics was more than happy to be included — this was the chance to redeem itself for the F-111 debacle and for being too late with too little on the F-15. Harry Hillaker's friendship with Boyd, which went back to 1962 at Eglin, was paying off.

As an aside, the "Y" designation was another ploy to keep the Air Force in the dark about the true nature of the research project. Were this aircraft going into production it would have only the "F" designation. The "Y" meant that it would be one-of-a-kind — a prototype.

Boyd would call Hillaker at General Dynamics and a couple of engineers from Northrop at least once a week, sometimes more often, and ask them to come to Washington. If he summoned Hillaker, he then called Sprey and Riccioni to say, "Our friend from out West is coming to town. Tonight we'll be doing the Lord's work." Hearing Boyd on the phone solemnly talking of doing the Lord's work confused more than one secretary.

When called, Hillaker would work at General Dynamics in Fort Worth until the early afternoon, catch a flight to Washington, then meet Boyd and Sprey and Riccioni in his hotel room. They worked all night on plans for the YF-16, going over E-M charts and early designs. Sprey wanted the air intake under the nose and pushed far back. Usually the air intake on a single-engine jet is at the tip or side of the nose. Sprey's innovation saved weight and improved engine airflow during maneuvers. It also gave the aircraft a threatening, rapacious appearance.

After working all night, Hillaker would catch the first flight out of Washington National Airport back to Dallas. His counterpart at Northrop in California was doing the same thing. Since these two companies were competitive, each kept a lid of secrecy over the research.

People in Boyd's office wondered what was going on with him. Several days a week for month after month he did not come to work until almost noon. He yawned and gulped smart juice, trying to awaken. And every time his boss asked why he was late, Boyd said, "I was doing the Lord's work last night." Then he took a big drink of coffee, lit a Dutch Master, looked around, and said, "And goddamned good work it was."

In February 1970, a jaunty young first lieutenant named Robert Drabant reported for duty in Tom Christie's office at Eglin. "What's my job?" he asked.

Christie smiled. "You are Mr. E-M. Your sole job is to take phone calls from John Boyd in the Pentagon, listen to him, and handle his computer needs." Boyd called a few minutes later, was directed to Drabant, and said, "Tiger, we're gonna do some good work." For the next two years Boyd called every day. It was not unusual for a conversation to last two or three hours. Drabant generated more than 1,500 E-M diagrams for the Fighter Mafia. Boyd was never satisfied. He wanted every possible iteration. He had gone from the basic E-M charts to developing what he called the "Expanded Energy-Maneuverability Concept."

On January 6, 1970, Boyd again asked that his retirement date be extended, this time until July 1. He gave as his reason "to complete the final formulation and write-up of the Expanded Energy-Maneuverability Concept," which he said would have a "powerful influence on developing new fighter tactics and in developing new combat aircraft. . . ."

It is true he was working on the Expanded E-M Concept, but primarily as the rubric to cover his work on the lightweight fighter. He considered his official job monitoring the F-15 to be a nonjob. Was his retirement date extended because of the excitement he felt at working on the lightweight fighter, as the Acolytes contend? Or was it an attempt to leverage a promotion to full colonel? If the latter, it seems at first glance the bluff was not working, because the Air Force would have let Boyd retire had he not extended his deadline. But, in the light of what later happened, perhaps his bluff did work.

Perhaps no greater gulf exists in the officer corps of the Air Force than the one between a lieutenant colonel and a full colonel. It is in many ways greater than the gulf between a colonel and a brigadier general. If a man retires as a lieutenant colonel, he may be looked upon by his contemporaries as a man who never broke out of the herd. But a colonel is a commander, part of the leadership — no longer a "light colonel" but a "full bull" who is only one step from being a general.

The Air Force has a rule that after a transfer to another base an officer must serve a certain length of time before he can retire. The rule is to justify the expense incurred by the government in moving an officer. Boyd had transferred from the Pentagon to Andrews AFB. Never mind that it was only across town, that Boyd's residence remained the same, and that Boyd had been spending several days a week at the Pentagon. Rules are rules and Boyd had not served long enough at Andrews. In early May paperwork came down saying Boyd's request to retire had been revoked. He must have known it was coming, because several days before the request was denied, he filed an addendum to his retirement request asking that it be withdrawn. "I desire to remain on active duty because of the shortage of R&D officers in the Air Force with broad analytical skills," he wrote.

"Additionally I feel that I can contribute more to the Air Force and to the nation in this capacity than I could in private industry."

Boyd may have known that a promotion board had met and decided to promote him to colonel. This is conjecture because the workings of a promotion board are secret, but when a controversial name for promotion to colonel comes before the board — and Boyd's name certainly was controversial — board members have been known to call various generals to ask if they have any problem with this officer being promoted. The name of the contender often leaks.

Officers are promoted by date of rank; that is, a senior lieutenant colonel is promoted before one with less time in grade. Officers promoted below the zone are the last, as they are most junior. It is not unusual for these officers to know twelve or fifteen months ahead of time that they are being promoted.

A few days after Boyd's request for retirement was disapproved, he received an extraordinarily strong ER that laid the groundwork for a promotion. It is clear from the ER that the reviewing officer believed few lieutenant colonels in the history of the Air Force have had such an impact as Boyd. During the previous year he received two awards that brought credit on the Air Force "in a manner rare for an officer of his rank and experience." From a nationwide pool of candidates, he won the 1970 Hoyt S. Vandenberg Award for "outstanding contributions to aerospace technology." The ER said Boyd was "one of the best minds in the Air Force." He won a Legion of Merit with Oak Leaf cluster for his advanced E-M Theory, which the reviewing officer said "constitutes the most powerful evaluative tool for fighter aircraft analysis known to date and has provided industry with one of the most effective tools generated in the history of aeronautical engineering." The review ended with: *"Definitely promote below-the-zone to Colonel — now."*

It was Tom Christie who set in motion the events leading to Boyd's promotion. Christie and an Air Force colonel wrote an eight-page memo for General James Ferguson. As a three-star, Ferguson had been deputy chief of staff for Research and Development and knew Boyd's contributions. When Ferguson received his fourth star and was given the Systems Command, it was he who had Boyd transferred from the Pentagon to Andrews to monitor progress on the F-15.

Christie's memo said Boyd was about to retire and that the Air Force could not afford to lose an officer who had made so many contributions and who would make still more. Ferguson agreed and asked for a letter that he could sign and submit to the promotion board, a letter recommending Boyd be promoted to full colonel. Christie obliged.

Here the issue of Boyd's promotion becomes even more cloudy. First, a promotion board theoretically is free of command influence. In fact, some say a hint of command influence is enough to prevent an officer from being promoted. Second, four-stars rarely send letters of recommendation to a promotion board. When they do, the letter is received as Holy Writ.

It would seem the Finagler had pulled off his finest coup; he still was protecting Boyd, still operating outside the vision of those in the middle of a fray. He believes that Boyd never knew of his involvement.

It would be a year before Boyd pinned the silver eagles of a colonel on his shoulders. But he knew he was on the promotion list. The irony is that by promoting Boyd, the Systems Command made it possible for him to subvert its most cherished fighter project.

By December 1970, Riccioni, as the self-anointed godfather of the Fighter Mafia, was receiving a lot of attention. While some colonels in the Pentagon affect a swagger stick, Riccioni stalked the halls with a hunting arrow wedged under his arm. He used it as a pointer and waved it about in meetings.

"Why does Colonel Riccioni carry that arrow around?" someone asked Boyd.

"Hell, I don't know. Ask him."

"Because I am a warrior," Riccioni said. "It never lets me forget that I am a true warrior."

Riccioni liked the attention. He referred to himself in the third person, as in "Riccioni told several generals yesterday that they should be careful of the Fighter Mafia." But Riccioni did not understand that the very phrase *Fighter Mafia* enraged the Blue Suiters. Careerists saw the Fighter Mafia as a band of insurrectionists, plotters, and elitists. Riccioni's need for recognition and his naïveté were becoming a dangerous combination. He began writing inflammatory memos to superior officers, the contents of which called too much attention to the Fighter Mafia. Once he wrote a letter in which he blasted the F-14 as a grossly inferior aircraft and said that the Navy should consider buying a lightweight fighter. He sent copies to top admirals. In Riccioni's diatribes he positioned himself as the creator of the Fighter Mafia and even hinted at the true purpose of the study for which he had received funding. There were veiled references to an airplane that one day would embarrass the Air Force by defeating the F-15.

Boyd and Sprey were bewildered. On one hand it seemed Riccioni was a glory hound. On the other hand he was so innocent and genuinely sweet that it was impossible to be angry with him. One day Boyd went to him and said, "If you insist on getting credit for the work you do, you'll never get far in life. Don't confuse yourself with the idea of getting credit."

Riccioni agreed. But he continued writing incendiary memos.

An exasperated Boyd marched into Riccioni's office and said, "I have a special project and I need all the pencils you have."

Riccioni handed him the pencils from atop his desk. "You need more?"

"I need all you have." Riccioni dug more from his desk.

"You still have two in your shirt pocket. Give me those."

Boyd took the pencils, broke them in half, and tossed the remains in a waste can. A startled Riccioni looked up at him.

"Rich, you owe me. I've saved your ass more than once. Now it's time to collect."

Riccioni by this time had learned that Boyd had saved his career. He agreed that he owed Boyd and said, "What do you want?"

"No more goddamn memos. I don't want you to write anybody about anything."

Riccioni could not change his nature. He could not work behind the scenes. He became increasingly outspoken about the virtues of a lightweight fighter and he criticized the F-15 as needlessly complex and outrageously expensive. At a Christmas party, General John Myer, the then vice chief of staff, questioned Riccioni. The godfather listed everything wrong with the F-15 and said America needed an alternative, a small, cheap, high-performance aircraft.

"Are you telling me we have the wrong airplane?" the general asked.

Almost any other colonel in the Pentagon would have realized that a colonel does not tell the vice chief that the most prestigious acquisition project in the Air Force is a mistake. Riccioni said, "I can give you a better airplane for one-third the price." The general wheeled and walked away.

Several days later the godfather got word he was being transferred to Korea.

Sprey, too, was leaving. He was disillusioned with the Department of Defense and with how Bigger-Higher-Faster-Farther always seemed to prevail. He had decided to join a start-up company that studied air and water quality and analyzed environmental trends. He remained a consultant on the A-10 and still worked closely with Boyd, pulling all-nighters in motel rooms with contractors, still doing the Lord's work. In the Building, only Boyd would be found, and then as a visitor.

Few secrets remain secrets in the incestuous world of defense contractors. Word was now out about the study contracts, and other players wanted in. Lockheed and LTV and Boeing started taking seriously the study contracts awarded to Northrop and General Dynamics. The lightweight fighter could turn into a contract worth hundreds of millions of dollars.

In May 1971, Congress issued a blistering report on both the F-14 and F-15 and recommended spending $50 million to begin development of an alternative lightweight fighter. Pentagon generals fumed. There was information in the report that the Air Force and Navy considered proprietary. It had to have come from inside the Pentagon.

Talk of the lightweight fighter frightened generals far more than would the sudden appearance of a enemy bomber over the Pentagon. It was all the things that careerists fear. It signified change. It went against everything the Air Force held sacred. The brand-new, expensive, gold-plated F-15 was the heartthrob aircraft, the best in the world, they thought. And now the Fighter Mafia was saying it had a better and — *quelle horreur* — cheaper airplane.

Contractors took the congressional criticism of the F-15 and F-14 as a further sign that the lightweight fighter might be worth pursuing. Boyd cautioned those in his office that contractors always wanted to buy lunches and dinners and could easily corrupt the unwary. One contractor who wanted a piece of the lightweight fighter project announced it was sending a delegation of top officials to see Boyd, but first the contractor sent Boyd a massive stack of data to analyze. The data contained conclusions about aircraft performance that were so optimistic Boyd knew they were false. Then the vice presidents and top engineers descended upon Boyd's office and it was like a visit from royalty. The executives were coifed and tailored and their shoes gleamed and they were trying hard not to be patronizing toward this rumpled, scruffy-shoed colonel who happened to be the point man on the aircraft project. Boyd singled out one part of their proposal, a wing design that he knew created enormous wing-tip vortices. The proposal said nothing about the vortices.

In a calm and mildly curious voice, Boyd asked, "How did you get this data on the wing design?"

The vice president charged off the cliff. "Wind-tunnel tests," he said.

"Fuck a wind tunnel," Boyd roared. He pointed up. "The biggest wind tunnel in the world is up there. It's called reality. This is not reality."

Boyd paused. The vice presidents and engineers looked at each other. The senior man was about to speak again when Boyd said, "I had NASA check you people out. They can't duplicate your performance claims."

Such a statement is akin to saying the performance claims are bogus. The senior man drew himself up and said, "Colonel, we've had dozens of engineers on this for months." He tapped the desk. "It is correct. You need to go back to NASA and —"

Boyd stood up and pointed to the door. "You people are lying to me. Get the fuck out of my office."

"Colonel —"

"Out, goddammit!"

Officers and secretaries in the office were horrified. No one spoke to defense contractors like this. Boyd stood in the door, eyes glaring, daring any of the corporate executives to defy him. They collected their leather briefcases and all their data and stalked down the hall. Boyd raised a clenched fist and moved it up and down. "Stroking the bishop. You guys are just stroking the bishop. Come back when you get it right."

Boyd worked for Uncle. He was doing America's business and he had no time for defense contractors who bellied up to the trough with half-baked ideas. Billions of taxpayers' dollars were at stake and he had a fiduciary responsibility to see that the money was spent wisely.

Several weeks later the vice president in charge of the delegation called and told another officer that Boyd was right, that engineers had made a mistake on the wing design. He said it was not intentional, simply a mistake. He was afraid to tell Boyd for fear of his reaction. He asked the officer to pass the word to Boyd that the mistake had been corrected.

Another contractor sent in its top engineer, a world-famous designer who had sold an extraordinary series of aircraft to the U.S. government, to make a bid for the proposed new fighter. The engineer presented a set of generalized plans with no supporting data. The aerodynamic estimates were broad and vague. The lift versus drag curves were wildly optimistic. Boyd realized the design was not for a new aircraft but simply an upgrade of an existing airplane. The designer was giving Boyd what he thought the Air Force needed and not what Boyd wanted. The contractor apparently thought Boyd would be awed by the famous designer.

Boyd loved to tell the story of what happened. He looked at the drag curves and shook his head in apparent awe. "This is amazing," he said. "I just can't believe this."

The designer smiled. His retinue of engineers smiled. The famous John Boyd, for all of his reputation from E-M, was still a fighter pilot. And fighter pilots are easy to confuse when they are out of the cockpit.

Boyd leaned over the lift and drag chart and his fingers moved to the left, beyond the edges of the chart. He looked up, wide-eyed. "I can extrapolate this thing back to where the wing has zero lift. Wow. This airplane is so good that not only does it have zero lift, it has negative drag."

The designer no longer was smiling. Perhaps he had underestimated this Colonel Boyd. Perhaps he should have spent more time on the design. Boyd was only warming to his subject. "If this thing has negative drag, that means it has thrust without turning on the engines." He paused as if in deep thought. "That means when it is on the ramp with all that thrust, even with the engine turned off, you got to tie the goddamn thing down or it will take off by itself."

The designer glowered at Boyd. Who would have thought anyone would extrapolate the curves back to zero and show, using the contractor's own data, that the engines had thrust even before ignition?

Boyd shoved the papers across the desk. "Goddamn airplane is made out of balonium." According to Boyd, the designer called the next day and invited him to lunch and asked him not to tell his superiors about the spurious design. "I have to tell them," Boyd said. Then the engineer made an offer that, stripped of all the circumlocutions and delicate language, amounted to a bribe for Boyd to keep silent. "That won't take," Boyd responded. Then came an open threat that the designer would use his company's considerable clout with the Department of Defense to have Boyd fired. "Take your best shot, you son of a bitch," Boyd said.

A week later the famous designer and his company withdrew their design from consideration.

Once an officer is promoted to colonel, he is automatically considered for general the next time the promotion board meets. It might be several months after his promotion or it might be a year. To be passed over the first time is not significant. But when a man is passed over the second time, he begins to have doubts. If he is passed over a third time, his chances have gone. Thus, the first ER after making colonel is crucial. It is here the colonel has the first intimation of whether or not generals want to admit him to their fraternity.

On October 13, 1971, Boyd received his first ER after making full colonel and it was devastating. On the front side he was downgraded in three categories. The narrative is a classic example of an ER that, to the uninitiated, is unsurpassed. "Colonel Boyd has continued to make outstanding, major contributions to the Air Force's analytical approach toward optimizing the design characteristics of aircraft." Here Boyd is praised for his *old* work. And "outstanding, major contributions" is nowhere near as strong as previous comments about the innovative, groundbreaking aspects of his work, or of his leadership role. The reviewing officer recommends Boyd return to school to obtain a doctorate and then teach at the Air Force Academy. This seems to indicate belief in an officer potential. But to a colonel with twenty years of service it is demeaning. Boyd has only an undergraduate degree. It would take him three or four years to get a Ph.D. For a colonel to be taken out of the operational loop for four years is to end his career. Even worse, generals do not teach at the Academy; they command the Academy. Finally, if superior officers think a colonel might one day wear stars on his shoulders, his ER talks of leadership, hints at his political abilities, his statecraft. It recommends him for an assignment that qualifies him to be a general. Boyd's ER has none of that. Boyd's fate is sealed by an additional indorsement from a major general who says simply, "I concur with the evaluation and recommendations of the reporting and indorsing officer."

John Boyd had contributed as much to fighter tactics, aeronautical engineering, science, the Air Force, and his country as any man in Air Force history. A list of Air Force original thinkers — and this is a short list — would begin with his name. But his enemies prevailed. He had shot down too many generals ever to become a general. This must have been a time of despair for Boyd. As always he sought solace in his work. And it was then that he had another epiphany, a marvelous and far-reaching epiphany.

In doing advanced conceptual design work on the lightweight fighter, he went over all his notes from the past, from as far back as Korea. He remembered his early E-M work and how difficult it was to prepare accurate E-M charts for the F-86. He remembered the F-86's countless battles with MiGs. He remembered how, on paper, the MiG was a superior aircraft in almost every respect. But the F-86 had a ten-to-one kill ratio against the MiG. Why?

Boyd pored over the notes again and again. Could there be something else, some other element, perhaps an element not covered by E-M, that held the answer? Boyd made a list of attributes of the MiG and the F-86. For days he went into frequent trances as he groped for the answer. In the end he came up with two significant advantages the F-86 had over the MiG. First, the F-86 had a bubble canopy that gave the pilot a 360-degree field of vision, while the MiG pilot's view to the rear was blocked. Thus, the F-86 pilot had a much easier time observing his enemy than the enemy had observing him. Second, the F-86 had full hydraulic controls, while the MiG did not. This meant that the F-86 pilot could control his aircraft with one finger, while controlling the MiG was so difficult that MiG pilots often lifted weights between flights in order to gain strength. The unboosted controls of the MiG meant that its pilot grew fatigued more quickly than the F-86 pilot but, far more importantly, the F-86 driver could go from one maneuver to another more quickly than the MiG driver. In a practical sense this meant the F-86 pilot could go through a series of either offensive or defensive maneuvers quicker than could his adversary. And with each maneuver he gained a half second or a second on his enemy until he could either break for separation or be in position for a kill. The MiG was faster in raw acceleration and in turning ability, but the F-86 was quicker in changing maneuvers. And in combat, quicker is more important.

These advantages — better observation and greater agility — would make the lightweight fighter an even more extraordinary aircraft. This concept of agility was an intimation of what in another few years would be the best-known part of Boyd's legacy.

Chapter Eighteen

A Short-Legged Bird

AMERICA'S newest fighter aircraft continued to take hits.

The news media wrote story after story about the extraordinary expense of the F-15 and the abysmal performance of the F-14. Senator William Proxmire, who was the bane of the military, issued reports savaging both aircraft. He echoed the idea that money be appropriated to fund a lightweight fighter. As the Proxmire reports contained confidential information about both the F-15 and the F-14, the Pentagon suspected, but could not prove, that Proxmire's source was the Fighter Mafia. That nonsense about the lightweight fighter could have come from nowhere else. Criticism of the two aircraft reached such a peak that the Nixon Administration ordered Secretary of Defense Laird to whip the military purchasing system into shape. Laird assigned the job to his deputy, David Packard.

At the time the findings of the Fitzhugh Commission must have been very much on Packard's mind. The commission had been appointed in 1969 to take a hard look at DoD management and the acquisition process. The group issued a report recommending that when building new weapons systems, the DoD should develop and test a prototype before sending the weapons system into production. This is because in almost every instance, a defense contractor underestimates costs and overestimates performance. (The practice of underestimating costs is so common that it has a name: "front-loading.") A prototype reveals design flaws, performance inadequacies, and true costs.

This was not a new idea. Before World War II most new fighters appeared first as prototypes. It made sense to test a design, decide whether it was good or bad, make modifications, redesign it, and then put it on the production line. But then came jet engines and swept wings and ever more exotic avionics, all of which caused larger Air Force and contractor bureaucracies. The development staff of an airplane went from maybe a hundred people to a thousand or more. Defense contractors said the business had become too complex and too expensive to make prototypes. Air Force bureaucracies agreed. They did not want tests that might cancel their projects. McNamara played into their hands when he brought to the Pentagon something called "Total Package Procurement Concept." He thought all the analysis and quantification could be done on paper. Design teams grew to two thousand people, then three thousand. And the cost of developing a new fighter rose to around $1 billion.

In the summer of 1971, Packard announced a budget of $200 million to be spent on prototypes from all branches of the services. The Air Force put together a group to pick projects to be prototyped with the intention of grabbing as much of the $200 million as possible. Colonel Lyle Cameron was in charge of the group. He came out of OSD, where he was one of the few career officers to earn the respect of the Whiz Kids. Not only did he have the respect of that intimidating group but Pierre Sprey was one of his closest friends. Cameron combed the Air Force's Research and Development labs and found more than two thousand possible candidates. The Air Force told Cameron to move fast. By August, Cameron recommended a short takeoff and landing (STOL) transport aircraft and the lightweight fighter. He picked these two because they were far enough down the design pipeline that they were ready for contracts to be issued. Packard approved both and in December the Air Force launched the lightweight-fighter prototype program.

The generals laughed and said the lightweight fighter, if it was like every other small airplane, would have such a limited range it would be good only for a five-minute demonstration at an air show. Let them build their prototypes. That will be the end of it because that little toy fighter will never go into production. The Fighter Mafia can even fly the prototypes a few times. When the excitement had worn off, the generals would park the things in an Air Force museum and get on with the business of America.

Defense contractors with big ongoing projects groaned about going back to prototyping. But contractors without big projects loved it. Boyd and Sprey thought they were entering the most exciting time in aviation industry in more than twenty years. Now was the moment for the Fighter Mafia to streamline everything, remove most of the bureaucracy. Boyd borrowed many of the ideas Sprey had implemented with the A-10. The request for proposal, for example, was fifty pages rather than the usual three hundred or so, and the industry response was limited to fifty pages. Not only was he going to develop an airplane that would be superior to the F-15, he would show the Pentagon a production process that would be as lean and mean as the lightweight fighter itself. He was going to develop an airplane that, for the first time in Air Force history, would cost less than its predecessor.

It was Sprey's idea to have a fly-off between the prototypes, as he had done with the A-X, so Boyd turned Sprey loose to devise the rigid, real-world scenario. There would be simulated aerial dog-fights. Each prototype would fly against a MiG kept at a secret base near Nellis. Each prototype would also go up against the F-4. Sprey did not want Edwards pilots as test pilots; he wanted real fighter pilots who would bank and yank without worrying about their clipboards, guys who could stand an airplane on its tail and make it skydance without worrying if they were writing down all the numbers, guys who did not need some engineering geek on the ground to radio instructions on how to turn and burn. And once the pilots flew the YF-16, they would move over and fly the YF-17. Having the same men fly both airplanes takes out any possibility of pilot bias.

Edwards pilots wailed, first at not being allowed to fly the air-combat tests and then at the idea of pilots going from one airplane to the other. Too risky, they said — a pilot can't go from the cockpit of one new airplane to the cockpit of another. Boyd laughed. Maybe you Edwards pukes can't, he said, but fighter pilots can.

When the fly-off was over, when one of the two new fighters emerged as the superior aircraft, it would be winner-take-all. And the best part was that the Navy might also have to adopt the winning design. The Navy was about to eat an Air Force airplane.

Which, John Boyd thought, was the way it was supposed to be.

Design studies showed the lightweight fighter would be superior in performance to the F-15, but this had to be kept secret. The Air Force would not allow even a prototype to outperform the F-15. But the biggest secret, the single most innovative and startling aspect of the design, was that the new fighter would have greater range than the F-15. Sprey and Boyd fought for months over this. Sprey, ever the purist, wanted less fuel. Less fuel means less weight and less weight means better performance. Boyd, as always, had planned move and countermove, and he saw a way to have enough fuel to beat the F-15 in range. This knowledge gave him a big stick. Usually if a man in a bureaucracy has a big stick, he uses it. But Boyd decided to hide his. He knew there would come a time, perhaps in a year or even two years, when the stick could be used to greater advantage.

The fuel fraction is derived by considering the weight of the fuel relative to the combat weight of the aircraft. The crucial thing about understanding fuel fraction is that it is the *relative* fuel and not the *absolute* fuel that is important in determining how far an airplane flies. That is, the percentage of fuel relative to the weight of the aircraft is more important than the absolute gallons of fuel carried. Boyd was adamant that the fuel fraction for the lightweight fighter not go below 30 percent. That was the sacred number, not to be violated, doubtless because the fuel fraction of the F-15 was 25 percent and Boyd wanted the lightweight fighter to be better. The new fighter would have about sixty-five hundred pounds of fuel, for a fuel fraction of 31.5 percent.

As mind-boggling as it sounds, the Air Force looked at the total amount of fuel carried and never considered the fuel fraction. The school of Bigger-Higher-Faster-Farther was so firmly ingrained that it was almost genetic: big airplanes have more range than small airplanes. The MiG-21 was a small aircraft and notoriously short-legged. So was the F-5, another small fighter. If the Blue Suiters had considered birds, rather than airplanes, they might have found a better example. There is a hummingbird that can fly across the Gulf of

Mexico, while birds many times its size can fly only a few miles. The hummingbird has a high fuel fraction.

Boyd told Sprey, "Tiger, they are gonna use what they see as the lack of range to try to kill this airplane. Let 'em. Let that be their main focus. At the right time we will tell them otherwise and they will have nothing left. We will hose them."

Boyd was right. Air Force generals and congressional critics and reporters friendly to the Pentagon looked at the amount of fuel the lightweight fighter contained and began describing it as "short-legged," a plane of such limited range it could defend only the airfield from which it took off, the "home drome." The focus of criticism against the lightweight fighter became its limited range, as predicted. Boyd once delivered a briefing on the lightweight fighter and afterward a general looked around, smiled, and said, "That's a short-legged little fucker, isn't it, Colonel?"

"Sir, it looks that way," Boyd said, ignoring the derisive grins of those in the room.

The Navy loathed Sprey, as did the Air Force, and had coached Senate Armed Services Committee members on how to fight him. He was bitterly attacked when he testified to the committee about how the military was gold-plating the F-14 and the F-15 with parts that could be bought for civilian aircraft at one-tenth what the military was paying. He said the lightweight fighter being prototyped by the Air Force was the proper course for the military. A Navy official said Sprey's work was filled with "fallacious assumptions, half truths, distortions, and erroneous extrapolations." The Navy questioned the proposed performance of the lightweight fighter and said for an airplane to have the sort of thrust-to-weight ratio that Sprey described, the aircraft would have to weigh at least fifty thousand pounds. No toy fighter could do what Sprey said the new fighter would do.

It would be several years before the Air Force realized that the lightweight fighter not only had greater range than the F-15 but had greater range *than any other fighter in the Air Force*. That knowledge would cause more than a dozen generals to explode in anger. Keeping secret the range of the lightweight fighter was one of Boyd's greatest cape jobs.

Rarely in Air Force history has the design of an Air Force fighter been supervised by such a vigilant eye. Any suggested design change

261

by the contractors meant a deviation from Boyd's requirements. Every suggestion caused him to "come apart," as Christie described it. Boyd lost one significant design battle. He wanted each of the competing aircraft to have only one engine. But a three-star at Wright-Pat found it impossible to imagine a single-engine fighter. Thus, the YF-16 on the drawing board at General Dynamics could remain a single-engine, but the YF-17 at Northrop would be a twin-engine.

Boyd's determination to keep the lightweight fighter pure had one unusual side effect. A colonel whose specialty was preparing computer models to evaluate airplanes clearly favored the Northrop design. He developed a model showing the YF-17 was the better aircraft and tried to have the model made part of the source-selection process, a highly improper action. One day Sprey was in the colonel's office when the phone rang. Sprey realized that whoever was on the other end was telling the colonel that his computer model was being cut from the selection process. As the colonel argued he grew more and more excited and began sputtering and then a froth of saliva appeared at the corners of his mouth. He turned white and fell out of his chair. Sprey rushed around the desk to assist. After a moment the colonel shook himself and motioned for Sprey to leave the office. A few minutes later Sprey ran into Boyd and said, "The most amazing thing just happened. I was with . . ." — he named the colonel — ". . . when he got a phone call. Then all at once he fell out of his chair and began foaming at the mouth. I thought he was dying."

Boyd looked at Sprey and said, "That was me on the line. I wondered why the phone went dead."

Afterward the incident became known as the "air-to-rug maneuver," and the Acolytes shook their heads in amazement that even on the telephone Boyd could cause a Blue Suiter to fall out of his chair. The story of the air-to-rug maneuver became a favorite at happy hour, especially after the colonel became a four-star and then the Air Force chief of staff.

Boyd arrived late for World War II, late for the Korean conflict, and late for the Vietnam War. It was not until the end of 1971 that Boyd received orders sending him to Thailand, to one of the most highly classified military bases in Southeast Asia, where he would be working on a project so secretive he could discuss it with only a few people who had both a need to know and a security clearance beyond "top secret" — a code-word clearance.

A man going off to war has a need to revisit his roots. So in February 1972, Boyd went home to Erie, where he was greeted by ice and snow and the perpetual gloom of an Erie winter. Boyd visited his mother, but their relationship was strained, almost formal, ever since that visit when Elsie would not allow Boyd and Mary and the children in her house and they had to stay in a motel.

As always Boyd looked up Frank Pettinato and tracked down two or three close friends. He told them about the F-15 and the lightweight fighter and all the generals he had to fight and what a constant battle it was to produce the greatest fighter aircraft in history. But he was there, right in the middle of it, and he was making sure it went well. He would win in the end; he knew he would. Pettinato nodded and smiled in approval. Much of this was far too complex for him. But Boyd was like his son and he believed what the man said. Many of Boyd's friends did not. Yeah, yeah, yeah, they said, not bothering to hide their disbelief that someone from Erie could ever do such things. Great story, John. And they looked at each other and grinned. Pure bullshit, their expressions said. Oh, and by the way, John, when pilots go to war, they fly jet fighters. So what will you be flying over there? Well, this is not a flying assignment, he said, I'm running an operation. What operation is that? Can't talk about it. They laughed again. Can't be too important, they said. It if were, a general would be running it and you sure as hell are not a general. Boyd was silent for a moment, then he changed the subject. He and his friends talked of the old times, of growing up in Erie, of boyhood pranks, of the milkshakes they bought at Stinson's.

When Boyd returned to Washington, he had only a few weeks to have a physical examination and to take care of the countless preparations involved in being assigned to a combat zone. In the middle of these preparations came his last ER from Andrews AFB. The reporting officer, a two-star, downgraded him in three categories on the front side. But a three-star wrote an indorsement that slammed the reviewing officer by upgrading Boyd in four categories on the front side. It is rare that one general humiliates another in this fashion. But once again a higher-ranking officer had salvaged Boyd's ER.

By now scholarly journals or papers presented at scientific conferences had begun to take note of Boyd's E-M Theory. In the

January–February 1970 issue of *Journal of Aircraft* was an article entitled "Energy Climbs, Energy Turns, and Asymptotic Expansions" that
made reference to Boyd. In 1972, papers or articles on "Differential
Turns," "Supersonic Aircraft Energy Turns," and "Aircraft Maneuver
Optimization by Reduced-Order Approximation" all used Boyd's
work. And while Boyd was in Thailand, attendees at various scientific
conferences heard papers on such topics as "Applications of Reachable
Sets Techniques to Air Combat Analysis," "Long-Range Energy-State
Maneuvers for Minimum Time to Specified Terminal Conditions,"
and "Energy Management Rules for Turning Flight," all of which
were based largely on Boyd's work.

And it wasn't just theory. There would have been an F-15 even if
there had never been a John Boyd, but it would have been an altogether different creature — probably a misshapen F-111–like airplane that more than likely would have died in the process and thus
forced the Air Force to adopt a Navy airplane. Boyd's E-M Theory so
shaped the F-15 that many were calling him the "Father of the F-15."
Finally, there was the lightweight fighter. On April 13, 1972, about the
time Boyd left for Thailand, Secretary of Defense Laird gave the Air
Force approval to build the prototype aircraft for the lightweight-
fighter program. This meant that, for the first time since World War
II, the U.S. Air Force had three new tactical aircraft in development at
the same time — the F-15, the lightweight fighter, and the A-10. All
were from Air Force designs and not foisted off by the Navy. Boyd
was largely responsible for two of them and Sprey the other.

When Boyd left for Thailand, he embarked on the first and only
command assignment of his career. It was his last war, so he had to
make the most of everything. He had to perform his duties in an outstanding fashion — no more critical ERs. While he was away, prototypes of the lightweight fighter would be built. The fly-offs would
take place about the time he returned and he wanted to have a role in
deciding which of the two aircraft the Air Force would buy.

But that was a year away. In April 1972, Mary and the children
drove Boyd to Dulles, told him good-bye, and left before he boarded
a transport of the Military Airlift Command. As always, per fighter-
pilot family tradition, Mary and the kids did not watch him take off.

Boyd flew to Travis AFB in California, where more military personnel boarded, and then it was on to Anchorage, Alaska, before

crossing the Pacific to Japan. The transport flew down to Clark AFB in the Philippines, where Boyd spent the night in the bachelor officers' quarters. The next morning he flew to Bangkok and loaded his bags aboard a C-130 that made the rounds of Thai Air Force bases before finally landing at Nakhon Phanom Royal Thai AFB.

Chapter Nineteen

Spook Base

IN every war there are military bases where activities are so secret that few people outside the base know what goes on there. These bases have a mystique, a hint of strange comings and goings, rumors of covert organizations that are a cover for even more covert organizations. In the Vietnam War that base was Nakhon Phanom Royal Thai AFB, commonly known as NKP or, by the more irreverent, as Naked Fanny. Activities at NKP were so highly classified that for the first three or four years of its existence the base officially did not exist. But by the time Boyd arrived in April 1972, the word was out: NKP was a spook base.

NKP perches on the east bank of the Mekong River in northeast Thailand, a few miles from the old market town of Nakhon Phanom. It is on the Laotian border, about two hundred miles south of the Plain of Jars. Numerous and varied military operations, all highly compartmentalized so that few people knew what others were doing, were based there. The Army had a heavily guarded compound from which the curiously named Studies and Observation Group (SOG) launched some of the most daring and still-secret activities of the war. Six special air-warfare squadrons were based there, and they flew such a bewildering assortment of antiquated propeller-driven aircraft that pilots called NKP "the flying circus." Helicopters of the special operations crowd clattered in and out at all hours of the day and night. Forward air controllers (FAC) flew nimble little twin-engine OV-10s. World War II–era single-engine A-1 "Sandys" — muscular and heavily armed aircraft — flew search-and-rescue missions and CAS missions, particularly for Special Forces units. (Pierre Sprey's A-10 was modeled in part after the A-1.) A-26s, World War II light bombers, flew frequent combat missions. Taking off day and night were the ungainly AC-119s, propeller-driven cargo aircraft that, with the addition of a big Gatling cannon firing out the side, became deadly gunships that could light up a target like a Christmas tree. And there were a host of bulbous-nosed, antennae-wearing surveillance aircraft found nowhere else in the Air Force.

No F-4s or Thuds were based there, but they often landed to refuel. After aggressive North Vietnamese pilots shot down a helicopter flying out of NKP, a fully-armed F-4 occasionally sat on runway alert, ready to launch if MiGs came close. NKP was one of the busiest bases in Southeast Asia. It operated perhaps more flights at night than during the day.

Various fenced compounds were scattered around the base and unless one had business there they were off limits. But, as a rule, the base was relatively open. Thais operated a tailor shop, laundry, a bar, and several other commercial establishments. One of the more curious facts about NKP is that it was overrun by packs of wild dogs. The dogs were more or less accepted — hey, we're in Thailand, we're at war, was the general feeling. Besides, the ravenous dogs were good at catching the big rats that lived under the hooches of junior officers.

Taking up much of the base was an enormous complex surrounded by two security fences topped with razor wire. Earth-filled revetments bordered the complex. Security police stood in towers and walked patrol along the fences. Admittance to the complex was tightly controlled. The main building, when constructed in 1968, was the largest single building in all of Southeast Asia. But most of the facility was underground, protected by thick concrete walls and operating inside a positive pressurized atmosphere to keep out dust and protect an enormous array of computers. Around NKP the complex was known simply as the "Project." The official name was Task Force Alpha. Various other code names were associated with the complex: Igloo White, Dutch Mill, and Muscle Shoals.

The heart of Task Force Alpha was the "Infiltration Surveillance Center," the purpose of which was to monitor acoustic sensors, seismic sensors, urine sniffers, and various other sensors planted along the Ho Chi Minh Trail for the purpose of observing the enemy. Banks of computers synthesized the sensor data and tried to form a picture of what the enemy was doing. Is that a convoy of trucks or hundreds of men marching down the trail? Where are they likely to stop for the night? Might a supply depot be there? Once the computers spit out the information, targeting experts decided what aircraft and what bombs or missiles to send against the enemy.

The Ho Chi Minh Trail was a network of trails and dirt roads that formed the main route by which North Vietnamese forces operating in South Vietnam were resupplied by cargo-carrying bicycles and small trucks. Seeding the trail with sensors had been the idea of Defense Secretary McNamara's R&D technocrats, and the project became known as the "McNamara Line." The $2.5 billion operation was a huge windfall for IBM. The technocrats convinced McNamara that if the trail were wired — as one Task Force Alpha worker said, like a "pinball machine" — the supply chain could be broken and America could win the war. This was America's first electronic battlefield. It was one of the most highly classified operations of the Vietnam War.

John Boyd came to NKP as the vice commander of Task Force Alpha.

Boyd arrived at a time when something happened almost every day to demonstrate the lunacy of the war. Drugs were so pervasive on base that when he went to the dining room he was given a knife and fork and then a plastic spoon. All the metal spoons had been stolen to use as small containers in which drugs were heated. One of the enlisted men who worked for Boyd in the top-secret underground chamber always wore a raincoat to work. Underneath he was naked. His job was to listen to Vietnamese radio transmissions and the man said he could not break their codes when he was dressed.

Boyd jumped into his first command job with considerable zest. Locating the position of enemy artillery was one function of Task

Force Alpha. The acoustic sensors could not pinpoint the gun location quickly enough. By the time attack aircraft arrived on the scene, the gun was silent or had been relocated. Boyd developed a grid system for implanting sensors. Now, sometimes less than five minutes after the first enemy shell was lobbed, FAC pilots were firing marking rockets and the jets were lining up to bomb the artillery position.

Boyd was so excited about his new system that he began flying as a passenger on some night missions. He probably flew in the OV-10, a small, 175-mph, propeller-driven aircraft used by FAC pilots. But Boyd was too valuable to be flying over enemy territory and his boss soon ordered him to stand down.

In addition to his Task Force Alpha responsibilities, Boyd was also inspector general and equal opportunity training officer — a job fraught with peril considering the racial turmoil in the military toward the end of the Vietnam War. But he still found time to use E-M to develop a briefing that compared the performance of the F-4 with enemy-fighter aircraft operating in the theater. He gave the brief at Air Force bases throughout Thailand and Vietnam. Boyd also was ordered to preside over a board of inquiry into one of several F-111 crashes. He believed the assignment was punishment for his years of criticizing the F-111.

Like every other officer arriving at NKP, Boyd went to the Thai tailor shop on base and ordered up a "party suit." These were often blue, but members of Task Force Alpha wore black. The garment was cut like a flight suit, with a zipper up the front. It had numerous pockets. Party suits were worn at the Officers Club for going-away parties or for other festive events celebrated at a combat base. No rules governed the ornaments or decorations or regalia or patches sewn onto party suits and as a result they were some of the most colorful attire ever seen on military personnel. Boyd had his big Fighter Weapons School patch sewn onto the breast, and unit patches were sewn onto each shoulder. One patch says PARTICIPANT IN SOUTHEAST ASIA WAR GAMES. On the back is the pièce de résistance, a coiled, bright yellow garden hose and written underneath, also in bright yellow, THE HOSER.

There were times at NKP when officers found little to celebrate. In the early summer of 1972, race relations at NKP took a dangerous turn. One of the senior officers on base was devoutly religious, very conservative, and was becoming unwrapped by the war. He found solace in American booze and Thai women. The guilt he must have felt, he visited upon his troops. After a fight between black and white enlisted men, the commander ordered the black troops onto a helicopter, and they were flown under armed guard to an army jail near Bangkok. Pretrial detention rarely is practiced in the military, and because white participants in the incident were not treated the same way, the base seethed in racial tension. Feelings ran so high that white pilots were afraid to walk near the barracks where black security police were housed. Numerous racial fights broke out.

The commander ignored what was going on around him and sought refuge in more booze and more women. That was when Boyd stepped in. As equal opportunity training (EOT) officer, he took his responsibility seriously. Although several layers of command existed between Boyd and the commander, Boyd ordered up a helicopter and told the senior lawyer on base to go to Bangkok and interview the black prisoners. "Find out what happened," he said in effect. "If those guys were not involved or if they did not start the fight, get 'em out of jail. If they started it, leave them there."

Arnold Persky, then a major in the office of the judge advocate general, was the lawyer Boyd ordered to Bangkok. Persky interviewed the prisoners and ordered one, identified as the provocateur, to remain incarcerated until his trial. The others not only were released but flew back to NKP aboard Persky's helicopter. When they returned Boyd sat down with all the black troops on base and told them it did not matter what had happened before, that now he was the EOT officer and things were different. The racial situation on base was defused. "The difference was night and day," said Persky. "Colonel Boyd turned it around."

Because this was Boyd's first operational command, he was evaluated by his superiors two months after he arrived. The letter of evaluation said Boyd "has a seemingly unlimited ability and stamina to effectively cope with stressed operational procedures." He "prevented a possible major problem" by "exercising unusually sound judgment" in a racially charged situation. But most important of all it said, "He is fully qualified for Command." Air Force generals in Southeast Asia must have agreed, because the commander who had caused the incident was relieved of duty and shipped back to the

States, while Boyd was pulled out of Task Force Alpha and given command of the 56th Combat Support Group, a job that included, among other things, being base commander.

On August 10, Boyd wrote Mary that he was working out, eating lightly, and trying to lower his weight to 170 pounds. He said he had been doing much thinking and felt he was "on the verge of a fantastic breakthrough on the thinking processes and how they can be taught to others." He said he had arrived at an "expansion and distillation" of what he had begun thinking about while still at the Pentagon. "Don't speak about it to others because as usual they'll think it's cracked," he said.

What Boyd was obsessing about — and that is not too strong a word — was trying to understand the nature of creativity. This had actually begun several years earlier as he wondered how he came up with the E-M Theory. E-M is at heart such a simple thing; why had no one else discovered it? What was there about his thinking that enabled him to be the first? His search ranged far afield. From the base library he checked out every available book on philosophy and physics and math and economics and science and Taoism and a half dozen other disciplines. He was all over the map, searching but not quite knowing for what. He hints at what he is working on when, in a letter dated September 28, he again writes Mary that he is on the "verge of a fantastic breakthrough" in the thinking process and how it applies to life.

On October 15 he writes, "I've expanded on the thought processes in directions that frankly amaze even me." He says if his theory is workable, "I may be on the trail of a *theory of learning* quite different and — it appears now — more powerful than methods or theories currently in use." He says he is not sure where the ideas will ultimately lead and that before he goes much farther he wants to discuss it with Pierre Sprey. Boyd says he has "a new direction to my life" and that if his theory holds true, "I think it will bring us closer together and provide an enrichment toward living that has eluded us in the past."

It was when Boyd left Task Force Alpha to become commander of the 56th Combat Support Group that he received his first ER in Southeast Asia. The first page is fire walled, with the exception of the box dealing with "skills in human relations," which doubtless meant that he sometimes was more frank than his superiors liked. Nevertheless, the all-important first sentence on the second page reads, "Colonel Boyd is the most dedicated officer with whom I have ever served." The reviewing officer says he had personal knowledge that Boyd's briefing comparing F-4 performance with enemy aircraft "not only saved one of our aircraft from destruction, but also the user was credited with a victory." Once again the efficacy of Boyd's outside-roll maneuver was proven in combat.

And no matter Boyd's feelings about the F-111, he obviously did a good job of investigating the crash. The reviewing officer says Boyd's report of that incident was "thorough" and "well-received." The ER dwelled on the racial incident Boyd defused and said, "Since that time we have not had even a minor incident of a racial nature in this unit." The indorsing officer, a major general, says Boyd's performance was "absolutely superior" and that "Colonel Boyd is a highly intelligent and dedicated officer who generates enthusiasm and instills confidence in those with whom he works and supervises."

It was as base commander, a job that made Boyd master of all he surveyed, that his creative flair for solving problems soon burst into bloom. Boyd was responsible for all civil-engineering projects on base, transportation, security, and just about everything else, from supervising the dining rooms to making sure religious services were available for all. The previous commander had ignored many of the housekeeping activities around NKP.

In his new job, Boyd saw problems that needed immediate attention everywhere he looked. But 7th Air Force sent down paperwork daily that took hours to answer. Boyd thought Air Force bureaucracy was keeping him from the job at hand. His solution was to respond but to add material that caused 7th Air Force more paperwork than 7th Air Force caused him. "Pain goes both ways," he said. In only a few weeks the time-consuming requests from 7th Air Force shrank to almost nothing.

One of the most immediate and most serious problems Boyd had to deal with was that a number of the wild dogs on base had become rabid. Boyd's solution was immediate, effective, and simple: every dog was shot on sight — no exceptions. He later said that security police, acting on his orders, even shot a dog being walked on a leash by an Air Force officer. Boyd's reasoning was that while a dog did not show any symptoms of rabies, he might have been bitten and soon would manifest the disease. An Air Force combat base simply did not have the leisure of placing dogs in quarantine and then waiting to see if they were infected.

When Boyd made a base inspection, he found more of the legacy of laxness left by the former commander: latrines used by enlisted men were covered with scatological graffiti. Boyd called in the senior sergeants from all units on base and said he wanted the latrines repainted and that there would be no more graffiti. They told him that repainting the latrines would only present a new canvas for updated obscenities. Boys will be boys, the sergeants said.

Boyd put on his hard face and wagged a long forefinger at the sergeants. "Here's what I'm gonna do," he said he told the sergeants. "First, I'm going to have the latrines repainted. Then I'm going to dig a trench off base, out in front of the main gate. And the first goddamn time I see any more obscenity on the walls I'm going to padlock every enlisted latrine on this base. If somebody wants to piss or shit — day or night, rain or shine — he's going to have to do it in that trench. In front of every Thai person passing by." He paused to let his message sink in. He knew what the sergeants were thinking. The busiest street in town led straight to the base. A trench dug in front of the main gate would be in sight of hundreds of people. Thais were notoriously finicky about personal cleanliness and privacy. Any Americans seen using the trench would be subjected to considerable disdain. Plus, it was the rainy season, a miserable time in Southeast Asia.

The sergeants were not alarmed. They had their own latrines. If this crazy colonel wanted to dig a trench for the enlisted men, it would not affect them. "That includes you sergeants," Boyd added. "I'll padlock your latrines, too. So by God you better make sure your troops get the message. Now get out of here and have those latrines repainted."

It is said that from November 1972 until the base was closed, NKP had the cleanest enlisted latrines in all of Southeast Asia.

Then there was the story of the junior officer who was having an affair with a Thai woman. There was nothing unusual about this. Thai women are extraordinarily beautiful and many American officers formed close relationships with them. But this particular officer was married and soon was overcome with guilt. He broke off the relationship. The woman in question was the daughter of an influential

273

village official who felt his family lost face when his daughter was spurned. He was about to charge the young officer with rape.

Boyd said he called in the young officer and gave him the big picture of how many base activities depended on the goodwill of Thai officials. He ordered the young officer, guilty or not, to continue the relationship. "I'm giving you a direct order to screw her every night until you are transferred out of here," Boyd said he told the officer.

"Sir, I don't believe that is a lawful order," the officer said.

"Goddammit, I issued it and you better obey it. We're at war and bigger things are at stake here than your guilt. Your dick can cause you problems but it is not going to cause problems for America. You do as I say or I will make your life a living hell for as long as you are in the Air Force."

Then Boyd called in the village official and told him the young officer had seen the error of his ways and that the relationship with the official's daughter would continue.

Rabid dogs and obscenity on latrine walls and wandering young officers may seem inconsequential. But these small stitches not only make up the tapestry of a wartime Air Force base, they go to the heart of Boyd's creative style of problem solving. They were all effective, and they all contributed to turning around an important American air base with a severe morale problem.

Boyd also thought the Base Exchange (B-X) at NKP was an unnecessary indulgence. He said a store selling everything from hair dryers to television sets to stereos had no place on a combat base — that such things made Americans "soft." Persky recalls that once, he and Boyd were talking when Boyd pointed at the B-X and said everything in the store should be loaded aboard C-130s and parachuted into North Vietnam. "Let them get used to the good life and then we can just walk in and take over," he said.

Boyd also dealt with situations of great consequence. He said the McNamara Line was an expensive failure and shut it down. He claimed that a four-star general later told him he was sent to NKP solely because Pentagon generals knew he was the only man in the Air Force with the guts to close down the boondoggle.

Boyd, as a senior officer, lived in a trailer. By all accounts he worked eighteen- and twenty-hour days. He bought a reel-to-reel tape deck, and every night as he did paperwork his trailer was filled with the ominous "Ride of the Valkyries" or the majestic "Entry of the Gods into Valhalla." It was at night that Boyd made his phone calls to America, to Sprad or Christie or Sprey and once to Mary. These calls were made on the ham-radio network called MARS, a system that necessitated saying "over" after speaking and then waiting to accommodate the interminably long pause; Mary found it terribly confusing. And it was at night that he worked long hours on his "learning theory." It would be almost five years before this search culminated in one of the few things Boyd ever wrote, an eleven-page paper he called "Destruction and Creation," an unpublished work that some think is his most significant intellectual achievement.

In December, as the Christmas bombings began and Air Force bases were on high alert, Boyd received an emergency message from his brother Gerry. His baby sister, Ann, had breast cancer and was very ill. She might not live. Boyd must come to the hospital in New York.

The news hit Boyd hard. His mother was fighting a failing memory and Gerry had been talking about bringing her to Florida. And now this. He got an emergency leave and headed back to the States.

Ann lived with Marion in New York City. She still was influenced by her mother's admonition to keep all personal information close and did not want anyone in the family to know she had cancer. But Marion could not deal with a dying sister by herself. She said to Ann, "Gerry is coming up here on business. He will want to see you. I'll have to bring him by the hospital."

"Okay," Ann said.

Marion pressed ahead. "And John is coming back from Thailand for an important meeting here in New York. I can't keep him away."

"Okay."

So the four living siblings, the remaining sons and daughters of Hubert and Elsie Boyd, gathered in Columbia Presbyterian Hospital. After a few days, Ann seemed to rally. Boyd wearily crawled aboard an airplane for the long flight across twelve time zones, back to the war, back to a remote base in Thailand. But Ann's rally was brief. Boyd was at NKP little more than a week when he received another message: Ann is dying.

Ann was heavily medicated when Boyd arrived, in and out of consciousness. Gerry and Marion sat by her bed. Gerry suggested that he and John go out and buy Ann some ice cream, which she loved. Ann was sleeping so Marion nodded her assent. Gerry and Boyd slogged through the winter streets for almost an hour. While they were gone Marion noticed that Ann seemed unusually still. Marion jostled Ann's shoulder and got no response.

"Ann, are you asleep?" Marion said. No response.

Now Marion was frightened. She had always heard that the sense of hearing is the last thing to go when a person is dying. She leaned down and began shouting in Ann's ear. But Ann made no response. Nurses heard Marion shouting and rushed to the room. "My sister is not right. She is not answering me," Marion told them.

The nurses took one look at Ann and knew she was dead. "We'll take care of this," they said, and ushered Marion from the room.

When Boyd and Gerry returned with the ice cream, they found Marion standing in the hall, wishing she had been allowed to say good-bye to her sister.

Then Gerry and Boyd had to go to Erie to tell their mother her baby daughter had died of cancer. Since Elsie had not known Ann was sick, the news came as a considerable shock. But, with her usual stoicism, she endured it.

When Boyd returned to NKP, he had three months remaining on his tour and then it was back home, for good. How well he performed his duties is demonstrated in his final ER. The front side is fire walled, again with the exception of the box regarding his human relations, where he is graded "above average" rather than "outstanding." The narrative says his "sound and effective management practices" reversed a deteriorating racial situation, and that the improvements he had made in the living, working, and recreational facilities resulted in higher morale across the base. The ER also said Boyd's "high degree of rapport" with Thai officials had made possible the successful completion of numerous projects that depended on Thai–United States cooperation. It said Boyd's mission-oriented nature "contributed materially to the success of this wing's combat operations." The indorsement said that although Boyd came out of the R&D field, he had performed "in a superior manner" as a commander.

NKP was a pivot point in Boyd's career. For him the Vietnam War served almost as a vacation from the Pentagon war. It was a year in which he had the chance to wash everything clean. He had begun a voracious reading program and an obsessive search for the nature of creativity, both of which laid the foundation for what soon would become the major focus of his life.

Boyd's ERs from Southeast Asia are close to perfect. It is worth noting that in the cauldron of a combat environment, a place where men reveal what they are made of, and a place where — as his predecessor as base commander proved — some men collapse from stress, Boyd performed flawlessly.

But now he was going back to the Pentagon, back to the labyrinth of the Blue Suiters.

Chapter Twenty

Take a Look at the B-1

WHEN Boyd took off from Thailand on the long flight to Washington, he had little idea of how troubled America was and how significant were the changes taking place in the Pentagon and in the Air Force. President Richard Nixon was under siege, the vice president was about to be forced out of office, and an air of mistrust and uncertainty permeated the country. Throughout the Pentagon the command structure struggled to absorb the bitter lessons of Vietnam. And in the Air Force the long era of the nuclear bomber generals was ending. These generals still ran the Air Force, but they were retiring in large numbers and being replaced by a vanguard of fighter generals who brought a change, if not in philosophy, then at least in orientation.

Boyd had been in the Air Force almost twenty-three years and knew there was little chance he would make general. The Pentagon would be his last assignment before he retired. This was his last great opportunity to leave his mark on the Air Force. He thought his legacy would be the lightweight fighter, and all of his hopes and dreams centered around that project.

At the same time Boyd was reading widely and thinking ahead and searching for ways to get a grasp on his "learning theory." When he talked of learning, he did not mean studying but rather the process of creativity. Boyd did not then know it, but his learning theory would become the first bookend for an extraordinary series of intellectual accomplishments. He was about to begin a stormy ten-year passage into the rarefied realm of the pure intellectual. He also was about to step onto a stage where he would be joined in quick succession by three of the remaining four Acolytes. That stage was the Building, where, behind the scenes, extraordinary events were taking place.

James Schlesinger was the new secretary of defense — the "SecDef" in Building speak — and, like most secretaries, wanted to leave a legacy. To find out how to do that, he sought counsel with a man whose understanding of the military he deeply respected, Richard Hallock. Colonel Hallock was a paratrooper, a highly decorated combat hero who also was a close friend of the redoubtable Pierre Sprey. In fact, when Sprey first came to the Building, Hallock was his mentor.

Hallock sat down with Schlesinger and said in effect, "You must understand that if you want to leave a legacy it is vital for you to make a quick decision about what you want that legacy to be. If you don't make a quick decision, you will have no legacy. Because after several months you become so caught up in the business of the Pentagon, so enmeshed with the generals, so overwhelmed with the scope and enormity of the job that it will be too late. Pick a few projects and put the full weight of your office behind them. Guide the projects. Nurture them. Know from the very beginning that they will be your legacy. Force them through the bureaucracy."

Schlesinger agreed. But there were dozens, perhaps hundreds, of projects going on in each branch of the military. It would take months to sort through them. What should he choose?

"I can recommend several. Two of the most important are in the Air Force and the Air Force doesn't want either. You will have a fight."

"What are they?"

"The lightweight fighter and the A-10."

After reading Hallock's detailed analysis of the two projects, Schlesinger agreed.

Schlesinger's decision was the third serendipitous event that kept alive the lightweight fighter. Once again, remarkably, the project had been rescued. First there was Packard's decision to start a prototype program. Without Packard's decision, the lightweight fighter would have been stillborn. Second, when Colonel Lyle Cameron, head of the Air Force prototype selection committee and friend of Pierre Sprey, began looking for projects to prototype, the Fighter Mafia, working under the camouflage of Riccioni's study, was ready and handed him detailed specifications for the lightweight fighter. And now Hallock had recommended the lightweight fighter as a top priority of the new SecDef.

It might seem to anyone outside the Building that with such authority behind it, the lightweight fighter was a shoo-in to go from prototyping into full production. But this was not the case. The Air Force had two major acquisition projects underway — the F-15 and the B-1. A new fighter not only would take money from both of these, it would — as another fighter — compete with the F-15. As for Pierre Sprey's A-10, it was in prototyping but the Air Force was determined to kill the project. They wanted to forget both the airplane and the CAS mission.

Secretary Schlesinger could not have picked two more contentious projects for his legacy.

Boyd's new job in the Building was director of the Office of Development Plans. This office was one of several that conducted long-range planning for the Air Force, but in truth it was a dumping ground: the Air Force placed so little importance on long-range planning that the office never had developed a systematic approach. In yet another sign that Boyd would not make general, the Air Force had stashed him on a dead-end street.

But Boyd was about to use the job as a platform from which he would rock the foundations of the Pentagon.

Naturally, the people in the office enjoyed the status quo, so there was much trepidation when they heard about the new boss coming in from a tour at NKP — an Air Force superstar, a full bull with a reputation for creativity and for being an out-of-control maverick, a heavy hitting hard-ass. The word spread: put on a pressed Class A uniform, mind your manners, and walk softly.

Boyd lived up to his advance billing. First, his appearance was striking. Because of his disciplined diet and exercise program, he weighed only 170 pounds. Even though he had bulging biceps and a powerful frame, his clothes hung from his body. His sunken cheeks emphasized his beaklike nose. His high-wattage intensity gave his eyes an almost supernatural brightness. He was an intimidating and rapacious presence.

Boyd liked nothing about his new office. The long-range planning was done without budget considerations and therefore was largely irrelevant. Boyd called his new workplace the "office of no planning" and refused to sign most papers sent his way. Dozens of memos and plans and studies and directives crossed his desk and were tossed aside. The paperwork piled up, first in his desk, and then in a box in the corner. "If somebody asks me, I tell them the papers are here but I can't find them," he said. "I don't sign off on no-plans." He stalked the office, staring at his underlings, then suddenly walking up to them, sticking a bony finger into their chest, and saying things such as, "If your boss demands loyalty, give him integrity. But if he demands integrity, then give him loyalty."

They looked at each other in bewilderment. What the hell did that mean?

Boyd was in the office about a week when he called the first meeting of his department heads. He lit a cigar, took a long sip of smart juice, and leaned back in his chair. "Everything you people are doing is meaningless," he said. "Not a goddamn thing coming out of this office has any importance." They shifted uncomfortably and waited. "But that's what the Air Force wants. So keep on doing nothing. Just don't bother me with the bullshit." He dismissed everyone but one officer, a man he judged particularly ineffective. "If I never hear from you, you will get outstanding ERs," Boyd said. "Talk to me and your ER is downgraded. In fact, your ERs are going to be inversely proportionate to how often I hear from you." The officer stared at Boyd, not knowing what to say. Boyd leaned across the desk and pointed his finger. "I don't believe I'm getting through. In this office the only way for you to fuck up is to let me hear from you." He then waved his hand and dismissed the officer.

One bit of paperwork caught Boyd's attention. When he read studies and reports on the new B-1 Bomber, his antennae quivered. It could have been because he was a fighter pilot and simply did not like bombers. It could have been because the B-1 was a swing-wing aircraft and he felt contempt for swing-wing technology. It could have been because the B-1 was gold-plated in the extreme — so expensive that to build it would take money from the F-15 and the lightweight fighter. It could have been because the B-1 was so complex that Boyd knew it represented endless problems. Or it could have been that Boyd sensed that the project was fundamentally corrupt. He looked around his office and realized none of the careerists would dive into a project so prized by the Air Force. It would be up to him.

Boyd's new job made him a member of the Program Review Committee, a prestigious group of colonels and generals who sorted through hundreds of ideas to choose what programs the Air Force would adopt, what direction the Air Force would go. Again, all of this was done with no consideration for budget restraints. Boyd thought the discussions at these meetings were useless and refused to attend. When a general sent down word that Boyd, or a representative, had to attend the meetings, Boyd looked around the office and his eyes settled on a secretary. When she put paper in her typewriter and started moving her fingers, the typewriter sounded like a Gatling gun. She was one of the fastest typists in the Pentagon. But oftentimes her fingers were not on the home keys and when she ripped the paper from the typewriter and handed it to someone for signature, it was gibberish. Boyd sent her to the meetings.

In his first days back in the Building, he made numerous phone calls all over the country. He called Sprad out at Nellis and Tom Christie at Eglin. He called two of his favorite students, Everett Raspberry and Ron Catton. Razz was a lieutenant colonel serving as operations officer in a test squadron at Eglin. Catton was a full colonel who had been a wing commander and was about to go to the War College. He was on the fast track to becoming a general, but his wife was diagnosed with cancer and he told Boyd he was retiring early to take care of her. Boyd also called his old comrade Pierre Sprey and told him to gird for battle. "The lightweight fighter is in trouble, Tiger. We're gonna have to go to the barricades."

Boyd could not sit still for any length of time. Several times each morning he loped down the concourse to the cafeteria or the bookstore. He bought candy bars and read the *Washington Star*. He had been away for a year and suddenly faced the daily shock of Watergate. And as he returned to his office, he began to stop fellow officers in the corridors and open conversations with "You read the latest about that goddamn Nixon?" Usually he was met with shocked silence. Boyd then put a conspiratorial arm about the person's shoulder and said, "Let me tell you something. We got to get rid of that son of a bitch. He's a crook."

Active-duty officers almost never criticize their commander in chief in public. Boyd may have been the first colonel to stalk the halls of the Pentagon, urging fellow officers to "get rid of" a president. Usually the person to whom Boyd was talking spun and rapidly walked away. And if Boyd later met the person in the hall, more often than not the other person ignored him. At which point Boyd stopped and boomed out, "The son of a bitch won't even look me in the eye!"

Boyd had more than politics on his mind. The fly-off competition between the YF-16 and the YF-17 was about to begin and he frequently was off to Nellis or Wright-Pat. The lightweight fighter was Boyd's dream and he knew the Blue Suiters were lying in wait. But until the fly-off was over, there was little more he could do. He wanted to examine the B-1. His instincts told him something was terribly wrong with that project, and if he was right, that meant a skunk fight with the Air Force. There was nothing Boyd loved more than a good skunk fight. It kept the juices flowing. It kept him at a combat edge. Without a skunk fight, life was boring.

One day he charged down the hall to the general who was his boss and complained that his office was filled with bureaucrats and that he wanted someone, anyone, just one person, who could do "real work." The general and Boyd had a contentious relationship. Boyd's loud voice and desk pounding and language often bordered on insubordination. It probably was to avoid another exchange that the general told Boyd he could have a young captain who was coming to the Building. When the general said the captain had a Ph.D. in electrical engineering, Boyd said he would take him sight unseen. "Anybody with a Ph.D. in double-e must be reasonably smart."

Boyd did not tell the general he had a special project for the young officer. He did not tell the general that what he really wanted was someone not contaminated by careerism, someone who still had his idealism, someone he could wind up and send into battle against the Air Force.

The captain reported in June. He saluted and said, "Sir, Captain Raymond Leopold reporting for duty."

Boyd glowered over a cigar. He looked at a tall slender officer and bellowed, "Boyd. Like *bird* in Brooklynese. Got it?"

A Ph.D. can figure out such things. "Yes, Sir."

Boyd put his feet on the table and opened the captain's folder. He shook his head in dismay. Leopold was a graduate of the Air Force Academy, a "Zoomie." "You got a warped education. The Academy teaches its graduates to be elitists, to expect too much."

"Yes, Sir."

Leopold had walked into Boyd's office with the confidence found in many firstborn children, the self-absorption embedded in graduates of the Air Force Academy, and the intellectual pride of a twenty-seven-year-old with a Ph.D. in one of the most difficult fields of engineering. He was among the most talented and educated young officers in the Air Force and he knew it. He was an officer of exceptional promise. Everyone thought so. Everyone, that is, but Boyd.

Leopold was born January 6, 1946, and boasted that he was "the first of the baby boomers." Ever since he was twelve years old, all he had wanted was to grow up and go to the Air Force Academy. On the math portion of his college boards, he made 798, the highest ever in his northwest Chicago high school. While his classmates applied to three or four colleges, he applied only to the Academy. He graduated in 1967 and ranked 165 in a class of 524. The ranking is deceptive because while Leopold fared miserably in political science and English and history, he was a near genius in electrical engineering. The Air Force sent him to graduate school and by the time he was twenty-two he had a master's degree. At Williams AFB in Arizona he was second in his flight class to solo the T-38. Later, at a celebratory party, his classmates decided to throw him into a swimming pool. Leopold resisted and in the resulting melee he herniated a spinal disk. His flying career was ended. During the next three and a half years, on his own with no Air Force assistance and no change of duties, he attended night school and earned his Ph.D.

Men in their twenties whose lives have been spent in academics sometimes have a childlike naïveté. This seems especially true of those who study mathematics. And for reasons only psychologists can explain, many young people of extraordinary intellectual gifts and accomplishments also have a deep sense of insecurity. Even the most casual question brought a response from Leopold in which he emphasized his ranking: first of the baby boomers, highest math SAT in his class, second in his class to solo. Leopold was an overachiever, especially after his father died, a year before his Pentagon rotation. He was focused on his career and wanted to be first in everything.

But he was standing in front of this gruff, blunt colonel and realized that none of his accomplishments mattered. In fact, he sensed he was on probation as far as Boyd was concerned. Leopold went home thinking someone made a big mistake by assigning him to Boyd's office.

The next morning Leopold showed Boyd his new Hewlett-Packard calculator. Such gadgets were still rare in the summer of 1973. Leopold had the first one in the office.

"Tiger, take that calculator of yours and do me a budget analysis," Boyd said. "I want you to go through the entire Air Force budget. I don't want my ideas to contaminate your search, but pay particular attention to anything to do with the B-1. Anything you see on the B-1, pull it out." Boyd leaned forward and in a conspiratorial whisper added, "I think they're fucking with the budget."

Then Boyd delivered what was to be called his "To Be or to Do" speech. Leopold was the first person known to receive the speech, probably because Boyd, based on his experiences over the years, was solidifying certain conclusions about the promotion system within the military.

"Tiger, one day you will come to a fork in the road," he said. "And you're going to have to make a decision about which direction you want to go." He raised his hand and pointed. "If you go that way you can be somebody. You will have to make compromises and you will have to turn your back on your friends. But you will be a member of the club and you will get promoted and you will get good assignments." Then Boyd raised his other hand and pointed another direction. "Or you can go that way and you can do something — something for your country and for your Air Force and for yourself. If you decide you want to do something, you may not get promoted and you may not get the good assignments and you certainly will not be a favorite of your superiors. But you won't have to compromise yourself. You will be true to your friends and to yourself. And your work might make a difference." He paused and stared into Leopold's eyes and heart. "To *be* somebody or to *do* something. In life there is often a roll call. That's when you will have to make a decision. To *be* or to *do?* Which way will you go?"

Leopold did not realize it, but Boyd was laying the ground rules, testing him. All Leopold wanted was to do his job, get a good ER, and move up the ladder. "Yes, Sir," he said.

Leopold went to the Pentagon library and to the Library of Congress and examined the defense authorization budget and the defense appropriation budget with as much attention to detail as those two hefty documents had ever seen. He studied the annual Air Force budget, the Research and Development budget, and the procurement budget. He studied the budgets of the previous eleven years and used the data to put together a preliminary analysis. In the Research and Development budget and the procurement budget, one project stood out: the B-1 Bomber. It was drawing off a disproportionate amount of money.

Leopold came back to Boyd, who told him to look at a parametric analysis of the projected B-1 costs and to use three numbers for starters: $500,000 for each engine, $2,000 per pound for avionics, and $200 per pound for the airframe. These numbers came from Boyd's work on the F-15 and the lightweight fighter.

When Leopold put the numbers on a graph, they showed an inexorable and undeniable trend. Congress had mandated that the B-1 not cost more than $25 million per copy. But the chart showed the costs were more than double that amount. Not only was the B-1 taking a disproportionate amount of the Air Force budget, it was violating a congressional mandate.

Boyd was so excited he bounced from one foot to the other. "Great work, Tiger. Great stuff. Stay with it." He told Leopold to take a "metaview." He used *meta* in the mathematical sense of a different domain, a higher level.

Boyd did not want to take these numbers to the Air Force, not yet. He ordered Leopold to recompute everything as a "best case," that is, to give the B-1 advocates the benefit of every doubt. Every time Leopold had a choice of numbers, he was to use the most conservative. This meant that under scrutiny, and the Air Force would indeed subject the study to the most rigorous scrutiny, the numbers would only get worse; that is, any adjustments would show only higher costs.

Boyd had a brief interruption from supervising the B-1 investigation when ongoing flight tests of the F-15 required his attention. Although the F-15 was a bitter memory, Boyd perked up when an Air Force general asked him if he wanted a flight in the new aircraft. Boyd did not like what the F-15 had become, but the general's offer resurrected both his parental pride in the aircraft and the persona of Forty-Second Boyd. "Hell yes," he said. The general said he would get back to Boyd.

In the meantime Leopold discovered, as had others, that Boyd had little perception of time. Leopold might work at the Pentagon until midnight and then, as he wearily walked into his house in Dale City some thirty miles south, the phone was ringing. Boyd had calculated to the minute the time it took Leopold to get home. And he would have more questions, more directions for the B-1 study.

In August, Leopold wrote a classified memo saying that if the Air Force bought the 240 B-1s it was scheduled to buy, the cost would be $68 million per copy. When the costs of the B-1 were superimposed on a chart showing the costs of other aircraft, it caused a giant and unmistakable bulge. The B-1 Bomber was the costliest project in the Air Force.

Leopold gave Boyd the memo, then took a week of leave to drive home to Chicago and see his mother. She met him at the door, all aflutter of the barrage of phone calls from the Pentagon. Leopold was to call a Colonel John Boyd immediately. Boyd said the command structure of the Air Force, the top three- and four-stars in the Building, were thunderstruck over the implications of Leopold's memo.

Much of Leopold's vacation was spent on the phone with Boyd, explaining and expanding his budget analysis. When he returned to the Pentagon, two young colonels working for the chief of staff were there to ask pointed questions and to tear apart his memo. Once Leopold showed them the source for his numbers and how he had charted the results, they saw that any change would only make the B-1 look worse. They reported to the chief that Leopold was a young staff officer doing his job. He had presented the information in the most conservative manner possible. He had no agenda.

Leopold transformed his memo into a classified briefing for top Air Force officials. Most young captains, if they ever were allowed to brief three- and four-stars, would have told the generals what they wanted to hear. Leopold was respectful but did not let the generals browbeat him into altering his findings. That made a tremendous impression on Boyd, and as a result, Leopold's life changed. He was in an office of colonels and lieutenant colonels and majors, the junior member of the firm. But because he was Boyd's protégé, he was number one.

One morning Boyd arrived about 10:00 A.M. to find Leopold sleeping at his desk. Ordinarily, if a colonel finds a captain sleeping on the job, the captain finds himself on the receiving end of a royal chewing out. The captain probably will be transferred. The lieutenant colonels and majors waited and watched and wondered what Boyd would do.

He tiptoed through the office, finger to his lips, saying, "Shhhhhh-hhh. Everybody be quiet. Ray needs his sleep." Then he thought for a minute and in a stage whisper said, "Okay, everybody out. Go to the concourse and read magazines and drink coffee, walk around or whatever. Ray has to have his nap."

The lieutenant colonels and majors were not amused at being tossed out of their office so a captain could sleep. But Boyd knew what no one else knew, that Leopold had worked most of the night.

The flap over the B-1 seemed to have been absorbed into the bowels of the Pentagon. Now Leopold was working on other projects. Two or three days a week, about 1:00 P.M., Boyd went to Leopold and said, "Ray, let's go take a walk." And the colonel and the captain walked down to the concourse, bought candy by the handful, read the newspapers, and talked.

Leopold was supposed to work with Boyd for six months before going to another Pentagon office. Leopold's Academy classmates said to him, "Nobody is going to hold it against you that you worked for Boyd for six months. But you need to get out of there. If you stay longer, it will affect your career."

As Leopold approached the six-month deadline, Boyd asked him to consider staying. "I gotta tell you, it will be better for your career if you move on. But you're doing good work, Tiger, and I'd like for you to stay."

"Sir, I'd like to sleep on it."

The next morning, for the first time since Leopold was assigned to Boyd's office, he arrived to find Boyd already there.

"Sir, I can't imagine doing more anywhere else than I can do here," Leopold said. "I'd like to stay."

Boyd's face lit up. "Ray, I can't guarantee you any early promotions or special recognition. All I can guarantee is that you will be doing important work. And it will be fun."

Boyd had become Leopold's surrogate father.

And Leopold had become the next Acolyte.

Chapter Twenty-One

"This Briefing Is for Information Purposes Only"

By 1973 Tom Christie's shop at Eglin had grown to about one hundred people. In September he left Eglin and moved to the Pentagon, where he took over the Tactical Air Program in the Office of the Secretary of Defense. There must have been considerable speculation about whether the big crewcut fellow from the Hobby Shop down at Eglin was ready for the Building — especially for the TacAir job.

TacAir was part of the old Systems Analysis office, the home of the Whiz Kids. Under McNamara, TacAir had been extremely powerful because it confronted the Air Force and Navy and made them prove why each program was needed. It thus had great influence on which proposed Air Force programs made it into the budget. Not surprisingly, the military loathed Systems Analysis so much that the name was changed to Program Analysis & Evaluation (PA&E). TacAir was thought to have been neutered by the name change, but the power of the office, while dormant, remained.

That power depended on two things: first, whether the person running the office was willing to confront the Air Force, and second, whether the person had the confidence of the secretary of defense. Before Christie was hired, he met with Schlesinger, who told him his primary assignment was to make the Air Force accept the light-weight fighter. That put Christie on a collision course with the Air Force. But he had the backing of the SecDef.

Gearing up to do battle with the Air Force took a few weeks. In the meantime Christie took care of something close to his heart. He called in Chet Richards, a twenty-seven-year-old management intern, and assigned him a crucial mission: find a bar where Christie could continue the Eglin tradition of Friday night office parties. Richards was the youngest person ever to receive a Ph.D. in math from the University of Mississippi, so he was up to the challenge. But none of the bars Richards checked out seemed to have that intangible mood that would make it a home for Christie's office family. On Friday nights Washington bars are crowded and raucous — not the mood Christie wanted. Then Richards discovered the Old Guard Room in the basement of the Officers Club at nearby Fort Myer. And he picked Wednesday night rather than Friday night; Wednesdays were quiet and offered a midweek break. So Christie and the TacAir crowd, along with Boyd and the people in his office, began meeting in the Old Guard Room of Patton Hall at Fort Myer. Christie was the de facto patron of the group, almost a father figure, but it was Boyd who was the center of attention. For more than a decade, the happy hour gatherings were a crucial part of Boyd's life.

Christie had barely settled into his office when the Air Force launched a strike against the lightweight fighter, and in the most vulnerable part of any Pentagon project: the budget. In late 1973 the Air Force was putting together the 1975 budget and the lightweight fighter was not included. The Air Force planned to fly the prototypes in 1974, then shut down the program. The lightweight fighter was considered a "technology demonstrator" and not part of any long-range Air Force plans.

Christie, with the crucial assistance of Chuck Myers, director of air warfare, slipped $30 million into the 1975 budget to continue work on the lightweight fighter and move it into full-scale development. The Air Force found the $30 million and removed it. Christie and Myers put it back.

Christie's immediate boss was famous for writing scathing memos on tiny pieces of white paper called "snowflakes." Christie's budget battle with the Air Force brought him a blizzard of snowflakes, one of which said in effect, "The Air Force will decide to field the light-weight fighter when and if it wants to. Get off the Air Force's back."

It had never occurred to Christie's boss or to Air Force generals that the new civilian from Eglin had access to Schlesinger. The generals did not know that, through Colonel Richard Hallock, Sprey had intro-duced Boyd to Schlesinger and that he, too, was meeting privately with the SecDef. The generals did not know that Sprey was a special advisor to Schlesinger. And the generals did not know that Schlesinger was committed to making the lightweight fighter part of his legacy.

When Schlesinger said the money would stay in the budget, Air Force generals ground their teeth in anger. As the generals began making plans to go over Schlesinger's head and take the issue to sym-pathetic members of Congress, a young Air Force captain transferred to Boyd's office. His name was Franklin "Chuck" Spinney.

Spinney is a military brat, the son of an Air Force colonel. He was born at Wright-Pat but, like most military brats, moved often. To the extent that he is from anywhere, he is from Severna Park, Maryland, where he moved when he was ten and lived until he was fifteen. Spin-ney is a mathematician. His college boards in math were excellent, but the English portion was a disaster. He went to Lehigh University and graduated in 1967 with a degree in mechanical engineering. When he joined the Air Force, his father swore him in as an officer. Spinney was assigned to Wright-Pat and worked in the same building where his father worked during World War II. His job was to study the effects of bullets on F-105s shot down in Vietnam.

From the time Spinney entered the Air Force, he was considered a brash young officer. In 1968, as a twenty-four-year-old second lieu-tenant, he ran into Christie at Aberdeen Proving Ground, where both were after a $500,000 grant. Spinney outmaneuvered the Fina-gler, something rarely done. Christie thought Spinney was a "smart-ass lieutenant" but offered him a job at Eglin.

In the first staff study Spinney wrote, he recommended that the Air Force cancel a consulting contract with a national company. The CEO of the company took Spinney to lunch and said, "If you try to terminate my contract I will ruin your career." Spinney looked at the bars on his collar and said, "Ruin my career? I'm a lieutenant. I can't go down."

When a high-ranking civilian who worked for the Army promoted someone to chair an important working group, someone whom Spinney thought incompetent, he had the temerity to ask, "Why in God's name did you make that asshole the chairman? He doesn't know anything."

Another of Spinney's early actions demonstrated both his impatience with regulations and his intrinsic passion about fiduciary responsibility. He needed a place to store records, so he had an empty building at Wright-Pat assigned to his office. Because many of the records he wanted to store were classified, he needed a vault. Rather than issuing contracts, he figured he could save taxpayer money by having employees scrounge materials around the base and build the office. The office was built without paperwork, but when it came time to hang a door on the vault, for technical reasons Spinney had to issue a contract. The base engineer came to inspect the door and looked around in amazement. He was in a facility that officially did not exist. It did not matter that Spinney had saved thousands of dollars, he had bypassed the system, and that was unacceptable. But what really upset the base engineer, a senior colonel, was that the young lieutenant had his own conference room and a desk with a big flag behind it. Flags are a perk reserved for generals. Eventually, the Air Force decided to keep the building, but Spinney had to give up his flag.

The Air Force sent Spinney to graduate school, where he got an MBA with an emphasis on applied statistics. Then he went to the Pentagon, where he had a job his superiors thought commensurate with his education: he delivered mail. Spinney often ran into Ray Leopold. They were the same age and the same rank, the only two young guys in the office. They were similar in many ways; the big difference was that Leopold was quicker but Spinney was deeper. Spinney heard of what Boyd was doing and said to Leopold, "I'd like to work with you."

Boyd called Spinney in for an interview. Boyd was gaining weight because of all the candy and junk food he ate and was drinking a diet supplement called Metrecal. He drank two cans during the half hour they talked, then said, "Let's go eat lunch."

Spinney's eyebrows rose. Colonels do not invite captains to lunch. At the cafeteria, Spinney watched Boyd pick up a plate and pile on lettuce and tomatoes and cheese and peppers and carrots and mush-rooms and whatever else he could find. After Boyd stacked up a mountain of salad, he held up the line for almost five minutes as he tucked croutons into every nook and cranny and then lined the borders of his plate. Even though he walked slowly toward a table, he left a trail of croutons and vegetables. He sat down and tucked in. Spinney watched for several minutes and then said, "Colonel, I hope you don't mind my asking. Don't you enjoy your food?"

Boyd stopped shoveling for a minute. Puzzled, he stared at Spinney. Then, as if belaboring the obvious, he said, "It's just fuel," and resumed shoveling.

After lunch the two men talked further. Then Boyd said, "Okay, Tiger. We'll try it out."

The fourth Acolyte was now onstage.

He would stay in the battle long after the others moved on. And he would become the best known of them all.

The new year brought a stream of significant events into Boyd's life. The battle over the lightweight fighter raged on two fronts: Christie dealt with budget battles and the ebb and flow of power politics, while Boyd computed E-M data for the two aircraft and planned the fly-off.

The biggest obstacle to the lightweight fighter remained Air Force intransigence in approving the aircraft for full-scale development. Boyd tried to overcome the opposition with a series of briefings, the point of which was that the lightweight fighter was needed and should go into production. The plan was to brief widely among the lower ranks and then begin working up through the generals, culminating in a briefing to the three-stars, the barons who ran the Air Force. In early 1974, Boyd learned he was facing a crisis: the three-stars were lying in wait. He was to brief up the ladder to them and then, once there was an impression that he had received a fair hearing, they would scuttle the lightweight fighter once and for all.

Christie helped devise a plan that would bypass the three-stars. General George Brown, the Air Force chief of staff, was like the SecDef in that he wanted to leave a legacy for his time in the Building. The greatest single desire of the Air Force was to increase the force structure — that is, the number of wings in the Air Force. Christie convinced Schlesinger to allow the Air Force to grow from twenty-two to twenty-six wings if the chief of staff would push the light-weight fighter and the A-10 into production. Schlesinger insisted on one caveat: the lightweight fighter would remain an air-to-air fighter and would not be wired for delivery of nuclear weapons.

Brown quickly accepted the plan. But he had a small problem. His three-stars were going to object. Swallowing the lightweight fighter was bad enough, but when the ugly and ponderous A-10 was added, the medicine was too bitter for the Blue Suiters. They might stage a bureaucratic revolt. How and when to tell them about the deal was a serious political matter.

Sprey and Christie passed the word about the deal to Boyd. Boyd was elated. His briefing with the three-stars was soon. "Can I tell them?" he asked. Sprey and Christie saw no reason why not. The secretary had not told them to keep the agreement quiet.

On the day of his big briefing, Boyd waited in the spacious, well-appointed briefing room. He must have smiled to himself as he watched the parade of three-stars enter the room. These were the men who made things happen in the Air Force. They, too, must have been smiling.

One of the generals nodded and said, "Colonel, you may begin."

Boyd picked up a wooden pointer and strode to the front of the dais. He stood on the edge, his toes curling downward, and rapped the pointer against his palm. He nodded at the sober group of generals, paused a delicious moment, and said, "Gentlemen, I am authorized by the secretary of defense to inform you this is not a decision brief. This briefing is for information purposes only."

Boyd paused a moment and let the generals absorb this. They looked at each other and then looked at Boyd. He continued. "The secretary and the chief of staff have decided to go into production with the lightweight fighter."

The generals sat rigidly through the briefing. There were no questions. When Boyd finished, the generals stood up and filed out. As they left, one muttered, "That fucking Boyd."

And the next Wednesday night at the Old Guard Room, the story was told and retold of how Boyd did a cape job on a roomful of three-stars. He shoved his arms out as if he were holding a cape, wiggled his hands, and said, "They charged right off the precipice."

* * *

Two weeks later the Air Force struck back. A two-star was called to testify before a congressional committee. The Air Force saw this as a great opportunity and convinced a congressman who was sympathetic to the military to question the two-star about the uselessness of the lightweight fighter and then move to overrule the secretary of defense.

Answering obviously scripted questions, the two-star told Congress the lightweight fighter was not needed and that he was not at all sure how it might be utilized. The F-15 was the airplane the Air Force wanted. The general said that the lightweight fighter was being shoved down the throat of the Air Force by Tom Christie and the TacAir shop. The congressmen nodded and made veiled threats against the Air Force.

Christie and Spinney and Leopold soon heard of the testimony. Leopold called Boyd and told him what happened and then grew silent as Boyd began talking. Leopold's eyes grew wider and wider. He put down the phone and turned to Spinney. "You won't believe what Boyd just said."

"What's that?"

"He said he was going to have to fire his first general."

The two young captains stared at each other. The idea of a colonel firing a two-star simply could not be assimilated. Such things do not happen in the military.

But then the SecDef called the chief of staff and asked him whether or not he was in charge of the Air Force. A few days later the two-star was given twenty-four hours to clean out his desk and leave the Pentagon. Other Pentagon generals saw what happened to the two-star. The Fighter Mafia had struck back and the generals could read the tea leaves. There could be no more obstacles for the lightweight fighter. It was cleared to go into production.

That evening at happy hour, Chet Richards and a group of Marine aviators gathered around Boyd. Christie and Sprey were there, too. Boyd looked at the faces of his friends and nodded in satisfaction. "Nobody thought I would ever get beyond major," he said. "But here I am a colonel." He paused. "And I'm taking out generals."

A few days later the Air Force made a last-ditch attempt to shoot down the lightweight fighter. A big part of Schlesinger's sales pitch for the lightweight fighter, one particularly convincing to congress-men, was that NATO countries were lining up to buy it. The Air Force moved to kill the international sales by saying the lightweight fighter was too limited in range to do anything but defend the home drome.

At last Boyd announced the fuel fraction and range of the light-weight fighter. He added insult to injury by comparing it with the F-15. The lightweight fighter not only had greater range than the F-15, it had greater range than any fighter in the Air Force. Of course foreign purchasing officials were euphoric, while Air Force generals reeled in shock.

One bewildered general called Boyd in and said, "I thought this was a short-legged airplane. It flies farther than the F-15."

"Well, sir, it is short-legged. It's just that the F-15 is shorter legged."

Now there was nothing else the Air Force could do to stop the lightweight fighter and the A-10. Both were going into production. The Fighter Mafia had won.

For the moment.

In June, Lieutenant Colonel James Burton reported to Boyd as his new deputy. Burton was a Chosen One — a graduate of the first class at the Air Force Academy and the first Academy graduate to attend the Air Force's three professional schools: Squadron Officers School, Air Command and Staff College, and Industrial College of the Armed Forces. He had a master's degree in business and had done the course work for a master's in mechanical engineering. Every promo-tion had been below the zone and now he was five years ahead of his contemporaries in the race to the top. He was a water-walker, the ultimate Zoomie, the quintessential Blue Suiter who had the inside track at becoming general and a good shot at becoming chief of staff.

Spinney was dismayed. He thought Burton standoffish, too seri-ous, too remote, and too much a careerist. Even though Burton was perhaps ten years younger than Boyd, somehow he seemed older. Spinney went to Boyd and said, "Colonel, that guy is big trouble. Don't hire him."

"No, he's okay," Boyd said. "I checked him out."

Boyd saw something that both Spinney and Leopold had missed.

In later years people would say Boyd "converted" Spinney and Leopold and turned them from promising careers. But in truth they were not converted; they simply never lost the principles and idealism common in most young officers. Once they raised their hands and took an oath to serve their country, they never wavered. It was their contemporaries who were converted, who bought into the beliefs and mores of careerists, who slowly and insidiously were corrupted by the Building. Burton was different from Spinney and Leopold. He was not a young idealist. He was an honored member of the Brotherhood of the Building. But Boyd sensed that Burton had an unbending spirit, an uncompromising heart, and a backbone forged of carbon steel. He looked into Burton's eyes and saw a man with the persistence of a rutting moose. He knew that rarely is a Blue Suiter turned around. But if it happens, and if all the virtues that drove Jim Burton so fast on the road to *being* someone could be redirected into his *doing* something, the man could change the world.

Burton was the most improbable of the Acolytes.

Now they were all together, all save one: Christie the Finagler, Sprey the Intelligent, Leopold the First, Spinney the Brash, and Burton the Unbending. For the next decade they revolved around Boyd, asserting themselves in various degrees before coalescing into the most powerful ad hoc group the Building had ever seen.

Burton's conversion was slow, but when it finally came he would astonish the Acolytes as much as he astonished his Academy classmates. He would show that one man can make a difference. He was to have an enormous impact on the Building.

But first he had to go through his trial by fire.

Burton's parents divorced when he was young and he was raised by a grandmother. He never had a father. From as far back as he can remember, he had the desire to accomplish things. He was president of his senior class in Normal, Illinois, and a member of the national honor society for four years. An outstanding athlete, he was an all-conference and all-city quarterback and earned letters in baseball and basketball. He was offered a chance to play professional baseball but instead became one of the 10,000 Illinois candidates for the eight openings in the very first class at the Air Force Academy. There, he was captain of the baseball team and during his junior year was third in the nation in the college batting championship. Curtis LeMay was chief of staff when Burton graduated, and the general saw that members of that first Academy class were given special treatment at every step in their careers. They were the Chosen Ones.

If Spinney and Leopold looked at Burton with disdain, he looked upon Boyd and his captains with even more. "This guy is crazy," Burton thought. Boyd was usually late to work, was slovenly, and disobeyed orders. He referred to generals as "perfumed princes" or "weak dicks" who would put their lives on the line for their country but not their jobs. Burton cringed when Boyd told how he had been at a party and invited a general to hear one of his briefings and the general said, "No thanks. I don't want to be told how dumb I am."

Burton was further astonished when he heard Spinney say Boyd ordered him to the Pentagon at midnight to correct a single letter in a transparency that was to be used in a briefing the next day. Technicians in the Pentagon graphics shop hated to see Boyd come in the door. He made them stop whatever they were doing to take care of his needs. When they complained of their workload he said, "If there is a higher priority than mine, I'll be glad to wait. But this is for Secretary Schlesinger." It amazed Burton that Boyd had back-channel dealings with Schlesinger, that it was not at all uncommon for Boyd to receive a phone call, seize books or studies or charts, and say, "I have to go see Schlesinger."

It is the nature of a careerist to mold and fit himself to his commanding officer. So Burton resolved to adjust. He would try to understand Boyd and he would begin by using Leopold and Spinney as interpreters. "What does he mean by that?" became a frequent question. Or "Why is he doing that?"

The relationship between Boyd and the two young captains was not easily fathomed. There was very little military protocol. Leopold and Spinney joked about Boyd's loudness, his table manners, and his other idiosyncrasies. But it was clear that both men revered Boyd. They competed for his attention and approval.

Burton came to work one July morning and found Boyd and Leopold and Spinney finishing an all-night job: drafting a one-page letter for a general. The general wanted Boyd to write a policy letter that would give guidance in generating new ideas throughout the Air Force. Boyd wanted more time but the general said, "I want it bad," and ordered Boyd to have it ready the next day. Boyd worked until about 10:00 P.M., then called Leopold and Spinney at home and told them to report to work immediately; they had a big job. Leopold said, "Yes, Sir," and jumped into his car. But Spinney complained and said, "Why should I come down there at midnight? That's bullshit." Boyd fired back, "Because you're a fucking captain and I'm a colonel and I say get your ass down here now." Once Leopold and Spinney arrived, Boyd said they needed to relax before they began drafting the letter. It was hot and the Pentagon air-conditioning was turned off. Boyd opened the windows and the three men took off their shirts. Boyd began telling stories. He told of growing up in Erie, of burning down the hangars in Japan, of being Forty-Second Boyd, of Georgia Tech, and of how he stole a million dollars' worth of computer time at Eglin and then deflected the inspector general's investigation. He told how he hosed a big-shot civilian at Eglin and cleaned out a colonel who wouldn't pay overtime to a secretary. He told them of his work on the F-15 and the surrealistic stories from NKP. He had them holding their sides with laughter. After several hours of war stories, Boyd decided everyone needed to rest. So they slept atop desks until about 5:00 A.M., when Boyd awakened his charges and the three men drafted the letter. Boyd examined their work, then added a final sentence: "After this course of action is considered, we respectfully recommend that it be disapproved."

Spinney stared at Boyd. "We spend all night working on that and then you say it should be thrown out?"

Boyd signed the letter. "He wants it bad, he gets it bad."

On July 27, 1974, Boyd received the last ER of his Air Force career. It was fire walled on the front side and the narrative opened with "Colonel Boyd is a very unique and superior officer." The ER said Boyd was "singularly responsible" for developing the F-15 and that his E-M work formed the basis for the lightweight fighter. It said Boyd was "unique in his ability to study, dissect, analyze and assemble ideas in a useful form so they can be transmitted into future actions." The ER told how Boyd was working on a Development Plan that would be the basis for developing future airplanes and technology. The ER was indorsed by a three-star who said Boyd made an "immeasurable contribution" to the Air Force with his E-M Theory.

In August, Boyd finished a six-and-one-half-page draft of the Development Planning Report. It is significant in two respects. First, astonishingly, it marks the first time the Air Force ever had guidelines about matching planning needs with available budgets. Second, the report says if combat tasks are to be of any use to planners, the tasks should be related to needed hardware. Boyd explains that in combat, both at the highest command level and at the lowest, individuals first orient themselves so they can understand the situation, then they make a decision to direct their activities, and then they take action. These three ingredients — orientation, decision, and action — would be seen in Boyd's work again.

Boyd's E-M work was being diluted by the bureaucracy at Wright-Pat, so he never missed an opportunity to brief anyone, military and civilian, on the capabilities and potential of E-M. One such briefing was to the Defense Science Board, a collection of the most prestigious scientists in America, whose job is to advise the secretary of defense. Most members of the board were interested and receptive to Boyd's ideas. But when he told of the poor performance of missiles in Vietnam and said fighters should be more maneuverable, a physics professor took umbrage.

"Colonel, I heard what you briefed," the professor said. "But the maneuverability should be built into the missile and not the aircraft."

Boyd patiently explained again how this had not worked in Vietnam.

"Colonel, for your information, I am talking about a different kind of missile, a missile whose performance is such that it doesn't matter about the capabilities of the delivery aircraft."

"Oh, and what kind of missile would that be, Professor?"

"I'm talking about a lenticular missile."

"Sir, I'm just a dumb fighter pilot. I have to ask you what a 'lenticular missile' is."

The professor's disdain for this slow-witted fighter pilot was obvious when he said, "It's shaped like a lens, like a saucer."

Boyd nodded and said, "Oh, I get it." He appeared to be thinking for a moment. Then he said, "You know, Professor, you have a pretty good idea there. Might I offer an idea for a modification?"

"Of course."

"Instead of saucer shaped, why don't you make it boomerang

shaped? That way, you can fling the goddamn thing out there and if it misses it will come back and you can fling it again."

Members of the board laughed so hard the chairman had to call a recess. For months afterward Boyd was known as "Boomerang Boyd" in honor of his latest cape job. The lenticular missile was never heard of again, except at happy hour on Wednesday nights.

In October 1974, the B-1 again came to the forefront when word leaked out of Wright-Pat that the airplane would cost $100 million per copy, far more than Leopold's early $68 million estimate. This was a lot of money at a time when the F-15 cost about $15 million, the light-weight fighter $6 million, and the A-10 — which finally was under construction — $3 million. Air Force leadership knew they were facing a crisis. Ray Leopold had developed a graph of the real cost of future purchases, what he called a "procurement bow wave," that showed the unbridgeable chasm between what the Air Force was committing to and the money Congress was appropriating for the purchase. This meant that every year, more and more unpaid bills were pushed into the future. Not even the United States could afford to buy some two hundred bombers costing $100 million each. Nevertheless, the Air Force wanted the B-1; as a general told Leopold, "Our job is to see that the flow of money to the contractor is not interrupted."

So the Air Force took two actions to save the B-1. First, a general directed that Boyd write a paper championing the bomber. It would carry immeasurable weight in Congress if the officer responsible for the E-M Theory and the F-15 wrote a paper saying he thought the B-1 was a great airplane. Boyd refused. Exactly what he said is not known, but given his proclivity for bluntness and complete distaste for posturing, it is likely he was rather straightforward. The general then gave him a direct order to write the paper.

Boyd complied. Then he wrote a memorandum explaining in detail why he disagreed with his own paper. And he told the general he considered the two papers a package; if the first one were released, he would release the second.

The general never released the first paper. Afterward he frequently was heard to mutter the same words used by so many other generals: "That fucking Boyd."

The second thing the Air Force did was to convene a Corona. This is a rare gathering of four-stars that happens only for the most serious of issues. A three-star — Boyd's boss — would brief the four-stars. Boyd was at Wright-Pat, so it fell to Burton and Leopold and Spinney to prepare the briefing. Leopold was about to go home on leave, so Spinney took the lead.

While Spinney was working on the briefing, Leopold received a phone call saying the four-star in charge of the Tactical Air Command had requested him by name for a new assignment. There are few higher honors for a captain than to be "name requested" by a four-star commander. Leopold needed this affirmation. His name had been taken off the list for early promotion to major. Boyd had told him at the time, "Your name was taken off the list because of me. They can't get at me so they get you. Don't feel bad about it. You are doing great work."

Now Leopold called Boyd, who began to suggest that Leopold had become a different type of officer than he had been a year or so earlier and that this fast-track assignment might not be best for him.

Leopold broke in and said, "I will not accept the job. And if they insist I take it, I will resign my commission."

Leopold could almost see Boyd's smile of approval. A man who would put his career on the line ranked high with Boyd. Leopold knew at that moment his life was forever changed. Within days Boyd engineered another name request from another four-star, and Leopold had a job teaching at the Air Force Academy.

Burton was about to deliver his briefing to a two-star, who in turn would brief a three-star. The two-star clearly felt it was his job to keep the B-1, and he ordered Spinney to change the estimate of how much money Congress might appropriate in the future to make it more optimistic. Burton was stunned. He had been in the Air Force fourteen years and this was the first time a general ordered him to doctor a briefing in order to save an Air Force program. He was being ordered to lie.

Spinney came up with the idea of following the two-star's orders but also including the much less optimistic new findings. During the briefing, when the three-star looked at the charts, he was bewildered by the confusing array of assumptions. He said the Corona would want a simpler, more clearly defined course of action. He turned to Spinney and said, "Which set of numbers do you like?"

Spinney pointed to the numbers that showed the true cost of the B-1. The two-star disagreed, saying Spinney's numbers were too conservative and that Congress would appropriate enough money for the B-1, F-15, lightweight fighter, and A-10.

The three-star saw that his deputy was pressuring Spinney. He gathered together the charts and said, "We'll go with the captain's numbers."

What takes place in a Corona is known only to four-stars. Boyd speculated that the Air Force realized it had no choice: the B-1 had to go. But the Air Force does not kill its young in public. Someone else has to do it. The official position of the Air Force remained that the B-1 cost $25 million each. In early 1977, when Jimmy Carter assumed the presidency, one of his first acts would be to kill the B-1. No Air Force generals would resign or complain to Congress or wage a guerrilla war to keep the program.

What Spinney remembers most about the B-1 episode is his call to Boyd to tell him what happened at the briefing. When Boyd heard that the three-star had used Spinney's charts over the strong objections of the two-star, he was exultant.

"My captain fucked a two-star?" he roared. And then he laughed and said, "Way to go, Tiger."

Chapter Twenty-Two

The Buttonhook Turn

IN January 1975, the Air Force announced that the YF-16 won the lightweight fighter fly-off. Differences between the YF-16 and the YF-17 were so great that the fly-off had hardly been a contest; the YF-16 was the unanimous choice of pilots who flew both aircraft.

The results confused Boyd: E-M data and computer modeling predicted a much closer contest. Boyd met with the pilots and they got down to basics. They used their hands to demonstrate combat maneuvers and they used highly technical fighter-pilot terminology such as "shit hot" to describe the YF-16, and it did not take long for a consensus to emerge. They preferred the YF-16 because it could perform what they called a "buttonhook turn." It could flick from one maneuver to another faster than any aircraft they ever flew. It was born to turn and burn — the most nimble little banking and yanking aircraft the world had ever seen. When a pilot was being pursued by an adversary during simulated aerial combat, the ability to snap from one maneuver to another made it much easier to force the adversary to overshoot. It was, as the writer James Fallows later described it, a knife fighter of an airplane, perfect for up-close-and-personal combat.

Until the YF-16 came along, energy dumping — that is, pulling the aircraft into such a tight turn that it quickly lost airspeed and altitude — was a desperation maneuver. This was the last resort when a pilot could not shake an enemy from his six. He dumped energy and hoped he would get a shot as the crowd went by. But the lightweight fighter had such an extraordinary thrust-to-weight ratio and could recover energy so quickly that energy dumping became a tactic of choice rather than of desperation. A pilot could dump energy, then pump the stick back and forth as he regained the initiative — "dumping and pumping," it was called.

Now that the fly-off was decided, the "Y" designation was dropped and the winning aircraft became the F-16. In later years, when aviation magazines or fighter pilots listed the ten greatest fighters of all time, the F-16 always was near the top of the list. But in those early days, before the aircraft became so prized by the Air Force and before so many others began to take credit for it, Boyd was blamed rather than given credit. Air Force generals did not equivocate: the cheap little fighter was Boyd's airplane, Boyd's and the damned Fighter Mafia's. Few in the Air Force ever paused to consider that had Boyd's original version of the F-15, or even the modified Red Bird, been accepted, he would have been happy and there never would have been a lightweight fighter.

By now the woods and open fields around the apartment on Beauregard were gone and in their place were new and cheap apartments filled with the young and the poor. One day Boyd came to work and told Spinney, "You know, I keep reading in the paper about all the burglaries and robberies around where I live, but nothing ever happens to people in my building. Then I realized that's because all the burglars and robbers live in my building. I see these people every day and they nod to me and speak and are civil."

Boyd knew that Stephen had a deep interest in repairing electronic equipment. But he had only a vague awareness that, to improve his craft, Stephen repaired television sets and tape recorders and record players for people in the building free of charge. Many of these items had what their owners called "shipping damage." It was little wonder that Boyd and his family lived in an island of safety amidst a sea of burglars and robbers.

Boyd began referring to himself as the "ghetto colonel." His sister Marion in New York did not like the appellation. Neither did his brother Gerry. His mother's "forgetfulness" had swirled downward into dementia and forced her from Gerry's condominium into a nursing home. So she did not care what her son called himself.

In August 1974, a congressional directive had ordered the Navy to accept the winner of the lightweight fighter fly-off as a Navy airplane, but in the aftermath of the Air Force acceptance of the F-16, the Navy announced it would not buy the aircraft. Instead the Navy took the aircraft that lost the competition — the YF-17 — changed its name to the F-18, and said the name change meant this was a new airplane and the one the Navy wanted. The Navy loaded it with extra fuel, electronics, and hard points — the external fixtures to which missiles and bombs are attached — redesigned the air frame, and turned it into another big, beefy airplane.

Boyd took little notice. He had returned to studying the buttonhook turn. Oftentimes when a man makes a contribution to science, his work — at least to him — becomes sacrosanct and he fights off attempts to correct or modify it. Boyd was not of that ilk. E-M did not anticipate the buttonhook turn and the difference it made in performance. He began researching a briefing called "New Conception for Air-to-Air Combat" that focused on what he called "asymmetric fast transients" (his name for the buttonhook turns). Boyd had thought about this new variable, that of "quickness" or "agility," when he had studied the F-86, but now he began to think about it John Boyd style — that is, obsessively.

Soon, however, he was forced to turn his attention from the puzzle of the buttonhook turn back to the F-16. Now that the aircraft was going into engineering development, the Air Force set about to "missionize" it. This was a deliberate attempt to make the F-16 a bomber and keep it from competing with the F-15. About three thousand pounds of electronics were added, a large ground-mapping radar, and hard points and pylons on the wings. With all sorts of things hanging out in the slipstream, the airplane was getting "dirty," every addition degrading its performance. Then the Air Force had to add more fuel to make up for the increased drag and decreased range caused by the external additions. A fuselage extension was added to accommodate the fuel. The nose was fattened to accommodate the big radar. All of this increased the aircraft's weight and wing loading and necessitated expanding the wing area in an effort to recapture the maneuverability of the original design.

The F-16 was an altogether different creature than the YF-16; the thoroughbred was becoming a draft horse.

Boyd fought every change. He called Christie and Sprey and ranted about what the Air Force was doing to his airplane. He screamed to Leopold and Spinney and Burton that his pure and nimble little fighter was turning into another goddamned gold-plated multimission aircraft.

The Air Force failure to increase the wing area finally caused Boyd to turn his back on the F-16. The original F-16 wing was 280 square feet. Boyd thought that if the wing area were increased to 320 square feet, much of the original performance could be retained. But the Air Force wanted a wing of only 300 square feet. Rather, it wanted to make sure the F-16 could not outperform the F-15. Boyd had a friend, a young officer, at the F-16 development office. Perhaps the officer would use the authority of his office to fight for 320 square feet. Boyd called and for weeks the two men talked on a daily basis. Then after one phone call Boyd turned to Spinney, pointed at the phone, and said, "He flunked roll call." In the end the young officer had gone along with his superiors and settled on 300 square feet; he had decided to be someone rather than to do something. Years later, when the young officer was rewarded by being promoted to general, he called Boyd. He had been drinking and was contrite and apologetic about the decision he made on the F-16 wing. He asked, in effect, to come back into the fold and be Boyd's friend.

Boyd hung up on him.

Boyd's anger at what the Air Force did to the F-16 never abated. He had lost the last great battle of his Air Force career. And perhaps his bitterness at the defeat was the final catalyst in shifting his attention from hardware toward more cerebral pursuits.

Boyd's learning theory was now a partially formed paper he called "Destruction and Creation," but his efforts to finish it were pushed aside by events at the office. Two of the Acolytes were about to leave the fold. Spinney was disenchanted, both personally and professionally. His marriage was disintegrating and, as is often the case in such instances, he felt the need for professional changes. The idealism he felt since childhood toward the Air Force had been shredded when the two-star general told him to fudge the numbers on the B-1 in order to save the project. Not long afterward a general had called Spinney into his office, closed the door, and said, "When I was a captain, if I had gone through what you did with the B-1 budget, I would have resigned." Spinney was thinking of doing that.

Leopold was teaching at the Air Force Academy and began inviting Boyd out as a guest lecturer. Boyd began what would become years of teaching at the Academy by delivering early versions of "Destruction and Creation" to cadets. He listened to their response and to Leopold's comments, and when he returned to the Pentagon he asked Burton and Spinney for their thoughts as well. Then he made changes to the paper. It was always fluid. Sprad had found that it was almost impossible for Boyd to finish the "Aerial Attack Study" and Christie discovered the same thing with the E-M Theory. Boyd never wanted to finish an intellectual effort. He made changes and those changes made him see another fallacy or another place for elaboration, and the process began all over. But the value of this process, arduous though it was to all around Boyd, was apparent, both with the "Destruction and Creation" paper and the earlier "Development Planning Study."

Boyd spent much of 1974 trying to educate Jim Burton about the true nature of the Building and its denizens. Burton took it all in but there appeared to be no change in his thinking. Spinney and Leopold were convinced Burton would always be a Blue Suiter, that he was simply biding his time and doing what he had to do in order to get a good ER, that he would always be an officer who wanted to be somebody rather than an officer who wanted to do something.

Then one day Burton came to Boyd with a problem. He was working with a close friend, a fellow classmate from the Academy, another lieutenant colonel who also was a water-walker destined to become a general officer. The other officer's job was to take the changes in the Air Force planning process being devised by Boyd and Burton and see that they were implemented. The friend always nodded and agreed with Burton and said he would follow through. But nothing ever happened. Burton was confused. After all, his friend was an Academy man.

Boyd shook his head in disbelief. He stood up and went to the blackboard and outlined what should have happened and what did happen. He diagrammed events that could not be refuted. Burton wrote later that Boyd said to him, "Your friend is not a friend. He used you." Burton knew that Boyd was right.

Seeing it all on the blackboard made clear to Burton what Boyd and Spinney and Leopold had seen months earlier. And from that moment on, Burton had a new rule: judge people by what they do and not what they say they will do. The conversion of Jim Burton had begun. But it would take another, far more traumatic event before he became a true believer. And when he did, the hidden iron will would become a coat of armor. He would shock Spinney and Leopold and Sprey and Christie — everyone but Boyd. The quintessential Blue Suiter would turn his back on all that he had worked for and prove that he wanted to do something with his life rather than be somebody.

On June 25, 1975, Boyd won the Harold Brown Award, the highest scientific award granted by the Air Force. In Room 4E-871, in a ceremony presided over by Secretary of the Air Force John McLucas, Boyd received a citation stating how E-M was used in designing the F-15 and F-16. The citation said E-M gave the Air Force the means to "forge a superior fighter force in the decades ahead."

Afterward, at home, Boyd turned to Mary and shook his head in disbelief, almost in embarrassment, not so much that the Air Force had given him such a prestigious award but that he did not deserve it, that his accomplishments were not of sufficient magnitude to merit such acclaim. This was not the false modesty of a man talking to his friends. It was the heartfelt response of a man talking to his wife in the privacy of their home. It was the response of a small-town boy who never outgrew his childhood insecurities.

That summer was tumultuous for Boyd. Mary Ellen was making no effort to hide her heavy smoking. Tired of seeing his Snookums with a cigarette in her mouth, Boyd said, "Okay, here's the deal. You stop smoking cigarettes and I'll stop smoking cigars. We do it cold turkey. Now. Deal?" Mary Ellen agreed and Boyd gave up his trademark cigar. But Mary Ellen soon was smoking again. At the office Boyd constantly gnawed on carrots. He had to have something in his mouth. He drank Metrecal, then went to the cafeteria and had a big lunch. He went out to dinner with one of the Acolytes and ate a huge meal and drank wine. But he never again smoked a cigar.

Meanwhile, Spinney resigned his commission in June and left the Pentagon to become a consultant for a defense contractor. He entered night school at George Washington University and began working on his doctorate in business and applied statistics. He was in almost daily contact with Boyd.

Boyd, too, was talking of leaving the Air Force. He wanted to devote all of his time to "Destruction and Creation." The paper was one of the few things Boyd ever wrote, and it certainly was the longest. While the E-M Theory, for which he was most famous, had been written as a technical document, it was primarily a briefing. Even the "Aerial Attack Study" had been dictated and then transcribed by a typist; it was not written. The only things Boyd had written were a few articles for the Fighter Weapons School publication. But now he wanted to put his ideas on paper.

Boyd's vague talk of retiring was postponed when he was asked to do a highly classified study of the Soviet "Backfire Bomber." The CIA and the Defense Intelligence Agency, but especially the Navy and the Air Force, were conjuring up a tremendous capability for this new swing-wing bomber. The Navy said the Backfire was, like the B-1, a strategic bomber with accurate deep-strike capability and with such extended range that it was a threat to sea lanes between the United States and Europe. The Navy said the Backfire was capable of being launched from the area around Murmansk, flying down through the GIUK Gap (between Greenland, Iceland, and the United Kingdom), and attacking convoys. The Air Force used the threat of the Backfire to ask for more surveillance aircraft and more F-15s to defend Western Europe.

Exactly who commissioned the top-secret study is not known, but there was no doubt that an independent assessment of the Backfire was needed. Boyd prepared a briefing for Schlesinger and there was talk that Secretary of State Henry Kissinger wanted to know the results.

Stripped of the E-M comparisons and technical jargon, Boyd's briefing said the Backfire threat was highly inflated. He said it was not a strategic bomber but a medium-range bomber, and he summarized its performance by saying, "The Backfire is a piece of shit, a glorified F-111."

Soon after completing the Backfire research, Boyd walked into the personnel office and said, "I want to retire. Now."

On August 31, 1975, John Richard Boyd retired after twenty-four years in the Air Force. He was forty-eight years old. He told Spinney and Sprey and Christie and Burton that the secretary of the Air Force pleaded with him not to retire. He said the secretary promised to make him a general if he would stay in the Air Force. "I told him no. I don't want to get on the cocktail and pussy circuit."

But this was an effort to save face. Boyd could never have become a general. He talked of hosing generals so often that at office parties and birthday parties he was given garden hoses as gifts. Spinney and Leopold laughed at the idea of Boyd in what was called "charm school," the indoctrination course for colonels who have just been promoted to general. Even if Boyd could have been promoted to general, he would have been — at best — a different kind of general, most likely a terrible general. He was incapable of compromise. He had little patience with those who disagreed with him. And while he performed brilliantly as a commander at NKP, that was a wartime environment. He was a natural leader, but he did not have the sort of management skills the Air Force looked for when they promoted colonels.

One of the first things Boyd did after retiring was drive home to Erie. He went by himself and saw many of his boyhood friends. He told them he had retired, and that the airplanes he had been instrumental in producing — the F-15 and the F-16 — were in production and that now he was working on this new thing, this paper called "Destruction and Creation." Several asked what rank he had held at retirement and when he said "colonel" they laughed and chided him about not making general. How could he have been responsible for those two airplanes when he was not a general? Everyone knew that generals did all the important work in the Pentagon.

Boyd walked the beach out on the Peninsula, where already a hint of fall was in the air. He spent hours with Frank Pettinato, who still was the chief lifeguard. Pettinato was not like Boyd's childhood friends; he believed what Boyd told him about the F-15 and the F-16, and he believed "Destruction and Creation" would be a very important achievement.

The postretirement visit must have been an emotional trip for Boyd. The Boyd family no longer had a presence in Erie. And now his mother, the person who always held the family together, was sliding ever deeper into the dementia that seemed to plague her side of the family.

In his hometown, were it not for Frank Pettinato, Boyd would have been alone.

For several weeks Boyd stayed, walking the beach, thinking about his new project and how he would go about researching and writing it. He let the ideas bubble, mulled them over, turned them back and forth, and examined them from all angles and then discarded most of them and began again. By the end of his visit he was rejuvenated. The Peninsula did that for him. He was overflowing with thoughts about the books he wanted to read and the ideas he wanted to explore.

And then he returned to Washington. Even though he arguably had more influence on the Air Force than any colonel in Air Force history, his greatest contributions were yet to come. He was about to enter the most productive and most important part of his life.

In November 1975, President Gerald Ford fired Secretary of Defense Schlesinger.

Within days the Air Force resumed its efforts to kill the A-10. The chief of staff of the Air Force also ordered that the F-16s be wired for the delivery of nuclear weapons.

Part Three

SCHOLAR

Chapter Twenty-Three

Destruction and Creation

THE 1970s were a low point in American military history.

The Vietnam War had humiliated America's armed forces. The greatest superpower on earth used almost every arrow in its quiver, everything from multimillion-dollar airplanes to laser-guided bombs to electronic sensors to special-operations forces, and still was defeated by little men in black pajamas using rifles and bicycles.

Yet, there was little soul-searching among senior generals. They were managers rather than warriors. And when managers lead an army it is their nature to cast blame rather than to accept responsibility. The senior generals who prosecuted the war and the weathervane careerists under them never admitted their failure. They never admitted that their war-fighting strategy — both in the air and on the ground — was flawed. They never admitted they did not know how to fight a guerrilla war. Instead, they looked outside the military for scapegoats: politicians had stabbed them in the back or the media were out to get them. Then they put a fresh coat of paint on the strategy of the past, the strategy that failed in Vietnam, and they pressed on.

Military leaders of the 1970s were more familiar with business theory than with military theory. They read management books and talked at length of how things were done at the Harvard Business

School. But some had never heard of Sun Tzu and could not spell "von Clausewitz." They might have known the names of Douhet or Jomini or von Schlieffen or Fuller or Guderian or Lawrence or Balck, but few knew the theories espoused by these men. Many Civil War buffs knew more about military tactics than did the average senior officer in the mid-70s.

Not all officers were careerists. There were young men who believed there was a better way. Throughout the military were hundreds of company-grade and field-grade officers who were contemptuous of senior officers and of their outdated dogma. Unlike their superiors, they had done a lot of soul-searching about Vietnam. They came back from Vietnam and said, "We got our asses kicked." They had seen their friends killed because of the idiocy of their commanders, and they felt an obligation to their departed comrades to hang tough and fight for change. They looked at senior generals and saw men who had done nothing but get promoted. They were ashamed that these generals blamed everything on politicians and the media.

Young officers, primarily in the Army and the Marine Corps, talked often about strategy. But the talks swirled and eddied and all too often were vague and formless. There was no organized movement, no coalescing force. There were only small and widely scattered groups, most unaware of one another's existence.

These officers needed new ideas about war. They needed something they could hold in their hands and study far into the night, something they could debate and argue, something that had the power to galvanize them and the troops under them with new and powerful knowledge. In short, they needed a military theory that would enable them to win wars. They also needed a leader to whose flag they could rally. He must be untainted by the disgraceful past. He must be a man of far different character than their present leaders, a man uncorrupted by the system and committed to cleaning it up. He must love America more than he loves his career. Young officers emerging from the dank careerist swamps of the post–Vietnam era would accept no other.

When Boyd retired as a full colonel with twenty-four years of service, his retirement pay was $1,342.44 per month plus COLA — the cost-of-living allowance. Even in 1975 that was a pitifully small sum to support a wife and five children. Boyd could easily have followed the route of many senior officers and gone to a well-paying job with a defense contractor. But his real life's work lay ahead and he sensed the dangers of accepting a civilian job. Boyd knew he had to be independent and he saw only two ways for a man to do this: he can either achieve great wealth or reduce his needs to zero. Boyd said if a man can reduce his needs to zero, he is truly free: there is nothing that can be taken from him and nothing anyone can do to hurt him.

Boyd stopped buying clothes. The cars that he and Mary drove would, over the next decade, become rambling wrecks. He even refused to buy a case for his reading glasses; instead, he carried them around in an old sock. And despite the rising anger of his children, he said the family would continue to live in the basement apartment on Beauregard.

Boyd disappeared for about a year. But if he was not seen, he certainly was heard — in almost nightly phone calls that lasted hours. Sprey referred to these calls as the "pain" and said they were the price of admission for Boyd's friendship. One weekend Christie and Spinney and Burton were out of town and Boyd spent much of Friday and Saturday night on the phone with Sprey. On Monday, Sprey called the others to complain about their leaving town at the same time.

It was obvious from Boyd's phone calls that he was not only spending a disproportionately large amount of his retirement pay on books but was reading them all. Christie's phone might ring at 2:00 A.M. and when he picked it up Boyd would say, "I had a breakthrough. Listen to this." And without a pause he would begin reading from Hegel or from an obscure book on cosmology or quantum physics or economics or math or history or social science or education. Christie thought Boyd had taken leave of his senses. Except for the year at NKP, the past nine years of Boyd's life had been devoted to hosing his superiors. He was a man of action. But when he walked out of the Building, he walked into a world of ideas. There was almost no transition. One day he was on the phone checking on the progress of the F-16 and the next he was calling people at 2:00 A.M. to read German philosophy. And for what? What was this learning theory he kept talking about? He said he had begun work on the thing back at NKP and he still had nothing to show for it. Why didn't Boyd just *retire*?

Tom Christie now was a Pentagon superstar about to be promoted to deputy assistant secretary of defense. He knew how to say no to things not relevant to his work, and now he was growing impatient with his old friend. "John, I read that in college," he said. Or, "John, I can read it myself." Boyd ignored him and continued to read. When he was through with a twenty-minute passage he said, "Now, what do you think of that?" In the end Christie forgot how to say no and he and Boyd talked until the predawn hours.

When Boyd had drained Christie, he called one of the other Acolytes and went through the same process. All of these men were well educated and widely read. But by the end of 1975 and certainly by the early months of 1976, the depth of Boyd's study was moving beyond what any of them experienced in graduate school. Boyd was charging into esoteric and arcane areas of knowledge. And the Acolytes were far too proud to simply agree with Boyd on everything he said. If they were going to hold up their end of the conversation they had to buy whatever book Boyd was reading. They read and when Boyd called they were ready. And while the Acolytes did not discuss it with each other, they knew that Boyd was fortune's child, that he had passed beyond the E-M Theory and was venturing into more rarefied heights. They sensed he was about to give birth to his greatest work.

But they wished the birth were not so painful and protracted.

Boyd's calls tied up the phones of his friends for hours. Burton became the envy of the Acolytes when his wife installed a separate line for a "Boyd phone." Only Boyd had the number.

Boyd had less formal education than did any of the Acolytes. But he was their intellectual leader — not only in the number and substance of the books he had them read, but in his passion and his obsession and his iron discipline about getting to the truth. Boyd had a different relationship with each of the Acolytes. Christie served in an oversight capacity; that is, he suggested adding to one part, taking out from another, and doing more research on still another part. Burton and Spinney were like sons — very bright sons who contributed so much to his work that at times they seemed extensions of his brain. The cross-fertilization between Boyd and Burton and between Boyd and Spinney was extraordinary.

Sprey was in still another category. In one sense, he was closer to Boyd than any of the Acolytes. The two men were like brothers. But while the others encouraged Boyd's research into his learning theory, Sprey was not at all sympathetic. He said Boyd was wasting his talents. Sprey knew that Boyd, like many autodidacts, craved sanctification from academics, from those he considered "real" scholars. Sprey told Boyd the learning theory was far too abstract, another "philosophy of science sort of thing" that held no promise. Sprey had become increasingly interested in ground warfare since his work on the A-10, and he was convinced it was the only sort of warfare that really mattered. He urged Boyd to drop this dalliance and to study ground warfare. But Boyd was obsessed with the learning theory. He did agree to read a few of the books Sprey recommended, but that was the end of it. Or so Sprey believed at the time.

Boyd was sensitive to criticism from Sprey. Each time Sprey challenged him he plunged deeper into his research and dug up new references. He knew if his work passed through the Pierre Sprey buzz saw there would be little substantive room for anyone to criticize it.

Boyd wrote draft after draft of his learning theory on yellow legal pads. He called the Acolytes to discuss the meaning of a word for hours. "What do you see when you hear that word?" he asked. "What picture comes to mind?" It was an exasperating business. Boyd liked ambiguity, believing it opened new vistas and led in unexpected directions. Burton was uncomfortable with Boyd's lack of fix. "You are taking advantage of the fact words can have more than one meaning," Burton said. "You are using words and ideas and concepts in ways that people don't use those words and ideas and concepts."

It all became even more exasperating when Boyd told the Acolytes that he did not know where he was going with his research and that he deliberately refused to set a goal. He was simply letting it carry him along. The Acolytes reeled when Boyd said his work would link Gödel's Proof, Heisenberg's Uncertainty Principle, and the second law of thermodynamics.

Gödel's Proof holds that there are certain mathematical statements about a mathematical system that can be true yet cannot be proven or derived from that system. Or, as Boyd put it, the consistency of a system cannot be proven within that system. Heisenberg, a physicist, said it is impossible to simultaneously determine both the position and the velocity of a particle. As Boyd learned at Georgia Tech, the second law says all natural processes create entropy; that is, they go from order to disorder. Philosophers such as Jacob Bronowski sensed relationships among these disparate elements, but no one had ever linked all three, raised them to a higher level, and from them synthesized a new idea.

Boyd might read a paragraph aloud one night and the next night call, voice filled with excitement, to say he had another breakthrough. He would read the same paragraph. The person to whom he was reading could discern no difference. In a pained voice Boyd would say he had changed one word. The Acolytes joked among themselves about Boyd's "breakthroughs." Sprey said if Boyd moved a comma he considered it a breakthrough.

"If you want to understand something, take it to the extremes or examine its opposites," Boyd said. He practiced what he preached. He considered every word and every idea from every possible angle, then threw it out for discussion, argued endless hours, restructured his line of thought, and threw it out for discussion again. Creativity was painful and laborious and repetitive and detail-haunted — not just to him, but to a half-dozen people around him. Boyd needed the dialectic of debate. Often he abandoned the entire line of inquiry and went back to the beginning. Burton and Spinney and Sprey began to wonder if Christie was right, if Boyd was putting too fine a point on everything, if he was pushing his ideas into fruitless areas. "How long will this go on?" Burton asked. "At some point you have to finish it."

"That time will reveal itself," Boyd said. "I will know. But I am not there yet."

To complicate matters, Boyd received a small grant from NASA to determine why fighter pilots flew simulators differently than they flew airplanes. His findings accelerated work on "A New Conception for Air-to-Air Combat," a briefing he had begun researching in 1975. He also revealed, to Sprey's delight, that he was beginning to work on a briefing he called "Patterns of Conflict," a survey of ground warfare since the beginning of time. He continued to research and write drafts of his learning theory while he worked on the two new briefings.

It was an extraordinary burst of creativity, especially considering it came from a man who was retired, almost fifty years old, and entering a time of life when many people begin to slow down.

The Acolytes thought it would never end.

But it did. Or at least the intense work on the learning theory did when, on September 3, 1976, Boyd came forth with the eleven-page "Destruction and Creation" paper he had been working on since 1972. With the exception of those few articles for a Fighter Weapons School publication back in the 1950s, it is the only thing Boyd ever wrote.

The hosannas that had accompanied the E-M Theory were absent when Boyd finished "Destruction and Creation." In fact, considering the years of toil that went into the paper, finishing it was anticlimactic. Boyd simply passed out a few copies.

Burton and Spinney pleaded with Boyd to have the paper published. It would have been relatively easy for Boyd to do so in one of several military magazines. But he never submitted it. One reason is because he did not believe that intellectual works are ever finished; he would revise "Destruction and Creation" for years to come. A second, more speculative reason is that he might have been fearful of the criticism that comes to such works upon publication.

Because Boyd spent more than four years researching and writing and then distilling his work down to eleven pages, the result has a specific gravity approaching that of uranium. It is thick and heavy and ponderous, filled with caveats and qualifiers and arcane references that span theories never before connected. To read "Destruction and Creation" is to fully appreciate the term "heavy sledding." The most important part of "Destruction and Creation" is Boyd's elaboration on the idea that a relationship exists between an observer and what is being observed. This idea is not original. One of the oldest questions in philosophy concerns the nature of reality. But Boyd presented a new explanation of how we perceive physical reality.

A half-dozen people can look at the same process or the same event and each might see the process or the event in an entirely different fashion. For a simple example, a crowd streaming into a college football stadium is looked upon one way by a fraternity boy, another way by a television cameraman, another way by a beer distributor, another way by a security officer, and still another way by the college president.

Atop this insight Boyd placed an idea borrowed from Heisenberg: the process of observation changes what is being observed. To continue with the simplified example, people in the crowd, knowing they are being observed by a television cameraman, might wave or shout or begin spontaneous demonstrations. The same crowd, knowing security officers are observing, might become subdued and decorous. Or it might become confrontational. If we are aware that these changes take place we reassess and recalculate our relationship with whatever it is we are observing. In other words, the process not only shapes what is being observed but feedback reshapes the observer's outlook. The television cameraman searches out people who are not waving. Security officers become more vigilant because they know people in the crowd are disguising their behavior. Thus a cycle begins. And the cycle is repeated again and again.

Now, to go back to the beginning, Boyd said there are two ways to manipulate information gleaned from observation: analysis and synthesis. We can analyze whatever process or event we are observing by breaking it down into individual components and interactions. And from this we can make deductions that lead to understanding. Or we can synthesize by taking various sometimes unrelated components and putting them together to form a new whole.

Boyd thought analysis could lead to understanding but not to creativity. Taken to the extreme, he thought analysis was an onanistic activity, gratifying only to the person doing the analyzing. He talked of "paralysis by analysis" and said Washington was a city of ten thousand analysts and no synthesizers. "They know more and more about less and less until eventually they know everything about nothing" is how he put it.

Boyd's favorite example in "Destruction and Creation" was a thought experiment that took his audience through his exegesis on the nature of creativity. It went something like this: "Imagine four separate images. Let's call them domains. Each domain can be easily understood by looking at its parts and at the relation among the parts."

Boyd's four domains were a skier on a slope, a speedboat, a bicycle, and a toy tank. Under "skier" were the various parts: chairlifts, skis, people, mountain, and chalets. He asked listeners to imagine these were all linked by a web of relations, a matrix of intersecting lines. Under "speedboat" were the categories of sun, boat, outboard motor, water-skier, and water. Again, all were linked by the intersecting lines. Under "bicycle" were chain, seat, sidewalk, handlebars, child, and wheels. Under "toy tank" were turret, boy, tank treads, green paint, toy store, and cannon.

The separate ingredients make sense when collected under the respective headings. But then Boyd shattered the relationship between the parts and their respective domains. He took the ingredients in the web of relationships and asked listeners to visualize them scattered at random. He called breaking the domains apart a "destructive deduction." (Today some refer to such a jump as "thinking outside the box." But Boyd believed the very existence of a box is limiting. The box must be destroyed before there can be creation.) The deduction was destructive in that the relationship between the parts and the whole was destroyed. Uncertainty and disorder took the place of meaning and order. Boyd's name for this hodgepodge of disparate elements was a "sea of anarchy." Then he challenged the audience: "How do we construct order and meaning out of this mess?"

Now Boyd showed how synthesis was the basis of creativity. He asked, "From some of the ingredients in this sea of anarchy, how do we find common qualities and connecting threads to synthesize a new and altogether different domain?" Few people ever found a new way to put them together. Boyd coaxed and wheedled but eventually helped the audience along by emphasizing *handlebars, outboard motor, tank treads,* and *skis.*

These, he said, were the ingredients needed to build what he called a "new reality" — a snowmobile.

To make sure the new reality is both viable and relevant, Boyd said it must be continually refined by verifying its internal consistency and by making sure it matches up with reality. But the very process of making sure the reality is relevant causes mismatches between the new observation and the description of that observation. It is here that Gödel, Heisenberg, and the second law come into play. The mismatches are inevitable and expected because, as Boyd said, "One cannot determine the character or nature of a system within itself. Moreover, attempts to do so lead to confusion and disorder." This never-ending cycle of mismatches, destruction, and creation is the "natural manifestation of a dialectic engine." This "engine" is the relationship between the observer and whatever is being observed. The idea that a two-way relationship exists between the observer and the observed, that the process of observation changes what is being observed, and that our awareness of these changes causes us to restructure the relationship is present in subtle and often unseen ways in almost every facet of our lives. It is a vital part of how we cope with our world; it shapes our decisions and actions. The danger — and this is a danger neither seen nor understood by many people who profess a knowledge of Boyd's work — is that if our mental processes become focused on our internal dogmas and isolated from the unfolding, constantly dynamic outside world, we experience mismatches between our mental images and reality. Then confusion and disorder and uncertainty not only result but continue to increase. Ultimately, as disorder increases, chaos can result. Boyd showed why this is a natural process and why the only alternative is to do a destructive deduction and rebuild one's mental image to correspond to the new reality.

Thomas Kuhn, a philosopher of science, and Joseph Schumpeter, an economist, recognized the destructive side of creativity. But Boyd was unique in his explanation of how the process is grounded in fundamentals discovered by Gödel and Heisenberg and by entropy.

The dialectic engine, once refined and elevated, was to become the intellectual heart of the new war doctrine so craved by elements within the U.S. military.

Chapter Twenty-Four

OODA Loop

ONCE he completed "Destruction and Creation," Boyd was a man possessed. It seemed he could hear at some subliminal level the voices of young military officers crying out for change, for a manifesto that would make them victorious in battle. To Boyd, nothing less than America's national defense hung in the balance. Two more briefings tumbled from him within a month. People began moving into place and events began forming, the end results of which would not be seen for years and then would seem a mosaic of impossible serendipity. The fast-transients brief is dated August 4, 1976. It is the application of "Destruction and Creation" to an operational issue — that is, a better and more thorough definition of "maneuverability." The ability of an aircraft to perform fast transients does two things, one defensive and one offensive: it can force an attacking aircraft out of a favorable firing position, and it can enable a pursuing pilot to gain a favorable firing position. The advantage gained from the fast transient suggests that to win in battle a pilot needs to operate at a faster tempo than his enemy. It suggests that he must stay one or two steps ahead of his adversary; he must operate *inside* his adversary's time scale.

Even though it was the superiority of the YF-16 over the YF-17 that precipitated his research, Boyd went back to his beginnings for the brief — to Korea, where the F-86 achieved such a stunning kill ratio against the MiG-15, a superior aircraft in energy-maneuverability terms. He used additional examples: Germany's blitzkrieg attack against France in 1940 and the Israelis' lightning-fast raid at Entebbe Airport to free hostages seized by Uganda. In both instances the ability to transition quickly from one maneuver to another was a crucial factor in the victory. Thinking about operating at a quicker tempo — not just moving faster — than the adversary was a new concept in waging war. Generating a rapidly changing environment — that is, engaging in activity that is so quick it is disorienting and appears uncertain or ambiguous to the enemy — inhibits the adversary's ability to adapt and causes confusion and disorder that, in turn, causes an adversary to overreact or underreact. Boyd closed the briefing by saying the message is that whoever can handle the quickest rate of change is the one who survives.

The briefing revealed that the central theme of Boyd's work — a *time-based theory of conflict* — was beginning to take form. And it marked a significant transition in Boyd's work with its references to the blitzkrieg and the Entebbe raid; he was becoming interested in ground warfare.

A month after the fast-transients briefing, Boyd was ready with the first version of his "Patterns of Conflict" briefing. He was to give it hundreds of times in coming years, so many times that it became known as "Patterns" or simply as the "brief." "Patterns" was a work in progress that would evolve until more than a decade later, when the slides were finally put together in a booklet. Boyd designated the first version "Warp I" (after the references to "warp speed" in *Star Trek*, a favorite television program of his children). Modifications within a warp were referred to as "wicker." (*Wicker* is a bureaucratic term that means "weaving" or "patching together.") Boyd first wrote the contents of each slide on a legal pad, then had them typed. He saved changes and additions until he reached a critical mass, then retyped the entire brief and gave it a new warp designation. The brief went through a dizzying nomenclature that changed almost weekly. By December 8, he was at "Warp VI, Wicker 2." By September 16, 1977, he was at "Warp X." In October 1977, he changed the title: "Warp XI" was "Patterns of Conflict: Cheng, Ch'i, and Schwerpunkt." By "Warp XII" he was back to "Patterns of Conflict." After

"Warp XII," he stopped using the "warp" and "wicker" designations and used only "Patterns of Conflict." Each new version was dated and signed with his bold, sprawling signature. He did not keep every version and often called Burton to ask something such as "How did I say this in 'Warp Six, Wicker Three'?" or "What was the wording for this part in 'Warp Nine'?" Burton kept almost every version and, as far as can be determined, is the only person to do so; it is a stack of papers about two feet tall. In the beginning Boyd took an hour to deliver "Patterns." A decade later, when Boyd put all his work into a collection titled "A Discourse on Winning and Losing," he took about fourteen hours — two days — to deliver it.

The nature of Boyd's briefings changed radically after he became a civilian. He went from being one of the best briefers in the Air Force, a man known for his spare and elegant slides and his brilliant presentation, to a man whose slides were jumbled, dense with bullets, and packed with long sentences. They remained ambiguous because Boyd still believed ambiguity created opportunities for unexpected richness. Some briefs are self-contained; one can look at the slides and receive the full measure of the brief. That was no longer so with Boyd's; his briefs were virtually impenetrable without an explanation. Boyd also became uncompromising — some would say arbitrary, perhaps even arrogant — about delivering his briefing. A person's available time did not matter. If someone wanted to hear the briefing, they had to hear it all. That was okay when the briefing was about an hour in length. But as it grew to six hours, Boyd often was asked for a condensation. "Full brief or no brief" was his response. And he would not let anyone see a copy of the slides or the executive summary until after they heard the brief.

Even though Boyd was a civilian, he spent a lot of time in the TacAir office at the Pentagon. Sprey was there one day and overheard part of a conversation in which Boyd said, "I'd be glad to give him the brief. It takes six hours." The person on the other end obviously wanted a much shorter version. "The brief takes six hours," Boyd repeated. Sprey saw Boyd's face tightening and then heard him say, "Since your boss is so pressed for time, here's an idea that will save him a lot of time: how about *no* brief?" He slammed the phone down, turned to Sprey, and said, "That was the exec for the CNO." And that was how the chief of naval operations did not hear Boyd's briefing. After the same thing happened with the Army chief of staff, the chief's executive officer, a full colonel, marched to Christie's office in a state of high dudgeon and demanded that Christie order Boyd to give a one-hour brief to the CSA. The colonel was flabbergasted when Christie said Boyd was a civilian whom he could not order around.

Several things did not change. Boyd's method of research remained as it always had been. He stayed up much of the night reading book after book. The final source list for "Patterns" numbered 323. And Boyd's phone calls to the Acolytes continued. The breadth and depth of subjects covered was nothing short of phenomenal. Boyd dove into the history of warfare as few men ever have. To outsiders his course of study seemed rambling and disconnected. It seemed to lack focus, but only until they heard the briefing.

As with much of Boyd's work, the building blocks for "Patterns" are mostly well-known ideas. But the synthesis of these ideas produced a reality new to the U.S. military. "Patterns" is one of the most monumental snowmobiles ever constructed, one of the most influential briefings ever to come from a military mind.

"Patterns" is also an example of how Boyd thought by analogy, a process that Sprey, ever the pragmatist, found extremely unsettling. Reasoning by analogy not only is backward from the way most people think but is dangerous; one misstep, especially in the beginning, and the entire process can go careening off into idiocy. Sprey found it even more unsettling that Boyd was always right.

One cannot study modern military history without studying the German Army, especially the period from 1806 — when Napoléon defeated Frederick and the Prussian armies at the Battle of Jena and Auerstadt — through World War II. After Frederick was defeated, a group of five men set about to rebuild the Prussian Army and to institutionalize military excellence. They called themselves "Reformers." Scharnhorst and von Clausewitz are the best known of the group, Scharnhorst because of his military brilliance and von Clausewitz because of his book *On War*.

William Lind, a tall, roly-poly, ruddy-cheeked civilian who drops historical allusions by the bushel and knows more about warfare than do most people in the Pentagon, was a congressional staffer working for Senator Gary Hart when he heard "Patterns." Sensing a parallel between Boyd's intellectual circle and the Prussian military master-minds, Lind dubbed Boyd and his followers "Reformers."

As Boyd studied the blitzkrieg, he found historical references he did not understand, especially in his readings on the tactics of Tank Commander Heinz Guderian and in the book *Lost Victories* by Erich von Manstein. He had to begin at the beginning, go back to the earli-est recorded Greek and Persian battles, and march through history to properly understand the blitzkrieg. Four areas drew most of his attention: general theories of war, the blitzkrieg, guerrilla warfare, and the use of deception by great commanders.

Sun Tzu, a Chinese military theoretician, was thought to have written *The Art of War* about 400 B.C. Sun Tzu's ideas about conflict include such themes as deception, speed, fluidity of action, surprise, and shaping the adversary's perception of the world. Sun Tzu also talked of how a commander should use two thrusts, either of which could attain the objective. But perhaps the most significant element in Sun Tzu is the concept of *cheng* and *ch'i,* the orthodox and the unorthodox, the traditional and the unexpected. A simplistic expla-nation of *cheng* and *ch'i* comes from General George Patton, who in World War II said his plan for attacking the Germans was to "hold them by the nose and kick them in the ass." Holding them by the nose is the *cheng*. Kicking them in the ass is the *ch'i*.

The Art of War became Boyd's Rosetta stone, the work he returned to again and again. It is the only theoretical book on war that Boyd did not find fundamentally flawed. He eventually owned seven translations, each with long passages underlined and with copious marginalia. The translations of Samuel Griffith and, later, Thomas Cleary were his favorites. He insisted the Acolytes read and reread the book.

From Sun Tzu, Boyd moved to the campaigns of Alexander the Great around 300 B.C., Hannibal around 200 B.C., Belisarius around 500 A.D., Genghis Khan around 1200 A.D., Tamerlane around 1400 A.D., then Napoléon and von Clausewitz and on through World War I and World War II. He found that the campaigns of many of these great commanders, particularly the Eastern commanders such as Genghis Khan, demonstrated an understanding of Sun Tzu.

For example, Boyd was fascinated by how a vastly superior Roman Army lost to Hannibal and the Carthaginians at the Battle of Cannae.

In that battle, one of the most famous in military history, Hannibal lost around three thousand men while the Romans lost around seventy thousand. Boyd found many such instances in history, and in these victories by numerically inferior forces he found a common thread: none of the victorious commanders threw their forces head-to-head against enemy forces. They usually did not fight what is known as a "war of attrition." Rather, they used deception, speed, fluidity of action, and strength against weakness. They used tactics that disoriented and confused — tactics that, in Boyd's words, caused the enemy "to unravel before the fight."

Von Clausewitz is often acknowledged as the greatest of military theoreticians. Rarely has his book been studied as Boyd studied it. As with Sun Tzu, he bought various translations and made copious annotations. For months he compared what von Clausewitz says early in the book with what he says in the middle and at the end. This is laborious work, because von Clausewitz takes a dialectic approach and sometimes seems to argue in favor of polar opposites. Boyd was doing more than reading; he was engaging von Clausewitz in combat. It was his mind against that of von Clausewitz. Boyd called Spinney late one night and said he had a breakthrough. He began reading passages and explaining two crucial differences between von Clausewitz and Sun Tzu. First, von Clausewitz wants to bring the enemy to a big "decisive battle," while Sun Tzu wants to unravel the enemy before a battle. Put another way, von Clausewitz believes wars are decided by set piece battles more than by strategy, deception, and guerrillalike tactics. This means that even if he wins, there is a bloodbath. Boyd said von Clausewitz's second major flaw is that he spends a lot of time talking about how a commander must minimize "friction" — that is, the uncertainty or chance that always appears in the "fog of war." He does not deal with maximizing the enemy's friction — as does Sun Tzu — but only with minimizing his own. As Boyd said to Spinney, "Sun Tzu tried to drive his adversary bananas while Clausewitz tried to keep himself from being driven bananas."

Spinney sleepily muttered something about von Clausewitz's work being more than one hundred years old and that it was never completed and —. "Doesn't matter," Boyd shouted. "I got the fucker now. I got him by the balls."

Boyd said the strategies and bloodbaths of World War I were the natural consequence of both the von Clausewitzian battle philosophy and the inability of generals to adapt new tactics to nineteenth-century technology: line abreast, mass against mass, and linear defenses against machine guns and quick-firing artillery. The bankrupt nature of that doctrine was demonstrated on the first day of the Battle of the Somme, when the British suffered sixty thousand casualties. After more than three years of this meat-grinder form of war, the Germans began engagements with a brief artillery barrage with smoke and gas obscuring their intentions, then sent in special infantry teams. These small groups looked for gaps in the defense and advanced along many paths. They did not hit strong points but instead went around them, pressing on, always going forward and not worrying about their flanks. They were like water going downhill, bypassing obstacles, always moving, probing, and then, when they found an opening, pouring through, pressing deeper and deeper. (These tactics ultimately failed because German leadership did not have faith in them, nor did they have the communication and logistics to make the tactics a decisive form of combat. Also, because the Germans lost the war, the Allies failed to understand the significance of the new infiltration tactics. Then, between wars, the new German Army expanded the concept enormously.)

In World War II German forces used the same tactics, but this time with massive tank forces. Journalists called it the "blitzkrieg." The Germans bypassed enemy strong points — such as the Maginot Line — and, with the use of airplanes and radio communications, punched through enemy weaknesses following the path of least resistance, driving deep into the enemy's rear, cutting lines of communication, disrupting movement, and paralyzing the enemy's command and control system. They moved so fast the enemy simply could not understand what was happening and became unglued. Hitler took Poland, Norway, Denmark, Belgium, Holland, and France with about two hundred thousand casualties. The Allies had about three point five million losses, almost three million of whom were prisoners.

Boyd, borrowing from Sun Tzu, said the best commander is the one who wins while avoiding battle. The intent is to shatter cohesion, produce paralysis, and bring about collapse of the adversary by generating confusion, disorder, panic, and chaos. Boyd said war is organic and compared his technique to clipping the nerves, muscles, and tendons of an enemy, thus reducing him to jelly.

As Boyd studied German tactics, words such as *Schwerpunkt* and *Fingerspitzengefuhl* became everyday expressions. Neither translates well. *Schwerpunkt* means the main focus of effort. On a deeper reading it is the underlying goal, the glue that holds together various units. *Fingerspitzengefuhl* means a fingertip feel. Again, the fuller meaning applies to a leader's instinctive and intuitive sense of what is going on or what is needed in a battle or, for that matter, in any conflict.

All these small stitches, and hundreds of others, made up the tapestry that became "Patterns of Conflict."

The briefing begins with what was to become Boyd's most famous — and least understood — legacy: the Observe-Orient-Decide-Act cycle, or O-O-D-A Loop. Today, anyone can hook up to an Internet browser, type "OODA Loop," and find more than one thousand references. The phrase has become a buzz word in the military and among business consultants who preach a time-based strategy. But few of those who speak so glibly about the OODA Loop have a true understanding of what it means and what it can do. (Boyd preferred "O-O-D-A Loop" but soon gave up and accepted "OODA" because most people wrote it that way.)

For a time, Boyd and Spinney were reluctant to fully explain the OODA Loop; it was far too dangerous. If someone truly understands how to create menace and uncertainty and mistrust, then how to exploit and magnify the presence of these disconcerting elements, the Loop can be vicious, a terribly destructive force, virtually unstoppable in causing panic and confusion and — Boyd's phrase is best — "unraveling the competition." This is true whether the Loop is applied in combat, in competitive business practices, in sports, or in personal relationships. The most amazing aspect of the OODA Loop is that the losing side rarely understands what happened.

The OODA Loop is often seen as a simple one-dimensional cycle, where one observes what the enemy is doing, becomes oriented to the enemy action, makes a decision, and then takes an action. This "dumbing down" of a highly complex concept is especially prevalent in the military, where only the explicit part of the Loop is understood. The military believes *speed* is the most important element of the cycle, that whoever can go through the cycle the fastest will prevail. It is true that speed is crucial, but not the speed of simply cycling through the Loop. By simplifying the cycle in this way, the military can make computer models. But computer models do not take into account the single most important part of the cycle — the orientation phase, especially the *implicit* part of the orientation phase.

Before Boyd came along, others had proposed primitive versions of an OODA Loop. The key thing to understand about Boyd's version is not the mechanical cycle itself, but rather the need to execute the cycle in such fashion as to get *inside* the mind and the decision cycle of the adversary. This means the adversary is dealing with outdated or irrelevant information and thus becomes confused and disoriented and can't function.

Understanding the OODA Loop is difficult. First, even though it is called a "loop," it is not. A drawing of the Loop shows thirty arrows connecting the various ingredients, which means hundreds of possible "loops" can be derived. The best drawing of the OODA Loop was done by Spinney for Boyd's briefings. It shows a very large orientation part of the cycle. Becoming oriented to a competitive situation means bringing to bear the cultural traditions, genetic heritage, new information, previous experiences, and analysis / synthesis process of the person doing the orienting — a complex integration that each person does differently. These human differences make the Loop unpredictable. In addition, the orientation phase is a nonlinear feedback system, which, by its very nature, means this is a pathway into the unknown. The unpredictability is crucial to the success of the OODA Loop.

Only three arrows are on the main axis, and these are what most see when they look at the Observe > Orient > Decide > Act cycle. But this linear understanding and its common result — an attempt to use the Loop mechanically — is not at all what Boyd had in mind.

Even Boyd's Acolytes do not always agree on what Boyd meant with the OODA Loop. Understanding it can be helped by studying the illustration (see p. 344). Note that Boyd includes the "Implicit Guidance & Control" from "Orientation" with both "Observations" and "Action." This is his way of pointing out that when one has developed the proper *Fingerspitzengefuhl* for a changing situation, the tempo picks up and it seems one is then able to bypass the explicit

"Orientation" and "Decision" part of the Loop, to "Observe" and "Act" almost simultaneously. The speed must come from a deep intuitive understanding of one's relationship to the rapidly changing environment. This is what enables a commander seemingly to bypass parts of the Loop. It is this adaptability that gives the OODA Loop its awesome power. Understanding the OODA Loop enables a commander to compress time — that is, the time between observing a situation and taking an action. A commander can use this temporal discrepancy (a form of fast transient) to select the *least-expected* action rather than what is predicted to be the *most-effective* action. The enemy can also figure out what might be the most effective. To take the least-expected action disorients the enemy. It causes him to pause, to wonder, to question. This means that as the commander compresses his own time, he causes time to be stretched out for his opponent. The enemy falls farther and farther behind in making relevant decisions. It hastens the unraveling process.

The OODA Loop briefing contains 185 slides. Early in the briefing the slide "Impressions" gives the frame of reference for what is to come. Here Boyd says that to shape the environment, one must manifest four qualities: variety, rapidity, harmony, and initiative. A commander must have a series of responses that can be applied rapidly; he must harmonize his efforts and never be passive. To understand the briefing, one must keep these four qualities in mind.

After marching through the great battles of history, Boyd dwells a moment on T. E. Lawrence, who talks of how a commander must "arrange the mind" of the enemy.

Another important slide shows how the blitzkrieg — or maneuver conflict — is the perfect tactical application of the OODA Loop. Boyd asks: How does a commander harmonize the numerous individual thrusts of a blitzkrieg attack and maintain the cohesion of his larger effort? The answer is that the blitzkrieg is far more than the lightning thrusts that most people think of when they hear the term; rather it was all about high operational tempo and the rapid exploitation of opportunity. In a blitzkrieg situation, the commander is able to maintain a high operational tempo and rapidly exploit opportunity because he makes sure his subordinates know his intent, his *Schwerpunkt*. They are not micromanaged, that is, they are not told to seize and hold a certain hill; instead they are given "mission orders." This means that they understand their commander's overall intent and they know their job is to do whatever is necessary to fulfill that intent. The subordinate and the commander share a common outlook. They trust each other, and this trust is the glue that holds the apparently formless effort together. Trust emphasizes implicit over explicit communications. Trust is the unifying concept. This gives the subordinate great freedom of action. Trust is an example of a moral force that helps bind groups together in what Boyd called an "organic whole."

Boyd, like Sun Tzu and Napoléon, believed in attacking with "moral conflict" — that is, using actions that increase menace, uncertainty, and mistrust in the enemy while increasing initiative, adaptability, and harmony within friendly forces. As an example of the moral game played right, Boyd told how the appearance of a few Mongol horsemen often was enough to collapse resistance in the enemy and cause chaos and panic. Guerrilla leaders had to master moral conflict to ensure the support of civilians as they engaged larger and better-funded government forces.

The mental and moral aspects of maneuver conflict do not sit well with most military minds, particularly those who use a managerial approach or those who prefer the slugfest of attrition warfare. They don't like the mental agility, the intellectual innovation, the placing trust in subordinates. They don't like the rapidly changing, free-form tactics of probing for weak spots rather than concentrating more firepower on selected targets. Why tiptoe through the tulips, the conventional mind asks, when war is blood and guts?

The question would never be asked by a commander with a true understanding of the OODA Loop and its deadly power.

Boyd showed that maneuver tactics brought victory. To attack the mind of the opponent, to unravel the commander before a battle even begins, is the essence of fighting smart.

But most modern commanders have serious problems with maneuver tactics and, by extension, the OODA Loop. The experience of General George Patton in World War II is a good example. Patton was the American general most feared by the Germans. He out-blitzed those who made the blitzkrieg famous. His tanks rolled across Europe and into Germany and could have punched through to Berlin in a matter of days. In fact, the German high command thought the war was over. But Eisenhower did not understand this kind of conflict and, at the very moment of victory — egged on by jealous and conventional British officers — he grew afraid for Patton's flanks and supply lines and ordered Patton to stop. The Germans were amazed at the respite. One school of thought says that Eisenhower's timidity cost another six months of war and a million additional lives.

A crucial part of the OODA Loop — or "Boyd Cycle," as it has come to be known — is that once the process begins, it must not slow. It must continue and it must accelerate. Success is the greatest trap for the novice who properly implements the OODA Loop. He is so amazed at what he has done that he pauses and looks around and waits for reinforcements. But this is the time to exploit the confusion and to press on. Patton knew this intuitively. He ignored his flanks and kept his armored spear pointed at the heart of the enemy.

A little over halfway through the briefing, Boyd begins building his snowmobile. He looks back and rehashes attrition warfare as practiced by Emperor Napoléon (as opposed to the far more creative strategies practiced earlier by General Bonaparte). He talks of maneuver conflict and the moral weaponry of guerrilla warfare.

This begins the most difficult part of the brief. Now Boyd begins slicing the same idea from a different direction simply to provide another shading of the same point. And it shows why simply reading the slides fails to give a full understanding.

Boyd begins the section on maneuver conflict with two crucial words: "Ambiguity, deception . . ." — the essence of maneuver tactics. This is General Patton's approach to fighting the Germans. It is Muhammad Ali saying he will "float like a butterfly and sting like a bee."

One of the most important charts in the briefing is utilized when Boyd begins to pull everything together to show how the key to victory is operating at a quicker tempo than the enemy. While the briefing continues through 185 slides, for all practical purposes it ends some forty slides earlier, when Boyd begins a series of repetitious examples of how to use the OODA Loop in war. This latter part is of interest primarily to soldiers and military historians. The theme of this section is consistent: disorient the enemy, then follow with the unexpected lightning thrust.

Boyd's briefing, then, is an updating and affirmation of Sun Tzu and a repudiation of von Clausewitz. In fact, if the briefing could be reduced to two simple thoughts, they would be: 1) the essence of warfare is *cheng* and *ch'i,* and 2) to practice this most effectively a commander must operate at a quicker OODA Loop than does his opponent.

The briefing has a number of problems. It is repetitive in the extreme. Boyd often threw in a slide that said ? — RAISES NAGGING QUESTION — ? when, in fact, the question had not been raised except rhetorically by Boyd. Periodically he had a slide titled INSIGHT, which is little more than a platform for him to launch into a tangential cadenza. The cluttered slides were jammed with ponderous and virtually impenetrable sentences. None of the discipline of the academic existed. Boyd was force-feeding his audience, another hallmark of the autodidact and a characteristic manifest in his insistence of "full brief or no brief."

Considering the impact of the briefing, these are niggling faults. And they speak more to Boyd's personality than to the content of the briefing. The purpose of the briefing was not to reveal the "Answer" but to jar listeners out of complacency and into thinking on their own. Boyd abhorred the idea that his briefing might be considered dogma. In fact, he often said listeners should take the briefing out and burn it before they considered it dogma.

The brief followed the ink-blot theory of growth. First a small group of men — the Acolytes — heard it. Then congressional staffers led by Winslow Wheeler, who worked for Senator Nancy Kassebaum, heard it. Dozens of reporters heard it. A number of junior officers stationed in the Pentagon heard it. Slowly, day by day, week by week, the numbers grew. And then the groups began touching and merging to form larger groups. By now the core group, Boyd and the Acolytes, were known far and wide as "Reformers."

One day Boyd was in his apartment working on an update of the briefing when he received a phone call. Jim Burton was not only passed over for promotion to colonel but was fired from his job and told to leave the Pentagon. It was not entirely unexpected. Burton was unwilling to bend to the ways of the Building. When Donald

Rumsfeld became secretary of defense in November 1975, Burton prepared a briefing chart showing the F-16 had better turning performance than did the F-15. While true, this did not sit well with Air Force leadership and Burton was ordered to change the chart to show the two aircraft had equal turning performance. He refused to do so. Burton also advocated canceling the B-1 because it performed far below specifications and because the Air Force could not afford it.

When Boyd heard the news, he called Burton and asked, "How did you like that kick in the stomach?"

Burton was devastated. Throughout his career he had been one of the golden boys. Now, after sixteen years — not enough time for retirement — he had been passed over, a clear signal that his career had ended. In a year he would have another chance at promotion, but once a man is passed over, his chances are slim.

"I know you are disappointed," Boyd said. Then came the lines he had recited to Leopold long ago: "You still have an opportunity to be promoted. But now you are at a fork in the road with your life. You have to decide if you really want that promotion and all the trappings that come with it. You can't have a normal career and do the good work."

Boyd continued, giving Burton the "To Be or to Do" speech, and ended by saying, "Do you want to be part of the system or do you want to shake up the system?"

The water-walker decided he wanted to shake up the system. He wrangled an appointment to Andrews AFB and stopped thinking about promotion. He started thinking only of doing what was right. And he came to find that freedom from the concerns that governed the lives of most officers was remarkably liberating.

Not long after Burton left the Building, Boyd received a phone call from Tom Christie. The Finagler now was one of the top non-appointed civilians in the Pentagon, and he offered Boyd a job in the TacAir shop. It was clear from the way Boyd dressed — tattered Ban-Lon shirts, madras-patterned polyester pants, and slippers — that he needed money. But he refused to accept a salary from Christie. Boyd was horrified that he might be called a "double dipper" — a man who had both a government pension and a government job.

At the Pentagon, Boyd occasionally performed the duties expected of an analyst. But Christie hired Boyd more to give him a base of oper-

340

ations than anything else. Boyd needed access to telephones and copy machines. He worked about five years with no pay before word came down that the Pentagon could not have unpaid consultants. Boyd griped and complained and said he wanted the smallest salary possible, $1 per pay period. But the minimum time a consultant could be paid for and remain on Pentagon rolls was one day every two weeks. So henceforth Boyd was paid for one day's work every two weeks.

Boyd dove deeper and deeper into the study of war. He realized that while wars take place between nations, every person experiences some form of war; conflict is a fundamental part of human nature. To prevail in personal and business relations, and especially war, we must understand what takes place in a person's mind. And what better place to continue work on a study of conflict than in the Pentagon?

Boyd needed someone he trusted to work beside him. He talked to Christie and Christie called Chuck Spinney, who was now working for a think tank and studying for his Ph.D. "Come see me," Christie said. When Spinney arrived, Christie said, "Do you want to work for me in TacAir? You'll be working with Boyd." That was all Spinney needed to hear. To work with Boyd meant conflict with the Pentagon, and Spinney was born for conflict. He remembered what Boyd often said: "There are only so many ulcers in the world and it is your job to see that other people get them." Spinney said yes on the spot.

TacAir had no job openings but this was not a problem for the Finagler. He created a job and Spinney went to work two weeks later.

In the eyes of the Air Force, TacAir had been suspect ever since the old Systems Analysis days of McNamara. Now word was beginning to get around the Pentagon and to a few Air Force bases about Boyd's new briefing and the group of people around him. They were part of the old Fighter Mafia crowd, goddamn insurrectionists and seditionists, civilians all and not a team player among them. Calling themselves "Reformers" and saying they were part of the "military-reform movement." What the hell was there to reform? When officers dropped in to chide Boyd about his reform movement, they could not resist the temptation to ask him how his ideas fit in with a military placing greater emphasis on technology. "Machines don't fight wars," he responded. "Terrain doesn't fight wars. Humans fight wars. You must get into the minds of humans. That's where the battles are won."

The officers laughed and wondered why Tom Christie had brought Boyd back to the Pentagon. Didn't he know Boyd's background? And Christie had hired a new man by the name of Franklin Spinney. Wasn't there an Air Force captain by that name involved in the B-1 budget studies?

What the Air Force did not know was that the Finagler was flying top cover for Boyd and was about to unleash Spinney on a study that would put the Air Force on the defensive for years. The Air Force figured Christie was a team player — their team. But Boyd and Spinney were about to turn TacAir into a little shop of horrors, ground zero for the reform movement.

Because Boyd was paid for one day every two weeks, he was free to come and go as he chose. He continued to travel to the Air Force Academy, where he lectured to cadets in Ray Leopold's classes. In the beginning the lectures had taken the form of briefings on "Destruction and Creation." Now Boyd was introducing "Patterns of Conflict."

On one visit, Leopold picked Boyd up at the airport in Colorado Springs. As Boyd and Leopold walked down the concourse, Boyd looked out the window and saw two F-16s taking off. He stopped and stared, mesmerized, as the sleek little aircraft climbed into the Colorado sky. Then, almost as if talking to himself, he said this was the first operational F-16 he ever saw. He shook his head as he remembered another airplane. "You know, they told me I could fly in an F-15 when I was at the Pentagon. But every time I was scheduled they cancelled the flight."

Leopold drove Boyd to the Academy campus, nestled against the eastern slopes of the Rocky Mountains. As they drove up the knoll toward the famous "Bring Me Men" arch, Leopold looked in his rearview mirror and said, "The superintendent is behind us." Boyd twisted around and recognized Bob Kelly, a three-star whom he had known as a fighter pilot at Nellis back in the 50s. He rolled down the window, leaned out, and began pumping his right arm — middle finger erect — up and down.

Leopold was horrified. Cadets marching to class were even more horrified. They saw the superintendent's car, popped to attention, and snapped off salutes. But their eyes were on the shouting and shabbily clad civilian leaning out of a car window giving the finger to a three-star.

"Stop the car, Ray," Boyd insisted.

"John, don't do this," Leopold said as he pulled over.

Cadets stared as Boyd jumped from the car, shirttails flying, and held up his hand to stop the superintendent. "Hello, Bob," he said. Then, in a voice heard across half the campus, he said, "Three stars! Goddamn. Whose ass you been kissing?"

The two men shook hands and the general asked Boyd what he was doing on campus. After a few minutes of conversation about the old days, Boyd returned to his car and the cadets continued on their way.

Leopold was dismayed. "John, you shouldn't have given the super-intendent the finger."

"Ah," Boyd said dismissively. "That's a fighter pilot's salute."

The next day Leopold was summoned to the superintendent's office and was told, "Don't ever again bring someone from the military-reform movement on this base without notifying me in advance."

It was a harbinger of what was to come, a rampant paranoia among senior Air Force officers where Boyd and the reform move-ment were concerned. In a few more years the paranoia would be transformed into open warfare.

In June 1977, Boyd visited his mother in her nursing home in south Florida. The strong authoritative woman who had borne five chil-dren and ushered them through the depths of the depression could not be recognized. The woman who had buried her husband, a son, and a daughter was near death. Her passage through the world had been one of endless travail. Now she was worn out.

Boyd called his sister Marion in New York and said, "Mom is pretty bad. She is very weak. I think you better come down."

"Oh, she's got a strong heart," Marion said.

"I really think you should come down," Boyd repeated.

Marion said she would make airline reservations and call him back to give him her flight number and arrival time. But before she com-pleted the arrangements, Boyd called back and said, "Mom's gone."

She was buried next to Ann in Erie's Laurel Hill Cemetery. Her husband was across town in Trinity Cemetery. Her son Bill was interred in a single plot, all alone and separated from the other members of the family, in Erie Cemetery.

Boyd convinced Marion to come down to Erie from New York more frequently thereafter, to visit the house on Lincoln Avenue and put it back into shape after three years of being empty. Gerry, Marion, and Boyd, the three surviving children, would pool their resources and put a new roof on the house.

About the time Boyd returned to the Pentagon, the new promotion list for colonel was published. Burton again was passed over. Now his chances were statistically less than 3 percent to make colonel. Under the Air Force policy of "up or out," the next time he was passed over would be the last. He would be forced to retire.

Boyd called Burton and said it was their friendship that kept Burton from being promoted. Burton agreed, but he was not upset about that; he was upset because, like most men, he wanted to make a contribution, to do something significant with his life. And it now appeared that chance was lost. Unless he was promoted, he had only a year remaining in the Air Force.

The OODA "Loop"
Sketch

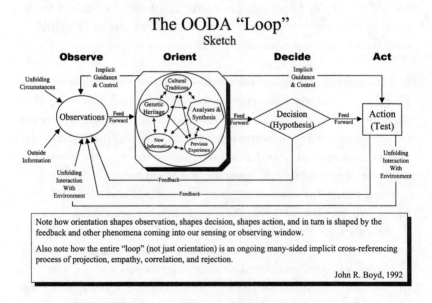

Note how orientation shapes observation, shapes decision, shapes action, and in turn is shaped by the feedback and other phenomena coming into our sensing or observing window.

Also note how the entire "loop" (not just orientation) is an ongoing many-sided implicit cross-referencing process of projection, empathy, correlation, and rejection.

John R. Boyd, 1992

The OODA Loop. Boyd sketched the original and then Chuck Spinney rendered a more professional version. Finally, Chet Richards drew this model to use on the Web site dedicated to Boyd.

Chapter Twenty-Five

Reform

By 1978, both officers and enlisted personnel were leaving the military services in large numbers. They left not because of pay, as military leaders had said for the past few years, but because they were displeased with what they saw as a lack of integrity among their leaders. They thought careerism inhibited professionalism in the officer corps. The military also was having readiness problems; expensive and highly complex weapons systems were fielded before being fully tested. These systems were not only expensive to buy but expensive to maintain, and they rarely performed as advertised. Stories began to appear in the media of America's "hollow military."

The military's answer was to place more emphasis on what it called the "electronic battlefield" by buying even more expensive and more high-tech weapons. Somewhere in the military there must have been those who sensed the system was headed toward a meltdown. If so, no one stepped forward to change it.

Then one day Christie called Spinney and said, "I want you to take a look at these retention and readiness problems." The results show why Boyd wanted Spinney working beside him. Spinney was young, brilliant, irreverent, and had the tenacity of a pile driver. It was only a matter of weeks before he began briefing the first version of what was officially called "Defense Facts of Life." Few people remember that title; what they remember is the "Spinney Report." From the beginning, those who heard the brief realized the impact it could have on the Pentagon.

Spinney gave his briefing to anyone who would listen. When the give-and-take of the briefing revealed that Spinney's presentation had flaws in logic and gaps where more data were needed, he went back, talked to Boyd, and fine-tuned the brief. The presentation had to be bulletproof. If Spinney were hosed one time — that is, if someone stood up during a briefing and delivered chapter and verse where he was wrong — it would be a devastating blow to the fledgling reform movement. Finally the brief seemed flawless, a seamless gathering of facts that came to an inescapable conclusion.

Then Spinney briefed Sprey. As Boyd had predicted, Sprey found dozens of flaws not seen by anyone else. Spinney revised the brief and presented it again. This time Sprey nodded in approval. If the brief could stand against the Pierre Sprey buzz saw, it was monolithic, impregnable against the blasts of heaven and Earth and all that the Air Force might throw at it.

There is nothing in the past to compare with the Spinney Report. For that reason alone, it is arguably one of the most important documents ever to come out of the Pentagon.

Spinney's basic point was that the unnecessary complexity of major weapons systems was wrecking the military budget. He made public what only a few people in the Air Force knew: throughout the 1970s much of the Air Force budget went toward procuring tactical air fighters and weapons while nearly all other areas suffered. So much money was being spent on overly complex weapons such as the F-15 and the F-111D that there was little money to operate and maintain the aircraft. Training flights for pilots were being replaced by simulators. Maintenance skills required to keep the F-15 flying were so high that civilian contractors had to be hired. Electronics systems failed far more often and took far longer to repair than predicted. Spinney showed that supporting the F-15 was more expensive than supporting the ancient B-52. He showed that readiness was at an all-time low; in a full-scale war, supplies of the Air Force's favorite munitions would last only a few days.

But the most significant part of the Spinney Report was that readiness problems were not caused by lack of funds; they were caused by Air Force leaders who deliberately bought such expensive and overly complex weapons that fewer and fewer of each model could be purchased. The leaders' incentive was to force increases in their budget and to funnel more money to defense contractors, and they said whatever they needed to achieve that goal. Spinney proved that virtually everything the Air Force had promised the American people about the F-15 and the F-111D was false.

The Air Force declared war on Spinney.

In 1978 Spinney was thirty-three, young to be the target of Air Force generals. But he had worked in the Pentagon under Boyd and knew the Building and its machinery better than many of those who were older and more senior. And he was brash enough that he never felt inadequate for the task of taking on generals. Like Boyd, he believed many of these men had never done anything but get promoted, that they had compromised their beliefs, that they were empty Blue Suits.

Spinney made no recommendations in his brief, so he was said to be a nihilist, a destroyer. But the omission was deliberate. Spinney knew that if he followed the usual procedure and included a list of recommendations, the focus would shift from the problem to which chores would go to what agency. He wanted the focus to remain on the problem. He chose to be the wrecking crew. He was tearing the domain apart and creating the destructive deduction. He was proving the fundamental point of the Reformers — that the Pentagon needed an overhaul.

Christie thought Boyd was putting Spinney out front as a target. Spinney shrugged off such comments. His attitude was "Maybe so. But if not me, who?" He was the right man in the right place at the right time. He had done his homework and knew his briefing was rock solid. He took great pride in knowing he was the first person ever to probe so deeply into the soft underbelly of the Pentagon. Plus, he had more than a little of the rock thrower in his character. He enjoyed a skunk fight.

The Reformers were united in their goals, but their approaches to reform varied widely. Boyd was the moral force that drew all the others. If Boyd was intense, Sprey was even more so. For him this was an Armageddon-like conflict in which the forces of good stood against the forces of evil. Christie was a survivor. He knew how to get the job done without appearing on anyone's radar screen. Burton, who against all odds had made colonel in his third and last chance, was quiet and remote, not given to the unrestrained antics of the Reformers. He was fueled by rectitude and guided by an unwavering sense of what was right. These men, and all the others gathered around Boyd, thought the Pentagon was off course and wanted to set things right. Spinney followed that belief. But for him it was also fun — a rollicking romp through the bosky fen that was the Pentagon. Never mind that billions of dollars were at stake, never mind that the most important weapons projects of the American military were the issue, never mind that the full force of the Building was about to come down on his head — it was a great, great time.

Part of Spinney's battle joy was that the Air Force did not know how to deal with his report. One of Boyd's fundamental dictums when waging bureaucratic war was to use the other person's information against him. Spinney's brief was built on Pentagon documents. He understated everything so that any revisions would only make his conclusions more damning. (Boyd's belief in using the adversary's information against him is the practical application of Asian writings, particularly *The Japanese Art of War,* in which translator Thomas Cleary talks of "swordlessness," or the ability to defend oneself without a weapon, a concept that by implication means using the enemy's weapon against him. Cleary says this technique can be used in debate, negotiations, and all other forms of competition. He says swordlessness is the "crowning achievement of the warrior's way.")

Since Spinney's briefing spoke to the readiness problem, something the media were beginning to write about, his report was becoming increasingly relevant to the stories appearing in the press. But Spinney was not yet known outside the Building.

It is here, with the advent of the reform movement, that Boyd's story becomes infinitely more complex. It no longer follows a linear path but rather explodes into various stories, some of which in the beginning may seem tangential. But taken together these stories demonstrate the tremendous reach of Boyd's ideas. Spinney is one story. The Marine Corps is about to become a separate story. The Army is another story. Jim Burton, still another. All these stories have two things in common: Boyd and "Patterns of Conflict." Boyd and his briefing were at the center of everything.

By now the "Patterns" briefing was the credo, the manifesto, the coalescing force for the reform movement. It was a briefing that continued to gather momentum over the years, a gleaming intellectual tour de force that caused enormous and profound change.

Spinney's brief was more immediate, more directly relevant. While it covered the full spectrum of Pentagon spending, it used the F-15 — America's front-line fighter aircraft and the darling of the Air Force — as the example of problems facing the military. The Spinney Report documented everything the Reformers had suspected.

Because of Boyd's coaxing and Sprey's critique, the Air Force could find no factual errors in the brief. Nor were there any flaws in the concept. Air Force generals used derision and sarcasm, hyperbole and misstatement, even personal attacks against Spinney. The Air Force referred to him as a "captain who has never been shot at," a silly argument but one thought to be devastating by officers who have been in combat. This tactic reveals a fundamental truth about the Building. Generals are allowed to indulge their egos as few people in business or government are allowed to do. A general is surrounded by people whose careers depend on what he says on their ERs. Every word he utters is considered as if Moses brought it down from the mountaintop. What in most of us would be harmless quirks seem rather bizarre when codified by a man with stars on his shoulder. And as the number of stars on a man's shoulder grows arithmetically, his bizarre behavior grows exponentially. Stories abound of a general who would let no one in his office who had a mustache, of a general who ordered a blinking red light be turned on in the hall before he entered as a signal to lesser mortals that they must disappear, of a general who ordered that the back side of traffic signs be painted brown, of a general who ordered that no one walk beside him but instead a respectful two paces behind, of a general who ordered that subordinates wear the same type of headgear he wore, then hourly switched between a cap and a hat. Generals rule with such absolute power that few dare confront them, so when someone has the audacity to point out they are wrong — as did Spinney — they often have no recourse but to fall back on hyperbole and emotion and personal arguments. The Air Force knew no other way to react toward Spinney.

Mary talked often of Florida. Ever since being stationed at Eglin, she had loved the state. She wanted the family to go there for several weeks every summer, but Boyd said he did not have time for "that sentimental vacation crap." For three or four years, Mary and the children went alone. Boyd went to Erie instead.

Spinney and Sprey and Christie and Burton sensed that things were not well in the Boyd household, but they divided Boyd's life into his work and his home life and did not want to know the details of the latter. "Mary is a saint," they said and left it at that. They sometimes felt a faint sense of embarrassment when they saw the way Boyd treated Mary, but they never asked questions. Boyd's friends knew little or nothing about Kathy's withdrawal, Jeff's collection of poisonous snakes, John Scott's confrontations with his father, or of the years when Mary Ellen and Boyd did not speak.

Boyd's attitude toward Mary puzzled his friends. She was so lovely and so winsome. Even though she had borne five children, she remained trim and had a sunburst of a smile that lighted a room. But there was something of the sleepwalker about her; she seemed to drift through life, oblivious of what was going on about her. At parties Mary was still the quiet one while Boyd dominated the room with his stories.

When Boyd talked to someone at a party, he gave them 100 percent of his attention. He did not look over the person's shoulder to see who else was in the room. But there were times at a party when Boyd might sit down and sleep for an hour or so. Mary tried to hustle him out quickly once he awakened. If she was not successful, Boyd, rested and raring to go, might hold forth until 2:00 A.M.

One day in 1979 Boyd received a call from a man who identified himself as the Washington editor of the *Atlantic Monthly*. The caller said that for years he had wanted to do a piece about national defense, a deep and wide exploratory piece about the state of America's military. The story was sidetracked when he spent two years as chief speechwriter for President Jimmy Carter, but now he wanted to resurrect the idea. The timing was perfect, as Carter was dueling with Republican challenger Ronald Reagan over defense spending. Reagan said he wanted to "re-arm America," a phrase that meant if he were elected, billions of dollars would flood into the Pentagon. Reagan knew the post-Vietnam military faced serious problems. He was going to fix everything with money.

The man who called Boyd had talked to Bill Lind in Senator Gary Hart's office. Lind recommended that he interview Boyd. Could he come over to the Pentagon and talk?

Boyd agreed, but only if the caller would spend enough time to hear "Patterns of Conflict." Boyd was not interested in any drive-by reporting; he wanted to make sure the writer was serious. The writer agreed; this was his first big piece for the *Atlantic* and he wanted to do it right.

A few days later, Boyd looked up at a tall, slender, thirty-year-old man in khaki pants and Polo shirt and blazer. The writer had graduated from Harvard and had been a Rhodes scholar. He could not have been more different from Boyd. He stuck out his hand and introduced himself. "Colonel Boyd, I'm Jim Fallows."

Neither man was terribly impressed with the other. Boyd later told Spinney that Fallows was a "goddamn preppy." Fallows looked at Boyd and saw a man with an ancient Ban-Lon shirt drooping from his shoulders, plaid pants that were hopelessly out of date, and slipperlike shoes of a sort rarely seen in the Pentagon. Boyd stood up and put his nose about three inches from Fallows's face, poked Fallows in the chest, and began talking in a voice loud enough to be heard far down the hall.

"Is this guy nuts?" Fallows asked himself.

Fallows heard the "Patterns" briefing and later spent more than four hours listening to an unclassified version of Spinney's "Defense Facts of Life." This was followed by a long session with Pierre Sprey. Fallows was overwhelmed by Sprey's intensity and intellect. "Is that guy for real?" he asked Spinney. Then he came back to Boyd for additional hours of interviews. By now Boyd had a growing respect for Fallows. Here was a writer who did his homework.

The *Atlantic* published "The Muscle-Bound Superpower" in the October 2, 1979, issue. It was the first of three events that launched the reform movement onto a national stage. While newspaper reporters had written a few articles about Boyd and the Reformers and the issues they espoused, Fallows was the first writer for a major national publication to tie it all together, to question the way the Pentagon spent billions of taxpayer dollars and to wonder if America's military was so burdened with high technology that it might fail in warfare.

Much of Fallows's fourteen-page story revolved around Boyd and "Patterns of Conflict." In the story, Fallows said he had come to "respect and value" Boyd more than anyone else he interviewed. Boyd and his followers "thought fresh thoughts" and were willing to take the impossibly rare risk that those thoughts might cause them to be labeled as fools. Fallows said Boyd's ideas were all common sense but were a "heretical departure" from current practices. Fallows made Boyd and the Reformers legitimate.

Boyd and Fallows became fast friends. Boyd respected Fallows's intellect and the depths to which he pursued a story. Fallows admired Boyd's integrity and single-minded devotion.

While the Pentagon was trying to figure out how to respond to Fallows, the second event that launched the reform movement was taking place on Capitol Hill. The Defense Appropriations Subcommittee of the House Appropriations Committee held a hearing. Congressman Jack Edwards of Alabama was the senior Republican on the committee. Readiness was a big issue with Edwards. He had sent an aide named Charles Murphy out on a fact-finding tour of Air Force bases. When Murphy went to Christie and asked what he should look for on his tour, Christie gave him the Spinney Report. Murphy briefed the congressman well. The hearing quickly focused on readiness problems of the all-weather, night-attack bomber: the do-anything-but-dust-crops F-111D. Congressman Edwards bored in on Secretary of Defense Harold Brown with detailed and specific questions. His probing queries revealed that America's premier fighter-bomber suffered from such a critical shortage of parts that in order to keep it flying, maintenance sergeants used their own money to buy parts from Radio Shack.

Ordinarily this would have been a relatively insignificant story, perhaps a "bright" used on the inside pages of a few newspapers. But suddenly the media had a symbol for the "hollow military" and the story achieved a life of its own. It ran in many daily newspapers, on the television networks, and in many smaller newspapers around the country. Follow-up pieces ran for days. The saga of enlisted men buying parts from Radio Shack to keep the F-111D flying was a story that would not go away.

The Air Force reacted by searching for a leak in the Pentagon. The questions asked of SecDef Brown revealed too much inside knowledge. They could only have come from inside the Building. Pentagon counterintelligence people threatened to withdraw the security clearance of anyone revealing classified information, and virtually everything involving readiness was classified. This was the first of many security investigations aimed at the Reformers.

In April 1980 came the third major event that gave the reform movement a national presence: Desert One, the debacle in the desert during the failed attempt by the Carter Administration to rescue hostages in Teheran. Eight men died, five more were seriously injured, and eight aircraft were lost. (Spinney had remarried and his wife went into labor as news of Desert One broke on television. Spinney pulled out a calculator and, using what he knew of helicopter reliability studies, began calculating how many helicopters the military should have used in order to have a successful mission. The data were complex and the calculator slow. Spinney's wife grew upset. "Let's go, Chuck!" she shouted. "I am about to have a baby." But Spinney was deep into his calculations and mumbled, "Just a minute. Just a minute." He calculated that the military should have used fourteen helicopters instead of the eight actually used. Then he took his wife to the hospital.)

These three events all happened in a six-month period and showed clearly that something was wrong with the U.S. military. These Reformers might be on to something.

Then, in May, Fallows weighed in with another piece titled "America's High-Tech Weaponry." He told of Spinney's "extraordinary report" and quoted Sprey at length.

The military simply could not refute what the Reformers were saying. They tried. Their most common response was that the Reformers were Luddites and antitechnology, the same argument used against the Fighter Mafia's complaints about the F-15. It was an equally spurious argument, overlooking the fact that Boyd, Christie, Sprey, and Spinney all came out of the technology community and that Sprey had insisted on the most high-tech cannon in the Air Force for his A-10. In truth, the Reformers argued not so much against technology as against the improper use of technology. One of the most valuable aspects of "Patterns of Conflict" was that it laid out a framework for assessing different technological approaches. It promoted the application of scientific and engineering knowledge to human needs. "Patterns" is about the mental and moral aspects of human behavior in war. That technology should reinforce that behavior, not drive it, was the argument of the Reformers. Boyd's mantra was "Machines don't fight wars, people do, and they use their minds." He also preached, "People, ideas, hardware — in that order." Thus, machines and technology must serve the larger purpose. The Reformers believed that America's technological advantages were being used incorrectly and had, in fact, become a liability.

Even decades later, the depth of Pentagon paranoia about Boyd and the Reformers is amazing. The idea that an institution as large and as seemingly omnipotent as the Pentagon would react as it did toward a handful of men is almost impossible to grasp. It is worth noting that neither Boyd nor Sprey held any portfolio or any official position in the Pentagon, private business, or academia. Boyd was retired and being paid for one day every two weeks. Sprey was a consultant to various businesses. It seems the most sensible thing for the Pentagon to do would have been to ignore them. But these men could not be ignored. The Pentagon has long dealt with the complaints of various organizations. But those groups often are single-issue groups whose members have no more than a surface knowledge of the military or of defense matters. Because their concerns are frivolous or tangential, they are easily dismissed. Now for the first time in history, Pentagon insiders, men who had the keys to the kingdom, men who knew the budgets and the issues as well as anyone in the Air Force, were attacking the Building. And they were building alliances with Congress and the media, the two institutions that can cause heartburn in generals. Reform was becoming a motherhood issue with the media. Publications from *Business Week* to the *New York Times* did stories about the Reformers. Congressmen and senators who were members of the Reform Caucus got more media coverage than they ever imagined. This fed their enthusiasm and, in turn, generated even more coverage. One Reformer described the process as a "self-licking ice cream cone."

Now Boyd was delivering his briefing to everyone from captains to colonels to four-star generals. One of the colonels was a Marine Corps officer named Al Gray. Gray later became a general and asked to hear the briefing several more times. He and Boyd had long private sessions in which they discussed the ramifications of "Patterns." Congressional aides heard the briefing and recommended it to the congressmen and senators for whom they worked. One quiet congressman from Wyoming, Dick Cheney, heard the "Patterns" briefing and then Boyd's other briefings — an investment of some twelve hours. He asked Boyd to come by his office for numerous private sessions to talk of tactics and strategy and how America might best conduct itself in the next war. "I was intrigued by the concepts he was working on," Cheney would later say. "He was a creative and innovative thinker with respect to the military." Cheney added that the Reformers had "great ideas" that were "a part of my education." He said the ideas of the Reformers were valuable to him then as a member of the House Intelligence Committee and later when he became secretary of defense. Asked if he and Boyd discussed maneuver warfare, Cheney said, "Maneuver warfare was embodied in the whole notion of what he was talking about."

The Acolytes sometimes had little respect for congressmen and senators, but even Pierre Sprey was impressed with Dick Cheney. He accompanied Boyd on some of the visits to Cheney's office and knew the congressman did his homework. Cheney studied deeply the intricacies of Boyd's approach to strategy. He was one of the founders of the Reform Caucus on Capitol Hill, a group that soon numbered more than one hundred congressmen and senators.

The amateurish bungling of the Air Force response to Boyd and the Reformers has been documented over the years, but one incident is worth repeating because it shows just how desperate the Air Force was. TacAir was a small office with a handful of civilian analysts as well as four officers, one each from the Air Force, Navy, Army, and Marine Corps. The Air Force representative was a lieutenant colonel anxious to be promoted. Because of the Pentagon structure, his efficiency reports were signed by the vice chief of staff. The Air Force lieutenant colonel was ordered to report on all activities of the Reformers in the office. He asked the secretaries to let him know the names of everyone calling Boyd and Spinney. He rifled desk drawers looking for memos. Boyd was suspicious and eventually caught the lieutenant colonel searching Spinney's desk. He confessed and told Boyd he was pressured by the office of the chief of staff. Christie demanded that the lieutenant colonel be reassigned. Boyd insisted that TacAir, not the Air Force, pick the Air Force officer assigned there. Boyd picked Ray Leopold.

He called Leopold at the Air Force Academy and said, "Ray, do you want to work with me in the Pentagon?"

"Colonel, I'm cut on orders to go to Europe. It can't be done."

"Ray, I didn't ask about your orders. Listen to me, Tiger. Do you want to come to the Pentagon? Yes or no?"

"Yes, Sir, but —"

"No *buts*. You just stand by."

Several days later, to his utter astonishment, Leopold's orders were changed and he was assigned to TacAir.

Then the Air Force chief of staff learned that Leopold had once worked for Boyd and that he and Spinney were close friends. The chief said Leopold was going to Europe.

Again, Boyd was at the center of a potential constitutional crisis. The deputy secretary of defense sent down orders for the Air Force chief of staff to come to his office. The chief was reminded that in America it is civilians who run the military. In so many words, the deputy secretary said, "If you wish to remain chief of staff, you will reverse the decision sending Major Leopold to Europe and you will send him to the Pentagon."

Leopold's orders again were changed and he came to TacAir.

The lieutenant colonel he replaced — the spy — was promoted to full colonel.

Leopold had a realistic understanding of how things worked in the Building. A few days after he arrived, he was walking down a hall when he saw an open door. The office was empty. He went in and wrote on the blackboard, "Duty Honor Country." Then he crossed out the words and under them wrote, "Pride Power Greed."

Now two of Boyd's Acolytes worked with him.

One day Boyd said to Spinney, "You know, I like the Pentagon more than I liked Nellis."

Spinney waited.

That feral grin sliced Boyd's face and he held a clenched fist in the air, then jerked it sharply downward and said, "More targets." His booming cackle filled the office; he was ready to do battle.

Acrimony between TacAir and senior Air Force generals became such that little work was getting done. The Air Force was bogged down fighting the Reformers. A three-star approached Spinney and said the Air Force wanted to make peace. The senior generals in the Air Force wanted to hear Spinney's briefing.

More than two dozen generals gathered in a large briefing room in the basement of the Pentagon. Spinney's every comment was ridiculed. Two hours later he was at a point in the briefing he usually reached in twenty minutes. All over the room, generals were interrupting, their faces contorted in anger. One two-star became so overwrought that he had an anxiety attack and collapsed. Boyd took charge and called for a white wagon. Attendants loaded the two-star aboard the white wagon and carted him off to the infirmary. All this was happening in the back of the room and Spinney was not aware of it until later on in the gym when an Air Force colonel approached him and said, "You are now an ace." He told Spinney how the briefing caused the two-star to collapse. "He's okay now," the colonel said. "But you downed him. He had two stars on each shoulder and we're giving you one for free. That makes you an ace."

Spinney's "white-wagon kill" was toasted again and again at happy hour the following Wednesday.

The Reformers were seen as a threat to national security. General Bob Mathis, the Air Force vice chief of staff, repeatedly referred to them as "dark and satanic forces."

That spring, Senator Sam Nunn of Georgia, the gnomish powerhouse of the Senate Armed Services Committee who had cultivated a reputation for brilliance simply by not saying much, heard of "Defense Facts of Life" and asked the Pentagon to send Spinney to his office to deliver the briefing. SecDef Brown refused. The Reformers were making too many inroads with Congress and the media. And Spinney's briefing was too dangerous to be heard by a U.S. senator. It might give him ideas not sanctioned by the Building.

Several times over the next six months or so, Nunn asked the Pentagon to send Spinney to his office. Brown was adamant in refusing.

Ronald Reagan was elected in November and almost immediately afterward Brown — under the threat of a subpoena — relented. In early December, Christie, Boyd, and Spinney went to Nunn's office and gave him the full briefing. They told Nunn the Reagan Administration was about to start throwing money at the Pentagon and that more money would only exacerbate already serious problems.

Nunn told Spinney to remove the classified materials from his briefing, write it as a report, and submit it to him. Spinney took leave and spent the remainder of December bent over a legal pad in his home office. After going through a security review, Spinney's report was cleared for release to the public. Spinney by now was infamous inside the Building, but this was the first the American public would hear of him.

In early 1981, the reform movement received another big boost, both in public awareness and credibility, when Jim Fallows published his first book, *National Defense,* to an extraordinary reception. The book was an elaboration of the articles he published in the *Atlantic Monthly.* It was a damning indictment of the Pentagon and the defense industry, and it portrayed Boyd and the Reformers as men who might have the solution to all that was wrong. One of the strongest sections of the book dealt with how Boyd originally had perceived the F-16 and what it had become in the hands of the Air Force — how "enhancements" had converted the once-nimble fighter into an all-weather bomber. The buttonhook turn was something of the distant past.

Various books on the Reformers and the reform movement followed *National Defense.* But Fallows was first, and his book gave the reform movement enormous credibility with the media and with the public. Not only did the book win the nonfiction category of what then was called the American Book Awards but it was runner up for nonfiction in the National Book Critics Circle. It launched Fallows's brilliant career.

Timing for the book could not have been better. Ronald Reagan came into office in January and no president could have been less interested in military reform. Upon taking office, one of Reagan's first actions was to resurrect the B-1 Bomber manufactured by Rockwell in his native state of California.

The B-1 later flunked its specifications for the radar cross section it presented to enemy radar, flunked its range specifications, and flunked its electronic countermeasures specifications. A combat-loaded B-1 cannot fly over many mountain ranges. Its altitude limitations are classified, but it cannot even reach the altitudes flown by commercial airliners. Design flaws create wind turbulence that prevents bombs in the rear bomb bays from dropping unless a rotary cylinder and long arms are attached. This modification means a bomb falls every few seconds, preventing carpet bombing, which means the B-1 must return over the target — not a pleasant prospect in heavily defended areas.

But none of this mattered. The aircraft that Jimmy Carter killed because its cost had risen to $167 million a copy was at last going into production . . . now at a cost of $287 million per copy.

Chapter Twenty-Six

The Great Wheel
of Conspiracy

THE February 1981 confirmation hearing for Caspar Weinberger as President Reagan's secretary of defense was reminiscent of a 1960s love-in. Senators knew a flood of defense dollars was about to cascade from Washington and each wanted more than his share. The senators were extraordinarily cordial to Weinberger.

But then Sam Nunn said he knew of people in the Pentagon who believed that throwing money at the armed services was not the answer to Pentagon budget problems. Nunn said those people were being squelched. He said he had an unclassified version of the Spinney Report and wanted to know if Weinberger had read the report. Weinberger had not been briefed to expect this question. He knew nothing of the Spinney Report.

Reporters covering the hearing were galvanized by Nunn's comment — first, because he was a pillar of the defense establishment, and second, the Pentagon had successfully blocked many of their stories, a tactic that built up enormous enmity. Now they were about to have their day. Not since the Vietnam War had such a large crush of reporters descended on the Pentagon.

During the next few days, hundreds of newspapers all over the world published news stories on the Spinney Report. Dozens more stories dribbled out in coming weeks in what reporters call "think pieces" or "thumb suckers." Chuck Spinney was catapulted from obscurity onto the national stage. With the exception of Weinberger, he suddenly was one of the best-known people in the Building.

In May, David Chu, head of PA&E, sent down word for Spinney to stop briefing "Defense Facts of Life" and to work on something else. For the next eighteen months Spinney worked on another briefing. It would be more politically explosive than the first.

In the meantime, Boyd continued to research and amend and add to "Patterns," briefing it often. Story after story about Boyd appeared in newspapers around the country. No one could counter Boyd's briefing because *no one in the Building was doing similar work;* the Pentagon had no military theorists. Boyd was out there all alone and gaining converts by the day. The Pentagon was under siege from reporters. Paranoia was a palpable presence in the Building.

The depth of that paranoia is best revealed by what Reformers called the "Great Wheel of Conspiracy." When President Reagan's civilian appointees came to the Pentagon, they were taken on tours and briefed — the Pentagon version of the Welcome Wagon. These briefings are largely self-serving, designed to make civilian leaders aware of the military's position on various issues and to show why the military position was the only one worth considering. By now Tom Christie was a deputy assistant secretary of defense, one of the highest-ranking nonappointed civilians in the Building, but the briefing book prepared by Lieutenant Colonel Walt Kross for Reagan's appointees was so sensitive that Christie could only look at it; he could not take it to his office. The five-inch-thick notebook concerned the "dark and satanic forces" that drove the reform movement. It opened with a depiction of a giant wheel with spokes radiating out from the center. Each spoke represented what the Air Force saw as a significant part of the reform movement. Christie laughed when he saw himself at the center of the wheel. Colonel Kross thought Christie was the leader of the reform movement, probably because TacAir was under his jurisdiction and was the front office for the Reformers. Therefore, in the top-down, rank-conscious Air Force, Christie had to be the leader. In truth, Christie protected Spinney and Boyd. He maneuvered Spinney's work into the political arena. He pushed the readiness issue so brilliantly worked by Spinney into the forefront of the

Department of Defense budget process. He was deeply involved in bringing the revelations about the F-111D to the attention of the SecDef. But in all of this he was very much in the background. He was not the leader.

The Great Wheel of Conspiracy illustrates how little the Air Force knew of the Reformers and how wrong they were in considering the movement an organized cabal. While there was some cross-fertilization between the Reformers and the Congressional Reform Caucus, mostly in the form of Boyd's briefing, the Reformers were still small, independent groups. They were organized only in the sense that they looked to Boyd as their leader. Even this most basic of facts, the Air Force got wrong. The Great Wheel of Conspiracy listed Boyd and Sprey on a spoke labeled "Consultants."

Still another spoke represented the media, where Fallows's name was the most prominent. He headed a list of journalists who wrote stories about the Reformers.

Senator Gary Hart and Representative Jack Edwards were listed on the spokes that included members of Congress whom the Pentagon considered Reformers. Winslow Wheeler, the congressional aide to Senator Nancy Kassebaum, was listed as leader of the congressional staffers in the conspiracy.

Christie has a near-photographic memory and at the next happy hour he went into considerable detail about the Great Wheel of Conspiracy. Laughter has seldom been louder in the Old Guard Room than it was that night. A possible exception was a few years later when the news came that the lieutenant colonel who developed the Great Wheel of Conspiracy was promoted to four-star general.

By now, some of the ideas in Boyd's briefing, particularly the OODA Loop, were popping up in various publications, often without crediting him. Boyd never seemed to care. He was a true guerrilla in that he only wanted his ideas to find acceptance. Nor did he care when, in the surging dialectic that was the reform movement, other men occasionally came to the forefront. In fact, he encouraged it. An incident involving Spinney and *Time* magazine is a prime example.

One of the significant battles in the reform movement began when Spinney finished his new briefing. He called it "Plans / Reality Mismatch." The point of the briefing was that year after year the Pentagon underestimated the cost of proposed new weapons systems.

When those systems went into production, the actual costs were much higher than the projected costs. Spinney showed that the Reagan Administration had underestimated the cost of the defense buildup by five hundred billion dollars. A couple of hundred million, maybe even a billion dollars, could be explained. But five hundred billion?

Spinney began delivering his new briefing throughout the Building. Curiously, Air Force generals were particularly interested. He briefed most generals on the Air Staff. Then David Chu ordered Spinney to stop the briefing while the Pentagon conducted an independent study of his work. Pressure on the Pentagon to finish the review of Spinney's work was enormous. Dozens of people wanted to hear the briefing. A year later the review said Spinney's briefing was accurate and that his conclusions could not be faulted. David Chu met with Spinney, ostensibly to talk about what he would do with the briefing. He said he would take some sort of action the following year. Spinney thought his work had been squelched.

By late summer of 1982, defense reporters for *Time* magazine were interested in the reform movement. This was due in large part to Hugh Sidey, then one of the grand old men of American journalism. Sidey, who wrote a column for *Time* titled "The Presidency," spent hours talking with Boyd and came away a believer. In fact, he organized a meeting of senior *Time* editors to hear Boyd's briefing and Sprey's ideas. It was largely because of Sidey that a team of *Time* reporters spent months researching a story on the defense industry.

Boyd was busy during those months. Not only was he a primary point of contact for the *Time* reporters but he was showing Spinney how to work within the bureaucracy to affect change in the Pentagon. Boyd believed the independent study that confirmed the accuracy of Spinney's work should "have lots of little brothers and sisters." Spinney knew what that meant: he should make dozens of copies of the study and send it to everyone in the Pentagon who had heard the "Plans / Reality Mismatch" briefing. The independent study was not classified and it mentioned Spinney by name. It mentioned the "Plans / Reality Mismatch" briefing. Spinney was simply letting people know they could now hear the briefing.

As Boyd knew would happen, news of the study found its way to reporters. It is safe to assume that this was leaked by a Reformer.

Again, dozens of reporters descended on the Building demanding copies of Spinney's newest work. Again the Pentagon launched a security investigation to determine the source of the leak. David Chu appeared at a press conference and told reporters there was no study — only a few scribblings that had been pasted together. The reporters suspected they were getting a runaround and called friendly congressmen and senators and had them call the Pentagon. They called every contact they had in the Building. The big squeeze was on. Coincidentally, about this time another study confirming Spinney's work popped out of the Pentagon. The Air Force had secretly conducted its own budget study and had come to the same conclusions as Spinney. The Heritage Foundation, a conservative think tank with close ties to the Republican Party, released still another study saying the Pentagon's budget process was in serious trouble.

By February 1983, the *Time* piece was finished. It was so powerful that it was scheduled as a cover story. Now *Time* needed both a news peg and someone from the reform movement to appear on the cover. By now congressmen and senators were weary of Pentagon stonewalling. Senator Charles Grassley of Iowa, a conservative Republican, called Secretary of Defense Weinberger and asked to see Spinney's study. To Grassley's astonishment, Weinberger refused. Grassley thought the role of the Senate was being usurped by a political appointee and he jumped into his old Ford Pinto, went to the Pentagon, and demanded to meet Spinney. He was denied.

Grassley returned to the Senate and called for Senate hearings. He was going to hear from Spinney even if he had to subpoena him. Now, once again, arose the constitutional issue of whether or not civilians controlled the Pentagon. That was not a battle the Pentagon wanted to fight, so the Building called upon one of its closest and most powerful friends. Senator John Tower of Texas, the Republican chairman of the Senate Armed Services Committee, was such a strong Pentagon supporter that the Reformers referred to him as "a wholly owned subsidiary" of the Building. Senator Tower said Grassley's budget committee had no authority to call for a hearing involving a Pentagon employee — that Pentagon issues should be heard before his committee. But Grassley, too, knew how to play the power game. He gathered enough support from fellow senators to force a joint hearing.

Now *Time* had a news peg for its cover story. But the magazine still needed a Reformer on the cover. *Time* wanted Boyd or Sprey but, to the utter astonishment of the magazine, both refused. Neither had any desire for publicity. Since Boyd was the point of contact for the *Time* reporters, they leaned on him to come up with a cover boy. Boyd pulled Spinney aside and said, "You're going to be on the cover of *Time*."

Spinney recoiled. "The hell I am."

"Listen very carefully to what I am about to tell you," Boyd said. "After you testify over on the Hill you are going to be vulnerable. They will be after you. This is your protection."

Boyd knew that when Pentagon bureaucrats seek vengeance the best strategy is not — as many believe — to keep a low profile but rather to become so prominent that any retribution will be seen for what it is.

Spinney put on a pinstriped suit and posed for a picture.

A story about Spinney appeared in the *New York Times* the week before the hearing. The next Sunday morning, Spinney's phone rang and a voice identified itself as Bosuns Mate somebody and said, "Admiral Rickover would like to speak with you." A moment later Admiral Hyman Rickover was congratulating Spinney about what great work he was doing. He wanted to see Spinney's latest study.

"I will send it over, Admiral, but I have to tell you it will take several hours to read."

"I don't read anything but executive summaries."

"I don't have an executive summary."

Spinney sent copies of his work and a few days later the admiral called and again congratulated Spinney. Then he mentioned the upcoming hearings and said, "Son, you are not going to win. But it will make a man out of you."

The call was very sobering to Spinney. For about five minutes.

Senator Tower was in charge of all arrangements for the hearing. He proved that he had the best interest of the Pentagon at heart when he scheduled the hearing for a Friday afternoon, a time when many senators have departed the capital for their home states. Even more important, Friday afternoon is one of the most difficult times to get media attention. Tower even tried to schedule the hearing in one of the smallest hearing rooms and to ban television cameras but was overruled by his colleagues.

To get a big turnout, *Time* reporters called their colleagues and said the hearings would be next week's cover story. While the reporters groused about having to work on Friday, they knew the cover story would drive the next week's news agenda for much of the Washington media.

On March 4, 1983, Spinney spoke to the joint Senate committees and the room was filled with print and television reporters. David Chu, Spinney's boss, sat beside him. If he was there as a looming presence to inhibit Spinney's presentation, he was disappointed. Spinney talked for more than two hours and held nothing back. The Reagan defense budget was going to be a fiscal disaster for America, he said.

Grassley and the senators on the Budget Committee were shocked, but Tower was calm and unruffled. The joint committee turned to Chu for a response. Spinney's work is historical, Chu said, and not relevant today. Trust us. The Reagan Administration will not repeat the mistakes of the past. Spinney's report is irrelevant.

As Senator Tower and the Pentagon had planned, press coverage was relatively light on Saturday and even less in the big Sunday papers. Many of the stories filed by reporters did not run. By Monday morning the Pentagon was gloating over how it had outmaneuvered the Reformers. Navy Secretary John Lehman said at a meeting, "Well, I guess we laid the Spinney thing to rest."

In the middle of the self-congratulations, the March 7, 1983, issue of *Time* magazine arrived in the Pentagon. Spinney was on the cover, identified as a "Pentagon Maverick." The cover line was underlined in red and said, "U.S. Defense Spending." Underneath, in bold type, was the question, "Are Billions Being Wasted?" Most of the eleven-page article was devoted to the reform movement, of which Boyd and Sprey were identified as "architects." Their ideas for alternatives to weapons proposed by the Pentagon were given great prominence. In fact, the article read as if they had written it.

The story said that, taking out the effects of inflation, the Army was spending the same amount of money in 1983 on new tanks as it had thirty years earlier, but the number of tanks produced declined by 90 percent. In 1951 the Pentagon spent $7 billion to buy 6,300 aircraft. Now the United States was spending $11 billion to build only 322 aircraft, or 95 percent fewer than in 1951.

Pentagon officials were in shock. All day long the magazine distributor brought shipment after shipment to the Building. An eleven-page story in *Time,* that powerful protector of Republican causes, had attacked the sacrosanct Pentagon and defense industry. And during a Republican administration? The impact was monumental.

Boyd smiled when he saw the cover, skimmed the story, and tossed it aside. He looked at Spinney and said, "Well, that's done."

As expected, the *Time* cover story caused still another flurry of stories in the national media about the Reagan budget and Pentagon spending and ineffective high-tech weapons. Not only that, but in the Möbius strip that is the congressional-media relationship, the House of Representatives and the Senate called for more hearings. Each hearing brought forth even more coverage. The coverage prompted congressmen and senators to call for still more hearings. This was suddenly the hottest issue in America and every person in Congress wanted to be involved. They were, as Boyd said, "climbing Mount Motherhood."

For months, Spinney, always followed by Chu, testified to congressional committees in what many in Washington called the "Chuckie-Chu Show." The script was always the same. Spinney's briefing brought a moment of stunned silence. Then the committee chair turned to Chu, who said the report was historical and therefore irrelevant.

Senator Grassley prompted the chairman of the Budget Committee to do what no one else thought of doing: ask Spinney to update his conclusions to include the current Reagan budget. The secretary of defense forbade Spinney to do so. This was still another direct assault on senatorial prerogatives and touched off another constitutional debate between the Senate and the Pentagon. That is an issue the Pentagon can push only so far. If one senator publicly raises the issue of civilian control of the military, newspapers all over the country will run cartoons comparing Pentagon generals with military strongmen in a banana republic, or show them jumping up and down on the U.S. Constitution.

In February 1984, Spinney testified before the House and Senate Budget Committees with a new briefing entitled "Is History Repeating Itself?" His testimony included three years of budget figures from the Reagan Administration. The answer to the question asked in the title of his briefing was a solid and undeniable *yes*.

Chu did not accompany him to this hearing.

As the reform movement reached its peak, a parallel chain of events was taking place in the military services. At first glance, the Army and Marine Corps' effort at reform are of questionable relevance to the life of John Boyd. But, as will be seen, Boyd and his ideas were at the center of each effort.

Years later, after John Boyd died, the Army would deny he had ever been involved in that service's effort at reform. The Marine Corps would claim Boyd as one of its own.

Chapter Twenty-Seven

Boyd Joins the Marines

THE Air Force has never made a serious study of warfare because every historically based effort to do so has come to the inescapable conclusion that the use of air power should be consistent with or — better yet — *subordinate* to the ground commander's battle plans, a conclusion that argues against the existence of an independent Air Force. And since Air Force doctrine is hardwired to the idea of independence from ground forces, this branch of the service remains unable to do any original thinking about how airpower should be integrated into the strategy of war.

Thus, while Boyd's ideas became increasingly well known and acknowledged, and while some Air Force generals thought it would be rather progressive to think about warfare instead of program management, Air Force efforts to change were little more than sophomoric public-relations stunts. Project Check Mate, the purpose of which was to create a think tank dealing with air warfare and strategy, quickly devolved into little more than a stage play. Then came the "Warrior of the Month" award, in which a large photo of the chosen one was displayed on the fourth floor of the Pentagon. Finally, the Air Force published a reading list of articles and books about war fighting, an idea taken from Boyd's source list at the end of his "Patterns" briefing. In short, the Air Force did not change at all. Even today, retired senior generals take pride in the fact that Boyd's ideas had no influence whatsoever on the Air Force.

Nor did his ideas have any effect on the Navy.

The Army, on the other hand, made a serious effort to change. No branch of the U.S. military was harmed more by the Vietnam War than was the Army — widespread drug use, pervasive racial troubles, and the "fragging" of officers being obvious examples. Plus, the senior noncommissioned officer corps was virtually wiped out by the war. The Army *had* to reinvent itself. But no one quite knew how to go about it.

In 1976 the Army made an attempt to change its ancient doctrine of attrition warfare, but the effort showed how very difficult it is for the military to abandon an old doctrine and adopt a new one. The new Army field manual still placed heavy emphasis on centuries-old ideas of firepower and orderly frontal assaults. The Army continued to rely on the idea that whoever has the biggest guns and the most soldiers will win; it favored a toe-to-toe slugfest with heavy casualties in which the winner is the last man standing.

Boyd constantly ridiculed the Army for spending months developing a new doctrine only to come up with essentially the same thing they had when they started. When Army generals were in his briefing audience, he would wave a copy of the 1976 doctrine overhead and, in his usual subtle and understated fashion, say, "It's a piece of shit."

Whether or not Boyd's frequent and devastating critique of the Army doctrine had any influence is not known. But — and perhaps this is coincidence — as Boyd's briefing gained more and more followers, the Army came under increasing criticism from both within and without. For whatever reason, in 1982 the Army again revised its doctrine. Donn Starry, the four-star general in charge of the Training and Doctrine Command, received credit for the new AirLand Battle Doctrine, but it was written largely by Lieutenant Colonel Huba Wass de Czege, a Harvard-educated, fast-rising young officer. In those days, Wass de Czege was considered a freethinking officer receptive to new ideas. He often invited Boyd out to Fort Leavenworth, the home of the Army's Command and Staff College, to lecture both to his colleagues and to classes at the college. He and Boyd talked frequently by telephone.

In 1982, Boyd and Wass de Czege ran into each other at a West Point symposium on the military-reform movement. Wass de Czege told Boyd the new doctrine was about to be announced and that it stressed four tenets: initiative, agility, depth of operations, and synchronization. Boyd thought the first three were splendid, a sign that the Army was indeed serious about discarding the old heavy firepower theories in favor of maneuver warfare. But what the hell was *synchronization* doing in the new Army doctrine? *Synchronization* is evening up the front line; it means an Army moves at the speed of its slowest unit. *Synchronization* is a fundamental part of the old doctrine of attrition warfare, and it obviates all the other changes. An army that relies on synchronization is not an army that practices maneuver warfare. "You synchronize watches," Boyd shouted, "not people."

Wass de Czege agreed. But he said his bosses had insisted that synchronization be part of the doctrine. Boyd pointed his finger at Wass de Czege and said, "Don't ever again let them do that to you." The Army had to change its ways, Boyd said. "They still believe in high diddle diddle, straight up the middle."

The Army not only adopted most of Boyd's theories regarding maneuver warfare, they even created the School of Advanced Military Studies — SAMS, for short — and placed Wass de Czege in charge. SAMS was for the top graduates in each class at Command and Staff College — an extra year for studying the history of warfare. Boyd's briefing was part of the curriculum up through the mid-1980s. From the beginning, there was an aura about the SAMS graduates; they were called "Jedi Knights" and were considered the brightest young officers in the Army. Spinney thought all this signified radical change. If the Army wanted to clutch the old security blanket of synchronization, well, it was just not that important. "You are overreacting," he told Boyd.

But Boyd was adamant. "This idea of synchronization will ruin the Army."

The time was drawing nigh when, in a very dramatic fashion, Boyd would be proven correct.

After the Air Force, Navy, and Army came the Marine Corps. What happened to the Marine Corps as a result of John Boyd is one of the great untold stories of modern military history. To understand the enormity of the changes Boyd wrought, one must know something about the Marines.

First, the Marine Corps, at about one hundred seventy-three thousand troops, is considerably smaller than the Air Force (three hundred fifty-seven thousand), Army (four hundred eighty thousand), or Navy (three hundred seventy-two thousand). Marines live with the constant fear of being subsumed into the Army or Navy. When the Navy, of which the Marines are a part, portions out dollars, Marines always end up holding the short end of the stick. Old equipment that nobody wants? Give it to the Marines.

The U.S. Marine Corps is a separate and distinct culture within the military. Marines are considered both primitive and elitist — primitive because all Marines are basically infantrymen, and elitist because they are so few in number and so good at what they do. They are warriors and for them there is no higher calling than defending their country in battle. The battle flags of these proud, sea-going troops go back to the "halls of Montezuma and the shores of Tripoli." They are the first to fight and they are given the dirtiest and bloodiest assignments. Got a beach held by vastly superior forces that needs taking? A country that needs taming? Send in the Marines.

Other services recruit by making promises. The Marines recruit by looking for a few good men. Almost from the beginning, the Marines have been considered the military's knuckle draggers, men who charge up a hill until they take it, classic up-the-middle troops who not only take horrendous casualties but boast of those casualties. No part of the U.S. military, however, has more esprit de corps, more respect for the military way, and more reverence for the individual than the Marine Corps. The Marine creed of *Semper Fidelis* — always faithful — is a living breathing thing. When a Marine agrees to do something, looks someone in the eye and says, "*Semper Fi,*" you know he will do what he promised. The Marines are more than a military organization; they are a national institution.

No two branches of the American military are farther apart than the Air Force and the Marines. It is a cultural chasm almost impossible for civilians to understand. There are the obvious differences: the Air Force is the youngest branch of the military and fights its battles in the skies, a place where wars rarely are decided, while Marines fought for America's independence in 1775 and still fight in the mud, where the fate of nations and the course of history are resolved. But there are less obvious differences as well. The Air Force is a technocracy while the Marines are a warrior culture. This all boils down to one thing: Marines are utterly contemptuous of the Air Force.

It is against this backdrop that Boyd's influence on the Marine Corps must be considered.

The education and training of Marine officers is conducted at Marine Base Quantico, about thirty miles south of Washington. Boyd came to Quantico through the offices of an extraordinary man: Lieutenant Colonel Michael Duncan Wyly. For a decade, Boyd and Wyly were Mr. Outside and Mr. Inside for the radical changes that took place in the Marine Corps. Boyd's ideas were the foundation and the impetus for the changes, but Wyly, as an active-duty Marine Corps officer, was the agent of change. Starting in 1980, Wyly became a critical player in Boyd's story.

Mike Wyly cannot remember a time when he did not want to be a Marine. He grew up in Kansas City, Missouri, hearing stories of his uncle Donald Duncan, a Marine Corps captain who, on June 6, 1918, led the 96th Company of the 6th Marines to a place in northeast France called Belleau Wood. Uncle Donald put on his service greens that morning, lit his pipe, and marched his men into battle. When he came upon a German machine-gun nest he took the pipe from his mouth, pointed it at the Germans, and said, "Hit their line together, boys. The guide is right."

The Marines lined up on the man on the far right. Uncle Donald stood out front and motioned for his Marines to follow, and they attacked the machine gun. Uncle Donald died that day. Belleau Wood became a hallowed name in Marine Corps history because that is where more Marines died than on any other day in Marine Corps history and because that is where Marines stopped the German advance. That is also where they acquired one of their most treasured nicknames: *teufelhunden* — "devil dogs."

Mike Wyly's relatives always finished this story by saying that if Uncle Donald had lived, he would have become commandant of the Marine Corps.

Wyly wanted to join the Marine Corps as an enlisted man. Even today he is not quite sure why. His father wanted him to go to

Annapolis and become an officer. Wyly was seventeen when he made a deal with his father; he would apply to Annapolis if his father would allow him to join the Marine Corps reserves. So Wyly sent in his application to Annapolis, then signed up in the Marine Corps and went off to boot camp.

The first thing an enlisted Marine learns is how to march and how to maintain "cover" and "dress." *Cover* is standing precisely behind the Marine in front of you so that when a drill instructor looks down a long column he sees only the first man in line. *Dress* is being lined up precisely with the man beside you so that the drill instructor can look across six or eight or ten rows of men and see only the first man. Dressed and covered, that's the rule. And when boots of a squad or company or even a battalion of Marines strike the pavement, there must be a single click. Marines take precise thirty-inch strides and their boots make one sound. A Marine who is a split second off is more annoying than one who is completely out of step. Dressed and covered and with hundreds of feet striking the ground as one — that's the Marine way.

Wyly was a private in the reserves when he entered Annapolis. He took his commission in the Marines, served a year on Okinawa, and then became an instructor in the guerrilla warfare school at Camp Pendleton. Instructors at Pendleton were an intellectual lot and read all they could find about any country that had known guerrilla warfare: Algeria, Indochina, Central America, Cuba, Kenya, and a dozen others. General Victor "The Brute" Krulak came to Pendleton and told the instructors that if America went to war in Vietnam it would be a long war and it would be different from other wars in which Marines had fought; it would wreak a terrible toll because the American military did not know how to fight a guerrilla war. Wyly went to jump school, to psychological-warfare school, and to special-warfare school, and he trained often with the Army. He read Bernard Fall's *Street Without Joy,* the classic book on the French in Vietnam, and stood on a platform and told Marines passing through Pendleton, "If we go to Vietnam, we are not going to make the mistakes the French made."

In 1965 Lieutenant Mike Wyly went to Vietnam as a psychological-warfare officer. His work was in the villages and he was pushed hard for body counts. At the end of his tour he knew the Marines were tough and disciplined and brave. But did they understand the war?

Washington was his next assignment. In 1969 he returned to Vietnam as a twenty-nine-year-old captain. Like his uncle Donald, he now was a company commander. He led Delta Company, part of the First Battalion of the 5th Marines, and operated out of An Hoa, west of Danang. Delta 1/5 was such a hard-luck group that it was called "Dying Delta." Wyly found that the war in 1969 was a different war than it had been in 1965. One of his Marines said, "Skipper, everybody here is the enemy." Delta Company was in a firefight every night. But the young Marines had learned how to survive — and not with traditional Marine Corps tactics. Marines in Delta Company knew how to disperse and how to use guerrilla tactics — how to fight like the enemy. Wyly remembered the lessons of Pendleton and saw how those lessons made sense. He sent out saturation patrols. His Marines were in the bush all the time. He kept the enemy off balance; they knew Delta Company could show up anywhere, anytime.

Senior Marine leaders had not learned the same lessons. One day Wyly flew to battalion headquarters and en route saw Marines advancing in a line across a field. The enemy let them pass and then attacked from the rear. Wyly sensed that something was fundamentally wrong with the way the Marine Corps did business.

Wyly had a platoon leader named James Webb. One day Lieutenant Webb was out leading a patrol. He waded across a shallow river and as he reached the far shore the men behind him were attacked. Webb came to their assistance so fast that a young Marine, in telling Wyly what happened, said, "Lieutenant Webb ran across the top of the water." It became axiomatic among Marines in Delta Company that Lieutenant Webb could walk on water. Later, Wyly recommended Webb for the Navy Cross, second only to the Medal of Honor as a recognition of valor.

Wyly and Webb would cross paths again.

When Wyly left Vietnam, Delta 1/5 was known throughout the Marine Corps as a savvy and aggressive bunch of troops, real mud Marines. The greatest compliment Wyly ever received was when, as he turned over command of his company, one of his young Marines said to him, "Skipper, we ain't the Dying Delta anymore."

Wyly now was a decorated combat veteran, a senior captain about to be promoted to major. In return for his education at the Naval Academy, he had pledged five years of service. That obligation now was over and he had to decide if he wanted to stay in the Corps or if he wanted to join the civilian world. His two tours in Vietnam showed him that the Marine Corps had fundamental problems in the way it conducted warfare. If he stayed in, there was much he wanted to change.

He chose the latter, and his next assignment was as a student at Quantico, where he went through the Amphibious Warfare School (AWS). The school is located in Geiger Hall, a two-story brick building atop a high hill overlooking a tributary of the Potomac. Amphibious warfare is unique to the Marine Corps; it is all that keeps the Marines from being swallowed by the Army or Navy. Amphibious warfare is what the Marine Corps is supposed to do better than any other military organization in the world. Yet, Wyly found the Marines were still teaching long linear attacks on beachheads, a tactic that produced the terrible casualties of World War II.

After graduating from the AWS, Wyly was assigned as an instructor at the Basic School, where young lieutenants are taught company-level tactics. The instructors were Vietnam vets, but they were ordered not to talk about Vietnam; why rehash that war when the next war would be against hordes of Soviets in Europe? The Marine Corps still taught the concept of advancing on line, just as Wyly's uncle Donald had done in World War I and just as Marines had done in World War II — the same suicidal tactics used in Vietnam. In fact, the worst criticism that could be leveled against a student during field exercises was that he did not advance his troops on line.

Saigon fell and no senior Marine Corps officer at Quantico realized that Marine tactics had not worked. One of them even said to Wyly, "We killed more of them than they killed of us." Officially, the Marine Corps won in Vietnam. But Mike Wyly and a host of other hard young officers, men who had been there and seen their friends die and who believed they were living on borrowed time, knew that was utter nonsense.

While the Marine Corps prided itself on being different, now the Corps was having the same problems as other services: race riots and discipline problems. Commandant Robert Cushman was so over-weight that young lieutenants joked that the Marine Corps fitness test was "three laps around Bobby Cushman."

After his tour as an instructor, Wyly was promoted to major. But he considered his tour at Quantico a failure. He had changed nothing. He went to Command and Staff College and was assigned to do a strategic study of a country. He picked Finland and studied the Winter War of 1939–1940. Wyly thought it was a good war to study because the Finns had prevailed over vastly superior Russian forces. His professor told him to return to college and study history. He entered the master's program at George Washington but soon was assigned to Okinawa. Then came another assignment to Quantico. Wyly had written a paper about the Battle of Tarawa in World War II, a battle dear to the heart of every Marine, and thus had come under the protective eye of Major General Bernard Trainor, the director of education in the Marine Corps. General Trainor placed Wyly in charge of tactics at the Amphibious Warfare School. "Tactics is the flat tire. It's your job to fix it," Trainor said. "And I don't want you to hide behind doctrine. Be out on the fringes. Use your mind." The assignment was a gem. The AWS is important to the Marines not just for doctrinal reasons but because only the brightest and most promising young officers are assigned there; it is where future leaders of the Marine Corps are first identified. Wyly was exactly where he wanted to be.

The lesson plans at the AWS dated back to the 1930s, to the very beginning of amphibious warfare. Wyly scrapped all the old lesson plans and began teaching famous battles from history. One of his favorites was the Battle of Austerlitz in 1805. Sometimes called the "Battle of the Three Emperors," this is one of the most significant battles in military history. Not only did Napoléon prevail against a numerically superior force, his victory was so decisive that it forced the Austrians and Russians to withdraw from the war. Napoléon was so successful at knowing what opposing generals were thinking that he wrote Josephine that there were times when he felt he was leading both armies.

Students at the AWS were captains and majors, not all of whom had decided to make a career out of the Marine Corps. They had lots of field experience and they were not reluctant to speak their minds. Under Wyly, for the first time in years, the tactics course received rave reviews. But Wyly wanted to do more than teach about ancient battles and how to deal with Soviet tanks on the plains of Europe. He was fascinated by the theme of armies winning against superior forces, of generals who controlled the thinking of their opposition. Somewhere there was a glue to bind all of this together into a different kind of warfare — but where?

Wyly turned to Bill Lind, the man who first called Boyd's followers "Reformers," and asked him to recommend someone with new ideas about warfare.

"Colonel John Boyd is your man," Lind said. Wyly looked at his khaki-covered Marine Corps manuals and he knew that whatever it was that Boyd offered, it had to be better. He called Boyd and said, "I hear you have a theory about warfare."

"It's not a theory. It's a briefing. I call it 'Patterns of Conflict.' It's five hours long."

Wyly laughed. "My class has only two hours."

"I can't do it in two. It takes five hours."

"We don't have five hours."

"Then you get zero."

Wyly relented. If his mandate allowed him to operate on the fringes of doctrine, why couldn't he stretch a class to five hours? Wyly opened the briefing not just to his class, but to all AWS students.

Boyd arrived in January 1980. Wyly had not heard Boyd's briefing, so he had no idea what to expect. But if there were no substance, if the no-nonsense students thought this retired Air Force colonel was wasting their time, the class could turn nasty. The more Wyly thought about it the more worried he became. What had he done? A retired *pilot* — and not even a Marine pilot but an Air Force pilot — lecturing mud Marines on how to fight a war, how to apply ideas that are relevant on the modern battlefield? The idea is ludicrous. These aggressive young captains and majors will make mincemeat out of this guy.

Wyly introduced Boyd. Boyd stood up and his eyes locked on the Marines and he took charge. His deep voice boomed out. The Plum began to weave his magic. He told them of Sun Tzu and the Battle of Leuctra in 371 B.C. and of Arbela in 331 B.C. and of Cannae in 216 B.C.

He told them of Genghis Khan and Belisarius and Napoléon, of Heinz Guderian and of what made great commanders. He defogged von Clausewitz and told them how to build snowmobiles. He told them the Army, despite its new AirLand Doctrine, still believed in "high diddle diddle, straight up the middle," and followed a doctrine that was a "piece of shit." He told them of OODA Loops and *Schwerpunkt* and *Fingerspitzengefuhl* and surfaces and gaps and mission orders and water going downhill.

The five hours came and went, but the Marines stayed. Now a half dozen Marines were on their feet, fighting for Boyd's attention, asking hard and thoughtful questions, but questions asked in respect. Their faces revealed their thoughts: *This old man may be an Air Force puke, but he knows warfare better than anyone I've ever heard.* The air crackled with excitement. Mike Wyly knew, as did the students, they were witnessing the beginning of something new and powerful and wonderful.

Six hours passed and the shadows lengthened across Quantico and a few Marines drifted away. Seven hours passed and the remaining Marines had forgotten Boyd was an Air Force colonel; they looked upon him as if he were the reincarnation of an ancient warrior. They were young and not saddled with the institutional memory of senior officers. They wanted ideas that would work and that's what Boyd gave them. Eight hours passed and now Boyd was sitting in a chair surrounded by eager young Marines. They leaned toward Boyd as if they could not get enough of what he had to say. And when the session finally broke up, night had long since fallen on the rolling hills of Quantico. But the young officers still were bright and eager. They wanted to know when Boyd would return.

Mike Wyly would remember this day for the rest of his life. Boyd had given him new ideas that validated the vague theories floating around in his head. And Boyd had given the young students ideas that could be translated into tactics that worked on the modern battlefield.

Mike Wyly had become the sixth Acolyte. He and John Boyd were about to take on the U.S. Marine Corps.

Chapter Twenty-Eight

Semper Fi

A FEW days later Wyly was introduced to the "pain," the long late-night phone calls from Boyd. He was immensely flattered. He was a lieutenant colonel being called by a man who had retired as a senior colonel. In the highly structured Marine Corps that is a big gulf.

Then Boyd returned to Quantico to talk with Wyly about his class. They met in Wyly's office under the picture of his uncle Donald leading the charge at Belleau Wood. "What should I be teaching?" Wyly asked. He showed Boyd the official khaki-clad Marine Corps lesson plans for the AWS. "You can't read these without going to sleep," he said. "We have the most exciting subject in the world: *warfare*. And we make it boring."

Boyd and Wyly decided the AWS was fundamentally an educational institution, and educational institutions are places where students consider *all* ideas. One of the best ways to do that is to have students read. So Wyly and Boyd put together a reading list. This was a radical step for the Marine Corps, the least-intellectual branch of the U.S. military. But General Trainor, by now widely recognized as Wyly's protector, blessed the concept and soon the young captains were reading *Victory at High Tide* and *Guerrilla* and *White Death* and *Strategy* and even books by World War II German officers such as

Attacks by Rommel and *Panzer Battles* by von Mellenthin. Boyd and Wyly were both combat veterans, so when they claimed there was a connection between books and the ability to lead men into battle, students listened. In fact, students began coming to class early so they could debate the ideas they had been reading. Soon students were recommending additional books for the reading list.

By now Boyd had collected all his briefings, along with "Destruction and Creation," and assembled them into a one-inch-thick document titled "A Discourse on Winning and Losing." Christie had printed several hundred copies. Because the document had a green cover it was referred to as the "Green Book." Wyly wanted copies for his classes but Boyd had only a few left. Wyly took a copy to the Field Print Plant at Quantico and said, "I want four hundred copies." He passed them out to Marine officers.

Boyd became a regular lecturer and took an active part in tactics classes. When the classes did amphibious exercises Boyd walked from group to group, studying their plans. Once, while the groups wrestled with how to put a landing force on the shores of Iran, Boyd realized the Marines were placing inordinate emphasis on *how* to establish a beachhead. "That beachhead is looming bigger and bigger," he said. "You guys are paying too much attention to terrain. The focus should be on the enemy. Fight the enemy, not the terrain."

The words echoed in Wyly's brain.

That beachhead is looming bigger and bigger. . . . Fight the enemy, not the terrain.

The fundamental content of the classes changed. Wyly now advocated fluid and fast-moving tactics that disrupted enemy thinking. During tactical exercises he told his students he did not want anyone to report that they had seized and were holding an objective. He wanted them to bypass resistance. Don't worry about your flanks, he said. Let the enemy worry about his. He gave them mission orders, *Schwerpunkt* exercises, and taught them how to lead from the front like Field Marshal Erwin Rommel. They should be everywhere on the battlefield so they could have an intuitive grasp of the ebb and flow of battle, *Fingerspitzengefuhl.*

"This stuff has got to be implicit," Boyd said. "If it is explicit, you can't do it fast enough." Boyd's teaching methods were different from those of a university. He abhorred guidelines or lists or rules or

381

deductive thinking; everything was intuitive. "You must have inductive thinking," he said again and again to the Marines. "There is not just one solution to a problem," he said. "There are two or three or five ways to solve a problem. Never commit to a single solution."

Boyd never said, "This is how Marines should fight" or "This is how you should conduct an amphibious landing." Instead he taught a new way to *think* about combat. His new way turned conventional military wisdom on its head. The military believes most of all in hardware. But Boyd said, "People should come first. Then ideas. And then hardware."

On Sunday afternoons a group of young captains gathered at Wyly's house, sat around a big mahogany table, drank wine, and talked of maneuver warfare. They met for additional seminars at Bill Lind's home in Alexandria. The cadre of Marines now known as "maneuverists" continued to grow. Those men were proud of the title. But at the Quantico Officers Club, senior officers turned their backs on maneuverists and laughed about Marines more interested in OODA Loops than in lifting weights, more interested in reading of ancient battles than in running five miles. Wyly was leading a guerrilla movement within the Corps, and sometimes he recalled a line from his lectures: "Guerrillas win wars but they don't march home to victory parades."

Trainor asked Wyly to write a new tactics manual for the Marine Corps, but Wyly's direct supervisor looked at the first three chapters and rejected them, saying with anguish, "It's all new." During the summer of 1981, Trainor transferred from Quantico and Wyly no longer had a protector. It would not be long before predators began circling.

About this time a story within the story, a story of crucial importance, and a story that would have a significant payoff in a few short years was beginning down in Camp Lejeune, the sprawling Marine Corps base in North Carolina. That summer, General Al Gray, who had heard Boyd's briefing as a colonel, was ordered to Lejeune as commander of the 2nd Marine Division. Gray was the son of a railroad conductor. He chewed tobacco and walked around in the fatigues Marines called "utilities" and, like Patton and Rommel, wore goggles across the front of his helmet. He was a warrior: a forceful, decisive, and highly unconventional Marine. He also was a devoted student of Boyd's and a man who believed in maneuver warfare.

Two young Marine Corps captains based at Lejeune, Bill Woods and G. I. Wilson, regularly hosted a group of officers studying maneuver warfare. The group was called the "Young Turks." When Wyly heard that Gray was coming to Lejeune, he called Woods and said, "You've got to get to Gray." Woods did. He and Wilson invited Gray to attend a meeting. Gray not only attended, he said, "This is no longer an informal study group. This is now the 2nd Marine Division's maneuver warfare board. The first thing you guys have to do is get John Boyd down here."

Boyd came down and delivered the briefing. Since Gray had heard the briefing several times, he left after about an hour. Soon thereafter other senior officers began to leave. But an enthusiastic core of true believers remained.

The scene at Lejeune was a microcosm of maneuver warfare within the Marine Corps; as long as it had the protective umbrella of senior officers, it was followed — reluctantly by many, enthusiastically by a few. Much of the reluctance was because of Bill Lind. Lind is a big fleshy man who, when he observed tactical exercises, favored an inverness and a deerstalker. He was a most incongruous figure as he lectured senior officers. Many of those officers had no patience with this pompous civilian; after all, he had never dodged a bullet, he had never led men in combat, he had never even worn a uniform. Inevitably, one of those officers rose in indignation and challenged Lind. And just as inevitably, Lind cut him off at the knees. One example was the time a heavily muscled, shaven-head officer interrupted Lind in the middle of a briefing and, with utter disgust, said, "*Schwerpunkt,* bilgepunkt, it's all the same to me." Lind smiled down at him and said, "Yes, it is. And, unfortunately, it will always be that way for you."

The concept of maneuver warfare could not have had a more polarizing patron.

Gray told Woods to set about planning a free-play exercise. Until that time, Marine Corps tactical exercises were choreographed operations. During the briefings, a battalion commander received orders saying, "You will assault and seize Objective Alpha. Then you will assault and seize Objective Bravo." This was fine with the lieutenant colonels who were battalion commanders. Being a battalion commander was part of getting the promotional ticket punched. After a year or two, if there were no mistakes, a promotion to full colonel was assured. But young officers heard the briefings and wondered, "What if the enemy is at Objective Alpha in unexpected force and we don't seize and hold? What then?"

In a free-play exercise — no scenario and no rules — the orchestrated performance was tossed out. There is no better way to select and test combat leaders than by free play. Free play means winners and losers; it means postexercise critiques by enlisted men as well as junior officers. No battalion commander enjoys being contradicted by a sergeant, especially if the sergeant is correct. And if a battalion commander loses a free-play exercise, he might lose his chance at promotion. Careerists hated free play and, by extension, maneuver warfare. True combat leaders loved it.

During the late summer of 1981, the Marines held their first free-play exercise at Fort Pickett, a little-used Army base near Blackstone, Virginia. Gray liked the base because it was unfamiliar to all involved; no one would have the advantage of knowing the terrain. Gray made sure the free-play exercise simulated the unexpected developments of combat as closely as possible. A battalion commander might be marching along and suddenly find that an element of the 82nd Airborne had parachuted on his flank. No one told him to expect an attack in force by paratroopers. Now what would he do?

The exercises were immensely popular with most junior officers and just as unpopular with most senior officers.

Boyd seemed to be everywhere during those years. He delivered his briefing hundreds of times, not just to Marines, but to members of the Army, Navy, and Air Force; to the various command and staff colleges; and at numerous seminars. Boyd was offered compensation for most of these lectures, but all he ever accepted was travel expenses. References to the OODA Loop were popping up everywhere from newspaper stories to the advice of business consultants. As had been the case with E-M, many of the references did not mention Boyd. His work had become generic. And as had been the case with E-M, he laughed and said he did not mind. The most important thing was that the ideas become known.

But "known" did not mean "accepted." Back at Quantico, Wyly was beginning to realize that his radical ideas on teaching were unpopular with the new director of the AWS. Wyly was not invited to meetings he should have attended. Numerous officers snubbed him. On February 25, 1982 — his forty-second birthday — Wyly came to work and was told he had been fired as head of tactics. His new job was as a member of the amphibious-warfare presentation team, a group that traveled around telling various groups how the Marine Corps conducted amphibious warfare.

Presenting the ancient and outmoded amphibious warfare briefings was the most painful time of Wyly's life. He read from the old AWS manuals all the traditional ideas of linear attacks, of seizing and holding a beachhead, of attrition warfare. He thought the Marine Corps was marching into the past. He called his office "Spandau" and plotted how to get out.

He was not the only one plotting. Wyly returned from one trip to find his office had been ransacked and his personal mail opened, the latter a federal offense. Papers were scattered all over the office and Uncle Duncan's picture was on the floor. Wyly suspected a burglary and called the military police but was astonished to hear them say there had been no burglary. A Marine officer fired from his job is considered wounded. He is prey for all predators.

The U.S. Military Academy at West Point held a conference on the military-reform movement during the spring of 1982 and invited representatives from all branches of the services. Wyly attended and was outspoken in proposing reform, but he was clearly operating on his own, far out in front with no support. He had only his belief in himself for sustenance. Other officers thought he was out of cover, out of dress, and out of step with the Corps — the single thunk of a boot — and let him know. When he spoke to Boyd a few months later, the frustration in his voice was clear.

"Mike, I can have you out of Quantico in a month," Boyd said.

Wyly laughed. "Colonel, I don't know how much you know about the Marine Corps personnel system, but —"

"I know about the Air Force personnel system," Boyd interrupted. "I don't think it's too much different. Just tell me this: what do you want to do?"

Wyly did not hesitate. "Meaningful work."

"Do you want to leave Quantico?"

"Colonel, leaving Quantico would surpass my wildest dreams."

Boyd laughed. "Okay. But remember, this conversation never took place."

Wyly sighed as he hung up the telephone. He was indulging a retired officer whom he respected. But what Wyly and so many other officers never knew about Boyd was that even at the height of the reform movement, when his name was anathema to the Pentagon, he still had admirers at high levels of government. And of course he still had close friends such as Tom Christie who knew all the back-channel ways of doing business in the Building.

A few days after Wyly and Boyd talked, an urgent message arrived at Quantico. It said, "Transfer no later than 15 September 1982 to Office of the Secretary of Defense, Lieutenant Colonel M. D. Wyly for duties essential to national security. Carlucci sends."

"Carlucci" was Frank Carlucci, the deputy secretary of defense.

Wyly was reeling. He was a mere lieutenant colonel caught in the bureaucratic backwaters of Quantico and suddenly he had been name requested by the deputy secretary of defense for a job in the Pentagon. It is rare for a *general* to be name requested by the SecDef's office; for a lieutenant colonel it is virtually unprecedented.

Wyly called Boyd and said, "Colonel, I received orders to get me out of here. A personal message from Carlucci."

Boyd laughed.

Wyly's orders were cut within days. For the next two years he worked in Carlucci's office, in a place referred to only as the "black hole," where he was involved in some of the most highly classified matters of the U.S. military. He was the only Marine in the group. Along the way, Wyly was promoted to full colonel. He probably would not have been promoted had not General Trainor, his old protector, been chairman of his promotion board.

Six months after becoming a full colonel, Wyly felt comfortable enough with Boyd to call him "John" for the first time.

In 1983 came the first opportunity for the Marines to put maneuver warfare into practice. The Marine Corps barracks in Beirut was attacked by terrorists and 241 people were killed. As this happened, a battalion of Marines was en route to Beirut to serve a tour of duty. The battalion was diverted to participate in the invasion of Grenada.

The battalion was led by Lieutenant Colonel Ray Smith, a maneuverist and graduate of the Fort Pickett free-play exercises.

Smith did two things in Grenada that demonstrated the efficacy of maneuver warfare. When intelligence reports told of a large building flying a curious flag, ranking officers assumed the building housed one of the Grenada revolutionary organizations. A Navy admiral ordered Smith's Marines to attack. Historically, a Marine commander receiving such orders would have done so without a second thought. But a fundamental tenet of maneuver warfare is to give the officer on the scene the authority to make tactical decisions. A young captain under Smith's command was not sure the building housed revolutionaries and suggested sending out a patrol. Smith had confidence in the captain and agreed. He could always call in naval gunfire to level the buildings. As the patrol approached the building, a civilian came out to welcome them. Dozens of guns were trained on the man. If he had twitched, if he had reached into a pocket, he probably would have died. He waved and said, "Gentlemen, I am glad to see you. I am the ambassador of Venezuela."

Smith's maturity and prudence that day saved the United States considerable ignominy.

Smith's overall performance in Grenada was even more illustrative of how a maneuverist works. Elite Army rangers were pinned down at the airport, largely by Cuban construction workers, and could not move. But Smith's Marines, a much smaller group, ripped around Grenada as if they owned the island. They bypassed enemy strongholds, put strength against weakness, and moved like water flowing downhill. They created such confusion and uncertainty that hundreds of enemy soldiers surrendered to Smith because, as one of them said, "The Marines are everywhere."

In his book *About Face,* retired Army colonel David Hackworth quotes an Army general as saying, "We have two companies of Marines running all over the island and thousands of Army troops doing nothing. What the hell is going on?" It was maneuver warfare. And in a few more years, the Marines would demonstrate, with far more force and clarity, the efficacy of this new-old concept.

After Wyly's Pentagon tour he asked to be transferred to the University of Kansas as head of Naval ROTC. It was not an assignment that helped his career, but his mother lived in Kansas City and was very sick, and this was something he had to do. Boyd came out often to lecture. So did James Webb, Wyly's former platoon leader in Vietnam who now was an assistant secretary of defense. General Al Gray also was a guest lecturer. It was quite an ROTC program. (Before being appointed to high office, Webb wrote *Fields of Fire,* a best-selling novel about a company of Marines fighting in Vietnam. "Dying Delta," they were called. One of the most important characters in the book is a heroic company commander who turned his hard-luck company into hard-charging Marines. That character, of course, is based on Mike Wyly's combat experience.)

In 1983 General P. X. Kelly became the commandant of the Marine Corps and spoke derisively of maneuverists and — in a reference to Bill Lind's study groups — "people who meet in basements." To survive, maneuver warfare needed support from the top level of the Marine Corps. Suddenly, that support was gone.

Except for the Marine Corps *Gazette.*

The *Gazette* is a monthly journal, much like the Navy Institute's *Proceedings,* the Air Force's *Aerospace Power Journal,* and the Army's *Parameters.* The *Gazette* is a curious little magazine. As early as 1941 it published a translation of Mao on guerrilla warfare. It also published articles on Sun Tzu, and in the period between 1955 and 1962 it ran twenty-five articles by the military theorist Liddell Hart. Nevertheless, until about 1980 the privately funded *Gazette* was a flaccid house organ, something of a cheerleading magazine largely without distinction even within the Marine Corps. Then retired Marine Corps colonel John Greenwood became editor. Greenwood is a modest and self-effacing man, a gentleman in the old sense of the word. Anyone who met him while he was in civilian clothes would never guess that he was a former regimental commander, a man with impeccable Marine Corps credentials. He has additional gravitas among Marines because his four sons serve as Marine Corps officers. Greenwood, perhaps more so than any other person — including the commandant — was Mr. Marine Corps. No one could question his devotion. No one could doubt that every publishing decision he made was based on what he thought best for the Marine Corps. And he wanted to publish articles that kept Marines awake at night.

So Greenwood did what great magazine editors have done throughout history; he kept alive a controversial idea. Greenwood opened the
Gazette to the maneuverists. And all during the 1980s, article after article on maneuver warfare appeared, along with spirited rebuttal from
senior Marine officers. The magazine became the vehicle that continued stirring intellectual ferment throughout the Marine Corps.

Wyly wrote many of the seminal articles of those years, one of the
most important being "Thinking Beyond the Beachhead," a piece
born of Boyd's comment, *That beachhead is looming bigger and bigger. . . . Fight the enemy, not the terrain.* In the article, Wyly said that in
an amphibious operation, getting on a beach was not the real challenge; getting *off* the beach and moving into enemy territory was the
challenge.

With each article Wyly became more out of cover, more out of
dress, more out of step with other Marines.

Just as it is difficult to separate some of Boyd's ideas from those of
the Acolytes, it is difficult on occasion to separate the ideas of Boyd
and Wyly. Even Wyly was confused at times. Boyd called to congratulate him after various pieces in the *Gazette* were published and Wyly
thanked him for providing an idea or a thought contained in the
piece. Boyd laughed and said, "It was your thinking and your ideas
that brought that out, Mike."

James Webb was named secretary of the Navy in 1987, and one of
his jobs was to appoint a new commandant of the Marine Corps.
Wyly and G. I. Wilson arranged for Webb to meet Al Gray, the
three-star who brought maneuver warfare to the 2nd Marine Division at Lejeune. "He's dynamite. We think he is a warrior," they told
Webb. Soon after, Gray, much to his surprise, was given a fourth star
and appointed commandant of the Marine Corps.

In 1987 Wyly received orders for Okinawa. He had two daughters,
and as military men have done for ages, he left his wife and children
at home when he went overseas. He had wanted to command a regi-
ment, but he was a pragmatist and knew that men who lead guerrilla
movements rarely lead regiments. His new job was as assistant chief
of staff, in charge of operations and training in the western Pacific.

Wyly continued to think hard about reform. After he wrote an
article about how generals need to study tactics, his boss came in and

shut the door — always a bad sign — and said, "Mike, this kind of article is not going to help your career." He was right: Wyly never had a command after he began publishing. Passed over for general, he began to think seriously about retirement.

Then old friends began writing letters saying, "Mike, it's beginning. You need to be at Quantico." Wyly had served more time at Quantico than most officers and did not want to return. But the letters kept coming. "The commandant wants you involved in the reforms at Quantico," he was told. Friends said, "Don't retire. Gray has a vision. Look what he did with the 2nd Marine Division down at Lejeune. He's bringing you back." Then came the orders. He had been name requested by the commandant. Wyly paced up and down the helicopter pad behind his house. This was the toughest decision he had ever had to make. Rather than asking, as others might, "How will this improve my career?" or "What's in it for me?" he instead said to himself, "My country is calling. I have to respond." If there was a chance to resurrect maneuver warfare, he would give his all.

When Wyly checked in at Quantico, the personnel office was packed with officers. A clerk stood up and asked, "Is there a Colonel Wyly here?" Wyly identified himself and the clerk said, "Sir, the commandant is calling." A dozen officers stared curiously at this colonel who was receiving a phone call from General Al Gray even before he unpacked. "My door is open," Gray said to him on the phone that day. "What you are doing is important. You can walk in anytime."

Wyly smiled as he finished checking in. Staying in the Marine Corps had been the right decision.

Gray gave Wyly two assignments, two dream jobs. First, he was to write a campaign plan for the Marine Corps. The plan was to chart the course the Corps should follow for the next five years. Second, Wyly was to follow through on an idea he had presented to Gray years earlier, to make plans for setting up the preeminent war-fighting university in the world, something called the Marine Corps University.

Wyly's immediate boss was Major General Mike Sullivan, one of the best aviators in the Marine Corps. Like most aviators, Sullivan didn't think much of maneuver warfare; he believed the doctrinal emphasis and the budget should go toward aviation. Wyly was not discouraged. As he began working on the campaign plan, he told his wife, "This is a mission. This is how George Washington must have felt en route to the constitutional convention." Wyly never imagined he would have this sort of opportunity. He was backed up by the commandant. Gray had, in effect, told Wyly, "Marine Corps warfighting doctrine is decades out of date. I want new ideas about war fighting codified into a manual. You and Boyd see to it."

Boyd and Wyly knew their names could not be on the book; they were far too controversial. And the new manual would be far more acceptable to junior officers if it bore the name of a young officer. They went to a young captain who already had the job of writing a new manual but who had become bogged down. Boyd and Wyly spent long hours with him. Boyd said, "Do not write it as a formula. Write it as a way to teach officers to think, to think in new ways about war. War is ever changing and men are ever fallible. Rigid rules simply won't work. Teach men to think." Boyd paused a moment and added a final thought. "And keep the goddamn thing simple so generals can understand it."

Originally the manual was to have a long number in the title, signifying the evolutionary process of Marine Corps tactics manuals. But Gray refused. "We want this to show that we are starting over, starting at the beginning. Put the number *one* on the cover."

The manual was called "FMFM-1 Warfighting."

Against the wishes of most officers on his staff, Gray simply signed on and said this is the way it will be, this is the way we will train, and this is the way we will fight. He decreed the manual as official Marine Corps doctrine. Shortly thereafter, Boyd and Wyly went to see General Gray. The commandant was immensely pleased and thought Boyd would be also. But Boyd looked at the ninety-eight-page manual and said, "Okay, General. Now you have to start changing it." He still loathed the idea of finishing an intellectual work.

All this time, Wyly continued sending drafts of the campaign plan to Sullivan. He said the first thing the Marine Corps should do was clean up the personnel system and stamp out careerism. He wrote of the need to provide professional education for all Marines, to instill a greater sense of ethics, and to promote unit cohesion. He stressed the importance of maneuver warfare.

Every idea was rejected. Sullivan slashed and edited and kicked back draft after draft for rewriting. He even wrote "Shit" on one version. He summed up his feelings toward Wyly with the greatest insult a fighter pilot can muster: "I don't think I'd want you for a wingman."

Then Wyly attended a meeting where some of his young officers were making a maneuver-warfare presentation to a two-star general. The general belittled every sentence. Wyly, as the senior maneuverist in the Marine Corps, felt obligated to come to their defense. He was not going to be intimidated by a general. He stood up and said, "General, let them finish before you begin criticizing."

In minutes Wyly and the general were standing toe-to-toe. "We have to keep the tried and true," the general shouted.

"You mean like Vietnam?" Wyly shouted even louder.

Other officers backed away. When the elephants are fighting, it is best to keep your distance.

Wyly later was told that his confrontation with the two-star ended his chances of being promoted to general. He did not believe it. The Marine Corps expected healthy debate, didn't it?

General Sullivan refused every idea Wyly had for the five-year plan. The commandant had given him the biggest job of his career but his immediate supervisor rejected his best efforts. It was clear that nothing but tired old doctrine would be acceptable to Sullivan. And Wyly wanted no part of this.

During Easter weekend of 1989, Wyly returned to Kansas City, where his wife and daughters lived in the Wyly family home. Mrs. Wyly had been waiting until the end of the school year to move to Quantico.

"I've decided to hang it up," he told her. She agreed. Her husband had been mistreated long enough by the Marine Corps. It was time to join the civilian world.

Boyd called the evening that Wyly returned to Quantico. His prescience was uncanny. Although he did not say so, the thrust of Boyd's conversation clearly revealed that he knew what Wyly was planning. Finally Wyly said, "John, I've decided to retire from the Marine Corps."

"Mike, you can't do that. It is not yet time. You still have a job to do, a big job. There is a mission here for you that you must continue." Boyd spent almost an hour cajoling Wyly, reminding him of the

OODA Loop, of bypassing resistance, of ambiguity, of making multiple thrusts against an enemy stronghold. "The multiple thrusts will confuse Sullivan," he said. "You know your *Schwerpunkt* but he doesn't." Boyd took Wyly to the mountaintop and showed him a rainbow-draped promised land, where Marines practiced maneuver warfare and where there were no generals to impede good ideas.

Wyly put down the phone, thought about what Boyd had said, then called his wife and said he was staying in the Corps. "Pack up and you and the girls come join me," he said.

He called again the next day and told his wife how much better he felt now that he had decided not to resign. "It was depressing to think that I was going to wake up a civilian. No more of those late calls from Boyd. No more OODA Loops or discussions about rapidity or fluidity. I would have missed those phone calls." He and his wife laughed; both at times were exasperated with Boyd's midnight calls.

Following Boyd's lead, Wyly decided to put the principles of maneuver warfare to work. He would continue to send drafts of his five-year plan to Sullivan, but while the general was occupied with that, he would make another thrust — this one straight toward the commandant. He asked Boyd to come to Quantico and bring the commandant up to date on his thinking about multiple thrusts and ambiguity, two concepts Boyd had begun emphasizing only in recent months.

Wyly knew Sullivan would refuse Boyd entrance to the commandant's office, so Wyly bypassed the chain of command. Wyly and Boyd talked to Gray for three hours. Aides kept trying to interrupt, to get the commandant back on schedule, but he turned them all away. He refused all phone calls. The next day Gray dropped in on a class at the Command and Staff College and talked to the students about multiple thrusts and ambiguity and *Schwerpunkt*. He told them of maneuver warfare and said, "This is where the Marine Corps is going."

Of course, two-star generals don't like being bypassed in the chain of command, so Sullivan braced Wyly and gave him a royal chewing out.

Several days later Wyly wrote a memo to Gray, attached it to a copy of his five-year plan — the project Sullivan kept blocking — and sent it to Gray's office. The copy was marked and edited and filled with Sullivan's derisive comments.

Wyly says he sent the plan to Gray not in reaction to Sullivan's chewing him out but out of frustration. Nothing was happening. He had to break the logjam. Besides, Gray told him earlier, "My door is always open. Come in anytime."

Wyly made a copy of the memo and stuck it in his desk. He thinks his desk was searched and the memo found and sent to Sullivan. This is possible. But it is also possible, especially in view of later events, that Gray, or someone in his office, sent Sullivan a copy of the memo.

However it got there, several weeks later a copy of the memo wound up on Sullivan's desk.

Wyly was again up for promotion to brigadier general. His contributions to the Marine Corps were such that he felt he might make it this time. He was feeling confident. Several days later he was escorting David Hackworth around Quantico. The two men were observing field exercises. At one point a messenger approached Wyly with a folded piece of yellow paper. "Call General Sullivan," it said. Wyly stuck the note in his pocket and continued escorting Hackworth. A second messenger brought another sheet of yellow paper saying, "Call General Sullivan." The note did not indicate any emergency. Wyly thought, "The general knows where I am. He knows what I am doing. He knows when I will be back." Wyly again stuck the note in his pocket.

Hours later, back at his office, Wyly's executive officer said, "Colonel, you really need to see the general."

Wyly looked at his muddy boots and wrinkled utilities and said, "I think I'll put on a fresh uniform before I go over there."

A few minutes later he stood in front of a mirror in his office and admired what he saw: starched utilities, polished boots, and a lean muscular physique. He looked like a Marine.

He reported to Sullivan's office, where the general handed him a fitness report, then pointed to a paper on his desk. It was the marked-up draft of the five-year plan he had sent to Gray.

"See that paper?" Sullivan asked him.

"Yes, Sir."

"Did you sign that?"

"Yes, Sir."

"You're out of here. I've arranged to have you moved out of your office. You're fired."

Wyly was cleaning out his office when Boyd called. Boyd always called in a crisis; Wyly was convinced he was telepathic. "How the hell you doing?" Boyd boomed.

"Not good, John." He told Boyd what happened.

"So you got your reward; you got kicked in the teeth. That means you were doing good work. Getting kicked in the teeth is the reward for good work."

Sullivan's fitness report on Wyly was so harsh that the three-star reviewing officer refused to send it to the promotion board. Later, the promotion board called Wyly to tell him it was missing. Wyly said that was General Sullivan's problem, not his. He asked Gray to write his fitness report, but the general never responded.

His new job was to do nothing. The man who came to Quantico with a mandate from the commandant again was adrift. He wondered if Gray even knew what had happened. Surely the man who brought him back to Quantico would come to his rescue.

A few days later he received a call from the commandant's aide saying, "Sit tight. You will be given meaningful duties. Don't be discouraged."

Then came the assignment: vice president of the new Marine Corps University. Wyly had hoped, since the MCU was his idea, that he might be the first leader. But a general was in charge and Wyly was the number-two man. His title of vice president was an unusual one in the Marine Corps; it meant Wyly was a thinker, a teacher, a man who developed concepts. Although it was not what Wyly wanted, he was perfectly suited for the assignment.

General Gray told Wyly he wanted to put together a list of books for Marines to read. Wyly took the reading list he compiled years earlier at the AWS, added books that Boyd recommended, solicited recommendations from others, and presto, the Marine Corps had its first Commandant's Reading List, a compilation that, while not mandatory, is read by most officers and enlisted personnel.

Wyly worked in his office until midnight five or six nights a week. He was only vaguely aware that the predators were circling closer.

One day in April 1991, the day after his father died, Wyly was ordered to report to a three-star general. As he was walking out the door, Boyd called.

"What's going on?"

Wyly was thinking only of his father's death. "I don't know. The general wants to see me in five minutes."

"What about?"

"I don't have the slightest idea."

Boyd paused. "Mike, this is imperative. Call me as soon as you get back. Got that? The minute you get back, you call me."

The general got right to the point. You've been passed over for general and you have to retire, he said. You have to be gone by October.

Wyly was numb with shock. He returned to his office and called Boyd. "Where am I supposed to go?" he asked.

Boyd loosed a volley of profanity.

"I don't think I'm going to tell my wife about this yet," Wyly said.

"No, you have to tell her."

The two men talked for a long time. And for the next several months, Wyly called Boyd four and five times daily. He was in the greatest pain of his life, lost and wandering. But he carried on as Marines always do. He chaired a symposium at the MCU when everyone in the audience knew he had been forced out of the Marine Corps.

It often seemed the fates conspired to heap even more indignity upon him. Wyly invited Martin Van Creveld, a renowned military theorist, to speak at the symposium. But his superiors said Van Creveld was too controversial and Wyly had to withdraw the invitation. He invited David Hackworth, the most decorated soldier in Vietnam, to speak. But Hackworth, too, was deemed too controversial and Wyly had to withdraw the invitation.

During his last days in the Marine Corps, Wyly got some satisfaction when young officers found a copy of his master's thesis in the MCU library and began briefing his ideas on amphibious warfare. Wyly told them not to use his name, that he was a pariah. The young officers came back to Wyly and told him the briefings not only were well received but there was talk of reworking amphibious warfare doctrine to be more in accord with the thesis and with the principles of maneuver warfare.

The plan for how Marines might conduct amphibious landings in future wars is highly classified. But today if anyone wants to know the philosophical underpinnings, the doctrine behind those top-secret plans, all he has to do is read Wyly's thesis. It does not call for row after row of amphibious craft moving toward a long beachhead in a linear attack. Rather it calls for swarms of amphibious craft landing maybe two or three at a time on a small beachhead, allowing Marines to move in fast and deep. Officers will lead from the front. They will have a clear *Schwerpunkt* and they will bypass hard points of resistance, always moving, ignoring their flanks as they press toward the enemy's rear area.

It was also a matter of considerable pride to Wyly that during the 1980s the Marine Corps evolved from being knuckle draggers who take the hill to the most intellectual branch of the U.S. military; even enlisted men were reading Sun Tzu.

When a Marine Corps colonel retires, especially a senior colonel who is a decorated combat veteran, there is a parade and a ceremony where he is presented with a Legion of Merit. His wife is given a large bouquet and there is a letter from the commandant thanking the colonel for his years of meritorious service.

Wyly got none of these. He drove out the front gate of Quantico unnoticed.

But then, guerrillas do not march home to victory parades.

Chapter Twenty-Nine

Water-Walker

Now we must go back to the late 1970s to pick up the thread of another story in which Boyd played a crucial role. This is the story of Jim Burton, a story that demonstrates, as does that of Mike Wyly, Boyd's great gift as a mentor. Because he had no father, he did not know how to be a father. But because of Art Weibel and Frank Pettinato he did know how to be a mentor. There is no doubt Boyd took tremendous pride in the work of Wyly and Burton. Through these two men, Boyd was able to continue his own work; he used Wyly and Burton to do what he no longer could do. And just as he had been receptive to the molding and the direction of his mentors, so these men were receptive to Boyd's molding and directing.

After making colonel on the third and last attempt, Burton knew he was no longer an Air Force golden boy. He would never make general. He would never *be* someone in the Air Force, but he still had the opportunity to *do* something.

The strongest possible indicator of Burton's rectitude and how he was perceived by his superiors is that after returning to the Pentagon in the late 1970s, he served as the military assistant to three consecutive assistant secretaries of the Air Force. The job of military assistant is one of the most sensitive in the military — so sensitive that those who fill it often last only for a year or so. Almost never do they go from one administration to another. But Burton served in both the Carter and Reagan Administrations.

A military aide rarely is loyal to his civilian boss because he knows that in a year or so he returns to regular military duties. If he has been loyal to his generals and protected the interest of his branch of the military, he usually is promoted. Some three-dozen military assistants work in the Pentagon. Their ostensible purpose is to act as a liaison between their civilian boss and their branch of the service. But in reality they are spies, there only to protect the interests of their generals and their branch. Every meeting of their civilian boss, every relevant phone call, even the areas of interest the civilians have, are all reported back to their generals.

Burton did not fit that mold. On numerous occasions he informed his civilian boss of how the Air Force was trying to deceive or mislead him. He saved his bosses from a host of embarrassing mistakes. That is why he was braced against the wall one day and poked in the chest by a general who said he was being disloyal to the Air Force and who reminded him that one day soon he would be returning to the regular Air Force and no longer would have the protection of the assistant secretary.

But instead Burton was assigned for his third tour in the Office of the Secretary of Defense and given a job overseeing the testing of various weapons. The vice chief of staff of the Air Force was not happy when he heard of Burton's new assignment; he knew Burton's background, that Burton was close to Boyd and the Reformers. He knew the harm that such a man could do to the Air Force and to other branches of the military. The vice chief was only three days from retirement when he got word of Burton's assignment. "Not while I am in the Air Force," he said to an aide. One of his last official acts was to cancel Burton's assignment and order him to Wright-Pat, where his job was taking care of parachutes and oxygen masks.

The assistant secretary of the Air Force said he wanted Burton in OSD. Once again, the battle lines were drawn. A group of Air Force generals totaling eighteen stars marched into the assistant secretary's office and said the Burton affair was an internal Air Force matter of no concern to the assistant secretary. It was a personnel matter. The assistant secretary insisted that he wanted Burton. The generals refused to back down.

To better understand why the generals thought this such a crucial issue, one needs a bit of background. Civilians unacquainted with the ways of the Building have only vague ideas about what it is the Pentagon does. They think the real business of the Pentagon has something to do with defending America. But it does not. The real business of the Pentagon is buying weapons. And the military has a pathological aversion to rigorous testing procedures because in almost every instance the performance of the weapon or weapons system is far below what it is advertised to be and, thus, far below the performance used to sell Congress on the idea in the first place. Weapons development is inherently risky and the costs can be difficult to predict. But the big problem is what Spinney calls "front-loading," the practice of deliberately underestimating the costs in order for Congress to fund the program. The weapons-buying business has few checks and balances; from beginning to end it is an advocacy proceeding. Not only do military rewards and promotions go to the officer in charge of a major program but he almost always finds a high-level job in the defense industry upon retirement, often with the company whose project he ushered through the Pentagon. This is the true nature of the Building. And this is why Air Force generals did not want an unbending and rectitudinous man such as Jim Burton in charge of testing weapons. This is why generals wearing a total of eighteen stars tried to intimidate the assistant secretary.

The assistant secretary found it necessary to do what several other civilian leaders had done in similar confrontations: he reminded the generals that civilians rule the military. The assistant secretary said if the generals continued to fight his wishes, he would call a press conference and resign. When reporters asked the reason, he would say it was over a fundamental constitutional issue. Only then did the eighteen stars fade away.

Burton arrived at the OSD testing office in June 1982. From the time he walked in the door, Pierre Sprey besieged him to conduct tests showing how vulnerable American aircraft and armored vehicles were to Soviet weapons. Sprey was one of the most vocal critics of the Army's new MI-AI Abrams Tank, and especially of how the vulnerability testing of tanks and armored vehicles was done largely by computer modeling. And the models were never verified by field tests. Thus, to Sprey, the model-based tests had no validity. *Subject our tanks and our infantry carriers to realistic battlefield tests,* he said. *The lives of American soldiers are at stake.*

Burton, with Sprey in the background, came up with the idea for a live-fire test program — that is, actually shoot live Soviet rockets and cannons at U.S. tanks to test their vulnerability. Such a program seems to be common sense, but in fact it was a radical departure from current practice. Boyd predicted that the Army would rise up in opposition.

For a year Burton briefed his ideas on live-fire testing to low-level Pentagon staffers and junior officers. After laying the groundwork and receiving the unanimous support of all branches of the services, Burton chose the first weapon he wanted to test: the Army's Bradley Fighting Vehicle. He could not have picked a weapon closer to the heart of the Army. The Bradley was supposed to be an advance over the traditional armored personnel carrier, which is just an armored box used to transport troops safely. The Bradley added a light turret to the armored box to allow it, in theory, to both carry troops and "fight." But the Bradley was too lightly armored to fight tanks: what it was supposed to fight had never been precisely detailed by the Army.

The Bradley was of crucial importance. First, it was the weapon whose safety affected the greatest number of soldiers; if America went to war, as many as seventy thousand soldiers might ride this vehicle into combat. Second, the Bradley program was in early production. This meant any problems could be corrected before thousands of the vehicles were sent to troops in the field. And third, the Bradley had never been tested for vulnerability to enemy weapons.

The Bradley was a tragedy waiting to happen. It was packed with ammunition, fuel, and people. The thinnest of aluminum armor surrounded it. So Burton sent the Army's ballistic research laboratory $500,000 to test the Bradley, and he insisted the testing use real Soviet weapons.

The Army agreed. But the first of the "realistic" tests consisted of firing Rumanian-made rockets at the Bradley rather than Soviet-made ones. The Army buried the fact that the Rumanian weapons had warheads far smaller than those used by the Soviets. To further insure that the Bradley appeared impregnable, the Army filled the internal fuel tanks with water rather than with diesel fuel. This guaranteed that even if the underpowered Rumanian warheads penetrated the Bradley's protective armor, no explosion would result.

"What are you going to do about this, Jim?" Boyd asked. "If you let them get away with this, they will try something else."

Burton still believed his job gave him the authority to force the Army to live up to its word. He tried to use persuasion and logic with Army officials, but to no avail.

When early tests detected large amounts of toxic gases inside the Bradley, the Army simply stopped measuring the gas. They jammed pigs and sheep inside the Bradley to test the effects of fumes after a direct hit. But the fumes had hardly dissipated before the Army slaughtered the animals without examining them and without allowing them the time to develop lung lesions, as had happened in other tests. The Army surgeon general's office then reported the animals had suffered no serious aftereffects.

Time after time the Army lied about the realism of its testing. But even the spurious tests were so damaging that the Army decided it wanted to postpone completing the live-fire tests for two years. This would insure that the contractor received a big portion of his money and would put the Bradley too far into its production run to discontinue, no matter what the tests revealed.

"Jim, you must like this," Boyd chided. "You are allowing it to continue." He looked at Burton and knew what was going through his mind. The issue now before Burton was orders of magnitude beyond anything in his previous experience. The Bradley was to the Army what the F-15 was to the Air Force. Eleven billion dollars were at stake, an amount that — to the Army — mitigated against honest tests. Boyd pressed Burton. "Jim, you can't have a normal career and still do the good work," he said. "You have to decide."

Burton knew he stood at a crucial point in his career and in his life. This was the place he had heard Boyd talk about so many times, the *to be or to do* fork in the road. From this point forward, no matter what his decision, there would be no turning back. If he did what the military expected — that is, if he allowed the Army to have its way — he would be a good soldier. If he challenged the Army, retribution was a certainty.

Rarely in his life had Boyd been so excited. He saw the coming fight as an operational field test for "Patterns of Conflict." What better way for Boyd to test his theories than to pit one man against the U.S. Army? At first glance, there could be no more unequal contest.

But the moral element of conflict is a crucial part of "Patterns." Boyd realized the Army was doing the wrong thing for the wrong reasons, guarding a program worth billions of dollars, "protecting the farm" in Boyd's words, while Burton wanted to protect the lives of American soldiers. The Army would try to steamroll Burton, to use the sheer mass of U.S. Army resources to crush him. It would be the crudest form of attrition warfare. Burton would have only his wits and the techniques of maneuver conflict. Boyd saw this as a chance for Burton to get inside the mind of the Army, to put the OODA Loop into action, to cause confusion and disorientation.

Boyd believed Burton could defeat the U.S. Army.

Burton knew he was being used as a test bed for Boyd's ideas, but he did not mind. In fact, he looked forward to it.

Boyd and Burton talked daily. Boyd wanted to know exactly what was said in every meeting with Army generals. He wanted to know who brought out which reports or studies. "Don't filter it with opinions or interpretations," he said. "Just tell me what happened and then we will talk of the implications." He listened and thought and told Burton where the Army was maneuvering to set him up and what he should be prepared for the next day. He and Burton spoke often of Churchill's comment in World War II that the truth was too precious a commodity to travel alone — that it had to be protected by a "bodyguard of lies." Boyd said Burton must break through the bodyguard of lies to find the truth. He told Burton to always keep the initiative. "And you must never panic. When they surprise you, even if the surprise seems fatal, there is always a countermove."

Boyd gave Burton three guiding principles. The first was the most difficult and most familiar to anyone who had worked with Boyd. "Jim, you can never be wrong. You have to do your homework. If you make a technical statement, you better be right. If you are not, they will hose you. And if they hose you, you've had it. Because once you lose credibility and you are no longer a threat, no one will pay attention to what you say. They won't respect you and they won't pay attention to you."

The second thing Boyd told Burton was not to criticize the Bradley itself. "If you do, you are lumped in with all the other Bradley critics. It is the testing process you are concerned with."

While Boyd and Burton might make such a distinction, the Army could not. To them, criticizing the testing process was the same as criticizing the Bradley. But the difference in the two approaches is not at all subtle. By staying focused on the testing methodology, Burton was protecting the lives of American soldiers; he held the mental and moral high ground.

Finally, Boyd counseled Burton not to talk to the media or to Congress, to stay inside the system. If you go outside the system, he said, you will be viewed as just another whistle blower. And whistle blowers get no respect; they get others to help them do something that they can't do themselves.

All of this advice and counsel should not be taken to mean that Burton was in any way Boyd's instrument. Quite the contrary: Burton was the man who had to walk into a room filled with Army generals and challenge them. He was the man on the mission. And he sometimes ignored both Boyd and Sprey.

In June 1984, Burton wrote what he called his "Rubicon Memo" to Secretary of Defense Weinberger. He said the Army was not performing realistic tests on the Bradley and was putting the lives of up to seventy thousand soldiers at risk. He asked that the Army be ordered to perform "full-up tests" — that is, tests in which the Bradley was loaded with fuel and ammunition, just as it would be in combat, and fired upon with real Soviet weapons rather than simulations.

On September 28, the Army agreed to conduct tests with a minimum of ten shots against a fully loaded Bradley. But two weeks later the Army realized how vulnerable the Bradley was and the under secretary of the Army cancelled the live-fire tests. Burton made an appointment to see the under secretary, and was persuasive. The under secretary again reversed himself; now the Army would conduct the tests as earlier agreed.

The Army did not want Burton around for those tests, however, so Army generals talked to Air Force generals, who sent down word that Burton was being transferred to Alaska. He was given a seven-day notice to accept the transfer or resign. It was just as Boyd predicted: a brutal, head-on assault. And it appeared effective. After all, if there is a bothersome employee, what better way to get rid of him than to transfer him? Burton thought the battle was over. But Boyd laughed. "Goddamn, Jim, this is the dumbest decision the Air Force can make. Whoever made this decision is general officer material." He told Burton to collect every memo and every letter and every study in his files that dealt with the Bradley controversy, to make copies, and to flood the Building with little brothers and sisters.

Burton protested. "I thought you wanted me to work within the system."

"Jim, part of working within the system means that everyone who has a right to know what's going on has a copy of all the paperwork." He paused. And when he spoke again Burton heard the laughter in his voice. "If something needs to leak outside the Building, God will take care of it."

Not even the most militant of Burton's opponents could fault him for providing information to those connected with the Bradley program, so Burton emptied the contents of a filing cabinet and made copies of every document. He delivered copies to a number of people. A cover memo explained that he had been relieved of his job and that these documents should bring them up to speed on the status of the program. When he handed the stack of documents to a senior Army general, the general blanched. He knew copies would leak. Burton was giving notice that he was not only still in the game but was raising the stakes.

Word came down to Burton that he was not being transferred. In an effort to resolve his conflict with the Army, his job description was being changed. The Army would conduct its own tests on the Bradley. But the tests would be exactly as Burton wanted. He could even observe.

Boyd told Burton he had won this battle and he had done it by working within the system. If the story breaks in the press, don't talk to reporters.

Several little brothers and sisters found their way to members of the Congressional Reform Caucus, who in turn told the press. Dozens of reporters showed up at the Pentagon wanting to know why Burton was being sent to Alaska. "Colonel Burton is not going to Alaska. There have been no such orders issued," said a Pentagon spokesman.

The reporters went back to their sources in the Senate and House who gave them copies of the seven-day notice. When the reporters realized the Pentagon spokesman had lied to them, they were in a state of high dudgeon. Burton's phone rang for several days. But he talked to none of the reporters.

Nevertheless, several days later the largest newspapers in America ran stories that Burton had accused the Army of rigging the Bradley tests and the Pentagon had retaliated by abolishing his job and then recanting. Burton still refused to talk to reporters, but the stories were written anyway.

The *Early Bird,* the Pentagon's internal newspaper, published a collection of stories from around the country. All told of the Bradley testing problems and how the Pentagon responded by abolishing Burton's job. The *Washington Post* and the *New York Times,* the two newspapers most feared by the Pentagon, sided with Burton and attacked the Pentagon for its heavy-handed ways. The Congressional Reform Caucus, headed by Nancy Kassebaum, joined the fray.

Not even the Pentagon could stand up against such forces. A Pentagon spokesman said Burton could supervise the Bradley program until all tests were completed.

By now Burton was a national figure. As with Spinney, this was to be his protection. But Spinney, despite the impact of his two major studies, had not changed the Pentagon. He had stopped the Reagan defense-budget increase, but that would have stopped on its own within another year or so. The Reformers had made the American public aware of just how reckless, even irresponsible, the Pentagon was with its money. But they had done nothing of lasting significance. Burton was the last chance. If he could not force permanent change on the Pentagon, the past few years would have been for naught.

The first round was a clear victory for Burton. The generals must have been bitter. Not only had a colonel defied them and won but he had done it in such a way that they could not punish him. Next time the military would not fail.

A brother officer, a colonel in Burton's office, began spying on Burton. He made notes when he heard Burton talking on the telephone. He kept a record of Burton's meetings. Every memo Burton wrote was copied and hand delivered to top Army generals. The memos were then copied and filtered down from four-stars to three-stars to two-stars and one-stars, even to colonels. Burton knew the military was building a file, the sole purpose of which was to justify firing him.

Boyd was elated. He saw this as a chance for Burton to wield great influence with the Army leaders behind the plan. He told Burton to keep in mind that when he wrote a memo, it was not for the person to whom it was addressed, but rather to the generals. Boyd called this a "reverse pump." Burton was feeding information to the people spying on him. This meant that accuracy in everything Burton said and wrote was even more critical. Again and again Boyd came back to one of his earliest admonitions to Burton. "Do your homework. If they hose you one time, they will never again respect you."

Burton did his homework so well he became known at the Army test site as a man who asked endless questions. He was up against Army experts who devoted their careers to covering up for the Army in such arcane areas as armor, terminal ballistics, medical effects of explosions on troops in confined spaces, effects of halon gases, and "vaporifics," the study of toxic gases that are byproducts of explosions. But the difference between Burton and the experts was that the Army relied on computer modeling to cover up the Bradley's dangers and Burton searched out the test data that confirmed these dangers.

While Boyd counseled Burton on tactics in dealing with the Army, Sprey provided the technical expertise. Sprey knew there was an entire range of literature on armored vehicles and combat results from wars in the Middle East. At his suggestion, Burton went to the Defense Technical Information Center and dug out every report ever written on the vulnerability of armored vehicles in war. He studied, took notes, and challenged everything. Time after time — either deliberately or from ignorance — Army experts made erroneous statements, thinking Burton did not know the truth. He let them proceed, let them justify their actions, then sprang the trap. "That's not what the data says." And then he reached into his briefcase and pulled out studies the Army experts had never heard of or preferred to bury.

Burton's research showed that fire and explosions inside a tank were the biggest source of casualties among tankers in World War II and among Israeli tankers in Middle Eastern wars. When he demanded more realistic testing procedures, he turned to an Army expert and said, "I want you to know there is nothing personal in what I am about to do." He took a deep breath and said, "Show me where your computer models deal with fire, explosions, toxic gases, and blast lung."

Army experts said these were not a consideration.

Burton reached into his briefcase, threw a report on the table, and said, "Then how do you explain the data from World War II, England, and Israel that show these are the main reason for casualties?"

The Army said, "Well, they do exist. But we can't model them on the computer so we ignore them."

In September 1985, Weinberger sent Burton a handwritten note asking that henceforth Burton keep him personally informed of all test results on the Bradley. General Colin Powell was then Weinberger's military assistant, performing the same duties for Weinberger that Burton had performed for three assistant secretaries of the Air Force. But Powell and Burton were cut from different bolts of cloth. Burton knew that when he sent a note to Weinberger, the Army's senior generals had copies before the SecDef did. The reverse pump was still working.

By now Burton knew as much about ballistics and vaporifics and blast lung and all the other arcane disciplines as did the Army. He was inside their minds and knew how they thought and how they reacted. He could walk into a room of civilian and Army officials and know when the game was afoot. He knew intuitively when and how the adversary would move. Burton had the *Fingerspitzengefuhl* to move rapidly through the OODA Loop and stay ahead of his adversary, and he found the experience exhilarating. It gave him something like a "runner's high" and he began to enjoy the confrontations. Each one began with his saying, "I want you to know there is nothing personal in what I am about to do." And then total devastation. He wrote memos to his superiors that someone always leaked to congressmen, senators, and the media, causing the Army another round of ever-increasing embarrassment. He was planting a demon seed, and the Army would reap the harvest.

It was not long before word got out that Sprey was the technical brains behind Burton's expertise. The Army hated Sprey for his criticism of the Abrams Tank as much as the Air Force hated him for his advocacy of the A-10 and complained to Weinberger, who lent a sympathetic ear. He changed the Building access rules so that people who did not have official badges could no longer come and go unescorted through the Pentagon's unclassified areas as they had in the past. It was a good and needed rule. But it was done almost entirely because of Pierre Sprey.

Hereafter, when Sprey had studies or reports he wanted to pass to Burton, they met in the Pentagon's south parking lot.

By now the entire Congress, not only the Reform Caucus, was interested in the Bradley. Congress was so concerned the Army might try to wiggle out of its agreement to let Burton oversee the testing that it passed a law saying all actions covered in Burton's agreement with the Army must take place.

Congressional affirmation was just one more sign that, by the summer of 1985, people in the Army testing program knew Burton was determined to make the Bradley safe for those who would ride it into battle. Only a highly principled man would have fought the Army for so long and at such a high personal price. Civilian personnel, many of whom were former Army enlisted troops, realized that Burton, unlike many officers involved in the testing program, had no self-interest at stake. He was not there to get a medal and a promotion for pushing the Bradley into production; he wanted only to clean up the system for the benefit of troops in the field.

Civilian test personnel began calling Burton at home. Almost every man called to tell Burton the specifics of how he was ordered to influence test results. Now Burton used his reputation for asking questions as a way to protect his sources. He returned to the test site and asked question after question until he officially received the information that had been passed to him unofficially.

Burton established a network of Army personnel who told him the truth about the tests. When he wanted to know what the Army was about to do, he called on those sources for information — "running my traplines," he called it. Then he returned to senior officers and said, "I want you to know there is nothing personal in what I am about to do."

By now that was a phrase that struck terror into the heart of Army generals.

Burton prepared an independent report in December 1985 showing that ammunition stored inside the Bradley was a major hazard to troops. If he were proven correct, the Bradley program would be in danger of being cancelled. The Army squelched Burton's report before its existence became widely known and countered with a report saying the ammunition posed little hazard.

Peter Jennings, the anchorman for ABC News, did a story about Burton's nonexistent report and how it threatened the Bradley program. Burton was mentioned in editorials in the *New York Times*. He was seen as one honest man fighting a corrupt Army system. When Burton's boss left government to begin a consulting firm, he was interviewed on *60 Minutes* and confirmed that he had threatened to fire Burton if he received one more call from Congress about him.

Reporters began calling the Pentagon, asking about Burton's report on the Bradley. The Pentagon knew by now that Burton would not talk to the media and took full advantage of this to deny he had written anything. But the little brothers and sisters were running loose. Copies found their way to reporters and once again the Pentagon was flayed.

One night an Army two-star called Burton at home. He praised Burton for what he was doing. "We should be doing these tests," the general said. "Your work is going to save countless lives." Then the general said that even though he agreed with everything Burton was doing, his job demanded that he attack Burton the next day.

By now Burton was growing weary. The unending pressure to be right was wearing him down. He drank a bottle of wine each night with dinner. And he wondered aloud to Boyd how much longer he could continue.

"Jim, you may not win," Boyd said to him. "But you can't give the bastards a free ride. You're doing the right thing. Stay with it, Tiger."

Congress ordered hearings on the Bradley. On one side would be the top generals connected with the Bradley program. On the other would be Colonel Burton. Sprey helped organize Burton's written statement, and when Sprey was through, Burton knew his position was unassailable.

Then the Army informed Burton that everything he planned to say was classified. He would not be allowed to say anything.

"If this decision is not reversed, I will inform Congress my testimony has been censored," Burton said. "And I will also testify that Army generals have revealed classified information to the media in order to support the Bradley."

Suddenly Burton's testimony was no longer classified.

Burton's testimony opened a two-year debate in Congress about the Bradley. Most in Washington and elsewhere now believed Burton was right. The lead editorial in the February 4, 1986, issue of the *New York Times* excoriated the Army for its attitude about the Bradley tests and its doctoring of the results. The editorial called on the Army to follow Burton's advice. When the Army opposed safety features Sprey and Burton had designed, Congress said Burton's ideas would be tested or the Bradley production line would be shut down.

Several years earlier the Congressional Reform Caucus had created what was to be the single lasting legacy of the reform movement, a new job in the Pentagon that supervised the testing of all military weapons. The Director of Operational Test and Evaluation, or "DOT&E," was unusual in that he reported directly to the secretary of defense and to Congress. The purpose of the job was to act as a counterweight to the weapons advocacy system in the Pentagon. The Pentagon vehemently opposed the new position and Congress had to force-feed it to the Building. Then for almost two years Weinberger refused to appoint anyone to the job. Finally, under great pressure, he asked Nancy Kassebaum to recommend someone. She said she would do so, but only if Weinberger promised that the nominee would not be persecuted solely because he was the Reform nominee — that is, solely because he had been nominated by her as chairwoman of the Congressional Reform Caucus. Weinberger said he understood Kassebaum's concerns.

She nominated Burton and promised him that if he were not accepted, she would see that the Pentagon did not punish him.

Not only did Weinberger refuse to accept Burton but the Air Force again tried to transfer him. He was given seven days to accept the new assignment or retire. Members of the Reform Caucus were furious and erupted in loud complaints. But Kassebaum remained silent. Boyd and Sprey went to her office to remind her of her obligation to protect Burton. But she said the pending transfer was not in retribution for Burton's name being nominated for the DOT&E job but rather normal Air Force rotation policy.

Winslow Wheeler, the Kassebaum aide who had for so long believed in reform, was there when Boyd and Sprey talked to the senator. He remembers the look of contempt on their faces and the look of shame on Kassebaum's face. And he believes the incident marked the beginning of the end for the reform movement.

Burton ran his trapline one last time and discovered that in the latest Bradley tests the Army had replaced internal ammunition boxes with cans of water in order to give false test results about what happened when a shell penetrated the inner compartment. An honest test would have destroyed the Bradley. Army officers were actually promoted for coming up with a way to provide better test results. In response, Burton wrote his most famous memo. He harshly accused the Army of cheating on the tests. He said the Army was not conducting tests in order to save the lives of American servicemen, but rather in order to buy weapons. Faced with such accusations, the Army chief of staff stopped the tests and the House Armed Services Committee called for hearings. But Burton's victory was, as he probably knew it would be, Pyrrhic. He received another notice saying he was about to be transferred to Alaska. If he did not accept the assignment, he would be forced to retire. He had seven days to decide.

The Army called in a panel of members from the National Academy of Sciences to validate its testing procedures. The panel, some of whom had contracts with the Army, did just that. Army generals now thought their testing methods had been sanctified. But Burton wrote to every member of the panel and said they were not scientists, but advocates. To the horror of the Army, the panel reconvened and this time said Burton's testing methods were best.

But by now Burton was physically and emotionally exhausted. He signed his retirement papers.

Pierre Sprey testified at the hearings against the Army. Sprey's specialty is statistics and the report he presented to Congress was one of the most devastating indictments of a military service — its chicanery, its outright lying, its lack of concern for its troops — that the Congress has ever heard.

But Burton was gone.

Chapter Thirty

They Think I'm a Kook

BECAUSE he often worked late at the Pentagon, Boyd sometimes did not leave his apartment until almost noon the following day. By then, the young entrepreneurs who lived in the complex were out in the parking lot, taking their first meetings of the day. They waved and nodded to Boyd and laughingly called him "Mr. President." He was, after all, tall and rangy, and he had the same craggy good looks as Reagan. But he did not have the same jovial sense of humor, at least not in 1984.

For about two years, Boyd and Mary Ellen had not been on speaking terms. Now Boyd extended an olive branch and asked her to work with him on revising "Patterns." She became his typist and Jeff drew the illustrations.

Mary Ellen worked with her father two and three nights a week and often on weekends. Boyd wanted to make sure every word conveyed precisely the right meaning. Mary Ellen recalls that once, she and Boyd discussed the difference between "swirling" and "whirling" for hours. At times the work became so intense that old animosities bubbled up and Boyd and his daughter had to walk away and let emotions settle down before they continued. But working

413

with her father was important to Mary Ellen; it was a way to make up for the years of not speaking.

By 1984 the military-reform movement was at its height. And the Wednesday evening gatherings were loud and raucous and filled with plans about generals to be hosed. Old stories were told and retold — of Spinney's white wagon kill, of a general's air-to-rug maneuver, of cape jobs and hot platters and the particularly effective techniques known as tube steaks and barbwire enchiladas. The Reformers did not win all the time; they often were on the receiving end of cape jobs, too. When this happened they laughed and shook their heads and said, "I let myself get fucked," then had a drink and planned a counterattack.

The Pentagon bureaucracy knew about the Wednesday night happy hour and on occasion sent spies. Standoffish and obviously not a part of the band of brothers, they were easily detected. Boyd might be in his transmit mode, holding forth with two dozen people circled around him, when someone would point out a couple of men across the room. "John, they're spies. Tone it down." Boyd said, "Fuck 'em" and talked even louder.

But the sessions had a very serious undercurrent. Boyd and the Reformers were fighting the largest and most powerful military institution in the world. They were outnumbered, outgunned, and had limited resources. Their victories came with a fearful price.

Spinney was a good example. Boyd knew that because the Building could not counter Spinney's "Plans / Reality Mismatch" briefing, the long knives would come out. He was right in insisting Spinney be on the cover of *Time* magazine. (He said the reform movement would not truly be accepted by America until one of the Reformers was on the cover of a Superman comic book.) But eventually that protection disappeared. By 1984, the thrust of the reform movement had shifted from Spinney to waste and fraud in procurement contracts — $600 toilet seats and that sort of thing. When Spinney no longer was in the media spotlight, the Building struck back. The man who had written two of the most important documents ever to come out of the Pentagon, the man who arguably had done more than any other individual to reveal the sloppy accounting procedures the Pentagon uses to disperse the taxpayers' money, was given a poor performance rating. This is a tactic used to set up an employee for dismissal: poor performance ratings over several years means an employee can be fired with no recourse. On the other hand, if the rating is proven to be retributive, it is illegal. A group of lawyers offered Spinney free legal service. They were about to seal the office of Spinney's boss and seize his records when one of the Reformers leaked the story to George Wilson of the *Washington Post*. When Spinney's boss said he had been pressured to give Spinney a low performance rating, Weinberger ordered that a new, favorable rating be issued immediately.

Spinney won the battle. But a long war of attrition lay ahead.

The Building soon struck again in the only way it knew how. David Chu's assistant told Spinney he no longer had a spot in the Pentagon parking lot.

In January 1987, Boyd turned sixty, an age when many men begin reflecting on their life. No matter how optimistic he is, when a man reaches sixty it is more difficult to cling to the idea that he is middle-aged. He stands at the threshold of old age and senses the increasing speed of time's winged chariot. Intimations of mortality grow stronger.

Jim Burton hosted a birthday party for Boyd. Most of the old crowd was there, some two dozen people. Mary worked for weeks on a skit that would give her a chance to show off what she called her "artistic side." Burton's wife played the piano as Mary read a long recounting of Boyd's career, everything from burning the hangars in Japan to stealing computer time at Eglin to all the hose jobs and hot platters and tube steaks. "Ride of the Valkyries" played at high decibels. Burton gave Boyd a model of the B-1 with a brick attached. As usual, Boyd received garden hoses as gifts. He was quiet and reflective during the party. But once he arrived back at the apartment on Beauregard Street, he went into a rage. He was furious at Mary for singing of his antics even though he had told those same stories for years. "People think I'm some kind of kook," he said. "They don't pay attention to my work because they think I'm a kook." He threw out his collection of garden hoses. Gag gifts, photographs, and many of his papers went into the garbage can.

By now everything was beginning to unravel. The Reform Caucus and the reform movement were deteriorating. Boyd must have remembered the days, only a few years earlier, when he and Sprey were two of the most influential men in Washington; they could get an audience with any congressman or senator. Neither had a portfolio; neither had the clout that comes with being an elected or appointed official — yet the power of their ideas made them all the rage in Washington. Boyd was sought out by members of the national media. People like Hugh Sidey and Jim Fallows and Alvin Toffler hung out in his office.

But it was all slipping away. Boyd began to talk of dying. "I want to go quickly," he said. "I want to go like a light turning off, a big bang and I'm out. If I thought it was going to be any other way I'd call Kevorkian and say, 'Hey, I got a job for you. Me.'"

Boyd, by the sheer force of his personality, might have kept the reform movement alive. But he chose not to do so. Congressmen and senators had other issues. The media were losing interest. Mike Wyly and Jim Burton were casualties. Spinney was a marked man who probably would never again be promoted. Sprey was gone, tired of going home angry every day. For years he had dabbled with amateur music recording; now he decided to open a recording studio.

In the summer of 1987, Boyd finished two new briefings. "Organic Design for Command and Control" was completed in May. Historically, briefings about command and control dealt with the "how" — that is, who reports to whom between various levels of command in fast-moving tactical situations. Boyd's new briefing dealt with the "what" of command and control — the implicit connections and bonds that form the foundation for the proper messages between levels of command. This was the first time that the *substance* of what was communicated took precedence over the hardwired connections of the past.

"The Strategic Game of? And?" Boyd finished in June. Here he deals with the themes of interaction and isolation. How do we physically, mentally, and morally isolate our adversaries while still interacting with others and with unfolding events? Much of the content of this briefing is a recycling of material from "Patterns of Conflict," "Destruction and Creation," and "Organic Design for Command and Control."

At the same time, Boyd was working on another briefing called "Conceptual Spiral," a work that elaborated upon "Destruction and

Creation" and thus more or less brought his work back to where it had begun.

Boyd often had counseled Spinney to have goals but to make sure the goals could not easily be reached. He talked of the desolation a man faced when he grew older and all his goals were realized. And now Boyd's work had come full circle. He had reached all his goals.

About this time Jeff Ethell, a well-known aviation writer, wanted to write Boyd's biography. But Boyd could never find the time and Ethell gave up on the idea.

Then began an alarming series of incidents involving Boyd's health. One day he was delivering a briefing at Andrews AFB when suddenly he could not breathe. His chest felt as if it was about to burst and he broke into a cold sweat. He stopped the briefing, sat in a chair for an hour or so, then drove home. About 3:00 A.M. Mary called Mary Ellen and said, "I think your father has had a heart attack. He needs to go to the hospital. He won't listen to me. He will listen to you."

"Put him on the phone," Mary Ellen said.

"Dad, I'm taking you to the hospital. Where do you want to go?"

Boyd mumbled vaguely that he did not need to go to the hospital, then said he would go to Andrews. He did not think Mary Ellen would want to drive into Alexandria, pick him up, and then drive out to Andrews. "Be ready," she said.

She and her dad arrived at Andrews before dawn. A doctor administered an EKG and found only a slight anomaly of no clinical significance. He said Boyd's heart was strong. Nevertheless, Boyd believed he had a heart attack. Overnight he changed his diet and stopped eating red meat.

Then he suffered a case of tinnitus, a loud ringing in the ears that is not uncommon in men of a certain age. Boyd must have suffered a severe case because he told Burton, "It won't quit. This buzzing is driving me crazy." He could not sleep. Medication did not help. He took powerful drugs that only brought on depression. Then he went to a psychiatrist who changed his medication several times, each time bringing even worse depression. Boyd decided the medications were aggravating his problem and, against his doctor's advice, stopped taking drugs. Both the depression and the tinnitus disappeared.

But months later a terrible depression, this one not caused by drugs, settled over Boyd. One day he was in Spinney's office when suddenly he started trembling. His eyes welled with tears. He reached into his pocket, pulled out a small vial, and quickly swallowed several pills.

"John, what is the matter?" Spinney said. He had never seen Boyd in such a state.

Boyd's voice shook and he seemed about to break into tears as he confided that at times a black-dog night descended upon him and enveloped him in such pain and foreboding that he could not cope.

When he told Christie he was depressed, Christie said, "About what?" Boyd could only shake his head in bewilderment. He did not know what he was worrying about or what he was depressed about. But it was real and it frightened him as nothing ever had.

About this time Christie's world turned upside down. His daughter reached puberty and ran away from home. Soon she was shuttling in and out of institutions. Christie used up all the benefits of his insurance plan but there was no relief in sight. His rank was the highest a nonappointed civilian could reach, but still he could not afford his daughter's increasing medical bills. He resigned his Pentagon job and went to work at the Institute for Defense Analysis, a think tank that works for the secretary of defense. By now Boyd rarely showed up at the Pentagon. But when he did, he spent most of his time talking to Christie about Christie's daughter. In fact, sometimes it seemed that was the only reason he came to work. Christie was puzzled by Boyd's interest. What Christie did not know was that by now Boyd was wondering if one of his own daughters, Kathy, should be institutionalized because of her severe depression. She would never be able to make her way in the world alone. And Boyd must have wondered if his family's history of mental disorders had fallen upon Kathy.

In late 1988, Boyd began looking for another place to live. He looked at apartments around northern Virginia but found nothing he liked. Then he drove to south Florida, met his brother Gerry, and picked out an apartment in Delray Beach, a community about halfway between Fort Lauderdale and Palm Beach. The apartment had two bedrooms, one for Boyd and Mary and a second for Kathy. Boyd returned to Washington and announced he was moving to

Florida the first of the year. His friends were astonished and wanted to know the reason.

The gist of his answer was that he was doing this for Mary. Ever since Eglin she had loved Florida. Mary had endured a lot from him, and now he was finally doing something for her.

As usual, in matters involving his family and personal affairs, Boyd did not reveal the whole truth. He had lived in the basement apartment on Beauregard Street for twenty-three years. Neighbors complained often about the Boyd family, first about Jeff's snakes, which escaped from time to time, then about Stephen's TV repair work being done in the apartment. Boyd thought all that was behind him, as both Jeff and Stephen had moved out. But Scott, now thirty, was in college and still lived at home. He developed a fascination for motorcycles — loud motorcycles — and he roared in and out of the complex with the blatting of the mufflers echoing off the buildings. Rather than park in the lot as tenants were required to do, he parked his motorcycle on the patio behind the apartment. Sometimes he even drove it inside the apartment. Eventually management had enough of the Boyd family. The official reason for asking them to move out was that after twenty-three years the apartment needed renovation.

But Boyd knew the real reason.

Chapter Thirty-One

The Ghetto Colonel
and the SecDef

BOYD sat in the cramped living room of his third-floor apartment in Delray Beach. The television was on. Any news story about the Pentagon or generals or weapons programs caused him to erupt with "Take him out" or "Cut his head off."

Boyd was surrounded by hundreds of books and copies of his briefings and the scattered yellow legal pages of revisions for "Patterns." He frequently retired to the bedroom, sprawled across the bed, and called Sprad and Catton and Christie and Sprey and Leopold and Spinney and Burton and Wyly. The apartment had two phone lines, one for Boyd and one for Kathy, but Boyd gave both numbers to his friends. He did not want to be on his line and miss a call.

On this day, Boyd called Pierre Sprey and with an almost ironic tone said, "Tiger, the pace of life down here is different. About all these people can handle is one project a day, like going to the supermarket." He told Sprey how he traveled to Montgomery, Alabama, where he lectured at the Air War College, and how he delivered his briefings all around the country. But he always had to come back to Florida, where he said he was "rotting." Sprey laughed and did not place too much significance on Boyd's comments.

The truth is that Boyd was miserable in Florida, and only Mary knew just how much. Six months after they moved to Delray Beach, Boyd told Mary he had been forgotten — that people thought he was crazy and that his work was insignificant.

When he was not delivering his briefing or talking on the phone, his days were spent prowling through bookstores, searching the non-fiction shelves for the growing list of books that mentioned him or his work. He leaned against a bookcase for hours as he read a book, then returned it to the shelf. Near the beach he found a restaurant he liked, Bimini Bob's, and he went there one or two days a week to eat conch chowder. No more Wednesday nights, no more prowling through the Pentagon. Boyd could sense himself deflating.

In early 1989, a group of Boyd's old comrades began talking about his ideas on maneuver conflict and how those ideas might presage a new form of war. They sat down and wrote a piece saying the first generation of war was the era of muskets and massed troops, the second was when massed firepower replaced massed troops, and the third was time driven, as exemplified by the blitzkrieg. And then they wrote of something new, something they called "Fourth Generation Warfare."

Marine Corps Colonel G. I. Wilson was one of the five authors. During his research he talked almost daily with Boyd about using strength against weakness, about how an enemy might use a low-technology or even no-technology offense to defeat a high-tech adversary, and how an enemy might win without a major battle. The piece was titled "The Changing Face of War: Into the Fourth Generation" and was published in the October 1989 issue of both the Marine Corps *Gazette* and the Army's *Military Review*. It may have been the only instance in military history in which two service publications ran the same article at the same time.

The article said Fourth Generation Warfare might emerge from "Islamic traditions" and that the "distinction between war and peace will be blurred to the vanishing point." It talked of terrorists moving freely within American society "while actively seeking to subvert it."

The piece was so futuristic, so against the grain of military thinking, that the Pentagon ignored it. But it elicited great interest and caused much debate with the Marine Corps and the Army's special-operations community.

Chet Reichert, Boyd's boyhood friend from Erie, spent the winters in Delray Beach and Boyd took him to various bookstores, where he pulled out book after book and opened them to the proper page and pointed with a triumphant finger at references praising his work. And he told Reichert about other books being written, books that would be published in a year or so, one of which would be dedicated to him. Reichert remembers that he and his wife occasionally invited Boyd and Mary out for dinner and that Reichert always paid. Boyd never reciprocated and never invited the Reicherts to his apartment. Reichert did not know how little money Boyd had in retirement, and since Boyd still lectured and gave his briefings around the country, Reichert assumed he was being paid well. But Boyd accepted only expenses, and when the expense checks arrived, he tossed them into a drawer and forgot about them. After he died, his children found a stack of several thousand dollars' worth of uncashed checks.

Boyd looked ahead and saw little about the twilight of his life that pleased him.

Then, on August 2, 1990, Saddam Hussein invaded Kuwait.

Less than a week later, American troops began arriving in Saudi Arabia as part of Operation Desert Shield.

Now began a phase of Boyd's life that for years was only whispered about.

Until Dick Cheney later spoke of that period, all the evidence was anecdotal and pieced together after the fact. The anecdotes pointed inexorably toward the idea that Boyd played a crucial role in the top-secret planning of what would become America's strategy for prosecuting the Gulf War.

Several weeks after Desert Shield began, Boyd suddenly was flying back and forth to Washington. He told Mary he had been summoned by then–Secretary of Defense Cheney. While in Washington, Boyd called none of the Acolytes, none of the men he spent hours every week talking to on the telephone — none, that is, save Jim Burton. When Burton asked, "What are you doing in town?" all Boyd said was, "I'm here to see Cheney." Burton waited but Boyd added nothing. Burton understood. He knew enough about classified operations and the "need to know" that he did not press for details. But he could put things together. The SecDef was working eighteen-hour days directing the buildup of Desert Shield and planning the coming war. He did not have a lot of free time. The only thing Boyd and Cheney had in common was "Patterns" and their numerous talks about war-fighting strategy. Therefore, Burton reasoned, if Cheney had summoned Boyd to Washington, the only possible reason was to talk about waging war.

Still another bit of anecdotal evidence involved Spinney. After the Iraqi invasion, he drew upon his encyclopedic knowledge of military tactics and spent weeks working on invasion plans, determining what he would do if he were in charge. When Spinney finished he was so excited that he called Boyd. Once he told Boyd what he wanted to talk about, Boyd grew strangely silent. Spinney hardly noticed at the time. "I've thought about this a lot," he said. "And there are only two options." Still Boyd did not respond. Spinney told Boyd of his first plan, which drew only a noncommital grunt. Then Spinney told him of his second idea, which he thought was best: have the Marines feint an amphibious assault at Kuwait and then, while the attention of the Iraqi Army was diverted, make a gigantic left hook far into the desert, then swing north, envelop the Iraqi Army, and annihilate them. "It's a classic single envelopment," he said. "Almost a version of the von Schlieffen Plan."

For a long moment there was silence. Then Boyd said, "Chuck, I want you to forget what you just said. You are not to discuss it with anyone else. Ever." Boyd used a tone Spinney had never heard before. He was not issuing an order. Instead he used a flat, no-nonsense tone that showed Spinney how deadly serious he was. Spinney was taken aback. He had been like a son to Boyd for almost fifteen years but had never seen this aspect of him. Spinney stuck his plans in a box and never discussed them.

Still another piece of the puzzle, one that the public would not become aware of until after the Gulf War — when books were written — was the growing awareness during Desert Shield that Cheney opposed General Norman Schwarzkopf's initial war plan. Schwarzkopf's plan was a head-to-head assault against the main strength of the Iraqi forces, the classic mind-set of Army commanders imbued with the theory of attrition warfare. Slug it out *mano a mano,* toe-to-toe, force against force, and the last man standing wins.

But Cheney, with the support of General Colin Powell, chairman of the Joint Chiefs of Staff, rejected the plan and asked Schwarzkopf to give it a second try. Young lieutenant colonels who were graduates of the Army's School of Advanced Military Studies, the famed "Jedi Knights," came in to revise Schwarzkopf's plan. The Jedi Knights were said to be well versed in maneuver warfare and Boyd's ideas. They offered Schwarzkopf a direct head-on attack and two variations of a less-than-ambitious left-hook envelopment. These plans were not only rejected but ridiculed.

In *The Generals' War,* a book written by Michael R. Gordon and Bernard Trainor after the war, Cheney is quoted as saying to Powell, "I can't let Norm do this high diddle up the middle plan." Not only did Cheney reject Schwarzkopf's plan but he used Boyd's language to do so.

It is rare indeed that the secretary of defense challenges the war plans of the on-scene commander. Even the Joint Chiefs of Staff are reluctant to do this. But in Dick Cheney the Pentagon had a rare SecDef. Cheney had enough one-on-one sessions with Boyd to give him the knowledge and self-confidence to second-guess even a headstrong four-star general such as Norman Schwarzkopf. Simply put, Cheney knew more about strategy than did his generals.

Cheney now says Boyd "clearly was a factor in my thinking" about the Gulf War. Cheney minimizes his role in changing Schwarzkopf's initial plan, saying "nobody" liked the idea of going "straight up the middle into the heart of Iraqi offenses." He says he had "no direct influence" on the final plan: "It was not my job to figure out the nitty gritty. That was Schwarzkopf's mission."

Nevertheless, it has become an article of faith that Cheney developed his own plan for fighting the Gulf War. The Marines would feint an amphibious assault while the Army would make a wide sweep through the western desert and then swing north to cut off the Iraqi Army.

What is still not generally known to the public is just how well the Marines performed in the Gulf. Brigadier General Mike Myatt, a graduate of the Fort Pickett free-play exercises and a man intimately familiar with Boyd's work, was then commander of the 1st Marine Division. Three days before the war officially began, Myatt's men raided deep behind Iraqi lines. They bypassed strong points, forgot their flanks, and penetrated so deeply and caused such confusion that the Iraqi Army rushed in reinforcements against what they anticipated would be the main thrust of the American invasion. Then they began surrendering by the thousands. Nowhere can be found a better example of Boyd's ideas on "folding the enemy in on himself" than in the fact that some fifteen Iraqi divisions surrendered to two divisions of Marines.

Spinney was sitting in the study of his home in Alexandria, Virginia, when Brigadier General Richard Neal, the American spokesman during the Gulf War, went on television to brief the press on the extraordinary success of coalition forces. He told of a confused Iraqi Army whose soldiers were surrendering by the hundreds of thousands. Asked for a reason, he said, "We kind of got inside his decision cycle."

"Son of a bitch!" Spinney shouted. He called Boyd and said, "John, they're using your words to describe how we won the war. Everything about the war was yours. It's all right out of 'Patterns.'"

He was right. Everything successful about the Gulf War is a direct reflection of Boyd's "Patterns of Conflict" — multiple thrusts and deception operations that created ambiguity and caused the enemy to surrender by the thousands. America (and the coalition forces) won without resorting to a prolonged ground war. America not only picked when and where it would fight, but also when and where it would not fight. Coalition forces operated at a much higher tempo than the enemy. The resulting crises happened so fast that opposing forces could not keep pace with them. The one-hundred-hour ground-war blitz against Iraq is a splendid example of maneuver warfare, a first-rate instance of *cheng/ch'i,* the conventional and the unconventional, all done so quickly the enemy was disoriented and collapsed from within.

The brilliance of Cheney's plan was proven in its success. But there were failures in execution, particularly by the Army, whose famous left hook simply stopped in the desert for three nights because a general was afraid to expose his flanks — in other words, he wanted his forces to be synchronized. This so slowed the Army that the retreating Republican Guard and much of the Iraqi Army escaped. Schwarzkopf and several generals have since spent much of their time blaming each other, but it was the slavish adherence to an outmoded attrition-warfare doctrine that allowed the Iraqis to escape.

Boyd's earlier predictions about synchronization in the Army were proven true.

Boyd rarely had been happier than he was in those euphoric days after the war, when his old friends called to congratulate him. Boyd never mentioned his visits to Washington to see Cheney. The closest he ever came to revealing his involvement was after General Schwarzkopf held his famous press conference and revealed the audacious sweep around the western flank of the Iraqi Army, what he called a "Hail-Mary plan." Boyd angrily disputed the phrase. "A 'Hail-Mary plan' implies desperation," he told Spinney. "There was nothing desperate about that envelopment. It was planned that way."

Boyd's friends also took great delight in pointing out that his long-time criticisms of the B-1 Bomber were confirmed in the Gulf War. The full inventory of Air Force combat aircraft saw duty in the Gulf — except the B-1. The aircraft resurrected by President Reagan could not answer when summoned for war. Once again, Boyd had been right.

Boyd's ebullience reached its peak when, on Monday, April 22, 1991, the House Armed Services Committee convened in the Rayburn House Office Building to conduct a hearing on the performance of high-technology equipment in Operation Desert Storm, and he was called to testify. Others testifying were former senator Gary Hart, who had been a member of the Senate Armed Services Committee and the Military Reform Caucus; John Lehman, former secretary of the Navy; Don Hicks, the Pentagon's under secretary of defense for research and engineering; and Pierre Sprey.

Chairman Les Aspin opened the hearing by saying that each of the panel members "shaped the forces, the doctrine, and the debate about our military structure that fought so successfully during Desert Storm." Boyd wore a bright-orange polyester sport coat and madras pants, an outfit guaranteed to make him stand out among the dark suits in the hearing room. But it was his eloquence that marked the day. He opened calmly with passing references to maneuver warfare and high technology. But then he segued into praising two officers who made a major impact on the services by promoting maneuver warfare: Huba Wass de Czege and Colonel Mike Wyly. Only days earlier Wyly learned the Marine Corps was pushing him into early retirement. Boyd saw the Wyly affair as the *Schwerpunkt* of his appearance.

That day, when Boyd turned a hearing on high-tech weapons into a hearing on military personnel matters, was one of his finest. He said that despite the success of maneuver warfare in the Gulf War, the Marine Corps still had senior officers with the old attrition-war mind-set. Boyd's eyes flashed and his chin jutted out in defiance. His eyes roamed the row of congressmen, lingering on each, singling out each one of them. His voice deepened. The Plum was back from retirement and holding center stage on behalf of a comrade, and he was never in better form. Boyd may have been sixty-four, but his personality had never been more magnetic, more commanding. His voice reached every corner of the hearing room, clear and dominating and insistent. He said he was "incensed and outraged" about what the Marine Corps had done to Mike Wyly. He told the congressmen if they did not act it would inhibit young Marine officers from proposing crucial new ideas and the Marine Corps would be ruled by "dinosaurs." People are more important than budgets or hardware, he said, and while the officer selection process is deemed sacrosanct, there are nevertheless ways for Congress to become involved. He would be happy to tell Congress just what it should do. He said gifted renegades such as Wass de Czege and Wyly must be protected or "it is high diddle diddle right up the middle again and we are going to be in deep yogurt."

Even though the other three men on the panel had held high public office and were skilled in debate, Boyd dominated the hearing. At the end of the day, nothing changed. But Boyd had defended Mike Wyly before the U.S. Congress, and when he walked out of the Capitol he was beaming.

His happiness soon passed. There was something far more serious with which he had to deal.

He was diagnosed with advanced prostate cancer.

The symptoms had been present for years, but Boyd had ignored them. He had not had a physical examination since 1975, when he retired from the Air Force. Now he was given five years to live.

He called the Acolytes and told them he had cancer, but he downplayed the prognosis. Only Pierre Sprey knew how tenaciously Boyd researched various treatments. Even though his brother Gerry strongly recommended surgery, Boyd rejected that option. He did not like the numbers: 50 percent of the survivors are incontinent. He told Mary Ellen that the idea of having no control of his bladder was anathema; "I won't wear a bag," he insisted. After leaning on the National Institutes of Health to reveal European clinical trial results that they preferred not to release, Boyd eventually elected to have radioactive pellets implanted in his prostate, a regimen then new in America.

In 1992, Jeff moved to Delray Beach. His earlier efforts at living with Scott and then with Mary Ellen failed. He could get along with neither. So he moved in with his parents and his sister Kathy. He slept on the floor in the living room. He wanted to bring his seven-foot Sri Lanka cobra, his forty tarantulas, the emerald tree boa, the canebrake rattlesnake, the timber rattler, and the tailless whip scorpion known as the *vinegarroon,* but Boyd said no. As a result, Jeff kept the vinegarroon and the tarantulas in his car. He always parked in a shady place and came out regularly to feed the scorpion and the tarantulas and to talk with them. He remains angry today that Boyd would not let him bring his collection into the apartment.

During his last years, Boyd's two great professional delights were the work of Chet Richards and a book being researched by Dr. Grant Hammond at the Air War College.

Richards was the mathematical whiz who came to the Pentagon in 1973, the man whom Christie assigned the job of finding a place for happy hour. Richards had reviewed all of Boyd's briefings. He later went to work for Lockheed and began studying the fabled Toyota production system, which he found "frighteningly familiar" from his study of maneuver conflict. But the Toyota production system began in the 1950s, about two decades before Boyd began work on "Patterns of Conflict." The underlying ideas of mutual trust, mission orders, and individual responsibility, and the concepts of "harmony" and "flow" and — most of all — the manipulation of time as a production tool were central ideas in both the Toyota system and the strategy of maneuver conflict.

About that time Tom Peters published *Thriving on Chaos,* a book that revolutionized management theories in America. Peters talked of creating and exploiting chaos — the essence of maneuver conflict — of shaping the marketplace and of mutual trust. Richards wrote Peters and said the book sounded very much like the theories of Boyd. Peters said he had read James Fallows's book and knew Boyd's work. He was embarrassed that he had not given Boyd credit, because his book had been shaped by Boyd's ideas. He later wrote a newspaper column in which he corrected the oversight.

Richards and Boyd talked for years about applying Boyd's ideas to business. But by 1993, when Boyd began his physical decline, Richards was beginning to lose interest. Boyd encouraged him to press on, to develop his ideas, and to write and publish papers on the subject. He saw this as an affirmation of the fact that his intellectual legacy encompassed more than war fighting; his ideas were universal, timeless, and could be applied to any form of conflict.

Richards found that lean production had the same impact on American business that maneuver conflict had on the U.S. military. While the idea became a much-talked-about fad in business, very few companies actually put it into practice. Because lean production depends on a certain cultural foundation, businesses, like the military, are reluctant to make the radical changes demanded by a full commitment to the doctrine. McDonnell Douglas, for instance, was like the U.S. Army. With much fanfare it adopted what it called "lean production." But just as the Army stopped in the desert because it clung to the idea of synchronization, McDonnell Douglas could not shake the adherence to top-down management and centrally controlled production, and the company wound up selling itself to Boeing.

Richards found that a famous observation by Taiichi Ono, the Toyota vice president who created the Toyota system, held true: companies performing reasonably well will not adopt the Toyota system, although they may showcase isolated elements of lean production. Boyd put it more succinctly: "You can't change big bureaucracies until they have a disaster."

With Boyd's encouragement, Richards wrote various articles applying Boyd's theories to business. He developed a briefing on the same topic and began delivering it to major corporations. He went to Denmark and lectured at the Copenhagen Business School, where Professor Ole Stromgren teaches courses designed around Boyd's work. Finally, Richards set up two Web sites (www.Belisarius.com and www.d-n-i.net) to showcase Boyd's ideas and how they relate to business. (Belisarius, the Byzantine commander, was one of Boyd's favorite generals and was an early practitioner of maneuver conflict; he always fought outnumbered, never lost a battle, and understood the moral dimension of war.)

By now Boyd must have wished he had listened to the admonitions of the Acolytes to transform his briefings into a written work. It is through a body of writing that a man such as Boyd is remembered. It is when academics pore over a man's words and then write learned papers that his ideas find permanency. And that may be why Boyd was so enthusiastic about the book being researched by Grant Hammond.

In the beginning, Hammond saw the book as a biography. But that changed when Boyd issued his only caveat: no personal information is to be included in the book. Boyd did not want to talk about Erie, about his family, or about the personal dimensions of his marriage and his life. Hammond's book *The Mind of War* was published in the spring of 2001. It is a study of Boyd's ideas and is written for an academic audience or for an audience interested in military affairs.

By 1994, Boyd was experiencing such discomfort in his legs and hips that he wondered if the cancer had metastasized to his bones. He spent an hour or so every day rubbing his legs with Ben-Gay.

Mary Ellen gave him a black cat named Pudding Pie and Boyd spent hour after hour sitting in his favorite chair with the cat in his lap. Even though Pudding Pie was grown and had belonged to someone else, the cat was extraordinarily attentive to Boyd. Clearly it was "his." He remained the indomitable John Boyd. He liked nothing better than calling Sprad out in Las Vegas, Ron Catton up in Spokane, Everett "Razz" Raspberry down in Fort Walton, and the Acolytes in Washington. Catton flew in to see Boyd and stayed several days, spending much of that time listening to the "full brief" of Boyd's work, about fourteen hours.

One of the few times Mary, Jeff, or Kathy saw Boyd display any emotion was when he saw *Legends of the Fall,* a movie about the relationship of a father to his three sons. Boyd wept with such grief that his shoulders shook and he cried aloud. Kathy did not understand how he could be so emotional about a family on-screen when he was so oblivious to his own family.

It seemed to Boyd's friends that he was winning his battle with cancer. But when he drove up to Erie to attend the 1995 reunion of his high school class from Strong Vincent, he was quiet and subdued. Before the reunion he found his way over to Lincoln Avenue and slowly drove up and down the street, looking at the neighborhood where he grew up. His car crept along in front of his old house. Then he went to the end of the street, looked out across the bay toward the Peninsula, then turned around and came back. Time after time he passed back and forth, almost as if he knew he would never see the house again. A vital part of Boyd's visits to Erie had changed; Frank Pettinato was retired and living in Florida.

That night the class reunion was down at the Yacht Club, only a few yards from where he and Chet Reichert launched their canoe as boys to go over to the Peninsula and work as lifeguards. Boyd wore the madras pants and orange coat, but he did not tell of his exploits in a voice that could be heard across the room. He was quiet, often staring across the darkness of the bay toward the Peninsula. Even when a few of his old friends chided him about never making general, he smiled and shrugged. When Chet Reichert's wife, Terry, said she heard that he had cancer but had defeated it, he looked away for a long moment. Then he moved closer and whispered, "It has come back."

Boyd did not know it, but by then he also had colon cancer.

The summer of 1995 was the last time Boyd ever visited Erie. And 1995 was the last time he updated "Patterns of Conflict." The pain in his legs was such that when he visited Mary Ellen in Washington, Ben-Gay and vitamin C and shark cartilage provided no relief. He was in constant pain. During the visit, Boyd asked Mary Ellen to drive him to the Vietnam Veterans Memorial, which, in all his years in Washington, he had never seen. There at "The Wall" he found the name of a friend who died early in the war and he wept.

The urologist whom Boyd had been seeing said he could do nothing more, that if Boyd wanted further treatment he should see another doctor. Boyd went to an oncologist in Palm Beach who was famous for prolonging the life of cancer patients. But there was nothing that could be done.

In 1995, as Boyd wrestled with what he now knew was a terminal illness, his firstborn son, Stephen, was diagnosed with melanoma. Mary was devastated. All she could think of were those long-ago days at Eglin when she spent so much time on the beach with her son. Stephen's cancer was so virulent and so advanced that Boyd thought his son might die first. He wanted Stephen to be comfortable and talked of buying him a big car, a Cadillac perhaps, that could more easily accommodate his wheelchair.

When Boyd talked of dying, it was always with much bravado. When he died he wanted a Viking funeral, his body tied atop an old wooden boat and the boat towed into the middle of Lake Erie and set afire. He worried constantly about his books and his records and the early versions of his briefings and what would happen to them when he died. At times he sat and looked at his books and wept.

By late 1996 Boyd was spending most of his time in bed. He did not want to go to the hospital. He fell frequently and Jeff occasionally took him to a hospital in Palm Beach for radiation treatments. As they drove north on I-95, Boyd stared at people in nearby cars and said, "Look at all these people. They are well. They are healthy. And I'm dying."

The skin of Boyd's chest broke out in frightening lesions. Radiation caused uncontrollable diarrhea. He wore a catheter. Darkly, Jeff took some delight in all this. The man who had dominated his life, the man who always had to be in control, now had no control.

Once Kathy came into Boyd's room and found him sitting in his chair, surrounded by his books and papers. Tears coursed down the folds of his face.

"What is it, Dad?" she asked.

"I won't get to see my friends anymore," he said. Uttering his thoughts made him weep aloud. His lips trembled as he said, "I won't get to see Tom and Pierre and Ray and Chuck. I won't get to see Mike and Jim. Not ever again."

Kathy fought back her anger. Why didn't her father say he would miss his family?

Almost as if he sensed what she was thinking, Boyd looked up and said, "I love you."

"I know," Kathy said. But she was even more angry. It was the first time her father had ever said that he loved her. And he waited until he knew he was dying. Why had he not told her years ago?

Now when the Acolytes called, Boyd was often too weak to come to the phone. He grew weaker and weaker and then, in late February 1997, entered the hospital. His family knew the end was near.

Jeff sat by his father's bed during those last days. By now Boyd was so heavily sedated that only rarely was he conscious. Jeff was there the night his father suddenly began talking of Tom Christie and reliving the days when they had stolen a million dollars' worth of computer time. Boyd drifted back into sleep. A few minutes later he called out "Pierre" and laughed and said, "Tiger, we hosed those bastards good." Again he drifted off. Then he called out "Chuck" and laughed about calling Spinney in one night at midnight. "Because I'm a god-damn colonel and I say so," he murmured. He called out for Leopold and Burton and Wyly. And Jeff realized his father was replaying his life, remembering one last time the comrades with whom he had fought the good fight. Jeff listened and waited for the name of some-one in the family. But his brother Gerry was the only name Boyd mentioned. Gerry was not there; he refused to visit because he was angry that Boyd had rejected his advice about having surgery.

Mary called Tom Christie and told him the end was near. Christie sent out e-mails to Boyd's friends. Sprey called Spinney and said, "We have to do something about John's books and papers."

"I know. I think they should go to one of the service schools."

"The Marines?"

"That's exactly what I was thinking."

Early the next morning Spinney sent an e-mail to Marine Corps Colonel G. I. Wilson, who forwarded it to Commandant Charles Krulak. Before noon, Krulak answered, "Let's do it."

By the next day, the top generals in the Marine Corps were planning not only how to handle a special collection of all Boyd's papers, but also a John Boyd exhibit at the Marine Corps Research Center at Quantico.

The Acolytes called daily to check on Boyd. He could not talk. Mary told Spinney not to visit, so Spinney sat down and wrote Boyd a long letter. It was difficult because, unlike Christie or Burton, he had a warm and loving childhood. He and his father were close, and he found it hard to articulate his feelings for Boyd without being disre-spectful of his own father. But he wrote the letter.

Then Jim Burton called at a time when Boyd was strong enough to talk. Burton said, "You are the father I never had. You made my life richer than it ever could have been without you." Burton is not a demonstrative man. But that night he said, "John, I love you." And he and Boyd wept as they said good-bye to each other.

Boyd wanted his friends to remember him as the man who burned down hangars in Japan, the bigger-than-life Forty-Second Boyd, the Mad Major, the Ghetto Colonel who presided over happy hour in the Old Guard Room, "Genghis John" who hosed a dozen generals and whose cape jobs and hot platters and tube steaks were the stuff of legend. He did not want them to see a withered old man with a catheter running into a container under his bed.

Two men ignored him and came to Good Samaritan Medical Center in Palm Beach. Ray Leopold came and sat on the bed and showed Boyd his new cellular telephone, one of the first of its kind in the country. It was one of Boyd's last good days. He and Leopold had a raucous evening.

Pierre Sprey flew in and sat on a chair in the corner of the room and talked quietly with the man he had known more than thirty years. There was much unsaid that night. But each heard what was in the heart of the other. These two men were brothers, the original Fighter Mafia who had been victorious in a hundred bureaucratic battles.

By now letters were arriving from all over the world, dozens of letters. Letters from Boyd's close friends, letters from those who knew Boyd professionally, letters from pilots and from soldiers and — most of all — from Marines. Many who wrote had never met Boyd. But they conveyed their respect and their great affection and said their lives had been changed by his work and by his example. Boyd never saw the letters. He was too sick.

On March 8, the day after Sprey visited, Mary called Mary Ellen in Virginia and said, "You better come down. I don't think your father is going to make it." Mary Ellen picked up Stephen and drove straight through to south Florida. Stephen was exhausted so she dropped him off at her mother's apartment and rushed to the hospital.

Boyd knew that Mary Ellen was on the way, but about 3:00 P.M. that day he told a nurse, "I'm not sure I can make it until she arrives." He slipped into a coma, and those were his last words.

When Mary Ellen arrived at the Good Samaritan Medical Center, a nurse smiled and said, "You must be the daughter he has been waiting to see. Where is the family?"

"What do you mean?"

"He's going. You need to get them here immediately."

Mary Ellen called home. But Mary, Kathy, Jeff, and Stephen could not get organized for the fifteen-minute drive to the hospital. Mary Ellen sat on the bed and clasped her father's withered hands and told him how much she loved him. By then Boyd could not speak, but his hand clasped hers. His Snookums was with him. Mary Ellen sensed how very tired her father was. She leaned over and whispered that she knew he had been waging a mighty battle to hold on until she arrived. "You know, Dad, it's okay. If you want to go ahead, go. It's okay." With tears streaming down her cheeks she told him that he should find the rest and peace he so desperately needed. "It's okay, Dad."

A moment later, at about 5:00 P.M., Boyd smiled. His face relaxed and the grasp of his hand loosened. Mary Ellen felt her father's soul pass through her and he was gone.

Epilogue

El Cid Rides On

JOHN Richard Boyd — as is often the case with men of great accomplishment — gave his work far greater priority than he did his family. The part of his legacy that concerns his family is embarrassing and shameful.

Today Mary and Kathy and Jeff continue to live in the two-bedroom apartment in Delray Beach. Except for workmen, no one who is not a member of the family ever enters. One reason is that Mary says the apartment is jammed and cluttered and she is too embarrassed for others to see it. Another reason is Jeff's collection of snakes and tarantulas and insects. He says that today he has only a seven-foot bull snake and a "few others," but as he says this, he ducks his head and looks around as if fearful someone might overhear him. Mary worries that word of Jeff's collection might get out and she wonders how the apartment management might react. Her friends have repeatedly asked her to kick Jeff out, but she can't bring herself to do that. She receives about sixteen hundred dollars monthly from social security and a pension, and she drifts along, wondering what will happen to Kathy and Jeff after she is gone.

Her concern is justified. Kathy's depression has deepened and her inability to cope with the world has grown. She says she was diagnosed with "schizo-affective disorder" and she talks of the voices she hears, critical and condemning voices telling her what a bad person she is. Occasionally she sees a psychiatrist who asks about her antidepressant drugs and sends her on her way. Three days a week she works at a facility for those with mental disorders. She is afraid to ride the bus so either Mary or Jeff drives her. She is well into her forties, but her anger toward her father is unabated.

437

For a while Jeff worked part-time at a nature preserve, but he was let go. He says he lost the job because he is principled and honest and these attributes make people uncomfortable. He is moving into his forties and, like Kathy, suffers from depression. He will not take medication. He says married women find him very attractive and that they frequently make advances but that he always turns them down. His portfolio is filled with drawings of spiders and snakes and insects, truly outstanding sketches. He could sell many of them, but refuses to do so. He spends hours every day lying across his mother's bed, talking on the telephone. He says Mary has helped him financially but not emotionally.

John Scott, who now uses only his first name, lives in California, where he works in the computer industry. His hobby is building motorcycles. Alexander, his young son, is named for Alexander the Great. John wanted to name him Alexander Genghis but instead named him Alexander John. The "John" is for his father. His animosity toward his father is such that the other members of the family wondered if he would come to the funeral. He did, but the anger lingers. Now he wants his son to grow up to be an Air Force fighter pilot. Sometimes he quotes his father and sometimes he admits that he misses him terribly. When things are not going well in business, he thinks of his dad's "sense of integrity and duty" and finds the strength to press on.

Mary Ellen writes computer manuals and lives outside Washington. Although she is the youngest child, she is easily the strongest person in the family. She handles all the details of her father's estate and watches closely over his papers and books at Quantico. She has Boyd's old phone book, which contains an unlisted number for the line between the Pentagon and Dick Cheney's home. She is very much like her father: direct, painfully honest, and at times loud and boisterous. Mary Ellen is divorced. She sometimes wonders if the depression that runs in the Boyd family might one day surface in her daughter, Rebah.

Mary Ellen and John Scott, the two children who for so long fought with their father, tried to join the military. Both were refused, Mary Ellen because of allergies and John Scott because of a juvenile run-in with the law.

Stephen died on June 3, 1998. In the aftermath of chemotherapy, he had a stroke and, like his uncle Bill, choked to death on his vomit.

Then there are the Acolytes. They remain an extraordinary group as they continue to shape and influence their world. In one sense, they are Boyd's greatest legacy. Through them, his work and ideas remain alive. Every year or so the Acolytes and more than a dozen of Boyd's old friends gather at Winslow Wheeler's West Virginia cabin for a Boyd Weekend. They eat and drink and tell the old stories and they laugh as they remember.

After Boyd died his family was making plans to bury his remains in Erie when Gerry, Boyd's older brother, said Boyd wanted to be buried in Arlington National Cemetery. Mary and the children were surprised. Boyd never mentioned Arlington to them; all he talked about was a Viking funeral on Lake Erie. But Gerry was so adamant that Mary Ellen called Tom Christie and asked for his help. The Finagler did not tell her that most of the available space in Arlington is gone and that it is very difficult to be buried there today. One more time the Finagler came through, a final favor for his old friend.

Christie lives in Vienna, Virginia, in the same house he and Kathy bought when they came to Washington about thirty years ago. In the spring of 2001, Christie was weeks away from retiring when he received a phone call from a representative of President Bush's administration. He was offered the job of Director of Operational Test and Evaluation in the Pentagon. This was the position created through the efforts of the Reformers in the early 1980s. The sweet irony of Christie's taking over a job that he indirectly helped create was not lost on the old Reformers.

Christie's decisions of the next few years will have a long-term effect on the defense industry. The happy hour crowd at Fort Myer wondered which Tom Christie would triumph: the ultimate insider, or the Finagler. Then came the war in Afghanistan and they stopped wondering. The U.S. military had the media believing that the Predator, an unmanned aerial vehicle, was the greatest technological advance in years, that it enabled commanders to monitor the battlefield in real time. Christie published a report saying the Predator was thrust into service without proper testing, that it was unreliable, and that the onboard surveillance cameras had severe limitations.

Pierre Sprey brought to his music recording studio in the Maryland countryside the same unbending ways he brought to the Pentagon. The corporate motto for Mapleshade Studio is vintage Sprey: "Music Without Compromise." He says the music is "rigidly empirical" in that every piece of recording gear is picked by ear, never by numbers or measurements. He does not use a mixing board, overdubs, compression, equalization, or reverb — none of the studio tricks to enhance music. It is all analog, live to two-track, and beloved by those who like their music warm and vital and pure. The loyalty of his customers is unwavering. His music is revered by audiophile magazines.

Sprey's son, John, is growing up hearing stories of the man for whom he is named.

Sprey rarely ventures into defense matters these days. All that is behind him. But his swan song in that area is one of which he is particularly proud: the sound of the A-10 Warthog screaming into battle like one of Boyd's Valkyries. Air Force General Charles Horner did not want to send the "Hogs" to the Gulf; they are cheap, ugly, and slow, and A-10 pilots go around posting signs that say THERE IS NO INTELLIGENT LIFE ABOVE 1,000 FEET. Much of the news about the aerial side of the war was devoted to the Stealth Bomber. But the A-10 had a bigger effect on the campaign than any other aircraft. It was the aircraft most feared by Iraqi troops. They called it "Black Death." Iraqi POWs said other aircraft came in, made a quick strike, and were gone. But the A-10 lingered over the battlefield, and when the pilot sighted a target, the deadly thirty-millimeter cannon released destruction such as ground troops had never seen. General Horner said, "I take back all the bad things I have ever said about the A-10. I love them. They're saving our asses."

One day during the Gulf War, Sprey saw a TV clip of an A-10 landing. The aircraft had gaping holes in the fuselage. Half of the tail was shot away and sky could be seen through an enormous hole in the wing. The pilot crawled down from the smoking airplane, then turned and kissed it. Sprey laughed. It was one of the greatest moments of his life to see that the airplane whose design he influenced was the only aircraft in the theater that could have brought its pilot home after suffering such damage.

Ray Leopold is vice president and director of technical enterprises for Motorola Labs, where he continues to be an achiever. He was one of three engineers who created the Iridium satellite-based cell-phone network and is a much-sought-after speaker at technical and telecommunications symposia. Leopold holds twenty-six U.S. patents and has patents issued or pending in about fifty countries. He is a senior lecturer at MIT. He lives in Arizona and keeps in touch with the other Acolytes.

As Boyd lay dying, Franklin "Chuck" Spinney wrote him a letter saying, "I will do my best to continue the good work you taught me to do." He lives up to that promise. Spinney stayed in the Pentagon, keeper of the flame and fiercely protective of Boyd's ideas. One of the best things written about Boyd after his death was done by Spinney — a piece in *Proceedings* called "Genghis John." As brash and uncompromising as ever, Spinney continues on at the TacAir shop, where he works in Boyd's old office, an office that some think is almost a shrine, what with framed quotes and pictures of Boyd on the wall. Spinney is the most feared and respected GS-15 in the U.S. government, a man whose very name causes defense contractors to tremble. The Pentagon gave up trying to fire him and instead adopted an isolationist policy: ignore him, give him no duties, segregate him from his colleagues, and maybe he will resign. A wall was installed between his office and that of several young civilians. The purpose of the "Spinney Wall," as it is called, is to keep Spinney from contaminating their minds. He has not been promoted since 1979. The last time he was assigned meaningful duties was 1989. He has received no awards or bonuses. Much of his time is spent writing insightful articles about the Pentagon, which he calls the "big green spending machine" or "Versailles on the Potomac." He calls the articles "Blasters" and sends them via e-mail to some of the most influential people in government and the media. The man who did not fare well on the writing side of his college boards has turned into a passionate and convincing advocate. His Blasters are not only unshakable in fact and logic (he has never been caught out on a major factual issue) but they have caused change in government. It was Spinney who made the wing problems of the F/A-18 a national issue. Spinney also has become a prolific writer of op-ed columns for the *Washington Post* and

Los Angeles Times. He laughingly served notice on Tom Christie that if he doesn't do the right thing as DOT&E, he gets hosed.

Spinney is one of three living people who can deliver the "Patterns of Conflict" briefing (the others are Chet Richards and Pierre Sprey), and he drives down to Quantico occasionally to give the briefing to young Marine officers. He and Richards are writing a commentary on the briefing in an effort to make it more accessible. They want to make sure Boyd's greatest work lives on.

Jim Burton, the man who might have been a general, moved into the village of Aldie, Virginia, and lives in an old house near the base of Bull Mountain. After he resigned, Congress ordered the Army to complete the live-fire tests exactly as Burton had ordered them. In addition, Congress threatened to kill the Bradley program unless the Army implemented more than a dozen of Burton's recommendations. Finally, Congress mandated that all weapons systems be tested in the same realistic fashion as the Bradley. One change alone to the Bradley — the addition of a Kevlar lining inside the troop compartment — doubtless saved many lives in the Gulf War. It took almost three years, but Jim Burton won his battle with the U.S. Army. When Lieutenant General Donald Pihl of the Army testified before Congress about the live-fire tests, he said the Army had "learned much" and "much of the credit must go to Colonel Burton for pushing us in that direction."

Burton wrote a book called *The Pentagon Wars* that, on February 28, 1998, aired as an HBO original movie starring Kelsey Grammer. The book's epilogue was largely about the failures of the Gulf War and was published as an article in *Proceedings*. For eight months after the article was published, senior Army generals wrote letters taking Burton to task. He used the information in the letters to put together a devastating briefing about the failures of the U.S. military in the Gulf War.

After he moved to Aldie, Burton grew dismayed at the rapid pace of development that was destroying the rural nature of the Virginia countryside. Loudoun County is the fastest-growing county in Virginia. His ideas of controlling development resonated with a group of citizens, and they asked him to run for the post of county supervisor. "I will run but I will not solicit funds," he said. "I will not be beholden. You raise the money and I will run." He was elected and lived up to his campaign pledge so well that a major developer, one of the wealthiest men in Virginia, held a clenched fist in Burton's face and said, "I'm going to build houses. Nothing you can do will stop me. I am a fighter."

Burton looked him in the eye and said, "I haven't had a good fight in about six months. Let's see how this turns out."

A few months later the developer left the county. "It's the same game as in the Pentagon," Burton says. "Except there are not as many zeros."

Burton learned from Boyd that if a man does the right thing, it does not matter how overwhelming the odds against him. There always is a way to victory. "No matter what the situation is, no matter how bleak or how dark things appear, how scary, there is always a way out," Burton says. "It works every time. And it all goes back to Boyd's ideas on maneuver conflict."

Mike Wyly bought a farm near Pittsfield, Maine, planted grapes, and made big plans for what he called "Wilderness Vineyard." But then he heard that the local ballet was in debt and in danger of being disbanded. The board of directors spent more time squabbling and trying to make sure their children had starring roles than they did in good business practices. Wyly volunteered to take over the ballet. He sounded the call to his Marine Corps friends, and James Webb and Colonel G. I. Wilson and a dozen others responded. Wyly put Marine Corps thinking to the ballet and turned it around, and today the Bossov Ballet Theater is a great success story. The *Wall Street Journal* even did a front-page story about the retired Marine colonel who runs a ballet school.

Wyly hosted a Boyd Conference the summer after Boyd died, and more than two dozen of Boyd's friends journeyed to Maine for a week. In early 2001, he called a board meeting to coincide with a per-formance of *Cinderella*. Board members and advisors came from as far away as California and Georgia to a small town in central Maine. After the performance, Wyly and his friends visited a bar, where they stood and drank a toast to Colonel John Boyd.

Every morning when Wyly arises, he asks himself, "What is my *Schwerpunkt* today?" And every morning he misses not being able to put on his Marine Corps uniform.

The Wednesday evening happy hour at Fort Myer is still running strong after thirty years. Many of those who attend are getting a bit long in the tooth: G. I. Wilson, Winslow Wheeler, Jim Stevenson, George Wilson, Don Vandergriff, Chuck Myers, Chris Yunker, Dan Moore, and Greg Wilcox. They are laughed at now as old cynics and troublemakers and antitechnology types. But America owes them a great debt. The occasional knowledgeable guest who knows their backgrounds looks around in awe, aware that he stands among living legends. There are nights when several dozen people gather and the beer flows and the old stories are retold and everyone laughs as if it were the first time they ever heard them. In 2001, the Air Force announced that its fleet of some ninety-three B-1 Bombers was being reduced to a force of about sixty. "Boyd called that one back in the early seventies," someone remembered.

Boyd's work has been cited in almost three hundred magazines, journals, and books. His legacy to science and to aviation, though he does not always receive credit, is exemplary and lasting. He contributed as much to fighter aviation as any man in the history of the Air Force. He single-handedly moved the Air Force away from aircraft designed to fly at high speed in a straight line and toward the highly maneuverable aircraft of today. And more than any other person he deserves credit for creating America's tactical Air Force of the past thirty years: the Air Force F-15 and F-16 and the Navy and Marine Corps F-18 rule the skies because of Boyd. This is a claim that causes retired four-stars, whose own accomplishments are minimal, to grow livid. They say Boyd was unprofessional, unreliable, and an embarrassment to the Air Force — a man who happened to have a flair for math, and that's all.

Boyd's Energy-Maneuverability Theory did four things for aviation: it provided a quantitative basis for teaching aerial tactics, it forever changed the way aircraft are flown in combat, it provided a scientific means by which the maneuverability of an aircraft could be evaluated and tactics designed both to overcome the design flaws of one's own aircraft and to minimize or negate the superiority of the opponent's aircraft, and, finally, it became a fundamental tool in designing fighter aircraft.

In the May 6, 1991, issue of *U.S. News & World Report* was an article about the innovative tactics that won the Gulf War. And it said the men behind the tactics were John Boyd, Mike Wyly, and Huba Wass de Czege. The January 4, 1998, issue of the *New York Times Magazine,* the annual issue called "The Lives They Lived" that marks the passage of those who have made a great contribution to society, includes a piece about Boyd.

The academics who know of Boyd agree he was one of the premier military strategists of the twentieth century and the *only* strategist to put time at the center of his thinking. That is as far as they will go. But Boyd was the greatest military theoretician since Sun Tzu.

Academics snort in derision at such a claim. Von Clausewitz remains their favorite even though those who know the work of both Boyd and von Clausewitz agree that Boyd revealed the gaping flaws of von Clausewitzian theory. Another reason that academics are reluctant to rank Boyd with Sun Tzu is that he published so little. His ideas — while broadly disseminated by word of mouth — still received relatively limited circulation (though not as limited as the circulation of many professional journals). Academics dismiss Boyd because he left no text for them to analyze. They say that since his war-fighting strategy was never subjected to critical review, they find it difficult to support the position that he ranks with Sun Tzu. Academics are a cautious group that like to qualify their judgments. The absolute nature of ranking Boyd with Sun Tzu bothers them. "You just can't say that" is their final rejoinder.

But as the years go by and Chet Richards continues to deliver his lectures to large corporations, the word will spread. Richards — considering that he has a Ph.D. in mathematics and is a retired intelligence officer — has a rather unusual assessment of Boyd: he thinks Boyd is the most recent link in a chain that began with Sun Tzu and continued with Musashi, the sixteenth-century samurai, and then with Mao Tse Tung. Richards says the similarities between Musashi and Boyd are many: Boyd's shiny fighter aircraft was like the lacquered armor of a samurai. Both went into battle one-on-one. Both had personal habits that caused others to think them uncouth. Both lived by an austere code of honor and self-sacrifice. Both believed that if they confused an enemy before the battle, they had won even before the fight. In combat, neither ever lost a battle. Both read widely and were single-minded in their search for enlightenment. Both loomed large in their times. Both evolved from fighters into teachers and both left works that lived long after their death. Musashi's famous work was *A Book of Five Rings* and Boyd's was the OODA Loop. The

OODA Loop is in five pieces, the "Loop" itself being the fifth. "Boyd *was* the old warrior," Richards says.

Graduate students now are writing papers on Boyd. The two Web sites created by Chet Richards receive three hundred thousand visits annually and the numbers continue to increase.

Boyd was not as interested in his career as he was in the fate of the American fighting man, the man who — as the military says — is at the pointy end of the spear. He wanted these men to have the best possible equipment, whether it was an airplane or a tank. That was his life.

Boyd made men believe they could do things they never thought they could do. And most of them were men of integrity and accomplishment even before they met Boyd. He encouraged all that was good in them and galvanized them and sent them forth renewed. Boyd's ideas and work are out there, still germinating, still spreading in an inkblot fashion, with the isolated and widely separated blots coming together and forming even larger pools of knowledge. Some say Boyd has become a cult figure. But no one who knows the Acolytes or the U.S. Marines or the growing use of Boyd's ideas in business believes this is cultish activity.

After the initial media coverage of the September 11, 2001, attack on the World Trade Center and the Pentagon, newspaper and magazine reporters began mining their sources for the deeper meaning of the tragedy. A few weeks later stories began appearing on Fourth Generation Warfare and the October 1989 piece in the Marine Corps *Gazette* was rediscovered. The article, written more than a decade earlier, was so frighteningly prescient in its description of how terrorists might operate in America that it was reprinted in the November 2001 issue of the *Gazette*. Colonel G. I. Wilson suddenly was perceived as a prophet.

One of the Web sites devoted to Boyd suddenly was receiving as many as sixteen hundred hits per day, many visitors pulling up the 1989 article. A surprising number of the visits originated from the Pentagon, where a mighty battle was waged over how to respond to the terrorist attack. The deployment of B-1 and B-52 Bombers meant the traditional Air Force mind was at work. But Vice President Dick Cheney and Secretary of State Colin Powell advocated following Boyd's ideas. Powell appeared on national television and talked of a response involving multiple thrusts and getting inside the adversary's decision cycle.

Vice President Cheney has his own ideas about Boyd's place in military history. "We could use him again now. I wish he was around now. I'd love to turn him loose on our current defense establishment and see what he could come up with. We are still oriented toward the past. We need to think about the next one hundred years rather than the last one hundred years."

The military itself does not have such certitude.

After Ron Catton delivered his emotional eulogy at Boyd's funeral, he stopped by the office of his congressman, George Nethercutt, to ask a favor. Catton wanted the Air Force to recognize Boyd in some formal fashion. Today Catton is a multimillionaire financial consultant and one of Spokane's most prominent citizens. If he asks something of his congressman, chances are, he gets it. The initial response from the Air Force was that Grant Hammond, who teaches at the Air University, was writing his book and that should be enough recognition for Boyd. Nethercutt disagreed and on September 17, 1999, the Air Force dedicated Boyd Hall at Nellis AFB. It is a small building across the street from the Weapons School. The original version of the dedication speech was twenty minutes, but a retired general said Boyd was not worth twenty minutes and ordered the speech cut by half. This same retired general read the prologue to this book on the Internet several years ago and sent an e-mail to friends in which he denigrated Boyd and said when Boyd was at the Fighter Weapons School, "I had to wax his ass" in simulated aerial combat. The claim brought howls of derision from those who knew both men.

The Fighter Weapons School has gone through a name change. Because crews for the B-1 Bomber and the B-52 and other aircraft are now trained there, the "Fighter" was dropped and it is now the "Weapons School." In the summer of 1999, to celebrate the fiftieth anniversary of the school, the Air Force published a special issue of *USAF Weapons Review*. The featured article was titled "Air Combat Maneuvering" and was from Boyd's "Aerial Attack Study." His name was not mentioned.

At the Air Force Academy, seniors take an advanced course in aeronautical engineering. The textbook is primarily an explication of the E-M Theory. Boyd's name is not in the book and those who teach the course do not give Boyd credit. When a group of graduating seniors was polled, not one cadet knew the name of Colonel John Boyd.

The U.S. Army has forgotten that one of its generals stopped three nights in the desert during the Gulf War and today proudly proclaims that it practices maneuver warfare. The Army also says that Boyd had nothing to do with the doctrinal changes of the late 1970s, that those changes came from within.

And then there is the Marine Corps. When Boyd died, Commandant Charles Krulak wrote a moving tribute in a defense journal saying Boyd was the architect of America's victory in the Gulf War. He later elaborated, saying it was "the concept of maneuver, intent, and agility that led to victory." Young Marine officers know of Boyd and study his work. Twice a year retired Marine officer Chris Yunker sponsors a Boyd Symposium to discuss Boyd's ideas.

The Marine Corps Research Center at Quantico is a soaring building of brick and glass. Mike Wyly greatly influenced its design. When a visitor enters the large airy lobby, straight ahead are two brass cannons gleaming as bright as the day they were cast. On the walls are pictures of stern-faced Marine generals and of battle scenes dating back to America's beginnings. Wings of the building and the conference rooms are named for famous three- and four-star Marines. This sacred and hallowed hall is the repository of the mystique surrounding one of America's most elite fighting forces. This is a hall that commemorates Marine warriors. But the eye quickly roves past all of this and is drawn straight ahead and to the left, to the most prominent display in the lobby: the figure of a man in a blue flight suit. Behind the figure is a model of the F-16 and on his shoulders are the silver eagles of a colonel. The name tag over his right breast is in big bold letters and says JOHN BOYD. In his outstretched arms rests a thick briefing book with a faded green cover: "A Discourse on Winning and Losing."

And finally there is Erie, Pennsylvania, where Boyd returned year after year, finding renewal and seeking approbation. A half dozen or so of Boyd's boyhood friends read his obituary in the *New York Times*. They might have later seen Jim Fallows's glowing tribute in *U.S. News & World Report* and perhaps even the widely reprinted eulogy written by David Hackworth. They were amazed. John Boyd, the fellow they grew up with, the man they considered a loud-talking salesman, really did all those things he said he did. They journeyed down to Washington for the memorial service and heard the eulogies from Ron Catton and Pierre Sprey, and they were proud that a boy from Erie had gone so far.

They wished they had known earlier.

The house on Lincoln Avenue has gone through several owners and today is empty. While the *Erie Times-News* did a full-page story about Boyd several years before he died, and while the publisher occasionally mentions Boyd in his columns, the city has never formally recognized Boyd. Erie has a statue commemorating Colonel Strong Vincent, a man generally overlooked by historians. The city is proud of how in the War of 1812 Oliver Hazard Perry fought aboard a ship built in Erie. Yet Erie does not recognize its most accomplished son. The children of Erie do not know of John Boyd.

But then, Erie always was a hard town.

Appendix

Boyd was obsessed with wanting to understand how he had developed his Energy-Maneuverability Theory when many far better educated engineers had not discovered it. "Destruction and Creation," one of the few things he ever wrote, is his effort to understand his own thought processes. It is a window into his mind.

DESTRUCTION AND CREATION

John R. Boyd

September 3, 1976

Abstract

To comprehend and cope with our environment we develop mental patterns or concepts of meaning. The purpose of this paper is to sketch out how we destroy and create these patterns to permit us to both shape and be shaped by a changing environment. In this sense, the discussion also literally shows why we cannot avoid this kind of activity if we intend to survive on our own terms. The activity is dialectic in nature, generating both disorder and order that emerges as a changing and expanding universe of mental concepts matched to a changing and expanding universe of observed reality.

Studies of human behavior reveal that the actions we undertake as individuals are closely related to survival, more importantly, survival on our own terms. Naturally, such a notion implies that we should be able to act relatively free or independent of any debilitating external influ-

451

ences — otherwise that very survival might be in jeopardy. In viewing the instinct for survival in this manner we imply that a basic aim or goal, as individuals, is to improve our capacity for independent action. The degree to which we cooperate, or compete, with others is driven by the need to satisfy this basic goal. If we believe that it is not possible to satisfy it alone, without help from others, history shows us that we will agree to constraints upon our independent action — in order to collectively pool skills and talents in the form of nations, corporations, labor unions, mafias, etc. — so that obstacles standing in the way of the basic goal can either be removed or overcome. On the other hand, if the group cannot or does not attempt to overcome obstacles deemed important to many (or possibly any) of its individual members, the group must risk losing these alienated members. Under these circumstances, the alienated members may dissolve their relationship and remain independent, form a group of their own, or join another collective body in order to improve their capacity for independent action.

In a real world of limited resources and skills, individuals and groups form, dissolve and reform their cooperative or competitive postures in a continuous struggle to remove or overcome physical and social environmental obstacles.[11,13] In a cooperative sense, where skills and talents are pooled, the removal or overcoming of obstacles represents an improved capacity for independent action for all concerned. In a competitive sense, where individuals and groups compete for scarce resources and skills, an improved capacity for independent action achieved by some individuals or groups constrains that capacity for other individuals or groups. Naturally, such a combination of real world scarcity and goal striving to overcome this scarcity intensifies the struggle of individuals and groups to cope with both their physical and social environments.[11,13]

Against such a background, actions and decisions become critically important. Actions must be taken over and over again and in many different ways. Decisions must be rendered to monitor and determine the precise nature of the actions needed that will be compatible with the goal. To make these timely decisions implies that we must be able to form mental concepts of observed reality, as we perceive it, and be able to change these concepts as reality itself appears to change. The concepts can then be used as decision-models for improving our capacity for independent action. Such a demand for decisions that literally impact our survival causes one to wonder: How do we generate or create the mental concepts to support this decision-making activity?

There are two ways in which we can develop and manipulate mental concepts to represent observed reality: We can start from a comprehensive whole and break it down to its particulars or we can start with the particulars and build towards a comprehensive whole.[28,24] Saying it another way, but in a related sense, we can go from the general-to-specific or from the specific-to-general. A little reflection here reveals that deduction is related to proceeding from the general-to-specific while induction is related to proceeding from the specific-to-general. In following this line of thought can we think of other activities that are related to these two opposing ideas? Is not analysis related to proceeding from the general-to-specific? Is not synthesis, the opposite of analysis related to proceeding from the specific-to-general? Putting all this together: Can we not say that general-to-specific is related to both deduction and analysis, while specific-to-general is related to induction and synthesis? Now, can we think of some examples to fit with these two opposing ideas? We need not look far. The differential calculus proceeds from the general-to-specific — from a function to its derivative. Hence is not the use or application of the differential calculus related to deduction and analysis? The integral calculus, on the other hand, proceeds in the opposite direction — from a derivative to a general function. Hence, is not the use or application of the integral calculus related to induction and synthesis? Summing up, we can see that: general-to-specific is related to deduction, analysis, and differentiation while specific-to-general is related to induction, synthesis, and integration.

Now keeping these two opposing idea chains in mind let us move on a somewhat different tack. Imagine, if you will, a domain (a comprehensive whole) and its constituent elements or parts. Now, imagine another domain and its constituent parts. Once again, imagine even another domain and its constituent parts. Repeating this idea over and over again we can imagine any number of domains and the parts corresponding to each. Naturally, as we go through life we develop concepts of meaning (with included constituents) to represent observed reality. Can we not liken these concepts and their related constituents to the domains and constituents that we have formed in our imagination? Naturally, we can. Keeping this relationship in mind, suppose we shatter the correspondence of each domain or concept with its constituent elements. In other words, we imagine the existence of the parts but pretend that the domains or concepts they were previously associated with do not exist. Result: We have many constituents, or particulars, swimming around in a sea of anarchy. We have uncertainty and disorder in place of meaning and order. Further, we can see that such an unstructuring or destruction of many domains — to break the correspondence of each with its respective constituents — is related to deduction, analysis, and differentiation. We call this kind of unstructuring a destructive deduction.

Faced with such disorder or chaos, how can we reconstruct order and meaning? Going back to the idea chain of specific-to-general, induction, synthesis, and integration the thought occurs that a new domain or concept can be formed if we can find some common qualities, attributes, or operations among some or many of these constituents swimming in this sea of anarchy. Through such connecting threads (that produce meaning) we synthesize constituents from, hence across, the domains we have just shattered.[24] Linking particulars together in this manner we can form a new domain or concept — providing, of course, we do not inadvertently use only those "bits and pieces" in the same arrangement that we associated with one of the domains purged from our imagination. Clearly, such a synthesis would indicate we have generated something new and different from what previously existed. Going back to our idea chain, it follows that creativity is related to induction, synthesis, and integration since we proceeded from unstructured bits and pieces to a new general pattern or concept. We call such action a creative or constructive induction. It is important to note that the crucial or key step that permits this creative induction is the separation of the particulars from their previous domains by the destructive deduction. Without this unstructuring the creation of a new structure cannot proceed — since the bits and pieces are still tied together as meaning within unchallenged domains or concepts.

Recalling that we use concepts or mental patterns to represent reality, it follows that the unstructuring and restructuring just shown reveals a way of changing our perception of reality.[28] Naturally, such a notion implies that the emerging pattern of ideas and interactions must be internally consistent and match-up with reality.[14,25] To check or verify internal consistency we try to see if we can trace our way back to the original constituents that were used in the creative or constructive induction. If we cannot reverse directions, the ideas and interactions do not go together in this way without contradiction. Hence, they are not internally consistent. However, this does not necessarily mean we reject and throw away the entire structure. Instead, we should attempt to identify those ideas (particulars) and interactions that seem to hold together in a coherent pattern of activity as distinguished from those ideas that do not seem to fit in. In performing this task we check for reversibility as well as check to see which ideas and interactions match-up with our observations of reality.[27,14,15] Using those ideas and interactions that pass this test together with any new ideas (from new destructive deductions) or other promising ideas that popped out of the original destructive deduction we again attempt to find some common qualities, attributes or operations to re-create the concept — or create a new concept. Also, once again, we perform the check for reversibility and match-up with reality. Over and over again this cycle of Destruction and Creation is repeated until we demonstrate internal consistency and match-up with reality.[19,14,15]

When this orderly (and pleasant) state is reached the concept becomes a coherent pattern of ideas and interactions that can be used to describe some aspect of observed reality. As a consequence, there is little, or no, further appeal to alternative ideas and interactions in an effort to either expand, complete, or modify the concept.[19] Instead, the effort is turned inward towards fine tuning the ideas and interactions in order to improve generality and produce a more precise match of the conceptual pattern with reality.[19] Toward this end, the concept — and its internal workings — is tested and compared against observed phenomena over and over again in many different and subtle ways.[19] Such a repeated and inward-oriented effort to explain increasingly more subtle aspects of reality suggests the disturbing idea that perhaps, at some point, ambiguities, uncertainties, anomalies, or apparent inconsistencies may emerge to stifle a more general and precise match-up of concept with observed reality.[19] Why do we suspect this?

On one hand, we realize that facts, perceptions, ideas, impressions, interactions, etc. separated from previous observations and thought patterns have been linked together to create a new conceptual pattern. On the other hand, we suspect that refined observations now underway will eventually exhibit either more or a different kind of precision and subtlety than the previous observations and thought patterns. Clearly, any anticipated difference, or differences, suggests we should expect a mismatch between the new observations and the anticipated concept description of these observations. To assume otherwise would be tantamount to admitting that previous constituents and interactions would produce the same synthesis as any newer constituents and interactions that exhibit either more or a different kind of precision and subtlety. This would be like admitting one equals two. To avoid such a discomforting position implies that we should anticipate a mismatch between phenomena observation and concept description of that observation. Such a notion is not new and is indicated by the discoveries of Kurt Gödel and Werner Heisenberg.

In 1931 Kurt Gödel created a stir in the World of Mathematics and Logic when he revealed that it was impossible to embrace mathematics within a single system of logic.[12,23] He accomplished this by proving, first, that any consistent system — that includes the arithmetic of whole numbers — is incomplete. In other words, there are true statements or concepts within the system that cannot be deduced from the postulates that make-up the system. Next, he proved even though such a system is consistent, its consistency cannot be demonstrated within the system.

Such a result does not imply that it is impossible to prove the consistency of a system. It only means that such a proof cannot be accomplished inside the system. As a matter of fact since Gödel, Gerhard Gentzen and others have shown that a consistency proof of arithmetic can be found by appealing to systems outside that arithmetic. Thus, Gödel's Proof indirectly shows that in order to determine the consistency of any new system we must construct or uncover another system beyond it.[29,27] Over and over this cycle must be repeated to determine the consistency of more and more elaborate systems.[29,27]

Keeping this process in mind, let us see how Gödel's results impact the effort to improve the match-up of concept with observed reality. To do this we will consider two kinds of consistency: The consistency of the concept and the consistency of the match-up between observed reality and concept description of reality. In this sense, if we assume — as a result of previous destructive deduction and creative induction efforts — that we have a consistent concept and consistent match-up, we should see no differences between observation and concept description. Yet, as we have seen, on one hand, we use observations to shape or formulate a concept; while on the other hand, we use a concept to shape the nature of future inquiries or observations of reality. Back and forth, over and over again, we use observations to sharpen a concept and a concept to sharpen observations. Under these circumstances, a concept must be incomplete since we depend upon an ever-changing array of observations to shape or formulate it. Likewise, our observations of reality must be incomplete since we depend upon a changing concept to shape or formulate the nature of new inquiries and observations. Therefore, when we probe back and forth with more precision and subtlety, we must admit that we can have differences between observation and concept description; hence, we cannot determine the consistency of the system —

in terms of its concept, and match-up with observed reality — within itself.

Furthermore, the consistency cannot be determined even when the precision and subtlety of observed phenomena approaches the precision and subtlety of the observer — who is employing the ideas and interactions that play together in the conceptual pattern. This aspect of consistency is accounted for not only by Gödel's Proof but also by the Heisenberg Uncertainty or Indeterminacy Principle.

The Indeterminacy Principle uncovered by Werner Heisenberg in 1927 showed that one could not simultaneously fix or determine precisely the velocity and position of a particle or body.[14,9] Specifically he showed, due to the presence and influence of an observer, that the product of the velocity and position uncertainties is equal to or greater than a small number (Planck's Constant) divided by the mass of the particle or body being investigated. In other words,

$$V\,Q \geq h/m$$

Where:

V is velocity uncertainty

Q is position uncertainty and

h/m is Planck's constant (h) divided by observed mass (m).

Examination of Heisenberg's Principle reveals that as mass becomes exceedingly small the uncertainty or indeterminacy becomes exceedingly large. Now — in accordance with this relation — when the precision, or mass, of phenomena being observed is little, or no different than the precision, or mass, of the observing phenomena the uncertainty values become as large as, or larger than, the velocity and size frame-of-reference associated with the bodies being observed.[9] In other words, when the intended distinction between observer and observed begins to disappear,[3] the uncertainty values hide or mask phenomena behavior; or put another way, the observer perceives uncertain or erratic behavior that bounces all over in accordance with the indeterminacy relation. Under these circumstances, the uncertainty values represent the inability to determine the character or nature (consistency) of a system within itself. On the other hand, if the precision and subtlety of the observed phenomena is much less than the precision and subtlety of the observing phenomena, the uncertainty values become much smaller than the velocity and size values of the bodies being observed.[9] Under these circumstances, the character or nature of a system can be determined — although not exactly — since the uncertainty values do not hide or mask observed phenomena behavior nor indicate significant erratic behavior.

Keeping in mind that the Heisenberg Principle implicitly depends upon the indeterminate presence and influence of an observer,[14] we can now see — as revealed by the two examples just cited — that the magnitude of the uncertainty values represent the degree of intrusion by the observer upon the observed. When intrusion is total (that is, when the intended distinction between observer and observed essentially disappears),[3] the uncertainty values indicate erratic behavior. When intrusion is low the uncertainty values do not hide or mask observed phenomena behavior, nor indicate significant erratic behavior. In other words, the uncertainty values not only represent the degree of intrusion by the observer upon the observed but also the degree of confusion and disorder perceived by that observer.

Confusion and disorder are also related to the notion of entropy and the Second Law of Thermodynamics.[11,20] Entropy is a concept that represents the potential for doing work, the capacity for taking action, or the degree of confusion and disorder associated with any physical or information activity. High entropy implies a low potential for doing work, a low capacity for taking action or a high degree of confusion and disorder. Low entropy implies just the opposite. Viewed in this context, the Second Law of Thermodynamics states that all observed natural processes generate entropy.[20] From this law it follows that entropy must increase in any closed system — or, for that matter, in any system that cannot communicate in an ordered fashion with other systems or environments external to itself.[20] Accordingly, whenever we attempt to do work or take action inside such a system — a concept and its match-up with reality — we should anticipate an increase in entropy hence an increase in confusion and disorder. Naturally, this means we cannot determine the character or nature (consistency) of such a system within itself, since the system is moving irreversibly toward a higher, yet unknown, state of confusion and disorder.

What an interesting outcome! According to Gödel we cannot — in general — determine the consistency, hence the character or nature, of an abstract system within itself. According to Heisenberg and the Second Law of Thermodynamics any attempt to do so in the real world will expose uncertainty and generate disorder. Taken together, these three notions support the idea that any inward-oriented and continued effort to improve the match-up of concept with observed reality will only increase the degree of mismatch. Naturally, in this environment, uncertainty and disorder will increase as previously indicated by the Heisenberg Indeterminacy Principle and the Second Law of Thermodynamics, respectively. Put another way, we can expect unexplained and disturbing ambiguities, uncertainties, anomalies, or apparent inconsistencies to emerge more and more often. Furthermore, unless some kind of relief is available, we can expect confusion to increase until disorder approaches chaos — death.

Fortunately, there is a way out. Remember, as previously shown, we can forge a new concept by applying the destructive deduction and creative induction mental operations. Also, remember, in order to perform these dialectic mental operations we must first shatter the rigid conceptual pattern, or patterns, firmly established in our mind. (This should not be too difficult since the rising confusion and disorder is already helping us to undermine any patterns.) Next, we must find some common qualities, attributes, or operations to link isolated facts, perceptions, ideas, impressions, interactions, observations, etc. together as possible concepts to represent the real world. Finally, we must repeat this unstructuring and restructuring until we develop a concept that begins to match-up with reality. By doing this — in accordance with Gödel, Heisenberg and the Second Law of Thermodynamics — we find that the uncertainty and disorder generated by an inward-oriented system talking to itself can be offset by going outside and creating a new system. Simply stated, uncertainty and related disorder can be diminished by the direct artifice of creating a higher and broader more general concept to represent reality.

However, once again, when we begin to turn inward and use the new concept — within its own pattern of ideas and interactions — to produce a finer grain match with observed reality we note that the new concept and its match-up with observed reality begins to self-destruct just as before. Accordingly, the dialectic cycle of destruction and creation begins to repeat itself once again. In other words, as suggested by Gödel's Proof of Incompleteness, we imply that the process of Structure, Unstructure, Restructure, Unstructure, Restructure is repeated endlessly in moving to higher and broader levels of elaboration. In this unfolding drama, the alternating cycle of entropy increase toward more and more disorder and the entropy decrease toward more and more order appears to be one part of a control mechanism that literally seems to drive and regulate this alternating cycle of destruction and creation toward higher and broader levels of elaboration. Now, in relating this deductive / inductive activity to the basic goal discussed in the beginning, I believe we have uncovered a Dialectic Engine that permits the construction of decision models needed by individuals and societies for determining and monitoring actions in an effort to improve their capacity for independent action. Furthermore, since this engine is directed toward satisfying this basic aim or goal, it follows that the goal seeking effort itself appears to be the other side of a control mechanism that seems also to drive and regulate the alternating cycle of destruction and creation toward higher and broader levels of elaboration. In this context, when acting within a rigid or essentially a closed system, the goal seeking effort of individuals and societies to improve their capacity for independent action tends to produce disorder towards randomness and death. On the other hand, as already shown, the increasing disorder generated by the increasing mismatch of the system concept with observed reality opens or unstructures the system. As the unstructuring or, as we'll call it, the destructive deduction unfolds it shifts toward a creative induction to stop the trend toward disorder and chaos to satisfy a goal-oriented need for increased order. Paradoxically, then, an entropy increase permits both the destruction or unstructuring of a closed system and the creation of a new system to nullify the march toward randomness and death. Taken together, the entropy notion associated with the Second Law of Thermodynamics and the basic goal of individuals and societies seem to work in dialectic harmony driving and regulating the destructive / creative, or deductive / inductive, action — that we have described herein as a dialectic engine. The result is a changing and expanding universe of mental concepts matched to a changing and expanding universe of observed reality.[28,27] As indicated earlier, these mental concepts are employed as decision models by individuals and societies for determining and monitoring actions needed to cope with their environment — or to improve their capacity for independent action.

Bibliography

1. Beveridge, W. I. B., *The Art of Scientific Investigation,* Vintage Books, Third Edition 1957
2. Boyd, John R., "Destruction and Creation," 23 Mar 1976
3. Brown, G. Spencer, *Laws of Form,* Julian Press, Inc. 1972
4. Conant, James Bryant, *Two Modes of Thought,* Credo Perspectives, Simon and Schuster 1970
5. DeBono, Edward, *New Think,* Avon Books 1971

6. DeBono, Edward, *Lateral Thinking: Creativity Step by Step,* Harper Colophon Books 1973

7. Foster, David, *The Intelligent Universe,* Putnam 1975

8. Fromm, Erich, *The Crisis of Psychoanalysis,* Fawcett Premier Books 1971

9. Gamow, George, *Thirty Years that Shook Physics,* Anchor Books 1966

10. Gardner, Howard, *The Quest for Mind,* Vintage Books 1974

11. Georgescu-Roegen, Nicholas, *The Entropy Law and the Economic Process,* Harvard U. Press 1971

12. Gödel, Kurt, "On Formally Undecidable Propositions of the Principia Mathematica and Related Systems," pages 3–38, *The Undecidable,* Raven Press 1965

13. Heilbroner, Robert L., *An Inquiry into the Human Prospect,* Norton and Co. 1974

14. Heisenberg, Werner, *Physics and Philosophy,* Harper Torchbooks 1962

15. Heisenberg, Werner, *Across the Frontiers,* World Perspectives, Harper and Row 1974

16. Hoyle, Fred, *Encounter with the Future,* Credo Perspectives, Simon and Schuster 1968

17. Hoyle, Fred, *The New Face of Science,* Perspectives in Humanism, World Publishing Co. 1971

18. Kramer, Edna E., *The Nature and Growth of Modern Mathematics,* Fawcett Premier Books 1974

19. Kuhn, Thomas S., *The Structure of Scientific Revolutions,* University of Chicago Press 1970

20. Layzer, David, *The Arrow of Time,* Scientific American, December 1975

21. Levinson, Harry, *The Exceptional Executive,* Mentor Books 1971

22. Maltz, Maxwell, *Psycho-Cybernetics,* Wilshire Book Co. 1971

23. Nagel, Ernest, and Newman, James R., *Gödel's Proof,* New York U. Press 1958

24. Osborne, Alex F., *Applied Imagination,* Scribners and Sons 1963

25. Pearce, Joseph Chilton, *The Crack in the Cosmic Egg,* Pocket Book 1975

26. Pearce, Joseph Chilton, *Exploring the Crack in the Cosmic Egg,* Pocket Book 1975

27. Piaget, Jean, *Structuralism,* Harper Torchbooks 1971

28. Polanyi, Michael, *Knowing and Being,* University of Chicago Press 1969

29. Singh, Jagjit, *Great Ideas of Modern Mathematics: Their Nature and Use,* Dover 1959

30. Skinner, B. F., *Beyond Freedom and Dignity,* Bantam / Vintage Books 1972

31. Thompson, William Irwin, *At the Edge of History,* Harper Colophon Books 1972

32. Thompson, William Irwin, *Evil and World Order,* World Perspective, Harper and Row 1976

33. Tse-Tung, Mao, *Four Essays on China and World Communism,* Lancer Books 1972

34. Waismann, Friedrich, *Introduction to Mathematical Thinking,* Harper Torchbooks 1959

35. Watts, Alan, *The Book,* Vintage Books 1972

36. Yukawa, Hideki, *Creativity and Intuition,* Kodansha International LTD 1973

Sources

This book came largely from the sources listed below and from the partial bibliography that follows.

Some interviews lasted minutes, some hours. Some people were interviewed once and some dozens of times. Interviews took place over the telephone, via e-mail, and face-to-face.

A number of those listed retired as colonels or generals but were interviewed about events that occurred when they were lieutenants or captains; thus, to avoid confusion, I have omitted all military ranks.

Arbuckle, Jack
Barshay, Donald
Bellis, Ben
Booth, Jim
Boyd, Jeffrey
Boyd, Kathryn
Boyd, Marion
Boyd, Mary
Brantley, A. L.
Brooks, Mrs. Ralph
Burke, Harold
Burns, Michael
Burton, James
Buttleman, Hank
Byron, Dick
Cameron, Lyle
Case, Jack
Case, Ted
Catton, Ron
Cheney, Dick

Christie, Kathy
Christie, Tom
Colbath, Jeff
Collins, Richard
Cooper, Charles E.
Cowan, Jeff
Creech, Wilbur
Dayton, Allen
Dorsett, Tracy K. Jr.
Drabant, Robert
Fallows, James
FitzPatrick, Hal
Greenwood, John
Grossman, Elaine
Guild, Richard
Hallock, Dick
Hammond, Grant
Hillaker, Harry
Holton, Mary Ellen
Horner, Chuck

Hosmer, Bill
Ingvalson, Roger
Isham, Marty
Jones, John C.
Kan, Bobby
Knox, Robert
Krulak, Charles
Leopold, Ray
MacAlpine, James
Maitland, Jock
McDowell, Robert
McGarvey, Michael
McInerney, Thomas G.
McKinney, Cindy
Michel, Marshall
Mogan, Bill
Moore, Daniel
Morrisey, John C.
Morrison, Blake
Mortensen, Dan
Moser, Dick
Murphy, Charles
Myers, Chuck
No Kum-Sok
Nordeen, Lon
O'Donnell, John
Persky, Arnold
Peterson, Douglas B.
Pettinato, Frank Jr.
Pyle, Joe Mike
Raspberry, Everett
Reichert, Chester
Riccioni, Everest
Richards, Chet

Shanahan, Jack
Smith, R. L.
Sparks, Bob
Speir, Bob
Spinney, Alison
Spinney, Franklin C.
Spradling, Vernon
Sprey, Pierre M.
Stevenson, James
Street, Frank
Stromgren, Ole
Tedeschi, Jim
Thompson, Jim
Thompson, Wayne
Titus, Robert
Toperczer, Istvan
Vandergriff, Donald
Vincent, Hal
Wass de Czege, Huba
Weinert, Charlie
Whatley, James
Wheeler, Winslow
Whitcomb, Darrel
Williams, Lynn F.
Wilman, Jane
Wilson, George
Wilson, G. I.
Winer, Ward O.
Winters, John
Wolford, Connie
Woods, Bill
Wyly, Mike
Yates, Dave
Yunker, Chris

Bibliography

Air Warfare Center. Office of History Headquarters. *A Brief History of the Nellis Air Force Range*. Nellis AFB, Nev., 1997.

———. *A Chronology of Nellis Air Force Base*. Nellis AFB, Nev., 1997.

———. *A Concise History of Nellis Air Force Base Nevada*. Nellis AFB, Nev., 1997.

Barnett, Correlli, ed. *Hitler's Generals*. New York: Quill / William Morrow, 1989.

Baugher, Joe. "General Dynamics F-111 History." Online posting. August 9, 1999 <http://www.f-111.net/JoeBaugher.htm>.

Berent, Mark. *Phantom Leader*. New York: Jove Books, 1992.

Beyond the Wild Blue. Written by Walter Boyne and John Honey. The History Channel. VHS.

Blesse, Frederick. "No Guts No Glory." *Fighter Weapons Newsletter* (March 1955).

Booth, Jim. "John Boyd: An American Patriot." *Erie Daily Times* (July 4, 1994).

Boyd, John R. "A Discourse on Winning and Losing." Briefing. 1987.

———. "Air to Air Missile Analysis." Study. Circa 1968. Possession of Tom Christie.

———. "Fundamentals of Air-to-Air Combat." Briefing. 1965. Possession of Tom Christie.

———. "New Conception for Air-to-Air Combat." Briefing. August 4, 1976. Possession of Tom Christie.

———. *U.S. Air Force Oral History*. Interviewed by Jack Neufeld. Washington: Office of Air Force History, 1973.

———. *U.S. Air Force Oral History. Corona Ace Interview*. Interviewed by John N. Dick Jr. Maxwell AFB: Office of Air Force History, 1977.

Broughton, Jack. *Going Downtown*. New York: Orion Books, 1988.

———. *Thud Ridge*. New York: Bantam Books, 1985.

Burton, James G. "Desert Storm: A Different Look." Briefing. June 21, 1995.

————. *The Pentagon Wars*. Annapolis: Naval Institute Press, 1993.

Carter, Gregory A. "Some Historical Notes on Air Interdiction in Korea." Santa Monica, Calif.: The RAND Corporation, September 1966.

Casti, John L., and Werner DePauli. *Godel*. Cambridge: Perseus Publishing, 2000.

Clausewitz, Carl von. *On War*. Edited and translated by Michael Howard and Peter Paret. Princeton: Princeton University Press, 1976.

Coulam, Robert F. *Illusions of Choice*. Princeton: Princeton University Press, 1977.

Cowan, Jeffrey L. "From Air Force Fighter Pilot to Marine Corps Warfighting: Colonel John Boyd, His Theories on War, and Their Unexpected Legacy." Diss., United States Marine Corps Command and Staff College, 2000.

Creech, Wilbur L. *U.S. Air Force Oral History*. Interviewed by Hugh N. Ahmann. Maxwell AFB: Office of Air Force History, 1992.

Creveld, Martin Van. *The Transformation of War*. New York: The Free Press, 1991.

D'Amato, Martin J. "Vigilant Warrior: General Donn A. Starry's Air-Land Battle and How It Changed the Army." *Armour* (May / June 2000).

"Defense Technology." *The Economist* (June 10, 1995).

Dorfer, Ingemar. *Arms Deal*. New York: Praeger Publishers, 1983.

Dupuy, T. N. *A Genius For War*. Falls Church, Va.: Nova Publications, 1984.

Fadok, David S. *John Boyd and John Warden: Air Power's Quest for Strategic Paralysis*. Maxwell AFB, Ala.: Air University Press, 1995.

Fallows, James. "America's High-Tech Weaponry." *Atlantic Monthly* (May 1980).

————. "A Priceless Original." *U.S. News & World Report* (March 24, 1997): 9.

————. "I Fly with the Eagles." *Atlantic Monthly* (November 1981).

————. "Muscle-Bound Superpower." *Atlantic Monthly* (October 1979).

————. *National Defense*. New York: Random House, 1981.

Fastabend, David A. "That Elusive Operational Concept." *Army Magazine* (June 2001): 37–44.

FMFM-1 Warfighting. Washington: U.S. Marine Corps, 1989.

Gabriel, Richard A. *Military Incompetence*. New York: Hill and Wang, 1985.

Gentry, Jerauld R. "Evolution of the F-16 Multinational Fighter." Research Report No. 163, Industrial College of the Armed Forces, 1976.

Goodwin, Jacob. *Brotherhood of Arms*. New York: Times Books, 1985.

Gordon, Michael R., and Bernard E. Trainor. *The Generals' War*. Boston: Little, Brown, 1995.

Gordon, Y. W. "Mission Bolo." *7th Air Force Working Paper 67/3* (February 1967). USAF History Support Office.

Gray, Colin S. *Modern Strategy*. Oxford: Oxford University Press, 1999.

Hackworth, David H. "Col. John R. Boyd: A Fighter on Many Fronts." *New York Times Magazine* (January 4, 1998): 32.

Halberstam, David. *The Best and the Brightest*. New York: Ballantine, 1993.

Hammes, Thomas X. "Rethinking Air Interdiction." *Proceedings* (December 1987): 50–55.

Hanson, Victor Davis. *The Wars of the Ancient Greeks*. London: Cassell, 1999.

"Harry Hillaker: Father of the F-16." *Code One*. (July 1991). Fort Worth: General Dynamics.

"Harry Hillaker: Father of the F-16. Part II." *Code One*. (July 1991). Fort Worth: General Dynamics.

Higgins, J. W. "Military Movements and Supply Lines as Comparative Interdiction Targets." Santa Monica, Calif.: The RAND Corporation, July 1970.

Hooker, Richard D. Jr., ed. *Maneuver Warfare*. Novato, Calif.: Presidio Press, 1993.

Kaplan, Fred. "Beast of Battle." *Boston Globe Magazine* (July 21, 1991): 12.

Keaney, Thomas A., and Eliot A. Cohen. *Gulf War Air Power Survey*. Maxwell AFB, Ala.: Air University Press.

Keegan, John. *A History of Warfare*. New York: Alfred A. Knopf, 1993.

———. *The Face of Battle*. New York: Penguin, 1976.

Kofsky, Frank. *Harry S. Truman and the War Scare of 1948*. New York: St. Martin's Press, 1993.

Kross, Walter. *Military Reform*. Washington: National Defense University Press, 1985.

Krulak, Victor H. *First to Fight*. Annapolis: Naval Institute Press, 1999.

Leader, C. A. "Lambs to the Slaughter." *Marine Corps Gazette* (January 1982): 38–43.

Lind, William S. *Maneuver Warfare Handbook*. Boulder: Westview Press, 1985.

Lind, William S., et al. "The Changing Face of War: Into the Fourth Generation." *Marine Corps Gazette* (October 1989): 22–26.

———. *Maneuver Warfare*. Novato, Calif.: Presidio Press, 1993.

Llinares, Rich, and Chuck Lloyd. *Warfighters: The Story of the USAF Weapons School and the 57th Wing*. Atglen, Pa.: Schiffer Military / Aviation History, 1996.

McKenzie, Kenneth F. Jr. "On the Verge of a New Era: The Marine Corps and Maneuver Warfare." *Marine Corps Gazette* (July 1993): 63–67.

McMaster, H. R. *Dereliction of Duty*. New York: Harper Perennial, 1998.

Millett, Allan R. *Semper Fidelis: A History of the United States Marine Corps*. New York: The Free Press, 1980.

Minutaglio, Bill. "Tales of the Fighter Mafia." *Dallas Life Magazine* (May 3, 1987).

Moore, Daniel E. Jr. "Bosnia, Tanks, and 'From the Sea.'" *Proceedings* (December 1994): 42–45.

Muller, Mary M. *A Town at Presque Isle: A Short History of Erie, Pennsylvania, to 1980*. Erie: The Erie County Historical Society, 1997.

Murray, Williamson. *Air War in the Persian Gulf*. Baltimore: The Nautical & Aviation Publishing Company of America, 1995.

Musashi, Miyamoto. *A Book of Five Rings*. Woodstock, N.Y.: The Overlook Press, 1974.

Myrer, Anton. *Once an Eagle*. Carlisle, Pa.: Army War College Foundation Press, 1997.

Neufeld, Jacob. *The F-15 Eagle Origins and Development 1964–1972*. Washington: Office of Air Force History, 1974.

No Kum-Sok. *A MiG-15 to Freedom*. Jefferson, N.C.: McFarland & Company, 1996.

Operation Desert Storm Evaluation of the Air War. Washington: United States General Accounting Office, 1996.

O'Shaughnessy, Hugh. *Grenada*. New York: Dodd, Mead & Company, 1984.

Prados, John. *The Blood Road*. New York: John Wiley & Sons, Inc., 1999.

Richards, Chester W. "Agile Manufacturing: Beyond Lean?" *Production and Inventory Management Journal* (Second Quarter, 1996): 60–64.

———. *A Swift, Elusive Sword*. Washington: Center for Defense Information, 2001.

———. "Riding the Tiger: What You Really Do with OODA Loops." In *Handbook of Business Strategy*. New York: Faulkner & Gray, 1995.

Robinson, Clarence A. Jr. "USAF Studies Fighters for Dual-Role." *Aviation Week & Space Technology* (January 3, 1983): 36–40.

"Rollover Beethoven . . . Bail Out! Bail Out!" *Lost Birds* (Jan / March 1998): 13–16.

Romm, Joseph J. "The Gospel According to Sun Tzu." *Forbes* (December 9, 1991).

———. *The Once and Future Superpower*. New York: Morrow, 1992.

Salter, James. *The Hunters*. New York: Vintage International, 1999.

Schwarzkopf, H. Norman. *It Doesn't Take a Hero*. New York: Bantam Books, 1993.

Sherry, Michael S. *The Rise of American Air Power*. New Haven: Yale University Press, 1987.

Smallwood, William L. *Warthog*. Washington: Brassey's, 1993.

Smith, Hedrick. *The Power Game*. New York: Ballantine, 1988.

Smith, Perry McCoy. *The Air Force Plans for Peace 1943–1945*. Baltimore: The Johns Hopkins Press, 1970.

Spector, Ronald H. *U.S. Marines in Grenada 1983*. Washington: U.S. Marine Corps, 1987.

Spick, Mike. *The Ace Factor*. New York: Avon, 1988.

———. *The Complete Fighter Ace*. London: Greenhill Books, 1999.

Spinney, Franklin C. *Defense Facts of Life*. Boulder: Westview Press, 1985.

———. *Defense Power Games*. Washington: Fund for Constitutional Government, 1990.

———. "Genghis John." *Proceedings* (July 1997): 42–47.

Sprey, Pierre M. "Austere Weapons Systems." Briefing. Late 1960s.

———. "F-XX and VF-XX — Feasible High Performance, Low Cost Fighter Alternatives." Staff Study, Office of the Assistant Secretary of Defense, June 9, 1969.

Stevenson, James P. *The Pentagon Paradox*. Annapolis: Naval Institute Press, 1993.

Stevenson, William. *Zanek!* New York: Bantam Books, 1971.

Sun Tzu. *The Art of War*. Edited by James Clavell. New York: Delacorte Press, 1983.

———. *The Art of War*. Translated by Samuel B. Griffith. London: Oxford University Press, 1963.

———. *The Art of War*. Translated by Thomas Cleary. Boston: Shambhala, 1988.

———. *The Art of Warfare*. Translated by Roger Ames. New York: Ballantine, 1993.

Taylor, Maxwell D. *The Uncertain Trumpet*. New York: Harper & Row, 1959.

Thomas, Robert M. Jr. "Col. John Boyd Is Dead at 70: Advanced Air Combat Tactics." *New York Times* (March 13, 1997): 22.

Thompson, Warren, and Joe Mizrahi. "Air War over Korea." *Airpower* (September 2000): 8–39.

Tilford, Earl H. Jr. *Setup: What the Air Force Did in Vietnam and Why.* Maxwell AFB, Ala.: Air University Press, 1991.

"The United States Strategic Bombing Survey." September 30, 1945.

Watts, Alan. *Tao: The Watercourse Way.* New York: Pantheon Books, 1957.

Watts, Barry D. *The Foundations of U.S. Air Doctrine.* Maxwell AFB, Ala.: Air University Press, 1984.

Webb, James. *Fields of Fire.* New York: Bantam Books, 1979.

Wells, Linton II. "Maneuver in Naval Warfare." *Proceedings* (December 1980): 34–41.

Williams, Michael D. *Acquisition for the 21st Century.* Washington: National Defense University Press, 1999.

Wilson, George C. *This War Really Matters.* Washington: CQ Press, 2000.

Wilson, G. I. "The Gulf War, Maneuver Warfare, and the Operational Art." *Marine Corps Gazette* (June 1991): 23–24.

———. "Maneuver / Fluid Warfare: A Review of the Concepts." *Marine Corps Gazette* (January 1982): 54–61.

Wilson, G. I., and W. A. Woods. "The Controversy: Attrition or Maneuver?" *The Word Publication* Marine Corps Reserve Officer Association (January–February 1984): 38–42.

Wolfe, Tom. *The Right Stuff.* New York: Farrar Straus Giroux, 1979.

Woods, William A. "A Reevaluation of Doctrine: Applying Infiltration Tactics to the Water-Borne Assault." Amphibious Warfare School. Quantico, May 1, 1981.

Worden, Mike. *Rise of the Fighter Generals.* Maxwell AFB, Ala.: Air University Press, 1998.

Index

Index

moral conflict, as war strategy, 337
Murphy, Charles, 352
Musashi (samurai), 445–446
"The Muscle-Bound Superpower" (Fallows), 351
Myatt, Mike, role in Gulf War, 424–425
Myer, John, questioning Riccioni, 250–251
Myers, Chuck, 291, 443–444

Nakhon Phanom Royal Thai Air Force
  Base (NKP)
  aircraft used at, 267
  Base Exchange at, 274
  Boyd as base commander at, 271,
    272–274
  described, 266–268
  latrines at, 273
  officer's love affair, 273–274
  paperwork at, 272
  race relations at, 269–270, 272
  Task Force Alpha at, 268–269, 271
  wild dogs at, 267, 272–273
Napoléon I, at Battle of Austerlitz, 377
National Academy of Sciences, 412
National Defense (Fallows), 358
Navy. *See* U.S. Navy
Neal, Richard, 425
Nellis Air Force Base
  combat training at, 46–47
  haven of fighter pilots, 60–63
Nethercutt, George, 447
"New Conception for Air-to-Air
    Combat" briefing, 307, 322
Newman, Ralph
  and "Aerial Attack Study," 112–114
  confronted by Boyd, 103–104
  and Ronald Catton, 107, 110, 111
New York Times, and Bradley testing, 406,
    410–411
New York Times Magazine, 444–445
Nixon, Richard, 282–283
"No Guts, No Glory" (Blesse), 70
Northrop company, and lightweight
    fighter, 245–246
nuclear explosions in Nevada, 60
Nunn, Sam, 360
  and Spinney Report, 357–358

Office of Development Plans, Boyd's
  approach as director of, 280–281
Officer Efficiency Reports (ERs),
  described, 56

Officer Efficiency Reports, Boyd's
  at Andrews AFB, 248, 263
  at Eglin, 159, 166, 184, 185–186
  in Korea, 56–57
  letter of evaluation, 270
  at Nellis AFB, 69, 71, 78, 101–102,
    118–119
  at the Pentagon, 195, 210–211, 243, 300
  and promotion to full colonel, 243, 248
  in Southeast Asia, 271–272, 276, 277
  undercutting his promotion to general,
    254–255
Old Guard Room, happy hour gatherings
    at, 291, 414, 443–444
Olds, Robin, 213
Ono, Taiichi, 429
On War (von Clausewitz), 330, 332
OODA Loop, 334–339
  blitzkrieg as application of, 336–337
  briefing, 336–337, 338–339
Operation Desert Shield. *See* Gulf War
"Organic Design for Command and
    Control" briefing, 416
OV-10 aircraft, 267, 269

Packard, David, 257, 258, 280
Parker, Jerald, recollections of Boyd, 54
party suit, Boyd's, 269
"Patterns of Conflict" briefing, 6–7, 322,
    330, 354, 361, 378, 383. *See also*
    OODA Loop
  at AWS, 378
  and Boyd's study of battle tactics,
    331–334
  changing titles of, 328–329
  and Dick Cheney, 355
  exemplified in Gulf War, 425
  field test: Burton vs. Army, 402–403
  James Fallows and, 351, 352
  post-Boyd, 442
  and reform movement, 349
  revising, 413–414
Patton, George, 331
  war tactics of, 337–338
Pentagon
  budget underestimates of, 362–368
  issue of civilian control of, 364, 367,
    399–400
  nature of, 188–191
  paranoia of, 354, 361–362
  role as weapons procurer, 400
The Pentagon Wars (Burton), 442

Index

"Study to Validate the Integration of Advanced Energy-Maneuverability Theory with Trade-Off Analysis" (Boyd, Riccioni, Sprey), 239–240
Stuka Pilot (Rudel), 235
Sugarplum Fairy (Boyd's nickname), 163
Sullivan, Mike, 390, 395
  blocking Michael Wyly's campaign plan, 391–392, 393
Sun Tzu
  Boyd ranked with, 445
  Boyd's study of, 331
  von Clausewitz's battle tactics contrasted with, 332
supersonic flight, with F-100, 83–84
Sweeney, Walter Campbell, Jr., 134
  briefing on E-M Theory, 169–170, 171–176
swing wing, 155
  failings of, 156, 157
  F-X and, 230–231
swordlessness, 348
synchronization
  as Army maneuver doctrine, 371
  in Gulf War, 425–426
synthesis
  vs. analysis, 324
  as basis of creativity, 325

TacAir. *See* Tactical Air Program (TacAir)
Tactical Air Command, favoring "Aerial Attack Study," 113–114
Tactical Air Program (TacAir)
  described, 290–291
  Raymond Leopold assigned to, 356
  and reform movement, 341–342
  Thomas Christie and, 240, 290–291
tactics manual. *See also* "Aerial Attack Study"; Training Research and Development manual
  for Marines, 382, 391
tanks
  casualties in, 407–408
  comparative costs/production, 366
  computer-model testing of, 400–401
Task Force Alpha, Boyd as vice commander of, 268–269, 271
Taylor, Maxwell, influence on JFK, 136
test pilots vs. fighter pilots, 61–62, 259
thermodynamics. *See also* entropy, law of

laws of, 127–128
"Thinking Beyond the Beachhead" (Wyly), 389
Thriving on Chaos (Peters), 428–429
Thud. *See* F-105 fighter
Thunderbirds, Boyd's denunciation of, 77
tiger (as accolade), 62
Tigers Airborne (Riccioni), 238
Time magazine, defense industry story, 363–367
Titus, Robert, 243
"To Be or to Do" speech (Boyd's), 285–286, 340
Total Package Procurement Concept, 258
Tower, John, Senate hearing on Pentagon budgets, 364, 365, 366
Toyota production system, 428, 429
Training Research and Development manual, vs. Boyd's "Aerial Attack Study," 113–114
Trainor, Bernard, 377, 380, 382, 386, 424
tropospheric discontinuity, 177
T-6 "Texan" trainer, 41
  Boyd and, 41–42
turbofan and turbojet engines contrasted, 154–155
"Twenty-Second Boyd," legend of, 87–88

U.S. Air Force
  competition with other branches, 228–231, 233–234, 239
  contrasted with Marines, 372–373
  efforts to change, 369–370
  in 1950s and 1960s, 58–59, 136
U.S. Army
  and Bradley testing. *See* Bradley Fighting Vehicle
  changes to warfare doctrine, 370–371, 448
  and computer-model weapons testing, 400–401, 407–408
U.S. Marine Corps
  campaign plan, 390–392, 393–394
  collection of Boyd's papers, 433
  contrasted with Air Force, 372–373
  Delta Company, 375
  described, 371–373, 374
  honoring Boyd, 8–10, 433, 448
  role in Gulf War, 424–425
  tactics manual, 382, 391
  warfare tactics of, 373, 375, 376

About the Author

Robert Coram is the author of three nonfiction books and seven novels.